VISION 3000

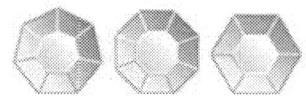

VISION 3000

The Transformation of Humanity
In the New Millennium

Michael Aschenbach

Emerging Vision Media LLC
Coatesville, PA
www.emergingvisionmedia.com

© 2006 by Michael Aschenbach

All Rights reserved. No part of this book may be reproduced in any form or by any means, electronic or mechanical, including photocopying, recording, or by information storage and retrieval system, except for brief quotations in reviews, without permission in writing from the publisher.

Emerging Vision Media™, the Emerging Vision Media logo, Universe Modeling™, and Universe Model™ are trademarks of Emerging Vision Media LLC

Cataloging Data

Michael Aschenbach
Vision 3000: the transformation of humanity
in the new millennium – 1st edition.
Includes bibliographical references.

ISBN 0-9787905-0-2 (softcover)
ISBN 0-9787905-1-0 (hardcover)

LCCN 2006906534

To Sarah

And to all those who have reached beyond what already is, to what might be.

Why Read This Book

This book talks about the future, but it is designed to provide value to the reader right now. Here are some of the benefits:

1. It offers a clear vision of human evolution and the forces that move it forward.
2. It offers well-founded reasons for hope, without avoiding the difficult challenges. It shows how our disasters actually serve to move us forward.
3. It explains the what, why, and how of human spiritual progress and how it relates to technological progress.
4. It explains the stages of human psychological maturation and how they move social progress forward.
5. It provides new specific knowledge about human science, spiritual culture, emerging technology, media development, wealth economics, and wisdom governance and how these areas will be transformed.
6. It gives guidance for individual transformation and how to align our lives today with the mighty changes that are sweeping through our world.
7. It provides plans for aligning social and organizational transformation with the true human potential.

A clear vision of why things emerge the way they do gives us strength and courage to live positively and rise above the difficulties we may suffer. This book inspires people to transform, to embrace transformation, and to accept their duty to help transformation move forward in ways that minimize the worst possibilities and maximize the great opportunities. We enjoy the privilege and the challenge of living in the most important time in human history. Read, and find out more....

Contents

Preface: How This Book Came About i
    Encounter in the Woods i
    The Message and the Book iii

PART I. Vision Logic 1
    Introduction 2

    Chapter 1. The Human Flower 5
        Vision of The Year 3000 6
        The Human Logos 12
        The Power of Far Vision 14
        The Logic of Transformation 16

    Chapter 2. The Reasons 19
        Why The Transformation Will Occur 19
        Reactions to Change 21
        Helical Cycles 24

    Chapter 3. The Timeline 27
        Time Patterns 27
        The Transition 29
        The Great Transformation 40
        The Counter-Transformation 44
        The Flowering 45

PART II. What Will Change and Why 49
    Introduction to Part II Social Functions (S_φ) 50

    Chapter 4. Human Science (H·S) 53
        The Convergence of Human Science 53
        What Is A Human Being? 54
        The Transformation Model 56
        Education and Lines of Development 84

    Chapter 5. Spiritual Culture (S·C) 99
        Awakening and Cultural Integration 99
        Spiritual-Religious Transformation 108
        Spiritual Qualities and Virtues 113
        Transformation Philosophy 117

    Chapter 6. Emerging Technology (E·T) 129
        Intersecting Technologies 129
        Technological Evolution 140
        Metamessage of the Technosphere 158
        Health, Enhancement, Environment 175

Chapter 7. Media Development (M·D) 179
- What Are Media? 179
- Media Convergence and Evolution 180
- Properties of Integrated Media 183
- Media Impacts and Consequences 190

Chapter 8. Wealth Economics (W·E) 195
- Transformation Economics 197
- The Innovation Economy 202
- The Future of Business 210
- Fairness and Equity 227

Chapter 9. Wisdom Governance (W·G) 233
- Planetary Governance 234
- Authority, Legitimacy, and Wise Governance 242
- Conscious Governance 256
- Leadership and Vision 269

PART III. What We Do Now 275
- Introduction to Part III 276

Chapter 10. The Transition 279
- From What – To What 279
- The Wave-Mix Model 280
- Phases of the Transition 282
- Conscious Transformation 295

Chapter 11. Individual Transformation 297
- Maps of Transformation 299
- The Soul Journeys 304
- The Awakening of Soul 320
- Transformative Practice, Soul, and Essence 324
- Emergence of Transformation Leaders 329

Chapter 12. Social Transformation 331
- Modeling Transformation Reality 334
- Organizational Change 343
- Transformational Tools 345
- The Great Transformation Vision 352

Summation 369

Selected Bibliography 373

Acknowledgements 391

Illustrations

Figures

Figure 1. Social Functions Diagram 50
Figure 2. The Transformation Model: Harp-Ladder Form 61
Figure 3. Crypto-Waves and Cultural Milieus 71
Figure 4. The Transformation Model: Flower-Gem Form 83
Figure 5. Lines of Development Diagram 85
Figure 6. Enneagram of Holy Ideas 116
Figure 7. Enneagram of Virtues 116
Figure 8. Libration Points and Halo Orbits 167
Figure 9. City Station Space Habitats 168
Figure 10. Media Convergence and VR/I 182
Figure 11. Universe Modeling Diagram 209
Figure 12. Value Network Optimization Diagram 210
Figure 13. Tracking Economic Quintiles 229
Figure 14. Economic Pyramid Models 230
Figure 15. Step-Wise Model of Socioeconomic Growth 231
Figure 16. Complexity Theory and Creative Evolution 238
Figure 17. Integrated Transformation Model 277
Figure 18. The Enneagram of Personality Identities 300
Figure 19. Journeys of the Soul 306
Figure 20. Group L_Δ Profiles 340

Tables

Table 1.	Time Periods of the Millennium	28
Table 2.	The Transformation Model - Tier I	58
Table 3.	The Transformation Model - Tier II	59
Table 4.	The Transformation Model -Tier III	60
Table 5.	Multi-Q Assessment Grid	97
Table 6.	Technology Categories, Dimensions, and Waves	142
Table 7.	Solar System Zones and Subzones	171
Table 8.	Technically Enhanced Elites	176
Table 9.	Virtual Reality Media Development Matrix	184
Table 10.	Wealth Values Matrix, Tier I: BL-OR-GR	198
Table 11.	Wealth Values Matrix, Tier II: GO-YE-TU	199
Table 12.	Estimated Population of Largest Cities 2015	222
Table 13.	Urban/Rural Population by Continent 2000 and 2030	223
Table 14.	The Wave-Mix Model	281
Table 15.	Enneagram Transformations	301
Table 16.	Social Function – Wave Matrix	335
Table 17.	Tier I to Tier II: Individual & Society	336
Table 18.	Tier I to Tier II: by Social Function	337
Table 19.	Development Lines – Wave Matrix	339

"Start a huge, foolish, project, like Noah.
It makes absolutely no difference
what people think of you."[1]
—Jalaluddin Rumi 1207-1273

"But I'll know my song well before I start singin'"[2]
—Bob Dylan

Preface: How This Book Came About

Encounter in the Woods

Several decades ago, an eleven-year old boy was walking in the Vermont woods a mile or so behind his home. The area was largely deserted, being bordered by a creek on one side and a mountain on the other. Few people ever passed that way, and for the boy it was a favorite place to be alone, surrounded by the peace of a beautiful natural wonderland.

On that particular day at a particular hour, the boy was wandering in a grove of hemlocks. The sun was shining through the boughs and reflecting off the creek below. As he came around a curve in the path, the boy paused, one foot half-lifted, about to take a step. Something in front of him caused him to freeze in his tracks and stare, transfixed. A powerful presence barely visible, like a ripple in the air, stood before him, perhaps twenty feet away.

He examined it wonderingly, observing a tall oval shape almost like the vague form of a man eight- or nine-feet tall yet hardly there. Through the form, which seemed like an energy field or a wave of heat

---

[1] From *The Illuminated Rumi*, translated by Coleman Barks, 1997.
2 From the song "A Hard Rain's A-Gonna Fall" by Bob Dylan, 1963.

in the air, he could see the trees, the water, and the field beyond. Though not much to look at, the form emanated an intensity of presence that utterly gripped the boy's attention. There was no question that something was there, but what was it?

As he stood stock still, he began to feel penetrating rays passing through him; he was utterly captivated and yet, after the first moment of startled awe, there was no sense of fear. Though the presence conveyed so much power over him, the boy knew somehow that it was a being of great goodness, like an angel, yet not what he had thought an angel would be.

The rays began to transmit waves of mysterious symbols into his mind. They seemed to flow along helical pathways centered in the being and passing by his awareness into some place deep inside his core. The symbols were rich, colorful, moving, and perfectly integrated in a logical web of meaning. He felt an astonished ecstasy as the wealth of knowledge they contained flickered by his conscious brain. They seemed to explain everything about the meaning of life in the clearest and most beautiful way imaginable.

The transmission continued to flow for a long time, perhaps half an hour, perhaps two, the boy couldn't say. He simply stood, riveted, with one heel lifted as at the first moment, and drank in the bliss of the transmission. Many mysterious explanations passed through in that indeterminate period. And then...suddenly it was over. Just the wisp of a goodbye lingered in his mind, and the boy could not tell if it was from the presence or from his own heart. Gradually, he came back to his normal awareness, shifted his weight, and eventually began to walk home, wondering. In some mysterious way, he understood that he was not to speak of the encounter at that time.

The boy grew up to be the author of this book. The boy was me. I have spent most of my life since then trying to decipher the meaning of the message I received that day. This book is an attempt to convey at least a small part of what I have come to understand as a result of my search. It is also part of my effort to fulfill a duty that has pressed upon my heart since that day, a sense of obligation to give something back in return for blessings received.

I still do not completely understand the events of that day or the full meaning of the transmission I received, but it has served as a catalyst, leading me to learn many things. It has taken its place alongside many other mystical experiences and a lifetime of visions. For whatever reason, it seems that I am wired such that I often live in a multidimensional way, aware of what people might call "visions" or (since they are more than visual in nature) "experiences." It has always been like this for me, even before that day in the woods. The reader should also know, however, that I live a quite normal life with a stable marriage and a career as an organizational consultant. Despite the many unusual ideas in this book, my personal preferences tend to be, in many ways, quite traditional.

The Message and the Book

This book is about human transformation: how we can move from lives of suffering to lives of freedom and delight. Although I am presenting an ecstatic vision of the possibilities for the next thousand years, this book is always about the present. Whether we consider visions of the future or histories of the past, we must always center our reality in the present. There is great value to learning about the past and great value to projecting vision into the future, but we apply that value in our immediate present.

Vision can be a transformative agency, especially in times of great change, when people feel confused about where things are going. A vision of the future that inspires can help us stay in contact with the present. The fact is, people have difficulty staying in the present. We tend to live much of our lives worrying about the past or escaping into the good old days, fearing the future or planning for the day when our ship will come in—anything but facing the daily grind. What we lose in all this escaping, hoping, and fearing is the aliveness in the details of immediate experience.

What is the point of living life, even with great material wealth, if we are not actually present to experience it? When we do show up to actually experience our lives, we discover that even a painful experience fully lived can give us a deep experience of meaning and aliveness. This level of presence takes transformative knowledge and practice.

Practicing conscious presence is in itself transformative in ways that open vast dimensions of life we normally don't suspect are there. The richness of experience I am talking about is worth far more than any amount of monetary wealth. It is the richness of life itself. Although wealth can provide comfort and pleasures, it cannot give us the level of aliveness that conscious presence can.

Presence is a transformative agency, and vision is a transformative agency. Experiencing where we are helps us understand where we are going. Understanding where we aim to go provides guidance that helps us stay present as we journey to get there. Learning to recognize presence in our own being leads us to know the presence of God, the one power that can truly transform.

This book is about being conscious of reality. It shows us the power of transformation at work in our lives and how it guides us to flower both as individuals and as a civilization. Our present situation requires us to understand things about our individual reality and about our circumstances as one human family. This understanding leads us to a great transformation.

The great work leading to the flower of humanity is emerging even now on levels way beyond our normal understanding. When we are in the midst of storm clouds, it can be hard to see the pattern that is already beginning to come to light. This vision serves to help us keep our eye on the real story through the dust of the storm.

When a new reality is emerging, as it is today, all the structures of the old reality feel threatened. This is why we see a marked rise of medieval fundamentalisms in many realms of life. The obvious example is the visible rise of religious fundamentalism and wars driven by fanaticism. After the rising expectations of a new age, this comes as quite a shock to some.

This vision shows why we should not fear. All the changes we see are part of a larger and longer pattern. Changes tend to bring out reactions and resistances within all people. It helps to look at the situation as a universal condition of which we are a part instead of pushing it off on "them," whoever our favorite bad guys are. When we see that the conditions of the times affect us all, we can see how to work on the one we can most easily change, ourselves.

Some ancient teachings say that we are nearing the end of one cycle of approximately 26,000 years and beginning a new cycle. This is how long it takes the wobble in Earth's axial spin to precess through the full circle of the zodiac. We are also said to be moving from the 13,000-year sleeping half of the cycle into the 13,000-year awakening half of the cycle, during which Earth's axis inclines toward the center of the galaxy.

We are also transiting from one astrological age (of approximately 2100 years) to another, from the Piscean Age to the Aquarian Age, with all the change of influences implied. And finally, we are starting a new millennium on our calendar. Even the biblical account in the Revelation of Saint John tells of a time of apocalyptic destruction followed by a thousand years of peace. Have we not yet seen enough of destruction?

All these grand cycles make the passage of a mere thousand years seem less impressive until we remember what history tells us of conditions one thousand years ago. It is almost unimaginable how much change has occurred in the last thousand years, so perhaps we can keep an open mind about what may occur in the next thousand.

A sober review of the documented technological and social changes over the last hundred years should be enough to convince the most skeptical that we live in rather extraordinary times. I have observed that most futurists and even science fiction writers have a hard time staying ahead of the curve of reality. It seems even pure imagination is being overtaken by the intensity and wonder of what is actually happening. During the years I spent writing this book, it often happened that events I thought would arrive many years in the future manifested almost before I could get them written down.

Even if we ignore ancient prophecies, it is clear that these are momentous times. In such times, a little vision is called for.

After criticizing our leaders for lacking vision, it became clear to me that the fault lay not with them. Executives are generally too busy dealing with immediate realities to invest the total commitment necessary to develop new vision. No, it became clear, the fault was with the visioners, that is, with people like me. If I wanted to see greater vision, I would have to do the work and bring it forth. For several years, I muddled around with these thoughts while I was busily engaged in other work.

Then, on the morning of February 27, 2002, I found myself scribbling some notes on a lined writing pad, a normal activity for me. When I looked at what I had written on that single sheet of paper, it struck me that I had just opened the door to a new chapter in my life. I knew that something important had been put in motion. That pad with its critical page of ideas became the start of this book.

As those who know me can attest, I have written hundreds of technical books and have file cabinets full of unfinished manuscripts on dozens of topics. Somehow, I knew that this time was different. This book would be written energetically from the start and carried directly through into publication, no matter what. Something beyond me is involved in this effort.

Within a couple of months, the process was moving at full tilt. I often woke with whole sections in my mind and had to struggle to get them written down before new material drowned out the old. It has come as a voice within me explaining things, but I call it "vision" because it is often accompanied with images and multidimensional diagrams. Sometimes it comes as a lucid dream in which I am giving a talk. The explaining voice seems to be my own, though, as I listen to it, I hear things I don't normally know.

Why have I been so captivated by this vision? Because what I see as possible for humanity is so beautiful it makes me cry. Though we will struggle as this unawakened world crumbles, we will see the fulfillment of the human flower before the end of the millennium. Even by the middle of this century, it should be clear to many people that we are making our way to a completely new and greater humanity.

Some of us are indeed waking up, and this will lead us to fulfill what we have always dreamed of. Waking up to our present reality has been coming about through the challenge of emerging technology and the resulting social and intercultural changes it brings. We are seeing our planet and our humanity more plainly and the first effect is that we are not so happy about what we see. After a period of shock and confusion, we will get down to making right what we do not like. Now, in the middle of the reaction period, it may be hard to see how this all works out, but that is why vision is not the same as news. This book can help you see how this transformation will happen.

Part I gives an overview. Part II gets into detail, describing particular areas of transformation and how they will unfold. Part III discusses the near future and how to align our individual lives, our organizations, and our societies to emerging realities.

My general approach has been to see where the human spirit is leading through vision, then to draw back timelines to the present to see how we got there and what stages occurred in between. Most likely, I will be wrong on some details, especially on exactly when a particular thing will occur, but in my bones I feel certain the overall pattern is right. You can decide for yourself if you think my confidence is reasonable. Now, on to the vision overview....

PART I.
Vision Logic

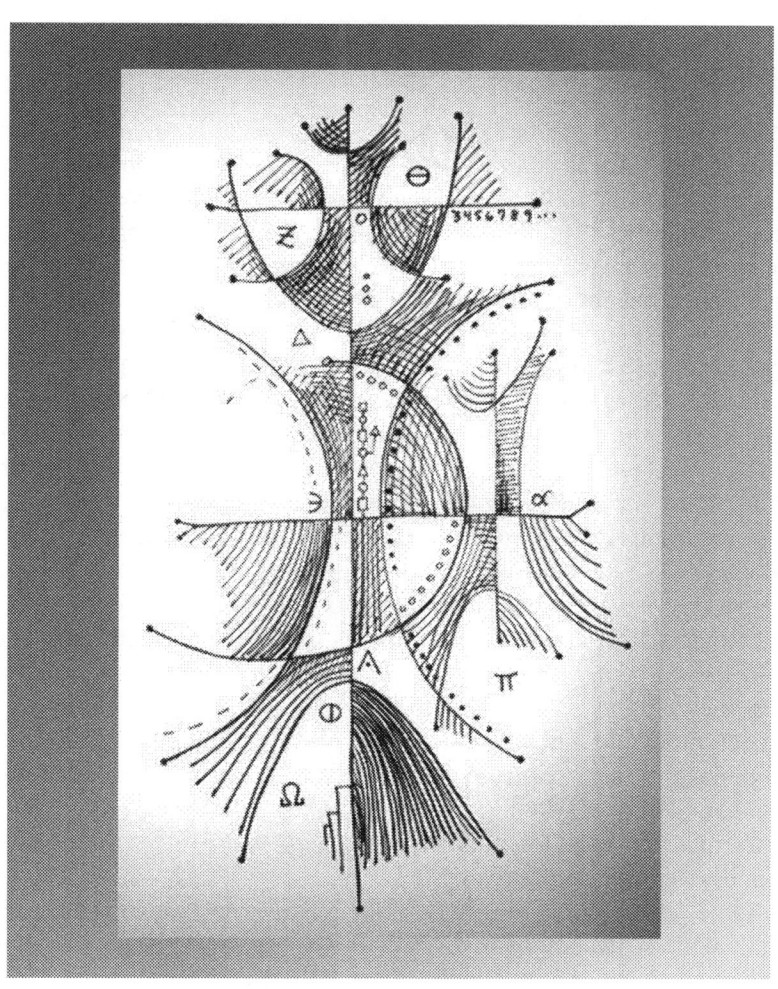

"Where there is no vision the people perish"
—Proverbs 29:18

Introduction

At present, our world is in a thicket of terrible dangers. We cannot decide which catastrophe will get us first. Before this book comes to your eyes, one or more new tragedies may have occurred already—nuclear terror in a major city, global flu pandemic, collapse of the economy, new wars in Iran and/or North Korea, asteroidal impact with Earth, severe weather disasters—all shown in great detail on television for those who are still alive to see. (And this was written before hurricane Katrina struck the Gulf Coast and New Orleans.)

Just as the tsunami disaster surprised us, other challenges are moving silently toward us. These tear at the foundations of our psychological well-being as they sweep over the walls of well-guarded castles. They shock us by coming from directions we have not foreseen.

Vision helps us to prepare for, and to recover from, the inevitable challenges and to be resilient in responding to those we have not planned for. We must use wisdom and forethought to find our way.

One driving challenge of our time is the collision of cultures as our world grows smaller and more interconnected. Traditional rules and authorities tend to collapse under this pressure, and people often react by becoming more fanatical and ethnocentric. Seeing the failure of traditional systems, some people may throw out all restraint. Social upheavals lead some to seek release in drugs, alcohol, or promiscuous sex, further breaking down family structures. War always brings with it innumerable other social ills.

Some imagine that the difficulties of this merging of cultures can be avoided by isolationism; others think we can thrive by imperial domination. Neither strategy can work. Our world has become far too interdependent, and there is no way back to an earlier age. Every society is feeling this stress and will experience more of it in the coming decades. This is a tsunami we can see and predict, though its impacts are likely to touch us more profoundly and subtly than we might imagine.

We are being forced to understand that we all live in one world; that what happens to one may affect all; that no one can feel confident that they are separate and safe from the dangers touching other parts of humanity.

From the comfort of their home, a wealthy couple in Europe or Asia or America watch a disaster on the news channel, unaware that their daughter has just volunteered to help and will die in the process. A civic leader in a quiet backwater of South America, Africa, or rural America suddenly sees his whole community destroyed by a new lumbering or mining operation, or by the loss of a major employer. A middle-class wife watches her husband deteriorate into alcoholism after a new technology wipes out his career. Families are torn apart by cults, churches by sex scandals, whole regions by religious conflict.

We know these kinds of catastrophes too well. They are the product of social upheaval. In their wake comes exhaustion and collapse. For the survivors, what often emerges too is a deeper, more inclusive sense of compassion and a willingness to grow.

Do not let the dark shadows of disaster or the news of corruption, greed, and venality turn your heart from the bright vision of this book. Humanity has passed through many dark valleys and has always pressed onward to greater heights. This vision looks through, over, and beyond short-term destructions to transformations of centuries and millennia. The vision of what is ahead for those who align with the awakening can give us faith and courage to sustain us through difficult transitions. Therefore, let us consider what is to come...

Chapter 1.
The Human Flower

This chapter gives an overview of the extended vision of humanity's future. It builds on the following principles:

1. The future will be more evolved than the present.
2. The present is more evolved than the past.
3. Long-range vision clarifies short-range forecasts.
4. Our vision frames include the possible, the probable, and the desirable.
5. We consider what the human spirit wants and where it is seeking to go. We contemplate long-term outcomes, then work back to the present time.
6. We weigh likely versus unlikely scenarios.
7. Negative events drive positive outcomes. The social metabolism responds homeopathically to crisis.
8. The centrality of media: Our thinking and communication tools condition our experience.
9. Human science becomes the key technology. Exponential technology multiplication drives transformation in all areas of life.
10. The solar system becomes our home.
11. We garden the Earth and become the healthy masters of our bodies and our biospheres.
12. The spiritual dimension is human destiny.

The Vision in the Night

There is a way to build things. We must follow a vision and keep working through every stage to bring it forward toward its fulfillment. In the middle, things usually get confused but, if we persist, the work can be brought back into alignment. Building anything good takes courage, and life has put before us all the difficult task of building a new human society. This book is not a big thing, only a small voice in a great chorus, but the song that is rising is the greatest humanity has ever sung.

A dark night is before us: wars over resources and wars to prop up economies, masquerading as wars of liberation that hide wars over culture, which are presented as wars of religion. Even those who imagine they are disguising the reasons seldom know the real reasons. In nations, communities, and even within families all over the world, desperate struggles take place over values, ideologies, and worldviews. Most world leaders are rational people, but life is not a ratio. The complexities and depths of our problems are beyond most of our leaders.

We must pray for the survival of the soul of humankind through this long night and the coming dawn. The way to build things requires that we hold on to the vision when things get muddled. It requires determined persistence, even when there seems little ground for hope. Every worthwhile vision goes through a period of apparent chaos before coming to its fruition.

The work humanity is now engaged in was set in motion centuries ago. We probably will not live to see its actual completion, but we can know it and see it in our hearts by being part of the building of it, even in the midst of the night of chaos, each in our small way. Just having the courage to hold the vision in our hearts is a significant contribution. This book presents a picture in simple, bold strokes and often leaves out the qualifying statements and detailed solutions that will take the efforts of lifetimes to work out. The first requirement in the way of building things is a big picture of the outcome, and that is what this book offers.

Vision of The Year 3000

A strong vision requires imagination and temporary suspension of disbelief. Since we are not talking about exact predictions of future events, but only exploring hypotheses of what is likely, it is appropriate to suspend critical analysis for the time being. With any scientific hypothesis, we begin by formulating the model, then we test it to see if it fits the data, whether it has explanatory power, and whether it suggests further research. So let us proceed with developing our hypothetical model, free of any worry about whether it fits our current assumptions. It is only a model.

Justice for All

Imagine a future where true justice is normal, so normal that it never, or very rarely, needs to be enforced because injustices simply do not occur. In such a society, to behave unjustly toward a fellow human being would be considered unthinkably primitive and pitiably immature, or perhaps be viewed as an illness.

Equity

Future society will have found ways of distributing wealth and goods equitably for all parts of society. Money will no longer be the motivation for striving to excel. People will seek to perform their chosen functions to the best of their abilities for the joy of it. To contribute to the well-being of the whole will be considered an honor. This will not be a capitalistic or a socialistic model, but a system built on a new transformative economics. Our motivations, needs, and wants will change. We will choose to migrate in this direction because it will meet the needs of both rich and poor for a stable happy human environment in which prosperity can flourish for all.

Well-Being

Both physical and emotional pain will be largely nonexistent, though there will remain yearnings for deeper levels of spiritual integration. The common experience will be one of great contentment by today's standards. Being discontent would be viewed somewhat the way we view being gravely ill today. There would be a profoundly compassionate response from everyone until the discontented one was returned to well-being.

Freedom

Everyone will be free to conduct their lives exactly the way they want. People will have matured spiritually to the point where they will know their chosen occupation and will always be working on unfolding their life plan to a higher level. There will be hardly a memory of compulsion. Most of the social constraints that we take for granted today will be seen as evils relegated to the past. In that future, compelling another will be viewed as a form of slavery and an abuse of the soul.

Peace

Nations as such will not exist, nor will wars. The only competitions will be toward reaching even higher levels of attunement, and even these will be primarily with oneself. We will strive to build things from within, rather than trying to take things from others. Of course, nations are still very important in the transformative processes we are undergoing today. It will take some time before we grow beyond the present-day structuring of national divisions.

Technology

Life and technology will be largely inseparable. The technology of that advanced time will be much subtler, more human, and more integrated into the flow of community life. A technological advance and its environmental and human impact will be seen as the same thing: the impact *is* the technology. Technology will become an integrated blend of the physical and the psychological, with more emphasis on the psychological. Even these terms will be replaced by distinctions we cannot imagine today. Think of how "software," "user interface," or "website" would have sounded in the eighteen hundreds.

Governance

The process of governing the flow and evolution of society will be a normal part of everyone's daily life activity, something like a daily internet referendum on a variety of issues, only much subtler and in effect automatically woven into every activity. Knowledge will be effortlessly gathered about the perceptions, insights, inclinations, and decisions of all citizens and fluidly woven into the policies that arise from this unfolding consensus. No one will feel that the direction of social policy is not attuned to their needs and wants.

News Media

Everyone will know anything they want to know. All information will be freely available. Today we have legal freedom of the press, but technological and economic suppression of information. Most people get their news passively from television and radio; they do not have access to the air waves. The internet is beginning to change that back to the way it was when "the press" was available to the citizens of every town. In the future, news and social communication will be fully integrated into the life of every citizen. No one will be deprived of access to the community attention.

Also, no one will be able to avoid experiencing the consequences of their actions. This factor is already leading to more equity and justice. It is embarrassing when your actions are revealed not to be equitable and just. Information will only become more public as time goes on. Loss of privacy will mean increased social responsibility and sensibility of policies. We are moving into a time of transparency. There will be no loopholes for hypocrisy. When all voices are heard, propaganda and media manipulation will be impossible.

Resources

Mainly, there will be a lot more resources as well as new kinds of resources that we are not aware of today. People will be richer in many ways. We will have moved from an economy of scarcity to an economy of universal abundance. At the same time, resource usage will be wiser and sustainability will be a requirement. Everything will be successfully recycled and conserved. Pollution will be managed at the source to the degree that it will almost seem to disappear as an issue. Pollutants will be either used as resources or not produced.

Religion

What we know as religion today will be transformed. It will evolve into a profoundly spiritual and scientific truth seeking. This will draw on all ancient traditional sources (the religions and scriptures of today) and will include a more personal and individual aspect. There will not be the same attitudes toward separate religions, per se, but people will work on their own personally suitable spiritual practices.

Spiritual experience and qualities will create naturally recognized leadership, but there will be no coercion at all. People will choose to study a particular teaching for as long as it helps them evolve, then they will freely migrate to another teaching. Values will be integrated in such a way as to allow maximum liberty to learn and explore. Ethics will not have to be imposed; they will be sought, and people will want to refine their understanding and their conduct. To be seen as spiritually evolved will be a source of honor and will replace money as the source of true status. However, this will not be a theocratic type of society with priests, ministers, or mullahs dictating the way of life. It will be so free and democratic that we would think ourselves a dictatorship by contrast.

Family

The boundaries between family and community will be far more permeable. The burdens of birth and child rearing will be shared and more intelligent. We are already learning more about childhood psychodynamics. In the future, this will be broadly extended throughout the community as common knowledge, and great care will be taken to raise the healthiest, sanest children possible. Child rearing, education, spiritual development, work, and everyday life will be pretty much the same thing. No child will ever be abused, and no adult will have the neurotic inclination to abuse.

All the normal activities of living will be a lot more fun, a lot less stressful, and a lot more meaningful than anything we experience today. Our love relationships will be deeper, healthier, more joyous, and more satisfying on every dimension. Our families will be like large groups of loving friends of different ages. We will understand each other in intimate detail and with great psychological precision. No one will feel alienated or alone, except as an aspect of spiritual transformation, that is, when they choose to experience solitude and seclusion.

Stress

Basically, we won't do it. We will recognize stress as a foolish waste of resources, as silly and barbaric. No one will rush to get anywhere or to get anything done fast. Instead, we will be interested in the quality of our experience in the present moment, and everything we do will be imbued with that beautiful quality of attention. We will love to do everything well. We will not see a difference between pleasurable activities and onerous duties. We will not feel compelled to do anything. We will get plenty of rest and good nourishment. Robots will do harsh and dangerous jobs. There will not be anything like what we now call stress. There will still be something vaguely like it, because life is always moving forward, but we wouldn't recognize it as stress any more than a cave dweller would recognize what we vacuum off our carpets as "dirt." But we will embrace spiritual stresses as a natural part of growth and transformation.

Speed, Time, and Space

We just won't look at these in anything like the same way we do today. We will be able to go almost anywhere within our domain, but we will never be in a hurry. All parts of human space will be in contact via advanced virtual reality internet. We just won't think of distance the same way. Everything will seem near.

Time will be treasured. We will be conscious of much more experienced time within each second. We will experience every cell in our bodies more completely and pleasurably, and we will live much longer, probably more than two hundred years. In other words, our lives will be richer, fuller, happier, and more meaningful than anything we can currently conceive. If we could experience one day in the life of a future human, we would nearly pass out from ecstasy by contrast with our present experience. When we returned here, today's most advanced environments would seem horribly primitive.

Space Colonization

We will have spread throughout the solar system and will have learned to live comfortably in space. Our homes will be huge orbiting city-stations containing gardens and even artificial wildernesses. In some regions off Earth, conditions may be somewhat rougher than what I have just outlined for life on this planet. Nevertheless, the conditioning power of evolved humanity will extend throughout most of the human domain.

Science, Art, and Higher Learning

These disciplines will be more integrated than they are today and will be considered part of spirituality and social governance. This body of knowledge will be readily accessible to all, and everyone will contribute to it every day. The whole concept of universities and separate disciplines will dissolve into a medium of group transformation, a kind of higher software of universal knowledge, that will always be growing and becoming more refined. Even the distinctions between knowing, doing, learning, and teaching will blur and disappear.

Our work will be the continuing deeper enlightenment of humanity, alignment with Being, and ever higher understandings. Human transformations will occur that are beyond our wildest imaginations.

***

Before you reject these projections as hopelessly utopian and unrealistic, read on. There are many reasons to believe that this vision is not only possible, but highly likely. It is easy to confuse the shadows of dawn for the dark shades of twilight, and it is hard to look directly at the noontime sun. Of course, we will not grow to these heights without moving through stages.

The Human Logos

Vision 3000 is a view into human destiny. It is a transmission from the Human Logos, that aspect of the Divine Being that holds the order and logic of human unfoldment.[3]

The entity I call the Human Logos has guided our species from the time of the earliest human emergence and will continue to do so until the final fulfillment of our ultimate potential. It is that within us that defines what we yearn for, what we seek, what motivates us in our ever unfolding transformation. It is the logic of what we are transforming into. It is the spiritual DNA of what we truly *are*. For the Human Logos, the next thousand years is a small chapter in our overall story, but it is a critical chapter. This is the era when we turn the corner into our greater reality.

The living manifestation of the Human Logos is like the thin layer of green bark that is the living part of a tree. Thus the Human Logos lives within the hearts of the living human population. But, like a tree, it has a firm historical structure and a destiny. Also, like a tree, it has seasons. It produces leaves, flowers, and fruit. The Human Logos seems to go through many profound transformations throughout the long life cycle of our species. The mystery is that it is both timeless and changeless, while also being responsive to the transformations we experience. When we speak of "the human spirit," we are referring to the Human Logos.

Behind the veil of our individual hopes and fears is a deep logic that guides what humanity is and what it is becoming. The spirit of that logic is the Human Logos. This spirit has brought us out of our primitive past to our present state of intense transition, and it will bring

---

3 Logos – Literally "word" in Greek, λογος; Also used in the gospels to refer to the cosmic Christ, "In the beginning was the Word ," John 1:1. In Greek philosophy, "Logos" meant the ordering aspect of life, hence "logic"; that which gives form and meaning to things.

us into our full flowering with unerring guidance. This compass is our true nature as beings. This spirit has always known what we truly are.

No matter how disorienting the blizzard of outer changes, the Human Logos never deviates from its path. Like the bellwether mountain goat, it leads the herd through the storm to the safety of the green valley. We have always traveled through storms of change, and we have always been guided by this deep reality. When I go to contemplate this vision, it is to the altar of our Logos that I go. There is a profound clarity here that asks only that we get out of the way and, when our personal veils are pulled aside, its splendor shines forth to show us what we need to see.

It is indeed the veils of our personal hopes and fears that obscure the message. Our belief that we already know is what prevents us from allowing a deeper, surer knowing to arise. The unfolding of the deep guiding logic is greater than us and emerges from a place beyond our control. Our desire to control it gets in the way of our conscious participation in the unfolding, the truly sacred great unfolding that moves behind and beyond all external manifestations of its action. While human individuals develop, build, and name movements like "the Renaissance" or "the Great Transformation," these are only passing approximations of the movement of the Human Logos as it unfolds its eternal plan.

Whether the Human Logos is an actual entity or a metaphor that describes a process is ultimately irrelevant. The effect is the same. Thus it is sensible to refer to the attractor around which the process of our transformation occurs as an actual objective being.

There appears, throughout all human history, to be a center that acts as if it were a conscious agent guiding humanity through a series of seemingly improbable transformations. While we also recognize an agency within all being, what we might refer to as "God" or "the Absolute," we see that the guidance of humanity seems more personal than the cool majesty of the Ultimate Reality. It is as if an aspect of the Divine were reaching out to speak to humanity in particular. Perhaps this is the one to whom is addressed the biblical question, "What is man that Thou art mindful of him?"[4]

This guiding power seems to be the sum of our living spirit and also somehow above and beyond us, drawing us forward through the patterns of a plan we can sense within us. It seems to nurture us. It

---

[4] Psalms 8:4

seems to want us to flower. At the same time, it *is* us, the very flower of us, just as the great spiritual teachers of history are seen as both man and God. Since the human being is said to have been created in God's image, when that image is made whole, the human being becomes godlike. Beyond the veil of our transition, we are moving toward this destiny.

The Power of Far Vision

For most futurist writers, a thousand years is considered an impossible time span for which to make meaningful predictions. Today very few venture to speculate beyond the next fifty years or so, and those who do are generally considered fiction writers. In actuality, I have found that it is easier to envision the farther future than it is to see the next few years. This is because the overall unfoldment has a definite direction and a destiny, but many varied pathways to get there.

Picture, for example, a hillside with a basin at the bottom. When it rains, water falling on the top of the hill flows down the hillside and inevitably into the basin to form a sparkling pool that reflects the sky. Seeing the empty hollow, the slope of the hillside, and the drops of rain beginning to fall, we can foresee the pool with considerable certainty, though not exactly the way each drop of water will flow.

The Human Logos defines this pool, which represents the next chapter in our unfoldment. By listening to its promptings and pressures, I have been brought to the place to write this book. It is certainly my book; it is not channeled, but it has been prompted. Its failings are the failings of my ability to understand or to translate the impressions I have received into exact language. Despite these inevitable frailties, I am confident that what is presented gives a clear outline that will accord with the reason and intuition of many who read this. Others will also carry the unfoldment of the vision further, as many have worked on this mission before me. We are carrying this vision together.

It is important that we see the far vision anew in every generation to help us endure the challenge of an era of great change. This is especially true now as we are making a hairpin-turn up the mountain of our destiny, our speed causing much fear and confusion. During the next hundred years or so, our evolutionary path is like the perihelion arc of a comet traveling around the Sun at maximum velocity before coming out the other side and slowing down again as it moves away from the Sun. In our case, the "sun" represents the gravitational force of our transformational crisis. The momentum of our orbit represents the drive of the Logos toward our destiny.

We are pulled inward by the forces of our traditions and of all the old structures that worked for us in an earlier era. These forces intensify as they are coming to the end of their time, just as a comet speeds up as it feels the pull of the Sun. They would pull us into the "sun" if there were not also another force that reaches beyond to the new era and swings us out and away from capture. The orbit of our history is the exact balance of these forces at any moment in time. Both are needed: a time of gathering in to complete an old cycle, then a time of going out in search of the new cycle. Much later there is another gathering in. Half the orbit is going out and half is coming back. But it does not merely repeat, for each turn is a helix moving through space, and each turn is a unique unfoldment of our nature and our potential.

By seeing the principles of the emerging new era more clearly, we are able to manage the stresses of the journey more gracefully. By understanding where we are going and why, we will be able to travel more serenely.

The first principle we are having so much trouble adjusting to is the principle of **one spherical planet**. Though the principle has been known for some time and was demonstrated by Magellan, it is only recently that the implications have begun to be felt directly by most of the inhabitants of our planet. Living on a finite sphere means that all paths and pressures are contained, that all motion comes back to its origins, and that therefore we must learn to live with each other. The new era will encompass the reality that we must function as one integrated humanity, and so we will. We really have no choice.

There is resistance to being absorbed into a one-world culture, so we have to come to grips with the second principle, which is **diversity within integration**. We will need to find ways to cherish the balance between the needs of the individual, the cultural group, and the whole planet. The new era will manage as much cultural variety as possible, knowing it as a great resource, but balancing it against universal values. The various ways local cultures define relationships between men and women versus our belief in the universal value of women's equality with men provides a notable current example of this struggle. The new era will find the balance of universal human values and pluralistic culture. Women are no longer tolerating patriarchal dominance, but each culture will find its own way of transforming and absorbing the pushes and pulls of all other cultures.

Along with each culture and each individual wanting the freedom of diversity for themselves must come tolerance of diversity for the other. The struggle here is to find how each can have as much freedom as possible while minimizing negative impacts on the freedom of others. We will learn to develop the highest respect for the neutrality of the public space and find ways to allow as much diversity as possible to coexist in the same environment. For example, by the use of headphones, many people can listen to different kinds of music in the same space, while others can enjoy relative quiet.

The Logic of Transformation

Flowering Is Built into Human Nature

It is natural for potential to be fulfilled. As humans, our spiritual DNA is based on divine essential qualities. We are constantly moved to grow and realize these virtuous qualities more fully. Our core reality contains the qualities of justice, compassion, peace, patience, truth, wisdom, brilliance, gentleness, subtlety, majesty, and true wealth. We are drawn to develop, unfold, and manifest these inner realities in our external lives, and many other virtues as well. It is, and always has been, our destiny to manifest the human flowering.

Causes: Social Impacts of Technology

It is not technology itself that is so fascinating; it is rather the effect it has on us and on our societies. We create technologies and they change us, then we change them in response. Technology is a mirror of human society. The thing we are fascinated by (as we should be) is ourselves. We are told we are created in God's image and we seek fulfillment by finding that image within. But to see it and become it, we must be transformed.

This book looks at technology not primarily for its own sake, but at how we change ourselves and our societies through it. It is the interplay of human with human through the medium of technology that has been the foremost visible cause of our continuing transformation. It is a mistake to say that "technology" changes us; the cause emerges from the human, not from the machine. Behind the system there is always human agency; it is only difficult to see because a lot of us are interacting on each other and technology is often in between.

Causes: Small Planet; Growing Population

Currently, approximately 6.5 billion people are alive on the planet. Although growth is slowing, estimates suggest that we will reach approximately 9 billion before growth stabilizes around 2050. That is a lot of mouths to feed and a lot of human longing to fulfill. The imperative to meet the needs of all these people on a relatively small planet is another great driving cause that will move us toward transformation.

Causes: Planetary Problems and Solutions

Many of our most pressing problems can no longer be solved on a national level. They require a planetary level of cooperation. This is why so many of the world's leaders are moving toward the concept of world governance. Although the steps are groping, this must and will come. There may be disagreements about the form and the approach, but the basic concept is inescapable. Many global organizations have been actively working in this direction for years.

Some fear this idea, and many abuses are likely before the system is settled, nevertheless, the alternative of failing to find unity and planetary solutions is much worse. Planetary problems are a major cause leading us, even pushing us, in the direction of transformation; and we will go because we must. Our survival is at stake.

Today's planetary problems will all be gone by the year 3000. We will discover new challenges in new dimensions. Today, however, we are faced with an agenda of challenges that can only be fully resolved on the planetary level. The list below gives an example of some of the planetary problems we confront:

1. Protection from asteroidal and cometary impacts
2. Population size, density, and control
3. Health of the biosphere: ecology management and global climate change
4. Economic equity, trust, and prosperity
5. Health of our bodies: ending pain and illness
6. Health of our psyches: soul fulfillment
7. Freedom and democracy versus dictatorship and oligarchy
8. Complexity management requiring larger vision

9. Planetary education for change at multiple levels
10. Technology impact shocks: preparation and resilience
11. Need for more resources: planetary development
12. Religious ecumenicism, tolerance, and diversity
13. Organizational effectiveness: flexible bureaucracy
14. Planetary policing: reducing violence and destruction
15. More equitable planetary law
16. Increasing creativity and innovation: human resources

These are just a few of the challenges the emerging planetary transformation must and will address.

Causes: Evolving Human Consciousness

Ultimately, the most important cause of transformation is the progressive evolution of human consciousness. As new challenges confront us, we discover new capabilities within us to respond to changing conditions. Human beings are creatively emergent.

The example of highly evolved individuals that have developed in advance of the rest of us (the great teachers of history) has left a record that shows the outlines of what we are all evolving toward. Each wave of consciousness moves us to a higher level with new capacities. As we will learn throughout this book, each level of unfolding awareness brings with it a completely new worldview, a new economy, a new social philosophy, and new technologies. The emergence of new consciousness transforms everything.

Changing Human Nature

Some say, "You can't change human nature." This vision says that human nature has always been evolving. We are the being that changes.

Human Nature Is Change!

This is part of what it means to be human.

Chapter 2.
The Reasons

Why The Transformation Will Occur

Here are some of the reasons that the extraordinary transformations described in this book will become the normal reality of our descendents:

1. The positive economic benefits of global cooperation and international exchange: Greater unity and peace will produce enormous wealth (especially as we learn to share prosperity more equitably).

2. Vastly increased intimacy of experience and information exchange via virtual reality media: We are going to experience our interdependence firsthand, in an up-close-and-personal way.

3. Rapid global transportation and intermingling of peoples of all cultures in all locations furthers cultural exchange: The society of planetary polyculture is a growing fact all around us and in all nations.

4. Pressure to solve global problems:
   - Climate and ecological changes
   - Oceans and pollution control; fisheries
   - International crime, terrorism, and drug trafficking
   - Global business law and intellectual property
   - Human civil rights and freedoms
   - Food distribution and energy needs
   - Space exploration, big science and technology
   - Population stresses and epidemic control

5. The expectation of progress: All populations expect new and greater thresholds of progress. We will be exhausted and sick of

greed, the wars that feed it, and the worldviews that drive these wars.

6. The explosive growth of education, scientific research, and technological development: New knowledge will give us the increasing ability to change, as well as the desire.

7. Better nutrition, prenatal care, and child nurturance result in stronger, cleaner physiologies and healthier psyches: Healthier people think more clearly.

8. Reduced physical pain and psychological stress: Neurotic drives will be reduced and people will be more humane. This has been the trend from the beginning, and there is no reason to believe it will not continue.

9. Deeper understanding of human psychology and wider application of its principles: Individuals and cultures will be healthier. We *shall* know the truth, and it *shall* set us free.

10. The spread of human science principles into electronic media culture will intensify and speed up cultural shifts: The discoveries of experts quickly become part of the planetary culture, especially in younger generations.

11. The ecumenical study and convergence of religions and spirituality will lead to increased unity and peace: We will stop warring and start sharing wisdom.

12. Human science, global cultural shifts, and spiritual unification influence changes in politics, governance, law, and economics (and vice-versa): Every small step toward unity will have many beneficial ripples.

For these and many other reasons, what might seem at first glance to be a fantasy is actually the most likely outcome for our future. The number of forces driving this process forward is beyond the scope of any individual's vision, but by looking at some of the most visible drivers, we can begin to get a sense of the magnitude of the wave now sweeping through our planet.

Sometimes I speak as though the transformation had a life of its own, for it behaves as if it does. Perhaps it does, or perhaps we can just as easily explain it as the collective actions of millions of people or millions of memes. (Richard Dawkins coined the word "meme" in his book, *The Selfish Gene,* to refer to idea forms, or elements of culture, that are understood to function in social evolution similarly to the way genes function in biological evolution.) Some say that a person is only the result of the collective action of millions of genes evolving through time, but such reductionism loses something in translation.

Therefore, I will unabashedly speak of the Human Logos, and the Great Transformation it is unfolding, as entities with lives of their own. If this is only metaphor, there is more meaning in it than there would be in any reductionist explanation of the phenomenon. We humans can hold only a few items of information in our attention at any one moment, so metaphors and abstractions have great value. We can even speak of our whole universe as being one with us and we with it. The specific numbers describing the universal forces present at the "big bang" are such as to create galaxies, stars, planets, life, and people. Any slight deviation from these numbers and none of this could exist.[5] We are of the origin; we are part of it, and it of us. Evolution is a pretty intelligent design.

Reactions to Change

Negative Events Are Reactions to Change

Wars, economic catastrophes, and political repressions have been stimulated at this time by reactivity to perceived change, an attempt to reject what is already here. Everyone senses, consciously or unconsciously, that momentous change is upon us, and some react to this by contracting. When this reaction is expressed socially, we experience it as a series of "negative events," such as terrorism, various fanaticisms, crimes, and wars.

This is just fear of change, but it actually has the ultimate effect of moving the change along even faster. Political and economic extremisms of right or left are reactive contractions that put pressure on the social flow, which in turn reacts by pushing forward, not unlike the birth of a baby. A homeopathic remedy is another metaphor that applies. Giving the body a bit of a substance that causes an illness stimulates the natural healing responses, and the body gets well, although suffering does occur during the transitional crisis.

---

[5] Martin Rees, *Just Six Numbers: The Deep Forces That Shape the Universe*, 2000.

We Are All Heroic Beings

It is hard to live in the stress of these momentous times. Just living daily lives and doing the best we can to get by makes us heroes. We may be viewed as such by future generations, though they won't comprehend the full extent of our stress.

Although I have no direct proof of this assertion, I believe that we are all very special souls who have been given the privilege to be alive on the planet at this one-time-only moment of transition, when humanity is awakening as a spiritual being and as a planetary species. We are the lucky few, all six-and-a-half billion of us; we have been given a seat on the fifty-yard line of the greatest game in human history, past or future. Even better, we actually get to play in the game. This is the greatest game in the life of our species, a game in which we learn to grow beyond selfish individualism and become the image of the Divine that was always meant for us.

It is right to look around your family, your community, your nation, and your planet and embrace everyone. We have been given the unique privilege to be alive at this critical point in our destiny. Whether we experience joy or pain, whether we live or die, just to have been here at this time is grace and blessing beyond measure and worth everything. Let us try to remember that we all share this wondrous honor and appreciate each other accordingly.

We Are All Resistant to Change

It can be helpful to appreciate traditional thinking and its resistance to the new paradigm as a cautionary slowing process that helps to ensure the integration of all concerns and interests. Resistance to change can keep us from plunging into something without considering all the consequences and, as such, it can lead to better planning.

We must not think of traditional resistance as only a right-wing reactionary stance. Traditional resistance occurs on both the right and the left. Instead of demonizing it, let us try to understand it and see it within ourselves. We can ask ourselves, "What will help more people evolve?" and "What will help *me* evolve?"

Like fish migrating out of the seas and onto the land, we resist change because it is hard. It demands adjustment to new realities. But if the new realities are inescapable, what else can we do but adapt or perish? The information presented in this vision is absolutely essential, but not because the process needs us to make it happen. It already *is* happening. It is a self-organizing process whose time has come as inexorably as a change of season. No, we need the information so we can understand the transformation and align our lives with it. The change will happen whether we are on board or not.

We need to understand the way the future is unfolding to help cure our resistance. If we resist without understanding, the coming changes will roll right over us. Our organizations will fail, and we will suffer. If we can better perceive what is coming, we can adjust and get sufficiently aligned with reality not to be run over by it.

We should all share our understanding of what is going on with the people we know. Sharing these ideas is helpful to people even if they don't always agree. It might be useful to develop your own vision statements based on the processes described in this book and discuss them with the people you care about. Form life-vision teams and organizational vision teams to help each other live more effectively.

Reactions Also Spur the Transformation

When greed, fear, and rigidity cause leaders in any culture to resist what is just and right, it may seem like a reversal for those who hope for the better day. Amazingly, the effect over time is that these reactionary responses actually stimulate the motion toward positive change. Cultivating this perception makes us unshakably strong in our hearts, even when confronted with negative reactivity.

There is nothing but reactivity and inertia holding up the old paradigm. The new paradigm that leads to the transformation of humanity is constantly fed by innumerable springs of fresh strength. Optimists have always had the power of positive thought. Now, that optimism is joined by a thousand supportive realities. When the time for a change has come, there is no stopping it.

The Most Compelling Vision and Leadership

The whole point is that the most positive vision is the most compelling vision. Why would anyone want to go to a depressing future when we can go to an ecstatic future?

Leaders inspire people to work together by presenting a desirable vision. Without the vision of a compelling goal, why would anyone want to make the effort and endure the sacrifices? Why give one's time and money for a vision, if it is not very inspiring? If we think back on the American revolution and the forging of our constitution, we can see an example of the great power of a compelling vision.

Given a choice of options, people will always move toward the most believably positive option. It must be both positive and believable. People want to trust that the good vision they are shown will actually manifest some day, even if after they are gone.

Leaders must address people's inclination to distrust positive visions to avoid getting their hopes dashed. A leader responds to this tendency by presenting compelling "proofs," reasons why the vision will succeed, and images of how we will experience the positive outcomes.

Another cause of resistance to positive vision is fear. People may fear it because of what it may demand of them. We may worry that we will not be up to the demand of the future, that we may be lacking. Leaders must address this fear and show people how the emerging future is part of all of us. We all need to learn how to evolve together.

None of us today are strong enough to live in the future this vision shows, but we can be strong enough to live fully and gracefully in the present as it unfolds before us. We will move toward the future as we participate in creating it, each in our small way. We are part of a greater whole that is achieving what no part can achieve by itself. No one is left out of this process.

Helical Cycles

Attitudes toward Change

Most people don't like change, not even positive change. We get accustomed to the way things are. Even those who complain get uncomfortable when something shifts. We build identities around the circumstances we are in and are reluctant to let go of those identities, even for something better.

We are sometimes cynical and assert that nothing ever really changes. And perhaps change is cyclic. Still, if all we have known is winter, the coming of spring seems like a great transformation even if, in the greater scheme of things, it is just a phase in a repeating cycle.

Cycles are actually helical, rather than circular. The seasons repeat, but each year has variations—floods one year, droughts the next. The helix model actually reflects the reality of our path in space. As we orbit around the Sun, the Sun moves around the center of the galaxy, thus our actual world-line is a series of nested helices.

Destruction and Re-Creation

Everything is being created and destroyed at the same time. One thing is subtly blended into another. The caterpillar begins to dissolve in places even before the cocoon is woven. The early igneous and sedimentary rock is broken up and blended into metamorphic rock.

Nation states arise and blend tribes into one national character. Empires rise and fall, blending and distributing culture and knowledge. Federations arise composed of many states bound by constitutions and laws. International organizations arise. Always the order that is destroyed provides refined raw materials for the new. The new order blends and preserves elements of the old.

Even when a form dissolves completely, its logos remains latent in the solution and gets rearranged and reanimated as new forms crystallize out of the solution. As the eighteenth century scientist LaVoisier said, "Nothing is created; nothing is destroyed; everything is transformed."

Every existing form struggles to resist dissolution because all forms have a natural drive toward self-preservation. When they begin to dissolve there is a great wailing and gnashing of teeth at the "destruction" of this good and familiar thing. Amazingly, if we look ahead, we see the apparently lost good thing re-emerging as part of a new, more refined synthesis; only the dross is left behind.

The great empires provided many good things for their citizens, yet in falling they distributed their culture even further. The classical literature of Greece and Rome, much of it "lost" to the West, was absorbed, preserved, and reintroduced to Europe by the Arabic empire. China introduced many inventions, such as paper, into Europe, which then transformed them through the industrial revolution and reintroduced the new version back into China. Recently, the Japanese learned manufacturing techniques from American experts, such as W. E. Deming, refined them, and taught the new version back to American manufacturers. We could continue such examples indefinitely.

Perhaps, as we digest the intuitive spirit of complexity theory, we will feel more harmonious with self-organizing processes and lose some of our fear of change. Perhaps we will learn to participate nimbly in processes of creative destruction. As we go toward this process, it will be good for us to be compassionate with ourselves and with others. We all tend to identify with familiar forms and try to cling to forms that are dissolving. We fear they are gone forever, that the most perfect flower of all creation is dying forever before our eyes and we are powerless to stop it.

We forget that flowers make seeds. That is actually their purpose as far as the plant is concerned. And we forget, in our lack of perspective, that spring does come again and that this flower, or one much like it, will bloom again. As we learn to internalize this understanding, we are more able to relax; we grow more flexible and agile to adapt to a time of change.

Seeing the synthesis of linear forward motion and cyclic return helps us align with change. This describes the helix, which is the form of both planetary motion through space and the form of the DNA molecule. Today we are both harvesting the old and planting the new. We must reap what was sown before, but we can choose what we now sow for the future, for our children and grandchildren.

Farming the Garden

Winter is a time for clearing weeds and preparing the garden for the spring which is soon to follow. Summer is a time of plenty and ease, but also of heat and rank growth. Every part of the creation-destruction cycle has its pros and cons. Nothing is all good or all bad. To the wise, every phenomenon of manifestation has its uses. Like good farmers, we can use every season to improve the garden.

So, we can look at the cycles shown in this vision and prepare accordingly. We can develop detailed vision plans, set aside needed resources, train, and prepare. Good preparation is what gives a farmer the advantage. If he says, "Oh, it's winter; we can't do any work now," when spring comes he will be unprepared. His neighbor worked all winter getting ready for spring, preparing tools and seeds, clearing new fields. When spring came, the neighbor soon had an early crop ready for market.

Today, most of our organizations don't think beyond the next quarter's profits or the next election. This is not a good formula for continuity. An organization that wants to endure must be flexible over a much longer cycle of activity. It must learn to invest appropriately for each cycle. To have vision and preparation is wealth itself, as history has demonstrated repeatedly.

Chapter 3.
The Timeline

Time Patterns

The timing of future events is not precisely predictable, but that is less important than getting a picture of what those events might be and in what sequence they would be likely to evolve. The phase-structured timeline offered below serves primarily as an aid to conceptualizing the potentialities.

We can consider an envisioned event and ask ourselves when it might be likely to occur. After we have penciled it in at a specific change point on the timeline, we can ask ourselves about the series of events that would necessarily lead up to it, then push the event farther out or pull it further in accordingly. We can also ask what further effects that event might have and extend a series of impacts further into the future.

The more people want a given event, the sooner it is likely to emerge. The less understandable the event, the longer it will take for it to be drawn into being.

Phases of the Human Flowering

The Transition (now to 2100)

This is the farthest that most technosocial forecasts extend. It is this realm that business and government, the primary funders of futurist work, are most interested in, especially the next ten to twenty years. What is often missed is that each future is affected by the farther future. To people in 2050, what seems likely to happen in 2100 will affect what they do, just as forecasts about 2050 affect our planning today.

The Great Transformation (2100-2700)

This will be a new renaissance for humanity, and it will change everything. It could begin earlier, possibly within our lifetimes. This transformation will be utterly compelling and represent the vision of everything humanity has longed for. A new belief system powered by new media and fueled by new economics will sweep the planet and create a new reality for almost everyone.

The Counter-Transformation (2700-2800)

This is the time of the reaction to the Great Transformation system, when its institutions have become brittle and begun to break down. It will open the way for a new transformation beginning in the final centuries of the millennium.

The Great Liberation (2800-3000 and beyond)

This period begins so far into the future that it is hard to see clearly. Many events and change points can be pushed out to this distant era; it is the backdrop to the whole canvas. Here, the dreams of today will be ancient. From this vantage point our highest imaginable aspirations will have been realized in the Great Transformation, then broken down and reacted to in the Counter-Transformation, leading to a new and wiser synthesis. I call this time the Great Liberation, the fulfillment of the human flower. We will look for new, more mature dreams that would be hard for us to grasp today, not having lived through the intervening eight hundred years.

Caterpillar, Cocoon, and Butterfly

The metaphor of the butterfly is often used in spiritual work to describe how we move from the egoic stage, through the confinement and dissolving of the spiritual practice stage, to the ultimate realization of liberated consciousness.

Time Period	Name	Metaphor
2000-2100	The Transition	Caterpillar
2100-2700	The Great Transformation	Chrysalis
2700-2800	The Counter-Transformation	Breaking out and Drying wings
2800-3000	The Great Liberation	Taking flight

Table 1. Time Periods of the Millennium

The caterpillar consumes much vegetation, laying waste to plants in its vicinity, as we do now to the world's environment. This present period is the Transition. We are preparing to gestate something new.

The strictures and internal growth of the Great Transformation period correspond to the chrysalis. We enter the confinement of the chrysalis as worms and come out as butterflies. The true human butterfly emerges in the period of the Counter-Transformation that breaks open the chrysalis.

We emerge from the Counter-Transformation like butterflies drying our wings. Then we fly into the life of the true human spirit in the unfolding metafuture of the Great Liberation.

The Fractal Timeline Pattern

This timeline pattern is fractal. The phases I have described: Transition, Transformation, Counter-Transformation, and Liberation repeat both short-term (within this century) and also long-term on many levels. This is one of the reasons it is hard to define exactly when a given change occurs; it occurs repeatedly at different levels of depth. In this timeline, I am referring to the whole of human society. Leading individuals will have made many of these transformations much earlier. A fuller, more detailed description of the Transformation Model is presented in Chapter 4, Human Science.

The Transition

Finding Balance in the Transition Times

Three main conditions influence humanity at this time: the old worldview of the previous millennium; the new worldview of the era to come; and the confused hybrid worldview of the Transition.

The main reason we are experiencing so much turmoil in the world today is that we are navigating that transitional condition. The going is tough because the hybrid worldview is not a smooth, homogeneous blend but rather a patchy mixture of two very different worldviews. The result is that we seem to be jerked violently back and forth from one perspective to another. These worldviews appear to be battling for control. Actually, the outcome is generally determined, programmed into our spiritual DNA.

This is not to say that we have no stake in the process or that everything is utterly predetermined and predictable, like a clockwork mechanism. I have described it as more like a change of season. This is a challenging time of transition. We are all experiencing war and strife and arguments over what is the right thing to do, which is normal for such a time. It benefits us now to calm our emotions and refocus on where we are going, what we want, our values, and our vision.

This book is about holding the star of human transformation before us as a guide and comfort during a stormy night. The proper way of conduct is to do what must be done at the appropriate time. When the storm is fiercest, we stay inside and prepare; when the wind and rain let up, we go out and see what we can get done. Since we can't do everything at once, we plan carefully the order in which to do things.

It is also important to remember that all parts of the process have their contribution to the whole. Both the old worldview and the new are part of this time. We will be less upset and more effective if we restrain our temptation to fall into judging and condemning other people. We can make our best determination of what is right and what is wrong and act accordingly, but we must leave final judgment to the All-Knowing One. We must come to peace with the reality that we are always making decisions based on partial knowledge and that therefore it is wise to have a little humility. When groups of people are arguing about the right course of action, it is always arrogance that turns winners into losers.

The Transitional Crucible and the Vision Beyond

One of the purposes of this book is to encourage people by reminding them that there is something good that comes after. Any transition period is often harsh and confusing; We are in a crucible, and all the cultural structures of the past are being dumped into the crucible like so much scrap metal. As the heat of events melts these things down, we feel brutalized because so many of our identity patterns are caught up in those old cultural programs.

Most people do not much examine the worldview they acquired while growing up. We absorb ideas from our families, schools, neighborhoods, and peers. By early midlife, a particular way of looking at things is embedded in our personalities. We tend to perceive this as something we ourselves have developed, rather than as a complex program that has been imposed on us. We identify with our cultural programming. While we lean this way or that by temperament, it is always in relation to a given cultural matrix. We gravitate to roles within that matrix according to aptitude, personality, and inclination. It is very difficult to step back and consider these psychological and cultural structures as something that can change. We tend to see them as cast in stone, the way things are, the "natural" order.

In recent times, every part of the traditional cultural order, in every society and in every nation, is being melted down in the crucible. Since it is the dross that rises to the surface, most of what we are faced with in the public discourse is about what is wrong with the present way of life. So our identity structures are burned by a continuous challenge to who we think we are.

We feel under attack and tend to project the source of this attack onto other cultures. It is very hard to see that they are feeling the same sense of attack, that no one is immune from this profound disorientation. Many people initially respond to this shock with expressions of anger, creating an attitude that pictures reality as a war in which we are the innocent victims.

Neither our old cultural structures nor any momentary reactive structure will be sufficient to provide us with a viable picture of reality. The intense pressures of the Transition will continue to pound us with shock after shock until our reaction capacity is worn down. Then a kind of numbness will set in, characterized by a noncommittal attitude toward the shifting events of life. Our focus will adapt to simply getting through the day. This is already evident in many people, but we will see even more of it in the near future. We will come to a place of surrender, where we have given up trying to defend old identities and begin to melt culturally.

This is a very hard time for the world psychologically, because many of the adaptive/reactive structures that emerge to try to fill the gap left by old codes that are no longer viable will themselves become quickly obsolete. We tend to lose trust in all ideologies, considering them transitory phenomena. Periodically, grotesque caricatures of old cultural patterns will arise only to be dissolved again by the heat of the fire.

This fire is no one's fault. It is not caused by one group of people and imposed on another, though it sometimes seems that way. It is inherent in the nature of the times we are in, and it affects all of us. Sometimes one group or another may be perceived as gaining an advantage from all of the change, but this is actually a delusion. When we look at the picture broadly enough, we see that advantage is soon changed into disadvantage. The angry majority pulls down the temporarily dominant minority. The kind of stable conditions that have allowed dominant minorities to sustain rule over long periods simply do not exist, which is not to say that many will not try, only that none will ultimately succeed. Technological and social changes have washed out the foundations for such dominance. Anarchy has more force than order in this time.

Nevertheless, the impression that there is no order is wrong. A mysterious order is indeed working below the surface. While the slag of old bigotry is bubbling to the surface and being shoved in our faces till we grow nauseated by it, the true gold of universal culture is settling into the center of the pot.

We are having to confront what has been wrong for so many eons so we can awaken to what is right. We will continue to be cooked until we lose the ability to hang on to anything false. The hypocrisy, greed, and prejudice of the past are being brought to confrontation with the truth. The fire of the Transition will leave the vast majority with no stomach for anything but the truth. We will learn to share the world with each other. We will learn to be gentle, humble, and kind to one another for the simplest of reasons: nothing else will work.

The small percentage of humanity that are not able to make this shift in consciousness will be managed institutionally. We will no longer tolerate being tormented by criminals. We simply will be fed up with that. But we will feel compassion for those who are still stuck in old, selfish ways. We will do what we can to help them adjust and to prevent them from injuring others. The new order will be a thing that emerges subtly from the gold that is left as the slag is poured off, layer by layer. No one group will impose it.

The emerging world governance system will resemble a global network of NGOs, associations, and organizations more than it will the United Nations. The UN, after all, is founded on the old idea of nation states. The helping ideals of some of its component programs are likely to re-emerge, recast in new forms. Since we will be in recovery and grieving, we will need everything that offers healing and comfort. These qualities will be the winning underlying order. Power and authority will flow to leaders who show genuine healing ability and true wisdom. This is the gold that is settling in the center of the pot.

On the surface, everything appears depressingly the same, perhaps even worse, as old banished horrors like torture and biological warfare return; but beneath the surface, the signs and outlines of the new world are visible. Changes are in motion. One example is our increasing concern for protecting civilians in warfare: this is new. A mere fifty years ago, in World War II, the idea of targeting civilians and indiscriminately bombing cities was common practice. The brutalities of soldiers were considered an unavoidable part of war. We don't feel this way any longer. Even the loss of combatants is no longer routine. Thirty years ago, America lost fifty thousand soldiers in Viet Nam. Though regretted, I'm sure, it was understood to be the price for war. Today, we are concerned about the loss of fifty or five or one. The mysterious self-organizing forces of a new way are stirring.

What makes it difficult to see "the new order" is that we still think in terms of the old structures. The whole idea of "new world order" is rife with echoes of corporate mercantile dominance and fascistic government enforcement. It may be hard to see, in the current climate, that this model is not a winner. All the central trends technologically and socially are moving in the opposite direction. It is only the eddies created by reactive structures that seem to be favoring such orders, but in truth, these old orders are melting down. Everything is becoming more transparent, and we simply will not accept hypocrisy and injustice from any side much longer. At this point, we might well ask, "How much longer?" demonstrating in our longing the very force of which I am speaking. Smart marketers, in business or in politics, capitalize on unaddressed desires by finding new ways to serve new needs.

The wondrous mystery is that the current "world government" of corporate globalist forces, with its tendency toward exploitation, has set up structures that will ultimately serve quite the opposite purpose; they will actually support and help the peoples of Earth become free, prosperous, and peaceful. Another wonder is that many of the "globalists" themselves will implement this shift as they see the writing on the wall. This shift in consciousness has already begun, and many already see the outlines of the new reality. We will move from a "global" view to a "planetary" view. Where the root word "globe" suggests a mathematically abstract sphere, the root word "planet" suggests a dynamic living ecology. The planet needs order; it does not need exploitative greed and slavery. People who get this point will win out over those who do not.

The Transition, with all its turbulence, may last thirty years or a hundred and thirty years. It is hard to say how much fire we will need to complete the melting process. Also, it will occur unevenly over the earth, with some areas or social domains experiencing transitional shifts before others. Uncomfortably, quite a lot of forward and backward motion is likely, as well. The experience of a "Prague spring" followed by a brutal repression may be common for awhile. Despite these disheartening events, however, and in some measure because of them, the Great Transformation outcome is highly likely. All the dynamic forces ultimately point this way.

During stormy times, it is helpful to remember the vision of what is to come. The Transition will flow into a planetary order unlike anything we have ever seen before, and this will mark the beginning of the Great Transformation which will continue, in institutional form, the work begun during the Transition. These two are really a continuity of motion. The difference is that during the Transition, the old worldview and its institutions will continue to falteringly try to cope with the problems of the world; by the time of the Great Transformation, a new worldview and emerging new institutions will be the prevailing way of life.

Back in the present, we have been experiencing over the past few decades the beginning of the transitional processes. Just in the last few years, the big news of the day has leaped from one major event to another in a dizzying kaleidoscope: the emergence of the internet, the dot-com boom and bust, the Clinton impeachment, the y2k computer crisis, the 2000 election crisis, the 9-11 attacks, the war on terrorism, and the war in Iraq. In the midst of each of these events, it seemed that we could see the complete reality of the future, then suddenly the old crisis was pushed to the back burner and the new crisis was everything. By the time you read this, other crises will probably be dominating the screen.

To some extent, this is because of the current dynamics of television news cycles. Even so, it still seems we have been pummeled with a barrage of real changes—future shock on steroids—and we have been learning to maintain a studied nonchalance, as if to say we are not as affected by these events as we really are.

The short list I gave above was focused primarily on American experiences. Meanwhile, Europe has been going through various stages in the integration of the EU, the adoption (or not) of the ecu, the admission of many new member nations, the division over the war in Iraq, and the questions facing NATO. And this is not mentioning German reunification, the breakup of Yugoslavia and attendant wars (Bosnia and Kosovo), the mad cow disease epidemic, the refugee crisis, and the Chunnel.

Japan fell from domination of world manufacturing to an intense internal financial crisis. China has been undergoing a shift toward a variety of market capitalism "with Chinese characteristics," the events of Tiananmen Square, a progressive changing of the guard to a younger leadership, and the North Korean crisis. India and Pakistan have come close to nuclear war over Kashmir. Indonesia has faced the crisis in East Timor, the terror bombings in Bali, and the tsunami. The Islamic world has been dealing with the struggle between theocracy, dictatorship, and modernist democracy. Africa and South America have experienced major change crises as well.

In short, the world has been a busy place of late. Perhaps the world has always been busy, but our new media technologies have made us more aware of the troubles and changes, and that has, in turn, tended to move them along even quicker. Earthshaking crisis? Get over it quickly, because the media has another one to serve up that will make you forget all about this one...sort of. In reality, we don't forget the past crises altogether. They continue to simmer in the back of our minds, and the accumulation "cooks" us.

We are left with a terrible thirst for something, and we are not always sure just what it is we want. Sometimes we want to get back to a fantasy of a better world "like in the good old days." Sometimes we want to hurry up and get on into the real twenty-first century, get this stuff over and get on with the good stuff. We want prosperity and peace, but maybe a little revenge first. Our emotions are unusually stirred up, and our thinking is often not very rational. We are not sure whether to believe a vision of Biblical end-times, a vision of technological utopia, or something else.

This book is about helping us find a positive future vision that realistically explains the relationship between the chaotic change we are seeing and a deeper underlying order.

Polarity Transforms into Alignment

We are shifting to a truly new way of thinking and being. Because it is new, and because we are all still at least partially enmeshed in the old mindset, it is difficult for us to see it clearly. We tend to think in polarity terms rather than in holistic terms. Economics, culture, politics and media coverage generally tend to be seen in terms of conflict between partisan poles.

Thus, "balanced" coverage means presenting a vociferous debate between opposing views, which usually generates more heat than light on the topic. We hardly know how to look at any issue in terms of how it will affect the whole social space from a diverse set of perspectives. Even when we do look at more than two points of view, we usually put them on a spectrum between polar opposites. For a very long time, our way of life has been oriented around binary conflict.

The emerging new mindset will be oriented first to the unity of the whole society and second to the enormously rich variety within it. It will be much more informative and less reactive. The idea in economics, culture, politics, and media will be to understand and nurture an unfolding reality that takes into account all stakeholders in the social space. Our model of reality will be a many-petalled flower, where the opening of all petals is seen as necessary for the beauty of the whole. The idea that there are only two poles of any issue, or that any one part can succeed without all the other parts succeeding as well, will seem primitive and wrong.

No ideal put forth as a solution to the world's problems will be able to succeed unless it wins the support of a significant majority. In the emerging world, even a small number of people violently opposed to an idea can cause great problems. Where today the idea has been to win a partisan majority of more than 50 percent and ignore the views of the losing half, this will soon be seen as unworkable.

The winning program will increasingly be the one that speaks to the needs of almost all the people. We will discover that we need to find ways of winning over resistant minorities on all sides of an issue. The winning platform will be based on a holistic model and will have some meaningful message for all parties. These platforms must always continue to search for and hold out options even to small minorities that are still rejecting the program.

Today, if a candidate, a social program, or a bill attracts a large majority vote, say 60 percent in favor, we call it "a landslide, a mandate!" But that only works in a world of polarity thinking. The other 40 percent has not been addressed. We may not convince everyone, but that does not mean we shouldn't try.

In the world of holistic thinking, we will look for solutions that are acceptable to all stakeholders. Picture a flower with all petals unfolded but one. The emphasis will be on helping that one last petal to unfold so that the whole flower can show its full beauty, even if it takes several decades of patient effort.

As I said, this is hard for us to see because we just don't normally think this way. It sounds idealistic, unrealistic, and even softheaded, but in the fairly near future it will sound like the only way to look at things, and our present way will seem barbaric, stupid, and distant. We are seeing the beginnings of this multistakeholder paradigm in current system-development processes, where requirements definitions try to capture the needs and concerns of all stakeholders to ensure a more effective system.

Economically and politically, the model we have today is like a steep mountain with a castle on top for the wealthy elite. Clinging to the sides of the mountain at different levels are the homes of the middle class. And around the base of the mountain is a vast swamp of slums filled with the poor. The great majority of decision makers that actually affect how the society evolves (and the main audience of books like this) are found among the middle class, who are struggling on the sides of the mountain; whether they are from the upper middle, middle, or lower middle matters very little. To this audience, I suggest that this configuration is unpleasant, unstable, and ridiculous. It is simply not a viable way of organizing the economic life of our society.

The broad middle class will soon come to understand that it really holds most of the power and that it has for far too long been manipulated into this precarious mountainside existence. At that point, a completely new economic and political model will begin to emerge, and we will begin to align to the needs and possibilities of the whole of humanity. The new landscape will ultimately look more like clusters of villages on low rolling hills.

In the new economic and political landscape, both the top and the bottom will be pulled toward the middle. We will see the value in having all human beings share a common environment rather than having one world for the rich and another for the poor, with the middle class suspended in between. The old polarities of class warfare will give way to a new and more complex, more realistic, and more human model. Both capitalism and socialism, as currently constructed, are of the old polarity view.

Ideologues of both left and right may be inclined to resist the new model; they are, after all, employed by conflict. The audience, hearing such critiques of the new model, should remember that polarists have a stake in maintaining conflict. The television news media also has a stake in drumming up conflict, wars, and fear to keep people watching. Allowing them to continue to manipulate the agenda—which, of course, we will not do—would lead to a very bad state of affairs. As new media such as internet news and new attitudes of distrust for centralized media become increasingly the mainstream view, we will experience a shift in the way news is understood. There is already beginning a confusing interregnum period in which control of the news is unclear.

Vigorous centrism will continue to draw adherents from all sides of the political and social spectrum as more people see the deep need to balance and damp down extremism in the stressful period of the Transition. Only centrists will be able to discover and develop the holistic model I have been describing and, as they do, they will win more and more of the allegiance of people around the world.

Let me make this clear: what is emerging is not just another partisan ideology. It will be deeply and centrally devoted to nonpartisan social justice, economic equity, prosperity, and global peace. This ideal will work only if it wins supporters from all sides of the social circle. The new economic models that are emerging must solve problems for business owners, entrepreneurs, workers, independent professionals, investors, and the chronically unemployed. It must be a model that truly sees all parts of the human family as legitimate stakeholders, and it must set goals for all, as well. All parts of our society must be able to contribute to the building of a new future.

The leftist systems of communist demagogues and bureaucratic machines doling out equal misery to all are not going to work. Neither is unregulated, unbridled, so-called "free-market" capitalism. (In reality, the capitalist market is never truly free.) The new model will take the best from all theories and add new concepts to synthesize a workable way. The vast majority of people seek a life of modest comfort and peace. Beyond a certain degree, what is the value to society of having huge sums of money tied up in the hands of the very few. On the other hand, some people will always have more ability and desire to achieve relative wealth. The emerging system must recognize that some will always live at the top of the hill and others at the bottom. In the new model, however, the slope must not be so steep, the bottom must not be so low, and the top must not be so high.

It is unjust and not aligned with any acceptable set of values for one person to hold oppressive power over another. Whenever a person's life and livelihood is controlled by another such that they have little choice but to submit to the employer's whims, this is slavery. This situation is prevalent today and inevitably leads to abuses that we prefer not to examine too closely because we get uncomfortable when our values are challenged. The systems we have been living under until now have enabled the economically powerful in all forms of corrupt emotional, physical, and sexual abuse.

The new model will insist on aligning us with our values, will expose hypocrisies and secret abuses, and will demand real justice and freedom of soul for all. And the times of conflict in the beginning need not last for long. Even in the darkest hour, know that this vision is certain to manifest. All who look honestly into their hearts know this is right.

When we integrate the clear view of both head and heart, we will come to understand that only such a vision is truly realistic for the world as it is now emerging. Nothing else will do. This is the true realism.

Unfortunately, clinging to ideas that are clearly on their way out can bring out a dangerous apocalypticism. Much of the conflict we are seeing is conditioned by an expectation of the devastating "end times," with "the rapture" as a magical salvation from destruction. This orientation encourages a self-fulfilling prophecy.

The amount of time we spend in this century, and possibly into the next, sorting out the conflict and bringing the new vision into reality will depend in part on bringing the meta-stories of all traditional religions out into the open. The global community needs to find ways for all communities to hear their stories in public and to consider the expectations that may be hidden within them.

When people consider the alternatives of apocalyptic religious wars versus a wise way forward toward a world where all are free to practice their beliefs without a need for polarized conflict, most will recognize the second alternative as more truly aligned with the highest teachings of their religions and also with their self-interest. All of the major world religions preach peace as among the highest values.

Increasingly leaders from all religions are seeing the value of reaching out in the ecumenical spirit and finding the common ground on which all religious teaching is based. As more and more writers and speakers emphasize the deeper truths in all religions and philosophies and the wrongness of attacking others, a calming influence will spread to all the multicultural communities of the world.

We must come to understand that killing, torturing, and robbing in God's name means sure destruction of our souls and is not at all aligned with God's plan. We will come to see that speaking in exclusionary ways is also a form of violence that often leads to physical violence. We could see that dawn in our lifetimes, or we could delay it—but not for long. Even in the darkest night, the dawn is near.

The Great Transformation

Even today, it is hard for us to see beyond the Great Transformation. It has not yet emerged, but already we are being pulled into its gravitational well. As this twenty-first century unfolds, we will see planetary unity and cultural pluralism materialize as the only viable reality in a world of shattering, high-technology changes.

The current form of the conflict embodied as the war on terror will ultimately end as emergent societies discover better ways of competing. Surprisingly, this will also lead to a progressive dissolution of the great powers—the US, the EU, Russia, Japan, China, and India—into a planetary governance network including regional centers such as Brazil, South Africa, and Indonesia. This shift is already well under way and very little can stop the process since it is driven by necessity.

The relatively peaceful transformation in South Africa from apartheid to a new way of life offers a moral example, since it was accomplished in a far better way than most postcolonial transitions. Networks of city states, regional commissions, and functional bodies are likely to gradually supercede nation states as this process unfolds.

As the semi-merged planetary system becomes widely accepted as the new reality, presided over by a network of planetary leaders and change agents, the conditions will be ripe for the formal emergence of the Great Transformation ideology. There may be several contenders in the beginning, all presenting similar ideas in various garb. Out of this political pack will emerge a frontrunner, possibly an individual champion, but definitely a planetary program, that promotes the ideals and policies that a large majority of the world's citizens will embrace.

These ideals will be presented through powerfully successful applications of an array of new communication technologies, such as what we call virtual reality (VR) today, only by then it will be much more evolved and compelling. Ultimately we will experience it as a great consensus conversation in which all participants feel they are part of defining the new reality. In fact, much of it will be carefully pre-scripted, but most of us will love it and believe we invented it (because it will take our needs into account).

This power structure will launch the Great Transformation. This will become a democratic planetary power structure that will control us very effectively by the simplest of means: giving us what we want—and what we need.

The combination of population control, super-virtual reality media, new resources from advanced technology, super healthcare, space exploration, depth psychology, and real organizational responsiveness (good government) will create an irresistible combination, and the new system will be founded. The great majority will love it. We will believe that the parts that aren't perfect yet soon will be, and meanwhile the benefits will be enormous.

Accomplishments of The Great Transformation

The Great Transformation will:

- Provide universal employment and education
- End war, violent crime, prejudice, and domestic abuse
- Create new health solutions and end most pain
- Conquer the solar system and its resources
- Create an ecologically sustainable world process
- Extend life span and psychological well-being
- Deliver awesome VR entertainment

Even if it takes a few hundred years to complete this system, we will delight in being part of it.

The conventional movie distopia of violent, smoggy, mega metropolises and barren deserts ruled by techno-militias will be more a phenomenon of the near future transition period in which we are getting ready. This will not emerge as the dominant paradigm; the reasons are many, but the main reason is that such unappealing visions of the future will not be able to compete politically for the minds and hearts and pocketbooks of the most powerful people in the world. (The war-aristocracy approach already will have failed.)

The Great Transformation ideal will appeal to the vast majority of educated people because it will be safer, happier, and a lot more fun. They in turn will use the new media to convince the rest of the world to go along, and it won't be a hard sell. New health technology, new psychology, new entertainment media, and relative peace will go a long way to making the more difficult challenges tolerable for the large global population.

We will be surrounded by subtle propaganda that weaves positive, forward-looking themes into both the "establishment line" and the various "rebellion ideologies." For example, programmers will design/co-opt several youth cultures and several cultural movements with themes that feel rebellious but actually integrate into the Great Transformation plan. The idea will be to pull as many creative new ideas as possible into the integrated program while guiding it in a positive direction. This is actually much the same concept as the representative constitutional democracy we know today. The difference will be that, in the Great Transformation period, people really will feel that they are part of an evolving new experiment. The media will reinforce this feeling by telling us it is so and by showing us a continuous stream of examples.

One of the most effective tools of the winner in the Great Transformation political game will be creating a new economics of near universal employment. The challenge will be to generate a booming economy and a declining planetary population at the same time. The key will be entertainment-education via cheap virtual reality units and powerful propaganda scripting 24/7. Another effective aid will be super advanced drugs, including feel-good-plus vitamins, antibiotics, anti-aging supplements, and so forth, with newer, better versions appearing regularly. Pharmaceuticals need not be as harmful to natural health or as expensive as they often are today.

Creating real as opposed to illusory global affluence, universal longevity, and full utilization of everyone's potential will take longer and will depend on several generations of population stabilization, plus massive pollution cleanup, depth-education, organizational advances, and many other tough accomplishments. However, the leadership will have plenty of time, because what they offer will be so much better than what we know today that very few will want to oppose them. They will also have very effective psychological policing and coercion powers. This governance system will last quite a while and will actually accomplish most of what it promises.

The Decline of The Great Transformation System

The ultimate decay and downfall of the Great Transformation institutions will arise from unresolved internal conflict in the hierarchy, which will lead to calcifying bureaucratic structures and complacency relative to the population's desires. They will lose sight of the very dynamic that brought them to power in the first place. While the attention of the leaders is turned toward internal political battles, the population will become restless, wanting more of the best perks, better longevity treatments, more actual power, more freedom, and greater individual expression for divergent ideas.

While the hierarchy originally will have championed freedom of expression, as power becomes consolidated this will be subtly eroded in the interest of keeping power and suppressing rivals. The conquest of the solar system and the undersea domain will create more far-flung and diverse populations who will begin to feel unevenly represented in the Great Transformation policy councils. Politicians looking for a wedge into the power elite will resurrect remnants of old divisions. Professional guilds and technology rivalries will begin to develop dangerous splits in the structural façade.

Eventually, these forces will converge around a challenge issue the hierarchy is not able to resolve. The first most likely result is a schism. This will lead to rapid further splintering and complex alliance shifting, possibly even low-intensity battles. The population will be shocked and will look to more localized belief systems to settle their anxiety and provide a new vision of how the world should work in the new disorder.

The intelligentsia who had previously championed the Great Transformation as the solution to all things will now begin to generate a host of "subversive" new ideas. There will be a feeling of breathing freer, colder air as cultures shake off the stagnation of the overarching, all-inclusive view of the Great Transformation ideology. It will be a more stressful time but also a time of new experiments.

In some conflict areas, the infrastructure will break down for awhile and, once again, people will have to struggle to survive. For the most part, though, the work of the Great Transformation will have provided a durable foundation, even when administered in pieces. The greatest areas of conflict will be ideological and psychological. Many people will feel disoriented and will have to do more thinking for themselves on these matters than they are accustomed to.

There will be a search for new ideals, which will be difficult because the mines of idealism will have been fairly well worked over during the Great Transformation. The emerging leadership will struggle to deal with a subtle feeling of depression, sadness, and betrayal, pervading the populace just behind the surface. There will be a rise in experimental behavior and adventurous entrepreneurial spirit as people break free of the standard ideology.

The Counter-Transformation

Counter-Transformation ideologies will have two components: first, generally accepted anti-Great Transformation ideas; and second, various local flavors. Off-world groups will develop a distinct set of new beliefs, undersea groups another set, and so forth. Various professional and technological factions will come out with specialized tenets that had remained underground when things were intact, and old historical divisions will partially reassert themselves, although we probably will not recognize them for what they claim to be.

What is difficult to perceive, from our vantage point in the pre-Great Transformation world, is that all of this will occur in a society that has been magnificently transformed. Many problems we take for granted today simply will not exist by then. Population will be relatively stable at sustainable lower levels on the planet. The majority of the human population will live in comfortable, off-world space communities. Pollution as we know it today will be nonexistent. Conflicts will occur in a much more civilized manner with very little of the extremes we consider part of life today.

The whole nature of the Counter-Transformation change point is different from anything we know. Despite temptations to compare it to the Reformation, the fall of Rome, or the end of the British Empire, none of these examples will fit the reality.

To try to grasp this era, imagine twenty to thirty generations of peace, prosperity, and extraordinary human accomplishments.[6] Imagine life spans of over two hundred years, good physical health, deep psychological health, very low stress, and widespread advanced spiritual development. Imagine the average educational level surpassing today's doctoral level. And imagine that all of this change is occurring in a population that cares deeply about humanity and feels a profound sense of unity and a commonality of values.

How will such people deal with divisions within the human family? And what will the divisions be? We might be tempted to wonder how such wonderful people could experience divisions after achieving so much, yet they will. Partly, the achievement itself will bring divisions.

Imagine a council meeting: Some of the delegates have become fully adapted to life under water, others to life in space or on other

---

[6] At an average generation value of twenty-five years, twenty to thirty generations equals five hundred to seven hundred fifty years. Note the distinction between "generation" and "life span."

planetary bodies; some have evolved highly specialized mental capacities; most have modified body and brain structures. They are all fully human, yet they have evolved a level of diversity well beyond any we know today. In some ways, they may have begun to diverge into distinct species that no longer interbreed.

Yet, at the same time, they feel a greater sense of human unity than we do now. They do not accept the prejudice and stereotyping that is so prevalent today. These are people of great psychological well-being who have been raised from birth into something like a religion of human unity that has demonstrated its greatness with wondrous works. And yet...the old order is not resolving the new challenges. The council meditates, discusses, and debates, applies all the tenets and practices that have made it great for hundreds of years, but something is not working, and they suffer a subtle sorrow and curiosity about what will come next.

The actual nature of this situation is not something we can grasp except to know that it is as likely that the Great Transformation institutions will break down eventually as it is likely that they will arise to begin with. These realities are built into the structure of our present time and can be read there clearly if we look with a steady eye.

Recognition of the nature of the Great Transformation that is already pulling us into its orbit and a preview of its accomplishments, as well as its eventual demise into something even greater, will help us navigate the current near-future process of the Transition. This recognition will help us understand some of the forces pulling at humanity today from its desire for future ideals and from its attachment to old traditions.

Ultimately the rising Great Transformation ideology will draw on the best from every old tradition and refine it into something new for a new millennium. Along the way we will struggle with old fears and prejudices, old habits and superstitions, and our own very imperfect and stressed-out natures. We will have to discover the momentum of the human spirit within us and submit to the purging fires of destiny to find our alignment with what is coming.

The Flowering

As the Great Transformation guided human evolution through the awakening of soul consciousness, the Great Liberation, or "The Flowering," will awaken us to the level of spirit toward the end of the millennium.

The Awakening and Spread of Spirit Consciousness

The dissolving of structures brought by the Counter-Transformation will coincide with the awakening of the spirit level of human consciousness. It will become apparent that the varied and far-flung ranges of human civilization need a new form of guidance. The awakening of the true spirit consciousness will shake us to the core and lead to the conscious dismantling of most of the control structures of the Great Transformation. They will have done their work; we will need freedom more than we need constraints. A new force will blow through the solar system out to the civilization growing on the inner edge of the Oort cloud, a vast cloud of planetoids and comets beyond the orbit of Pluto.

Having reached the fulfillment of soul consciousness, we will follow the path of mystics who have gone before and reach deeper into the divine mystery. We will begin to know the power of Divine Presence as a form of living energy. That is why I refer to this as an angelic era. The general mass of humanity will become responsive to an objective awareness of the Divine Presence in all of life. The learning of this period will continue to occupy us until well into the fourth millennium.

The advanced edge of humanity at the end of the third millennium will move beyond the first level of spirit consciousness to the level of knowing the divine attributes as objective entities. These flowering waves of consciousness will give us capacities we can barely dream of today. The depth of wisdom in these waves will require many centuries to absorb, carrying us almost halfway into the fifth millennium, or approximately 4300.

The Continuing Human Flowering beyond 3000

In the fourth millennium, humanity will have spread throughout the hundreds of thousands of icy bodies at the edge of our solar system called the Oort cloud. We will have discovered how to draw zero-point energy from the vacuum of space and be able to live comfortably far from the warmth of the Sun. Contemplation of the divine qualities will have given us vast abilities and enormous goodness.

Then the whole of human civilization will dive into a great contemplation of the eternal void and the nature of the Absolute. We will experience the Divine Being as an annihilation of our own consciousness. For many centuries we will live as a great community of contemplatives.

The middle of the sixth millennium (5500) will see the emergence of a dazzling wave of clarity and emerging omniscience. All existence will be seen through as a precise transparency. The absorption of this level will carry us through another thousand-year period to the middle of the seventh millennium (6500).

By this time we will have spread to the farthest reaches of the Oort cloud, almost a third of the way to the nearest star. A new consciousness will arise within us as we truly come to know ourselves as spirit. Humanity will have come to the point of receiving its established station as the crown of creation. Then we will begin a great diaspora across the galaxy and across the universe. Where the earlier waves of consciousness taught us about the Absolute, the next wave will awaken us to the nondual. We will know the Divine and the Human as one: matter, soul and spirit with no dualities, just one great moving life. This universal expansion will continue approximately another thousand years to 7500.

Then the final perfection of the God-Human station will appear. This wave completes the absorption of the nondual state as we explore the universe acting to awaken consciousness everywhere. Humanity will have become unified with God and will act as awakeners of all life everywhere.

These farthest images of the human flowering mean little to us in our current consciousness. But knowing that they are there for us to reach toward gives even greater courage and inspiration today. When we begin to see that even our smallest daily struggle is part of a great and holy unfoldment, all things get brighter. We can move with renewed focus in the little efforts of daily life. The small is part of the large, and the large is part of the whole. There is no difference ultimately between the divine motion in the universe and the divine motion in us as we go about living our lives. The more we understand this, the more we stop making false divisions and creating opposition for ourselves. When we live positively, without creating unnecessary adversaries, we experience much less adversity. Life becomes a wondrous unfolding of the miraculous; with every instant, everything is new.

These extraordinary transformations that the majority of human society will attain many centuries from now have already been experienced by the great teachers of our past. Many future leaders will awaken more quickly to higher levels of realization than the general populace and will use these advanced capabilities to help guide the continuing unfoldment of human society.

PART II.
What Will Change and Why

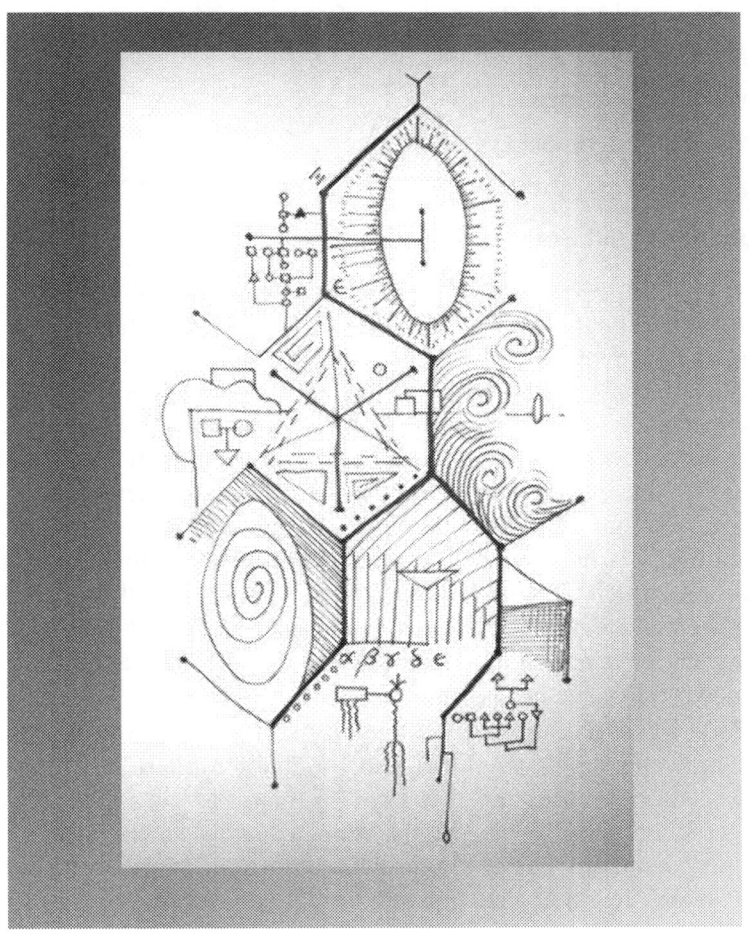

Introduction to Part II Social Functions (S$_\varphi$)

Part II of this book looks at our emerging transformation through the hexagonal lens of six intersecting social functions (S$_\varphi$):

1. Human Science   H·S
2. Spiritual Culture   S·C
3. Emerging Technology   E·T
4. Media Development   M·D
5. Wealth Economics   W·E
6. Wisdom Governance   W·G

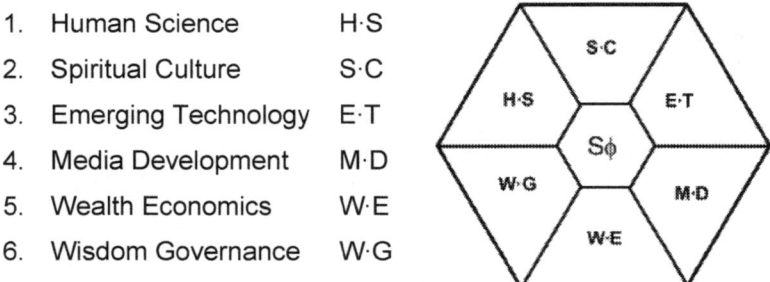

Figure 1. Social Functions Diagram

Each function is covered in a separate chapter. Of course, there are other social functions, but these six represent the main drivers of change. Other functions are subsumed within them or not addressed.

The chapter on **Human Science** introduces us to the Transformation Model: three tiers of development with several levels or waves in each tier. From the beginning of human history to the present, we have been developing the first tier, egoic "personality." The next millennium will be about developing the second tier, "soul" consciousness. The general mass of humanity will not fully develop the third tier, which I have called "spirit," until after the year 3000. Nevertheless, we human beings have always had the full structure of all three tiers present within us as our spiritual DNA, and some few advanced souls have unfolded these.

Part II examines how this hexagon of social functions will unfold as we move up the waves of the Transformation Model.

A central premise of this book is that evolving consciousness changes everything. From earliest human history to the present day, each time humanity has evolved to a new level of consciousness, these basic social functions have been transformed. The functions have remained relatively stable, but the ways in which they are expressed changes. Thus, we can extrapolate from the direction of evolving consciousness to future expressions of these social functions.

The chapter on **Spiritual Culture** describes our progressive integration as a diverse world metaculture. All of the world's spiritual traditions are contributing to an emerging integrated wisdom. Science and spirituality are also integrating into a unified philosophy of transformation. We will learn to use this wisdom to develop virtues and awaken to higher levels of understanding and being.

The **Emerging Technology** chapter explores the interactions and convergences of four categories of technology: physiotech, biotech, humantech, and mediatech. It describes some of the processes by which technologies evolve and how we can track their emergence. The most important thing about all technologies is how they affect us socially and as individuals, how they impact our lives. Some of the specific technology applications examined include space exploration, environmental biology, medicine and health, and the next big wave, nanotechnology.

One of the most powerful transforming agencies in the coming decades and centuries will be our rapidly evolving media technologies. The chapter on **Media Development** analyzes how our electronic media are developing and how they will affect us, both disruptively and later as positive tools for healing and transformation.

The chapter on **Wealth Economics** describes the growing innovation economy, network-based business, and our progressively more urban future. It presents a vision of the long-term trend toward greater economic equity in the world and the need to develop transformation economics to manage transitional disruptions and ultimate stabilization. Humanity is about to become much richer in many ways.

The **Wisdom Governance** chapter explains why we will establish a subtle new form of planetary governance by the end of this century. It describes why this structure will be far more democratic and transparent than anything we have seen before.

Part II uses these six social functions to track the stages of human transformation as we go forward to build a new world, which I call the Great Transformation society.

Chapter 4.
Human Science (H·S)

Human beings are the most complex and interesting phenomena in the known universe. The study of human beings will continue to consume ever more of our attention as we seek to understand our true nature and come to grips with our whole reality.

The Convergence of Human Science

The many disciplines converging into the domain called human science include:

1. Psychology, Sociology and Anthropology
2. Archeology and History
3. Philosophy and Religion
4. Mythology and Culture Studies
5. Communications and Media Studies
6. Linguistics
7. Education and Training
8. Library Science and Knowledge Management
9. Software Development, Cybernetics, and AI/IA (Artificial Intelligence/Intelligence Augmentation)
10. Neurology and Physiology
11. Demographics and Psychographics
12. Law and Law Enforcement
13. Future Studies
14. Memetics and Complexity Theory
15. Business Management and Organizational Development
16. Government, Diplomacy, and Political Science

Human Science will consider the parameters and integrations of all these fields as they move toward integration. In most cases, breakthroughs in any of these areas affect many of the others. The central questions of what human beings are, how they function, and how they interact with each other are part of all these fields. The more we look at them as an integrated whole, the more we will gain deeper understandings of how to solve human problems. The future era will be the era of human science. This convergent field will develop the most important new technologies of the future. In fact, it will redefine what technology means.

Even so, each of these fields will continue to evolve on its own, develop more varied subfields, and will enrich the whole of human science in the process. Many current-day disciplines on my list will be absorbed into other kinds of studies as breakthroughs create new ways of looking at things, but the central idea of the human being as the object of study is not likely to disappear any time soon.

Biological and physical sciences, mechanical technologies, and other disciplines not within the scope of human science will also play a role in the future. Nevertheless, the central challenges will pose questions for human science, and the answers will guide policies in other sciences as well as in government and business. We are increasingly asking ourselves questions about how the technologies we create are affecting us as human beings. This brings us to one of the most central questions to have engaged us throughout our history...

What Is A Human Being?

How we answer this question changes everything about how we view the world and what we are able to do in it. The more complete our answer, the more power we have over our lives. Throughout human history, as we have developed from one level to the next, our understanding of this question has grown. Each developmental wave has had a fuller answer to what a human being is.

Great spiritual teachers in every culture have brought gifts of deep knowledge about the vast wonder that is the true human being. Frequently, however, much of this wisdom has been diverted into the control of priesthoods, who have kept some of the most important parts secret. Knowledge that could empower people has been hidden away and eventually forgotten. (This process of losing deep meaning can also occur in the modern sciences as well.)

As we are often told, knowledge is power, and no power is more fundamental than knowledge of human potential. Organizations generally want to preserve themselves; thus, first by small measures, then by large, they begin to hold back some of the more liberating wisdom while promulgating teachings that empower the organization's leaders. This is the sad and beautiful story of religions. They begin with great gifts from a holy man, meant to liberate everyone, then, by increments, descend into esoteric cabals, formalistic bureaucracies, and administrative power structures. Another reason wisdom gets lost is that disciples are unable to fully understand the teaching they receive from holy teachers.

The time of secrecy is clearly over now; all the great wisdoms are being revealed. The way of transformation is being separated from the cultural structures in which it was once embedded. Now a universal teaching is unfolding in many forms so as to be available to the widest range of people. This book incorporates some of the many teachings that were once either secret or unknown.

One of the most important understandings is that human consciousness exists on many levels that we can discover as we grow. All human beings are children of the Divine Being, and in our highest levels of consciousness we become one with that ultimate reality. To know this, and to know the road map that guides our unfoldment, is to be empowered to transform our lives.

Many systems and road maps exist from the many spiritual traditions and teachers. Although they vary somewhat in details, they are mostly agreed on the basic premise: that human beings consist of many layers of consciousness and that we can realize greater awareness by learning to develop through these layers.

Some of this spiritual learning can be acquired in much the same way as any other learning. Nevertheless, realizing new states of consciousness cannot be achieved simply by cognitive study. Realization is a subtle and experiential thing; it requires guidance. Despite the fact that breakthroughs often come suddenly, they rarely occur without study and disciplined practice.

One of the first steps is to become familiar with the basic road map. The version presented here is what I call the Transformation Model, which has been developed from many sources including my own peak experiences.

The Transformation Model

This formulation of what a human being is remains only the barest sketch of what the full Transformation Model includes. Space in this book is limited, thus I have focused on those aspects most related to my subject matter.

After writing the first two drafts of this book completely from the vision as I received it, I paused to research into what others have said about the future of human evolution. Among these readings, I came across the model developed by Clare Graves, which was presented in the book *Spiral Dynamics* by his students Don Beck and Christopher Cowan and elaborated in the writings of Ken Wilber. Many writers in emerging fields of social transformation, such as Barbara Marx Hubbard in her book *Conscious Evolution,* have borrowed from and built on this model, as do I.[7] The spiral model corresponds, more or less, with what I had learned from other sources and meshes well with this vision because it extends the psychological and spiritual dimensions of human unfoldment into the social and cultural domain.

Beck and Cowan describe eight levels up to holistic consciousness and mention, without much elaboration, a ninth level as the next level to emerge. Wilber added to the spiral model in his integral model. I am further extending this work as the Transformation Model. Wilber also compared a large number of developmental road maps from various philosophers, psychologists, and spiritual traditions in the appendix to his book, *Integral Psychology.*

I have derived my understanding of the levels above the ninth level from vision, from my own spiritual experiences, and from my good fortune in knowing several highly evolved human beings, most notably the revered Sufi sage, Bawa Muhaiyaddeen. Living and studying with Bawa for many years gave me a nearby example of what a true human being could be, and the experience utterly transformed my life. I have also incorporated many of the understandings I acquired from over six years of study in the Diamond Approach, developed by A.H. Almaas.

I have named the three tiers of the model Personality, Soul, and Spirit for the aspect that is developed in each tier. The waves of development are represented by colors as follows:

---

[7] Beck and Cowan, *Spiral Dynamics*, 1996; Wilber, *Integral Psychology*, 2000; Hubbard, *Conscious Evolution*, 1998. The blogosphere includes a host of writers discussing these spiral/integral models.

I Personality	II Soul	III Spirit
1. Beige	7. Golden Olive	15. Amethyst
2. Purple	8. Yellow	16. Sapphire
3. Red	9. Turquoise	17. Onyx
4. Blue	10. Coral	18. Diamond
5. Orange	11. Teal	19. Ruby
6. Green	12. Gold	20. Emerald
	13. Indigo	21. Alpha-Omega
	14. Pearl	

The first tier addresses the stages humanity has gone through in developing the egoic personality levels of consciousness. Any particular person is a mixture of different levels of development.

With the exception of Golden Olive, which I added, Beck and Cowan describe the waves up through Turquoise. I will summarize some of this material along with my own thoughts, particularly on our present and near future situation, then move on to explain the future waves and the major shifts I believe will be associated with them. Of great importance, also, are the gifts each level leaves behind within us, as well as the repressed unresolved conflicts.

The dates I have given for the "era" of any given wave are, of course, approximate. All waves and levels are present at all times but in different forms. I believe that waves we have not yet attained as individuals or as societies are present as latent structures hidden in our spiritual DNA. These may be experienced by any human being at any level as a peak experience, such as a mystical vision, but, as Wilber points out, the memory of this experience will be interpreted by the capabilities of the person's normal level of consciousness.[8]

The major structures of the Transformation Model indicate that the third millennium will be primarily a period of soul development. We are moving into a level of realization that is transpersonal, that is, the realization that we are not our personalities and that personality structures are actually barriers to experiencing our true being, self, or soul. A central message of this transformational vision is that, as we

---

[8] Ken Wilber, *Integral Psychology*, 2000.

discover the satisfaction of knowing the soul level, we will completely change our whole human civilization in some very positive ways.

Tables 2, 3, and 4 below summarize human history and future evolution, based on vision and extrapolations of our direction of consciousness development. Each wave is represented by its color and a two-letter code. The *descriptors* column provides terms that describe the nature of each wave. The *era* column gives the estimated range of dates during which the wave is socially operational within the culture. The *events and civilizations* column summarizes the characteristic occurrences and the kinds of societies that each wave generates.

These concepts are explained in further detail in the pages that follow. The diagram in figure 2 following the table provides a condensed way of representing the developmental waves of the Transformation Model.

Wave	Descriptors	Era	Events and Civilizations
Green (GR)	Postmodern Pluralist Diversity	2150 1850 CE	Social welfare; Abolitionism; Women's suffrage; Civil rights; Ecology; The struggle and the exhaustion
Orange (OR)	Modern Rational Materialist	2040 1500 CE	The rationalist "enlightenment;" Democracy and science; Capitalism and Communism (dialectical materialism)
Blue (BL)	Conventional Rules & Roles	2025 CE 2000 BCE	Patriotic nationalism; Traditional religions; Obedience to the "one truth"
Red (RE)	Conquest Empire	6000 BCE	Early empires; Power and egoic expression; Freedom from tribal limitations
Purple (PU)	Tribal Kinship	35,000 BCE	New Stone Age; Tribal Cultural Explosion; Chiefdoms; Totems and superstitions
Beige (BE)	Primal Survival	2.6 Mil. BCE	Old Stone Age; Nomadic bands; Survival drives; Alert sensory awareness for food or threat

Table 2. The Transformation Model - Tier I

Tier I presents the waves of evolution we have gone through from our earliest history to the present day. It describes also the stages each individual goes through in developing a mature personality.

Wave	Descriptors	Era	Events and Civilizations
Pearl (PE)	Heavenly Gate Sublime Luster Judgement	3800 2450 CE	Mid-Kuiper Civilization; weighing the blended mature soul; Gate of awakening beyond soul
Indigo (IN)	Illuminated Transcendent Expectant	3500 2250 CE	Establish Kuiper civilization; Solar opulence impacted by rays of spiritual Illumination;
Honey Gold (HG)	Ontarchic Resonant Radiant	2850 2180 CE	Peak of the Belt Civilization; Rejoicing in prosperity and longevity; Outer belt and Jovian moons
Teal (TE)	Paxarchic Consolidative Lexiconic	2700 2080 CE	Consolidate Belt Civilization; Create new philosophy, law and religion to coordinate solar system
Coral (CO)	Avatarchic Solar Drive	2500 1980 CE	Strengthen the Great Transformation; Drive into solar system; Establish Belt Civilization
Turquoise (TU)	Holistic Planetary	2450 1920 CE	Establish the Great Transformation system; Planetary civilization; World peace
Yellow (YE)	Integral Flexible Flowing	2350 1900 CE	Transpersonal awareness; Systematic integration; Planetary negotiation; Psi-war recovery
Golden Olive (GO)	Seeking Transforming Awakening	1950 2280 CE	Transforming and awakening during the Transition; Helping people through the recovery

Table 3. The Transformation Model - Tier II

Tier II presents the waves of soul development that describe our emerging future. It also describes the stages of transformational growth that advanced souls go through as they unfold higher evolutions of consciousness. This is the story of the emerging third millennium.

Wave	Descriptors	Era	Events and Civilizations
Alpha-Omega (AΩ)	Beyond description	Eternal Timeless	Omnipresent
Emerald (EM)	Perfected Nondual Crown	10000 7200 CE	The perfected divine human fills the galaxy with conscious presence
Ruby (RU)	Established Nondual Spirit-Being	8100 6300 CE	God-Human spirit-self awakens, The stellar diaspora begins
Diamond (DI)	Transparent Omniscient Clarity	6900 4900 CE	Late Oort civilization; Sudden breakthrough of crystal clarity, precise knowing; All-seeing
Onyx (ON)	Annihilative Contemplative Absorption	5500 4300 CE	Mid-Oort civilization; Absence; Spiritual contemplation of the void; Concentrated still point
Sapphire (SA)	Essential Causal Attributes	4900 2900 CE	Early Oort civilization; Zero-point energy; Long tutelage in the divine qualities; Vast awakening
Amethyst (AM)	Angelic Archetypal Transclastic	4000 2800 CE	Late Kuiper civilization; Dissolving of The Great Transformation; Spiritual Shattering and Mystical Awakening

Table 4. The Transformation Model -Tier III

Tier III presents our spiritual far future and describes the realms of spirit that influence our awakening today. These domains represent dimensions of the divine Ultimate Reality. In addition to describing the end of the third millennium and the events of millennia to come, they also describe the states of consciousness of the spiritually awakened holy beings that have been our teachers throughout human history and who will continue to guide us in the coming centuries.

Figure 2 shows all three tiers of the Transformation Model: **I** Personality (6 waves), **II** Soul (8 waves), and **III** Spirit (7 waves).

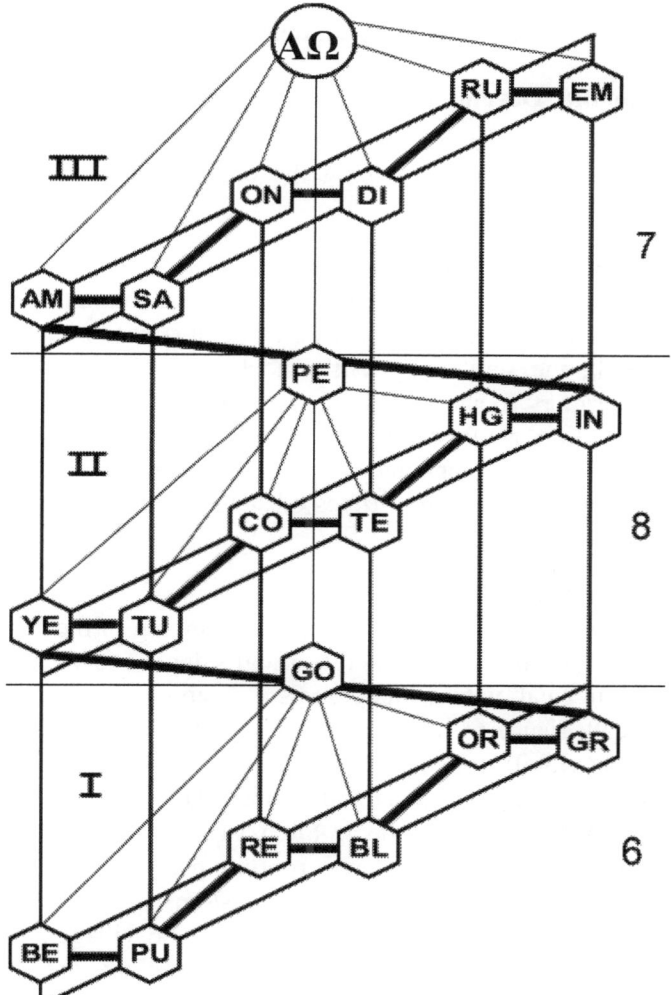

Figure 2. The Transformation Model: Harp-Ladder Form

Each wave is represented by its two-letter symbol inside a hexagon (representing social functions and lines of development). This "harp" form of the model also shows the harmonic correspondences between tiers, for example, second-tier Coral (Co) is the harmonic of first-tier Red (Re) and third-tier Onyx (On). The model represents the spiritual DNA of humanity as a historical and future collective whole, as well as the full potential of any individual human being. All waves are always present in some form, either actualized, repressed, or latent.

Tier I: Personality Development[9]

This is the tier of human history, describing the six waves through which we have grown in developing the complex structures of the contemporary personality.

Beige (Be): Survivalist and Instinctive

This wave describes the consciousness of the first human bands, of newborn infants, and of people regressed by great stress (street people, the mentally ill, the senile, the battle-shocked, victims of abuse or famine). The primary focus is on food, water, warmth, and safety. The gifts of this level are acute sensory attention and "animal" instinct for survival. This potential remains within higher levels as a hidden foundation that people call on in times of danger and privation. Beige is the color of savannah grasslands.

Purple (Pu): Tribal and Magical

As bands aggregated into larger tribes at the beginning of the Neolithic or New Stone Age, the focus shifted to tribal safety. The viewpoint is animistic and magical, with primary goals of keeping the spirits happy and showing allegiance to tribal chiefs. The order of tribal society is maintained by ritual, totem, and taboo.[10] Tribes are precisely structured along kinship lines even today, and relationships are defined by totemic symbols. The attitude is often superstitious with curses, spells, and the evil eye considered routine parts of life. Life is organized around seasonal cycles and tribal customs.

Today this wave is seen in extended family and village structures throughout the world, as well as in street gangs with their signs, athletic teams with their fans, corporate "tribes," and in royal heraldry. Purple is the color of tribal royalty. One gift of this wave may be its finely-tuned sense of tribal politics and social nuance. This level is also sensitive to the vitality of nature and the magical meaning it projects onto it. Purple emerged during the great cultural explosion of art,

---

9 First-tier descriptions are primarily drawn from Spiral Dynamics, plus Wilber and A.H. Almaas (multiple works), with additions of my own.

[10] Sigmund Freud, *Totem and Taboo*, 1913. Other analysts of this wave include Claude Lévi-Strauss, James G. Frazier, and Joseph Campbell.

decoration, and technological innovation that occurred some thirty-five to forty thousand years ago by current reckoning.

Red (Re): Impulsive and Mythic

As tribal life evolved into intertribal trade and warfare, war chiefs reacted to the rigid constraints and complex protocols of tribal ritual with a new feeling of self-expression. Ritualized contests and raids for wives were put aside for a new concept: outright conquest. The attitude of Red is, "I do what I please because I am strong." Red is about the ego and its id desires, sex, violence, and greed. This movement led to the founding of the early empires and the heroic tales of conquest by the god-kings.

As McLuhan points out, writing was the facilitative technology that transitioned the Purple-Red war chief into the divine emperor.[11] Even a primitive system of writing was necessary to run an empire, dispatch armies, tally tribute, and, of course, record victories. The Greek myth of Cadmus was that he sowed the letters of the alphabet like seeds and they sprang up as armed men. The oral sagas of early Purple-Red were transformed into the written victory accounts of full Red conquering emperors.

Psychologically, this level of consciousness is a necessary part of separation-individuation. The infant needs Red strength to say no to mommy and thereby define a self.[12] In spiritual development, unresolved issues repressed from the Red level cause enormous barriers to progress that almost always remain unresolved until the individual does shadow work to address and resolve primitive feelings of rage and lust.

Particularly among Green-wave people, we may see loss of energy, indecisiveness, and struggles with guilt over repressed anger and desire. The remedy is often to return to the Red in a controlled environment, such as psychotherapy or Golden Olive transformation work, and reclaim the gift of the Red. By coming to terms with primitive emotions and resolving them, we can recapture the strength and aliveness needed to leap to second-tier soul consciousness. As long as these energies are trapped, they remain untransformed and we will not know the authenticity of our true self or soul. (This means metabolizing these energies, not giving in to them.)

---

[11] Marshall McLuhan & Eric McLuhan, *The Laws of Media*, 1988

[12] A.H. Almaas, *Essence*, 1986, *The Pearl Beyond Price*, 1988, and *The Inner Journey Home*, 2004

Blue (Bl): Purposeful and Conventional

Into the world of egocentric kings and conquerors, the great teachers of the axial age (1800 BCE – 800 CE) brought a new wave of consciousness, the Holy Law. The founders of the world's religions were themselves of a much higher spiritual level, but what they gave to society was the idea of a God-given code of conduct that taught restraint against the unbridled ego lusts of warriors and rulers.

From Blue's viewpoint, the force of the "one truth" gives life an ordered meaning, direction, and purpose. Freedom of the self is sacrificed to the righteous way of life, which is precisely defined by laws and regulations and enforced by the order of the priesthood and the God-given scripture. Blue is about defining rules and roles. It brings sharply defined concepts of right and wrong and the authority structures to impose them.

Blue brought a degree of peace and order to society by restraining, to some degree, the whims of Red, but it also guaranteed war between societies with different religions. Conventional religion at the Blue level believes it must be absolute, eternal, and unique (the one truth), therefore any other religion is seen as a threat to be eradicated. Even when basic teachings were similar, the priesthoods could not tolerate deviations of ritual and still retain the absolute power required to restrain Red.

The Blue era, therefore, has been one of conflicts between religions and brutal repression of heresies, meaning any beliefs not in line with the dominant faith. Thus, it also saw the emergence of secret societies and esoteric teachings, hidden to avoid destruction by the Church. Activities such as alchemy were often fronts for research into the question "what is a human being?" using sources from many religions, especially the meeting point of Christianity, Judaism, and Islam. It is interesting to note that the Knights Templar, a secret society and a government in exile from the Kingdom of the Holy Land, was a precursor to the Freemasons and other sources of the next wave, Orange.

The gifts of the Blue wave are many and are the foundation of all later spiritual growth, even though Blue has created many barriers as well. One crucial gift of Blue is the discipline of restraint, without which we have only selfish impulses run amuck. Psychologically, Blue represents the emergence of the superego, when the child internalizes the image and voice of the parental authority in the form of the inner critic. As we will discuss later, this also creates barriers to further growth of the soul.

In present-day circumstances, whenever discipline and sharply defined order are called for, the gifts of the Blue wave are recalled. National patriotism, military discipline, and professional sports teams are all based on Blue principles. Blue's spiritual challenge is to restrain its own aggressive judgmentalism and to see the higher value in greater tolerance for other points of view.

Orange (Or): Rationalistic and Achievist

After centuries of Church dominance, a new wave of rational science began to emerge. At first, the inquisitors were able to control such discoverers as Galileo and force them to recant, but soon the new wave of rationalism became unstoppable. This worldview was expressed as the philosophy of reason in the 1700s Enlightenment era. Its most ambitious political project was the formation of the United States of America, the first modern democratic nation. Although Blue puritans established the American colonies, primarily Orange Freemasons, such as George Washington and other freethinking rationalists, founded the United States as a nation.

The viewpoint of this wave, which still holds most of the power in the world today, is "act in your own self-interest by playing the game to win." It is, both scientifically and economically, firmly materialist in perspective. The only God is seen as a deistic creator, or "Providence," who sets the universe in motion and lets it run according to natural laws which science can discover and use for human material happiness. In some respects, God is viewed as synonymous with nature.

The Orange wave believes in progress, change, and advancement as part of the natural order. As the foundation of capitalism, it gave rise to the bourgeoisie and the concept of upward mobility through self-reliance and merit. It believes in risk taking and social prosperity through technology, strategy, and competitiveness. This wave is also seen in the "dialectical materialism" of Marxist theories.

Orange has brought us most of what we know as the modern world and is the spirit behind corporate globalism. The gifts of this wave are almost too obvious and too numerous to see clearly, but chief among them are reason, freedom of speech and thought, democracy, rule of law, separation of church and state, and the dignity of the individual—especially the strong and resourceful individual.

Green (Gr): Pluralist Community

Into the sometimes harsh world of mercantile capitalism, the Green wave brought a demand for the abolition of slavery, women's suffrage, civil rights, rights for the handicapped, and gay rights. It has focused on caring and sensitivity for the rejected parts of society, the weak, the disenfranchised, and the poor. From its viewpoint, people should seek peace within the inner self and bond with others to discover the caring dimensions of community. It believes that feelings supercede cold rationality and that Earth's resources should be shared equally with all. It reawakens a spirituality of community ethics, social harmony, and human potential.

Green has been magnificent in the role of social critic, exerting tremendous influence and accomplishing major social change, and this it has done without ever being truly in charge. Today, Green exists in the position of perpetual heir: always prince but never king. Interestingly, this frustrating station suits Green just fine, though it chafes at still not having come to power. Orange still retains a firm grip on the major levers of power, even as Green exposes its corruptions and subverts its individualistic principles with concerns for the social good, and even as Orange is effectively forced to comply with consumer pressures.

Why does this situation suit Green? A broad-brush analysis drawn from object relations theory suggests the following psychological payoff: Green frequently adopts what is called the "rejecting object relation," which takes the parent (mother, father, or another object of authority) to be bad, hence rejected. The payoff is that the child (or adult who takes the position as victim to the bad authority) is by contrast, good. The powerful authorities, in this case the corporations, the government, the Americans, the rich people, and so forth, are seen as bad, corrupt, and victimizing; therefore, the victim identity can be seen as innocent and good.

Such a position provides a marvelously easy ethical solution to life's existential dilemmas. By identifying with the weak and casting themselves in the role of oppressed victim (which indeed they sometimes are), Green is absolved of guilt.

Of course this has a cost: Green is left in a state of being cut off from its full power. It is uneasy with situations in which it must take charge. In the Green worldview, to exert decisive authority is to be bad. It prefers to exert its considerable emergent-wave power in the form of unacknowledged regression to Red rebellion, rather than taking responsibility for making ultimate decisions, which it tends to leave to the "Orange father" or, increasingly, to the "Yellow son."

It is more comfortable with the familiar position of revolutionary opposition, hence it must continually search for new causes to champion, new flaws in the system to critique and deconstruct. When it is confronted with the burden of making decisions, Green prefers to use group consensus to diffuse the potential guilt of possibly victimizing someone. Alternatively, Green shifts back to Orange, or in extreme cases, to Red. A better alternative, which is now becoming available, is to evolve through Golden Olive to Yellow, but to do this, Green must see itself clearly and confront the profound transformation to soul consciousness, or second-tier awareness, and this is a difficult passage to accomplish.

Today most people in the developed world, and many in the emerging world, are a mixture of Blue, Orange, and Green, with Red and Purple seeping through under stress. It is partly through struggling to balance this somewhat schizophrenic collection of worldviews that we begin the evolution through Golden Olive to Yellow.

Tier II: Soul Development

Second tier is about the development of soul consciousness. This is the adventure of the coming millennium, the unfoldment of the soul and all that goes with the eight waves of this awakening. Evolving to second tier means these things:

- We know we are not our egoic personality structures.
- We disidentify with cultural incidentals and embrace a clearer view of humanity as a whole.
- We experience ourselves as consciousness, as free awareness, and we recognize that we are awake.
- We are authentic and true to our experience.
- We have the maturity to take responsibility for our lives and, in growing measure, for all life.
- We experience a sense of freedom and capability.
- We are aware of a higher level of mind, of knowing more, of understanding more, and of thinking more clearly.
- We experience fuller awareness of our senses and of our presence, that we are here *now*, experiencing life.
- We have an increased sense of vitality and aliveness.

There are many more signs of soul consciousness, some of which emerge with specific waves, but these give some indication of what this monumental leap can mean. People who are functioning primarily in Golden Olive, or even Yellow, may not experience all of these things all of the time. There are multiple lines of development that need to be stabilized, and the reality is always messier than the model. Nevertheless, these characteristics tend to become more constant as a person stabilizes in second tier. You know when you are experiencing this shift; there is generally very little doubt. If you are not sure, you are probably still in the in-between stages of Golden Olive, which are often difficult but always eventually rewarding.

The second-tier transformation is described further in Chapter 11 as a series of soul journeys.

Golden Olive (Go): Transforming and Awakening

Soul awakening means crossing a great divide between the world experienced through the ego structures of the personality and the reality experienced through essence. Normally, people experience life as a projection of their own personality dynamics, which generally produces a state of dis-satisfaction.

Disharmony within the personality is caused by "loss of essence," that is, being out of touch with our true nature.[13] This is a natural stage of development in early childhood when we are forming a personality, but development is arrested partway through the process because our whole civilization has not yet evolved to support the unfoldment of the essential being. As we grow up, we form a mask, a persona, and we see the world as a mirror image of this mask. We sense that something is wrong, but rather than see it as something in us, we project it onto the world.

The work of spiritual awakening is the process of regaining contact with our essential being. At this time, many people living within the advanced levels of both the Green and Orange waves are on the verge of crossing over into second-tier consciousness.

Both waves have something valuable to offer each other, something that can aid the transition to Golden Olive, but the cultural wars between them have created a barrier to integration. People at the advanced levels of Green and Orange have been able to integrate somewhat, and the right blending of the two produces a beautiful olive.

---

[13] A.H. Almaas, *Essence*, 1986.

When that olive is ripe, and under the proper kind of spiritual pressure, it produces the golden oil that opens the Yellow wave. This bridge to the soul level is the Golden Olive wave.

Green, of course, is poised on the brink of the second-tier divide, just below Golden Olive. But, for a number of complex cultural reasons, many in the Green wave are blocked and have been unable to make the leap to second tier. At the same time, many in the last stages of Orange who are naturally transitioning to Green are resisting full entrance into Green for some of the same complex cultural reasons.

Certain Greens are reabsorbing some Orange as a cultural balancing energy. Today, enormous creative energy is emerging between Orange-greens and Green-oranges. Most professional conventions and gatherings I have attended in recent years are full of these almost Golden Olive people, and they are energetically communicating with each other. Their terminologies differ, but the underlying issue is generally the same. It is a spiritual question (although usually not openly voiced): "How do we achieve fulfillment of the human promise?"

I would translate that as, "How do we regain contact with essence, with our true being?" or, "How do we get to second-tier consciousness?" This unspoken question also arises in people who *have* gotten to Golden Olive and don't really understand it yet as something like, "How do I understand and unfold what I am experiencing? How do I get more of this?"

This sizzling, questing environment of people from the business, scientific, cultural, academic, and spiritual domains is coming together around a host of issues and talking about the potential for human development. They are beginning to cross the Golden Olive bridge.

This book is devoted to supporting that bridge to the experience of true being and knowing its value. The Great Transformation, which is the flowering of humanity, begins with this stem and this bud, and they are swelling in anticipation of spring. All the forces described in this book converge to bring more and more people to the brink of second-tier consciousness and beyond with every passing day. We can choose to *consciously* support this process.

Despite the hazy confusion of the Transition, emerging generations are progressively more awakened and more pragmatically focused. Many people who are able to move into Golden Olive may continue to unfold to higher waves of Yellow, Turquoise, Coral, and above. The nature of the second tier is more fluid and thus nurtures development in a smoother way than first tier.

The key is to get to Golden Olive, but we must always understand that second tier cannot be maintained without embracing all of the first-tier waves as part of a living planetary process. For those working to contact their lost essence, what this means in practice is a lot of difficult psychodynamic work to relax identifications and contractions in the psyche (and in the body) that are blocking the way. The Golden Olive wave almost always involves training and disciplined work with a teacher in a school.

The three waves prevalent in the developed world today, Blue, Orange, and Green, have each built cultural milieus in which they thrive. But a distinction should be made between the levels of consciousness implied by these waves and the cultural milieus they generate. This is an important distinction, because the strains between the cultural milieus impede individual development.

I contend that some people are moving directly from Blue and Orange cultural milieus into the Golden Olive process, bypassing the Green cultural milieu. At the same time, the model distinctly implies that the levels are sequential; one cannot move beyond a level without moving through it and digesting its teaching. So what am I suggesting? Here is what I think is happening:

Green can move directly into Golden Olive by doing psychodynamic work, understanding its suppressed Red, integrating its Blue and Orange undertones, and reaching for the spiritual breakthrough. The question is, how does Orange get to Golden Olive when the way is blocked by a defensive Green culture? And how does Blue get to Golden Olive when the way is blocked by both Orange and Green cultural guards?

I suggest that the Orange culture develops a crypto-Green culture secretly within it, cloaked in Orange camouflage. The individual whose life is contained primarily within the Orange cultural domains of business and/or science may not easily be able to move into the Green culture, but may surreptitiously develop certain Green-wave values and understandings. In fact, business has developed many such cultural structures in recent decades (coaching, teams, sensitivity training). The net effect is people moving through the Green stage without moving prominently through the Green cultural milieu.

The situation for people working within a Blue cultural base appears to be even more difficult, but I'm not sure it is. What I have observed at any number of transformation gatherings is a distinct contingent of people who are coming from obviously Blue-wave environments, such as church or military backgrounds, but who are nevertheless exhibiting aspects of Golden Olive consciousness.

I am hypothesizing that these people have been able to absorb Orange and Green without completely immersing themselves in the cultures of those waves. The only way this seems possible is if crypto-Orange and crypto-Green domains are actually evolving within the Blue cultural milieu, but under Blue camouflage. It's important also to take into account that media have dispersed the worldviews of all three waves throughout much of global society.

Therefore, we should reach out to all three waves to support the people who are evolving within them. Even within nearby Green, Golden Olive is a foreign land, and the transition for Greens is also fraught with resistance, both from without and from within.

Ultimately transformation is about metabolizing psychic structures and social constructs. We learn to digest the ideas within us and to rearrange our lives to support our new understandings.

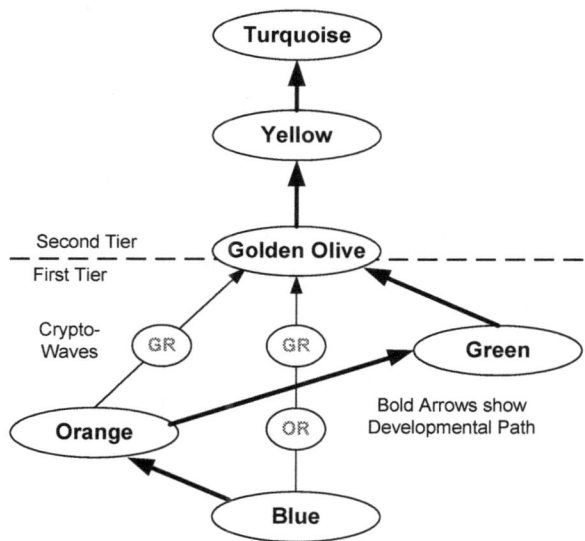

Figure 3. Crypto-Waves and Cultural Milieus

Yellow (Ye): Integral and Flowing
While Golden Olive pulls first-tier waves together and upward to second tier, Yellow reaches down to refine and clarify all first-tier waves. Golden Olive is like winding a cable out of first-tier wires;

Yellow is like a glowing welded bar of integrated qualities. Golden Olive presses out the oil; Yellow filters and purifies it, then discards the pulp.

The Yellow wave is emerging as a response to complexity and as an expression of capability. Yellow arises partly because it must, but mostly because it can. As Golden Olive releases the constraints and political correctness of social Green, Yellow begins to awaken, and we are able to explore a much wider kaleidoscope of experience. Yellow is responsible; it includes the compassion of the Green wave and the discipline of Golden Olive from which it has just emerged. While Green tends toward a depressed emotional tone, and Golden Olive a sense of searching urgency, Yellow radiates joy.

Yellow consciously integrates and refines the capabilities of all first-tier waves. While each first-tier wave identifies with its specific worldview and characteristics, Yellow sees them all as options to be selected according to the needs of the situation, like an array of outfits hanging in its closet.

This wave thinks in terms of complex systems and metasystems as it seeks to digest and coordinate its vast new abilities. Especially, it wants to arrange its life structures for maximum flexibility and spontaneity. It values the experience of "being" more than material possessions, although it has the ability to get whatever it needs. The emphasis is on functionality and competency. It tends to ignore formal rank and status in favor of ability and knowledge.

Yellow welds all the parts together and uses them to learn, grow, and enjoy its sense of potential. It is creative, it integrates feeling and thinking, and it combines analysis and synthesis. Yellow resolves complexity through its brilliant capacity for "vision logic," or multidimensional vision thinking. Its ability to solve problems looks almost magical to first tier, if it notices at all; Yellow subtlety and matter-of-factness tends to obscure the magic and make it look easy. This wave wants to get on with the next interesting challenge, the next thing it wants to play with. It is playful and utterly serious at the same time.

The desire to integrate attracts Yellow-wave people to situations that demand a mixture of diverse skill sets. They love the challenge of complexity and the pleasure of creating higher order within chaos. They are the quintessential chaos surfers. The Yellow wave is, frankly, more fun.

Although generally more disciplined than any previous wave, it is also more fluid. If it needs a break, it takes it, but it can also work night and day if it needs to. This wave is self-directed and completely true to its own authentic reality. It delights in experiencing the rich aliveness of its expanded level of awareness. People on the Golden Olive edge of second tier are drawn toward Yellow's aura of joy and vitality.

Attaining this transformation takes aptitude, disciplined practice, and psychological courage, but it is worth every possible effort. There is nothing in life more important or more desirable in this era than awakening to soul consciousness and stabilizing in that station, and this supreme achievement unfolds as a result of work done in the Golden Olive wave.

Although this level of satisfaction is worth more than any amount of money, people are either attracted to it or not. Even if you do not feel capable of completing this leap, it is valuable to support these efforts and to be around Golden Olive people who are evolving to Yellow. Some of the magic does indeed rub off and may make many things better in your life. Sometimes what seems impossible becomes possible by the grace of such contact.

Turquoise (Tu): Holistic and Planetary
As people begin to fulfill the Yellow mission to integrate the parts, they start to see that the whole is more than the sum of the parts, and Turquoise consciousness begins to arise. Because second tier is more conscious, transitions between waves are more fluid and less conflicted. There is less interwave tension and more understanding. Here Yellow sees beyond its own focus on flexibility and freedom to the needs of the whole of humanity.

The focus of Turquoise is planetary concern for everyone and every life form. People of this wave are the real ecosystem masters and the subtle diplomats who can bring about the consensus necessary to make planetwide ecological planning succeed. Turquoise is profoundly spiritual and compassionate, working across the great spectrum of life to bring about world peace, justice, and prosperity. It is really the first level to be truly capable of bringing these things into reality.

Turquoise knows and experiences the wholeness of reality through emotional, mental, intuitional, and spiritual awareness. It reaches out to support and nourish the healthy development of every level. People with a strong Turquoise component hold a compassionate understanding toward everyone around them. They appreciate the suffering and longing of all lives. These people have tremendous spiritual resources, and they use them to heal the world.

This wave sees the world as a single, dynamic organism with its own collective being. They see themselves as both distinct and part of the living whole. Everything is connected to everything else as energy and information permeate the entire environment. They are supremely effective at cooperative action.

People at Turquoise will work with Yellow, Golden Olive, and first-tier waves to smooth the transition to the Great Transformation system. They will be its natural leaders and ultimately will be supported by most of the world population in doing so because they are so clearly dedicated to the good of the whole. Although the egoic self is not entirely eradicated at this level, compared to first tier and even to Yellow, they will appear quite saintly and will be truly trusted and trustworthy.

The Turquoise system that establishes and extends the Great Transformation will be something we have never seen before. It will be founded on a consensus-based, civil society structure that gathers input from every category of stakeholders on the planet and, out of this, weaves carefully balanced policy decisions. It will use the power of advanced forms of internet and remote sensing technology to gather precise details at a level beyond anything we have seen. The majority of people will perceive the resulting governance as reasonable and fair, and from this it will derive its power.

It is largely because we are already seeing many people of the Turquoise wave in action, working to end disease, bring about peace and democracy, and elevate impoverished economies, that the vision of this book must be taken seriously as more than a fantasy. As a large enough number of people enter these higher waves of development, we will reach a tipping point and everything will change. This will occur before the end of the century and will establish a new way of governing the planet that will solve many problems.

Coral (Co): Avatarchic Solar Drive
As the fruits of peace and global prosperity spread and become the established way of life for humanity, a new wave will arise. Individuals on the advanced edge of Turquoise will begin to see the need to use the newfound power of a united humanity to accomplish bigger things. Partly this will be in response to dangers that Turquoise has not addressed because of its focus on diplomacy, and partly it will be the desire to grow and demonstrate what we can do.

The Coral wave will express the aspect of spiritual power in addition to the compassion of Turquoise. I have named it "avatarchic" because it will show the spiritual power of the avatars expressed in a governing capacity.

A number of precipitating challenges will thrust this wave forward, particularly the need to protect Earth from asteroid collisions, the one threat that could end the whole human experiment. To do this will mean a much more vigorous, and risky, drive into space and the development of complex, large-scale technologies for capturing and redirecting asteroids. We either achieve this level of cooperative technology or we go extinct from asteroidal impact with Earth. Humanity's final exam will decide if we graduate to our higher potential or not.

The payoff, aside from greater security, will be the ability to use these asteroidal chunks of material to build things in space. Coral will drive this into a major economic evolution and step from near-Earth object (NEO) protection to mining the asteroid belt. The mining and refining colonies established to do this will become the basis on which Coral will found the Belt Civilization.

Over a period of a bit more than a century, this wave will create a great ring of enormous space-station cities all around the inner edge of the asteroid belt. Imagine asteroids the size of Manhattan, linked with struts and rotated around a central spindle to provide gravity. These city stations will use robots and nanotechnology to mine and refine nearby asteroids. The main industries driving this economy will be real estate (creating more space habitats) and transportation (building space vehicles). These are discussed further in the Technology chapter.

Coral will also, true to its name, greatly expand human habitat under the seas of Earth. The continental shelf zones will become vast ocean farms and mining zones, all carried out with careful ecological planning.

The essence of Coral is its great charismatic power and its ability to inspire humanity to dare greater things. In the process, it will also convert the Great Transformation system into a stronger order that is focused on moving humanity forward. It will confront any structures that have tended to manipulate the Turquoise desire for diplomatic peace and demand that they align themselves to the greater good of the whole.

The era of Coral power will see enormous advances in technologies of all sorts and vast engineering projects that will transform deserts into gardens and conquer the solar system for all humanity. This wave will express great human courage and ingenuity. It will truly demonstrate what humanity can accomplish when we work together, and it will insist, with great persuasiveness, that we do.

Teal (Te): Paxarchic Lexiconic
At its crest, the Coral expansion will have extended human presence from the orbit of Mercury to the inner edge of the asteroid belt. We will have become solar citizens, and the great thrust of daring new technologies will have left us a bit bewildered and disoriented.

Specifically, we will have to deal with the problem of coordinating communication time delays of over half an hour from one side of the belt to the other. A message sent at light speed from one orbital city station to another could take anywhere from near zero delay (for a nearby station) to over thirty minutes one way (for a distant station). In addition, all the planets, moons, and orbital stations are moving relative to each other, thus increasing or decreasing the time-delay factor between any pair of human habitats. This relativistic scheduling problem will become something of a nightmare. We simply will not be accustomed to being so big and spread out. Like a gangly teenager, we will be having difficulty coordinating our limbs.

This and other challenges created by Coral's daring advance will trigger the emergence of the next wave, Teal. I have named Teal "paxarchic" because it will seek to pacify and calm the driving nature of Coral civilization, and "lexiconic," because it will create new laws (lex), new vocabulary (lexicon), and a new type of systematic imagery (icons) to coordinate the chaos. Just as Coral is the second-tier harmonic of Red, Teal is the second-tier harmonic of Blue.

Another term indicative of Teal is "consolidative." This wave will be intent on consolidating and bringing order to the gains of the Coral advance. It will also demand, and get, restraints on further exploration until it has tidied up and given us a new culture, religion, and philosophy to manage our complex new reality.

As Corals were the lords of space, Teals will be the lords of time. They will create the subtle technology for managing the relativistic clocks of the solar system and keeping everything flowing smoothly. Teal will set rules and regulations about what can and cannot be done. Teal will bring the Belt Civilization into balance and make it a nice place to raise kids. Under this wave's administration, the new frontier will be made truly civilized. It will use the most advanced media to instill its ideas into human culture as a new faith in doing everything according to precise and careful methods.

Generally, people will welcome the new order as a relief from the intense pace of change and the feeling of disorientation. They will embrace the new religion as a bulwark against the terror of facing our great accomplishments. After the heroic era of courageous advance, we will be feeling rather naked out among the stars and wondering just what we are doing there. In time-honored human tradition, we will turn to ritual to re-establish our sense of stability in a chaotic universe.

Teal's program will work as we slowly and methodically catch up to what we have built. All of our technological advances will be restrained and refocused on stabilizing the new normal. We will work to make the solar system and our new city stations homey and comfortable. Lots of new technology will be developed, mostly focused on creating familiarity, safety, and tranquility. This regime will preside over the middle period of the Belt Civilization and the Great Transformation it exemplifies. During this period, an attempt will be made to bring every human being to as high a level of development as possible, at least into second tier. Special programs will be created to allow people to transition through each wave in ways that are not disruptive of the Teal order.

Honey Gold (Hg): Ontarchic Resonant

After several generations, we will have become accustomed to the larger, more complex reality of life in space. The Teal scientific religion and cultural order will start to feel somewhat restrictive. Our desire to relax into a more intuitive approach to Being will catalyze the Honey Gold wave, which will be about experiencing Being and resonating to deep natural rhythms. I have called it "ontarchic" meaning *being governance*.

This wave is opulent, like sunlight shining through golden honey, and resonant like a long rich note from a bass cello. It expresses the full appreciation of soul consciousness at its peak and also presides over the peak of the Belt Civilization. It works to improve every aspect of life: longevity, health, enhanced capabilities, love and communion with friends, joy, and soul expression. Honey Gold is a wave of profound artistic, cultural, and technological creativity. Another word that expresses Honey Gold is "radiant."

The Honey Gold wave fulfills every dream of manifest life. This is a delicious time to be alive, and a very long and pleasurable life it will be, with life spans exceeding two hundred years. Honey Golds will be the lords of life and of knowledge. This wave will seek deep knowing of all aspects of existence and rejoice in a freer exploration of spirituality.

Honey Gold will experiment and expand in a slower, more appreciative way than Coral. Its great ships will colonize the Jovian moons, replacing the small research stations of earlier waves. Honey Gold will also complete exploitation of the entire asteroid belt. Its robotic advance explorers will begin to reach into the trans-Plutonian region of the Kuiper belt. It will strive to maximize the amount of solar energy collected and distributed throughout the system. It will also mine the gas giants—Jupiter, Saturn, Neptune, and Uranus—for hydrocarbons and other materials.

This will be a time of great wealth that is widely distributed among the human population, which will fill the whole solar system. By the year 2800, we will number more than 100 billion and the rest of the solar populace will dwarf the population of Earth.

Toward the end of this period, we will discover how to harness zero-point energy (ZPE), a technology that extracts energy from the quantum physics in the vacuum of space. This will allow us to live comfortably in the Kuiper belt, which is far from the warmth of the Sun.

Indigo (In): Illuminated Transcendent
Out of Honey Gold's search for deep knowing will arise a wave awakened at a new level and lit by rays of spiritual illumination. It will seek a purer, simpler way of life, far from the opulence of the inner solar system. The Indigo wave will reject Honey Gold's free-flowing experiences in favor of stillness and meditative inner focus. It also seeks the deep knowing of Being, but in a subtler way. The image of Indigo is the color of moonlight in a deep night sky. Approaching spirit now lights up the "moon" of the soul.

Societies led by Indigo consciousness will migrate like flocks of birds around the outer edge of the solar system. All city stations will be fully mobile "habitat ships," traveling in fleets along regular cyclic patterns. Periodically, great congregations or synods will be held, with many fleets gathering in the same zone to exchange wisdom, trade, people, and all the processes of social life. Indigo will be particularly focused on the accumulation of spiritual wisdom. Great teachers will be much revered and sought out by the most advanced seekers.

This society, approaching the edge of third-tier consciousness, will struggle with the deep forces implied by this impending shift. We can glimpse some of what this transition might be like by considering the writings of spiritually evolved individuals who have walked this path before. Indigo is filled with deep longing for greater communion with the Divine. The material world no longer fascinates, and all but the most necessary amenities will be ignored. Indigo is just not interested in the rich arts that Honey Gold brought into being. Rather, it uses technology in a passionate search for deeper truth.

The process this wave initiates, as Indigo sweeps through different parts of the system, is likely to be subtly disintegrative of the Great Transformation system. For one thing, the communication time-delay factor from one side of the Kuiper belt to the other is greater than ten and a half hours one way. Although information surely will be exchanged throughout the solar system, it will be difficult to maintain a sense of communicational intimacy at these distances. Physical travel time from the center to the periphery, even with great increases in propulsion speeds, is still likely to be a matter of years. Under these conditions, cultural divergence will tend to increase as different fleets and synods choose to follow their own paths to spiritual liberation.

Pearl (Pe): Luminous Gate
This second "half-tone" wave is the transition from second–tier soul to third-tier spirit. It is the upper harmonic of Golden Olive.

The Pearl wave blends all the colors of soul development into a pearly luster. It is a summing up and balancing of all the developments of the soul. All the great achievements are gathered, weighed, and brought to full maturity. If Golden Olive is a wave of spring, Pearl is a wave of the autumn harvest. The fruits of soul development are gathered into the spiritual granary. The produce is assessed and evaluated.

Pearl is the society of the human soul brought to judgment as we weigh and consider the meaning of human history, what we have attained and what remains undone. The luminous goodness of our great accomplishments provide comfort and strength to face the greater challenge of passing through the gates into third tier.

Tier III: Spirit Development

This is the tier in which we develop awareness of Divine Reality and actualize its nature. In this tier, humans unfold the waves of God-realization.

Amethyst (Am): Angelic Transclastic

The breakthrough into true third-tier consciousness is an enormously profound spiritual shattering of the soul and a deep mystical awakening. The Amethyst wave awakens to the presence of the Causal Spirit and, where this emerges, the remaining structures of the Great Transformation system will begin to dissolve. Because of this effect, I have named this wave "transclastic," or transformation-breaking, breaking beyond and through.

I also refer to it as "angelic" and "archetypal" because Amethyst experiences spirit as living causality. It perceives the Divine Presence acting everywhere through archetypal entities, spiritual beings, and angels. It will spread throughout the Kuiper belt as it learns how to live in the consciousness of spirit. This third harmonic of Beige and Yellow will explore how to survive on the causal level. It will integrate all of what was learned in the second-tier soul level into a new being in which both soul and personality are overwhelmed by spiritual presence. This is the realm of immortal holy beings, prophets, and saints, the domain of the seven heavens.

Sapphire (Sa): Essential Attributes

As Amethyst completes its integration, the level of holistic spirit begins to emerge beginning around 2900. The Sapphire wave will initiate humanity into a long tutelage into the divine qualities. We will research into knowing and learning from the divine attributes, not in the way the soul learns, but directly from the Divine Presence. The society of this time will be organized to unfold this extensive learning process in a structured and deliberate way. We will experience divine wisdom, compassion, power, peace, forgiveness, and all of the divine attributes as objectively existing realities. Our civilization will focus on exploring and learning from these profound spiritual presences.

This wave will expand the use of zero-point energy as it extends its presence out to the Oort cloud, a vast cloud of comets and rocks about one light-year out from the Sun. The Early Oort civilization will be founded some time after the end of the third millennium. This civilization will probably discover superluminal communication, finally ending the barrier of communication time delays.

Sapphire is the last wave to emerge in significant numbers before the end of the millennium, but I will give brief descriptions of the waves beyond this thousand-year period to put the whole model in context. The soul journeys, described in Chapter 11 will describe how all waves affect us even today.

Onyx (On): Annihilative Absorption
In the Mid-Oort civilization, after long immersion in the divine attributes, a shift will occur from the causal levels to the levels of the Absolute. The consciousness moves from knowing the Divine as qualities to contemplating the Absolute as void, hence it is represented by the pure black gemstone, Onyx. At this level, consciousness is concentrated at the deep still point and the state of being is known as "absence." All the functions of life are carried out, but it is as if no one is there. The being is totally overwhelmed by the presence of God and is thus mystically annihilated. This may seem undesirable to most people today, but for mystics it is a state devoutly sought. This is the realm of the many grades of space or emptiness.

Diamond (Di): Transparent Omniscience
The next stage of contemplating the Absolute is utter transparency. After annihilation of all the lower faculties, the consciousness clears and the Diamond wave emerges. This level sees every aspect of Being with a precise, sharp omniscience. All things are seen with diamond brilliance as aspects of one Being. There is a sense of total unity with the living presence of all reality. The whole universe moves as one living being, and we are that transparent totality. This is also the domain of light and many grades of luminosity. Here is an even more complete annihilation into divine effulgence.

Ruby (Ru): Established Relative Nondual
We may wonder how there could be anything beyond the Absolute, but then the first aspect of the nondual arises. In this level of realization, we see that the perceptions and presences of the relative world of "ordinary life" are not other than the Absolute. We grasp that there is no duality, no split between creature and Creator, no gap between human and divine. We become magnificently simple. The simple person is, at the same time, God incarnate, and also knows that every other life form is also an expression of God. There is no division in the nondual; everything just is. In this realization, we know there is no death. We are "established" forever in the eternal moment. We are beyond time and within time as well, no duality.

Emerald (Em): Perfected Universal Nondual
At the Emerald level, the nondual consciousness is perfected as the divine human being. The unity of God-Humanity moves forth through the universe, filling it with conscious life. This wave may also

contemplate the creation of a new universe beyond this one. This is the crown of creation and the complete flowering of humanity. Beyond that, it is the fruit of that flower. Beyond that, it is the taste of that fruit.

Alpha-Omega (AΩ): Absolute Divine Being
The Ultimate Reality. The unity that contains and absorbs everything, it is beyond description. Only God can know God. In the encounter with God in Diamond, we perish into oneness. Then we are resurrected into nondual Ruby and matured as nondual Emerald. There is only one eternal unity beyond beginning or end. Here it is called "Alpha-Omega," but It is beyond all names and all attributes

Vision has shown me the Emerald wave as the final flower of humanity, perhaps ten thousand years from now, or perhaps sooner.

Of course, what I have presented is only a sketch of a model, a map drawn on the back of a napkin. The reality is always messier and subtler, with mixtures of waves interacting in the same civilization and even within the same individual. In fact, I believe that all waves are always present in all individuals and societies, but the resonance focuses primarily on one wave at any given time. Some waves we have already actualized, and others are present as spiritual potentialities.

The Transformation Model as a whole represents the morphogenetic field of the human flowering, which is always calling and guiding us onward to the fulfillment of our destiny. This is our spiritual DNA. Time is just how we experience the unfoldment, but the whole flower is always present in the eternal now as the actual reality behind our experience.

Figure 4 below shows the flower-gem form of the Transformation Model. If we think of the model as both developmental, as shown in the harp-ladder form, and also as fully present, as shown in the flower-gem form, we will be able to appreciate a broader perspective of the reality behind the model. In this form, the Transformation Model is shown as an integral whole, rather than as a developmental ladder.

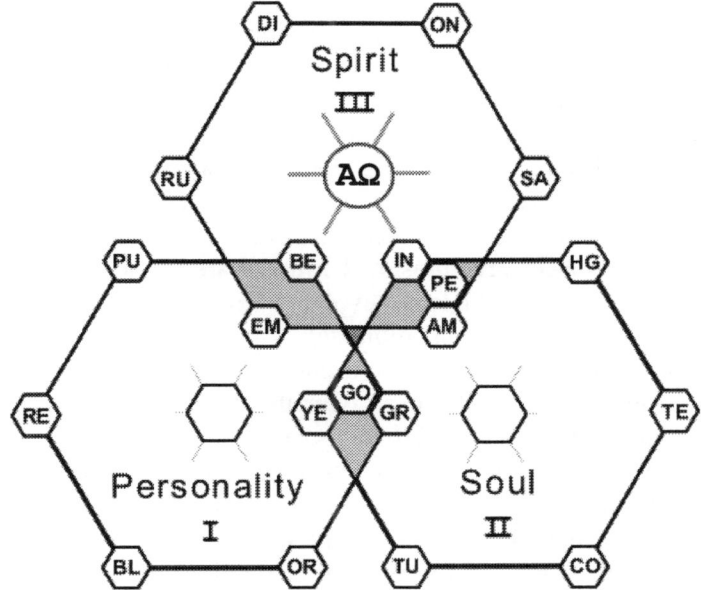

Figure 4. The Transformation Model: Flower-Gem Form

The end is the beginning, and the nondual consciousness flows freely on all levels as each wave is perfected in harmonic communion with every other. There is continuous deepening, but not in the sense of awakening unfoldment. All waves are awakened; only depth of integration expresses the perpetual, creative dynamic of essence.

The Wave-Mix Model of Future History

By looking at the characteristics of different waves that are active at any given time and place, we can estimate a general course of future history: such-and-such a wave mix is likely to generate a particular set of circumstances and ideas. (For example, our present wave mix in developed societies is BL-OR-GR with emerging Golden Olive plus traces of Yellow and Turquoise.) Conversely, a particular set of life conditions is likely to result in a specific wave mix. This is what I call the "wave-mix model" of future history.

I have used it in this book to coordinate and confirm various understandings that have come to me in vision. A review of wave-mix conditions has provided an analytical reality check to orient and locate ideas that have come through intuitive imagery and spontaneously arising stories. The model provides a context in which to situate intuitive understandings and a way to communicate them coherently. In Chapter 10, The Transition, I show a particular application of the wave-mix model to our immediate future.

The particular story I used to illustrate the emerging waves of the Transformation Model is only one possible way this model might emerge. The reality will be far more complex and surprising than anything that could be described in even a library of books. Nevertheless, the basic structures of the model are sound and likely to remain so. Human individuals do evolve from personality to soul to spirit, and our civilizations must ultimately follow the same path.

The basic patterns of consciousness unfoldment have been observed in many cultures from all over the planet. We may quibble about the details, but there is broad agreement on the larger picture. Therefore, any story of the human future must involve a progressive movement through these patterns. Even if we factor in periodic regressions, the eventual story pursues the same path.

For now, let us turn to the wave mix within individuals and the concept of "lines of development."

Education and Lines of Development

Lines of Development (L_Δ)

It helps us to understand how this model applies to real human beings in real situations when we realize that people evolve along many distinct lines and that these lines develop at different rates even within a single individual. We may, for example, make significant progress cognitively, while remaining stuck at earlier levels emotionally and morally. This familiar pattern in spiritual growth has frustrated many a seeker on the way.

One way of analyzing this includes the following lines of development:

1. Kinesthetic – Instinctual   K-I
2. Emotional - Affective   E-A
3. Cognitive – Mental   C-M
4. Empathic – Relational   E-R
5. Moral – Ethical   M-E
6. Aesthetic – Perceptual   A-P
7. Spiritual – Intuitive   S-I

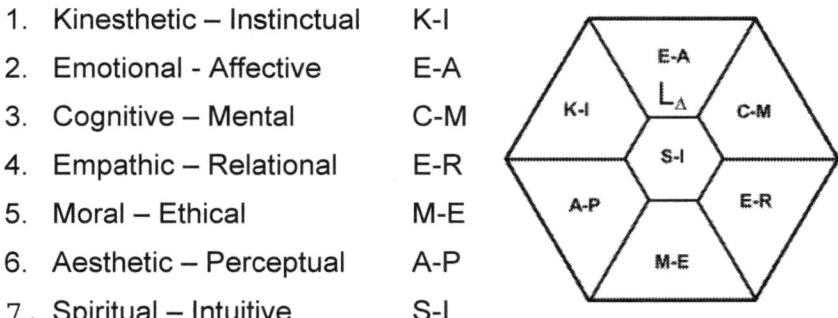

Figure 5. Lines of Development Diagram

Recognizing that people experience a mixture of developmental waves helps us to create more effective educational processes. For example, new methods for awakening higher capacities are already increasing the presence of second-tier soul consciousness and all it has to offer.

Future Education for Innovation

How we develop depends, in part, on how we are educated. The qualities that are rewarded in a person's learning environment determine which characteristics get developed and which do not.

Increasingly our economy moves away from material resources as the driving source of value and toward "soft" resources. What begins as the information economy moves toward the knowledge economy, the innovation economy, the psychological economy, and ultimately the wisdom economy. Investment moves toward organizations that have great business plans and also toward those that can nurture the most innovation from employees and the most enduring relationships with customers and suppliers. This is a form of human capital based on valued relationships.

This movement is one driving force behind current shifts toward a new model of accounting that includes creative and intellectual capital in the equation along with the classical components of capital and labor. These new economic forces produce, when properly managed, an exponential creation of value. Typical examples are software, pharmaceuticals, and fund management, some of the most successful sectors in recent markets.

The fact that early boom times have periodically overplayed the leverage of these factors and been subject to corrections in no way invalidates the profound shift the innovation or idea factor is having on economic theory and reality. Creative and intellectual property as a major driver of value is here to stay. In fact it was always present, but recently this "i-factor" has been more recognized in economics.

A primary driver of our current period of transitional change is society's struggle to catch up to an explosion of creative and intellectual energy emerging in people around the globe. A lot more innovation is circulating than we have previously been accustomed to managing. This is partly attributable to shifts toward higher levels of consciousness and the multidimensional systems thinking that naturally come with second-tier cognition.

We will come to understand that nurturing the best talents in all of our citizens is in everyone's self-interest. The current waste of creativity and intelligence is an enormous drain on our global well-being and, for individuals, a great source of frustration. We might at first think of people who never get a chance to go to college or learn to read, and this is very important, but we should also consider all of the "privileged" among us who are not able to develop our best abilities. Today this includes almost everyone.

In the future, the situation will be very different. Nurturing fully developed talents in as much of the population as possible will be a major planetary priority. We will become accustomed to living in a world filled with prodigies, geniuses, and multidimensional people. Most everyone will be an artist, scientist, writer, healer, and social leader. Leadership will be widespread because we will not separate leading and following so sharply. Most activities will be managed by teams wherein "leadership" flows to whomever has the best grasp of what is going on at any moment (the typical Yellow work style). Many business teams already operate this way.

Highly developed creativity in visual, musical, verbal, and body arts (healing, dance, and sports) will be as widely distributed as basic literacy is today. Mathematical and scientific inventiveness will also be a natural part of most people's daily activity. Leaning won't be difficult because our educational methods will be so much more sophisticated and effective. From prenatal infancy to the end of an individual's life, discovering and developing new skills and talents will be a natural and enjoyable process.

For awhile, this will have a competitive aspect. Societies, organizations, and individuals that do not invest heavily in all aspects of education and opportunities for learning will simply fall behind those that do. Soon, however, it will become obvious that this division is not good for any of us, and universal accelerated learning will become the planetary norm. The web and its evolving generations will quickly spread new discoveries around the world. As this takes off, generational divides will become a challenge.

New generations nurtured from birth (and before) with the most advanced technologies, such as what I call *superneural integration*, will quickly surpass the most highly educated adults, who will then require remedial adult education. The one thing we can count on is that some individuals will far outstrip others in learning capacity, and we will need to help others catch up. It is in the ultimate interests of all, including the fast learners, to help everyone move forward, and the emerging environment will increasingly reward sharing knowledge more than hoarding it.

How Superneural Integration Will Be Developed

From before conception, every effort will be made to provide both fathers and mothers with the best physiological and psychological health possible. Conception and all phases of gestation will be carefully monitored and adjusted. Nurturing methodologies may include customized proteins; maternal nutrients; specially designed music, light, and energy field environments; talking and singing to the growing fetus; meditation; and other concepts we can't imagine. The birthing process will be managed to minimize trauma and maximize infant comfort.[14] The early mother-child bonding environment will be carefully protected.

Precise knowledge of developmental psychology and physiology will inform the whole process of child rearing. Societies will learn that it pays to devote more time to childcare, especially in the first three to four years, for both the mother and the father. This is the period when basic identity foundations are being laid and, when these are well-established, the rest of the child's development will proceed more easily.

---

[14] See Chilton Pearce, *The Magical Child,* 1980, and Stanislav Grof's perinatal matrix studies in *The Adventure of Self-Discovery,* 1988.

Further in the future, larger groups of "parents" will be involved in the raising of an individual child. A child might have twelve parents instead of two, all involved in different aspects of caring for the child's growth. This concept may seem strange and unnatural to us, but much of what we take for granted today would have seemed equally strange to people of centuries past.

The principles behind enriched early childhood education will switch from today's competition-based efforts that force children into becoming superachievers to a more relaxed and playful approach. Providing all babies with enriched environments and subtler reward systems will produce much freer, less neurotic, and more effective results. The emphasis will move away from pressure to perform and toward true education, which draws out from within each child those things that particular child truly loves, thereby discovering and nurturing natural talents. The result will be to enhance innovation capabilities. In future society, most necessary rote learning will be handled by accelerated learning processes and appropriately programmed learning machines.[15]

VR Learning Machines

Here are some general specifications for developing such systems:

1. Increase the amount of sensory attention that is engaged, beginning with larger screens, for example, and extending all the way to total immersion virtual reality (VR). Use simultaneous integration of multiple senses: sight reinforced by sound and touch or, vice-versa, musical education reinforced by visual representations.

2. Increase the density and comprehensiveness of hyperlinks so learners can follow their own curiosity to investigate details. Current web links connect to pages that are too verbose for these purposes. Information needs to be chunked more efficiently to be truly effective in a learning space.

3. Use 3-D and dynamic animated models to explain dynamic structures and processes.

---

[15] For an early example, see Lozanov's "suggestopaedia" process for language acquisition described in *Psychic Discoveries Behind the Iron Curtain* by Sheila Ostrander and Lynn Schroeder, 1971. Also, *The Accelerated Learning Handbook* by Dave Meier, 2000.

4. Increase participatory involvement and kinesthetic reinforcement of concepts. Future learning will involve "dance" and related motion patterning to somatically integrate knowledge. Model the hand and body positions of experts.
5. Use multiple levels of symbolic abstraction, including the ability to "drill up," as well as "drill down," to add or subtract levels of detail.
6. Use powerful diagrammatic tools and symbolic notational structures. We are developing advances in symbolic language for this purpose.
7. Apply massive databases of real-time updated factual and statistical data. Provide multiple ways of visually representing data output.
8. Design systems for near instantaneous response time (no-wait state) to prevent rapid thinking from getting bogged down by machine processing.
9. Develop advanced, user-friendly interfaces that can be customized and personalized.
10. Use storytelling and story participation as part of the learning process at all levels. Incorporate ethical and moral decision-making into realistic story outcomes.
11. Integrate biofeedback systems and total physiology monitoring, including brain activity and total CNS activity. The system should respond to the monitored results.
12. Model the learning processes of the most effective students and develop ways to train others to use the same techniques.[16]

Precursors to such systems are already being developed today. Soon they will be part of our everyday environment.

We can't say with precision which technologies will be adopted and which will be rejected for technical or social concerns. We can predict with some certainty, however, that very advanced biology and psychology will be applied to the process of procreation, nurturance, and education of children (as well as adults). We will understand that

---

[16] This "modeling of experts" concept has been explored and developed in the neurolinguistic programming (NLP) literature, started by Bandler and Grinder, and carried forward by Dilts, Andreas, Robins, and others.

providing the best possible environment for babies will result in the best possible population controlling the world as each generation enters its retirement years.

People trained in these ways will be able to absorb large books in minutes and whole shelves of books in hours. Yet they also will be able to meditate on one sentence for months to discover its depth of meaning.

Building the best foundation for each human individual from the very beginning will result in naturally advanced superlearners who will continue to benefit all humanity as they grow. This effort will continue to improve exponentially from generation to generation. Superneural children educated by advanced learning methods will in turn apply their skill to the next generation. The process will be a self-feeding, accelerating, virtuous circle.

The resulting superneural and developmental integration will be the primary source of all the other resources and advances we will experience in the future.

Once this becomes clear to the world's leaders, implementing these processes will become an important planetary priority. The benefits will quickly repay every investment, further fueling greater educational investment and innovation. We will develop systems to install the necessary political and economic feedback loops to ensure that all of society receives these benefits. (This will become a reality only when second-tier consciousness becomes more widespread.)

With a firm foundation in the childhood formative years, the lifelong learning process will unfold easily. We will use many innovative methods to help people at all levels to bring out their natural talents and to develop the broadly rounded skill sets that will be necessary for life in the future world. Human teachers will focus on the psychological aspects of learning, while advanced virtual reality learning systems (AVRLS) will manage most of the knowledge and skill absorption tasks. Developing and improving these will be a major industry for awhile.

Such learning systems could teach mathematics along with sports and arts. Imagine a virtual golf game that teaches the physics and mathematics of ballistic trajectories along with the hand-eye coordination aspects of the sport. Imagine using virtual dance classes to teach trigonometry along with ballet. A virtual surfing program could make statistical concepts much easier to understand. If you have literally surfed the maxima and minima of statistical data, you understand it in a more than mental way. The knowledge would be embedded in your somatic memory. These sensory systems will also be combined with many levels of meditation training and ethical guidance to help students open higher dimensions of consciousness.

This gives a faint glimpse of what superneural integration will offer in the relatively near future. What also will come are the second and third generations of this process, designed and developed by those who have grown up with it. We may have some difficulty envisioning the long-term results, but it is not hard to see that they will be extraordinary by any measures we could dream up today.

We will need hundreds of millions of superneurally integrated, second-tier conscious people to complete the job of bringing the Great Transformation system into reality, and we will inevitably have them. This kind of capability is so powerful that selective emergent forces are certain to make them real and widespread. The process is clearly already under way with such comparatively primitive technologies as the world wide web, computer games, and educational TV.

In addition, a much richer human interaction process will nourish emotional intelligence. A large portion of future school activities will be focused on the social aspects of education, learning how to get along with, communicate with, and understand other people. By the time children are ten years old, a great deal will be known about their personalities. Their self-knowledge and their knowledge of others also will far exceed the level of most adults today. This kind of psychological curriculum will produce people who are much more effective at teamwork and relationships of all kinds.

I am not talking about people who are merely "well-adjusted." The result of this kind of education will be honest people who are not inclined to "adjust" to a bad situation but rather to change it. If faced with things that cannot be changed, such people deal with the reality frankly and openly. It is difficult for us to imagine generations of psychologically healthy people, since we are so accustomed to the norm of neurosis, but this is what will occur. We are seeing the first glimmers already, but it is camouflaged by media focus on the sensational failures in our present system. We haven't yet been able to measure the impact of new educational processes, for example, the evolving quality of the best educational television shows.

Many advances will continue to remain hidden by the traumatic effects of life in the transitional era and the complex politics of education. However, once this time has passed and we settle down into a more peaceful society with well-accepted goals, ideals, laws, and practices, we will see an explosion of optimism that will greatly nourish students. All the advances discovered over the years will come together for an enormous revolution in education, in children's lives, and in the lives of the adults they become. We can expect a level of satisfaction and inner peace almost beyond imagining.

It is difficult to measure whether television and games that show cooperative behavior between characters have a better socializing effect than violent programs, but intuition suggests that they do. In any case, media programming will continue to evolve until the main trend moves in a desirable direction. The fact that today's media often panders to lowest-common-denominator emotions in the short term will only underscore the desire for positive change in the longer term, and that change will come.

A factor that will influence this process is that we are gaining a deeper understanding of the shadow sides of the human psyche, partly as a result of Green rejection of hypocrisy. A lot of cruelty exists in most of us, which is only fueled by the frustration of our talents. As we understand more about how this works, we will also learn how to respond more creatively. One direction that shows promise includes suggestive mythological storytelling, Ericsonian hypnotherapy, and neurolinguistic programming techniques.[17]

At present, this work is still in its infancy but, as it evolves, it will meet and integrate with emerging new media to create a powerful synthesis. We may see the development of interactive virtual reality programs designed to help children, teenagers, and adults process and understand their feelings about difficult experiences and life passages. When coupled with psychologically valid ways of dealing with rejected "shadow" feelings, moral education about drugs, sex, violence, and money is likely to be much more effective than preachy sermons.

Morality that is not based on conscious, second-tier ethics is not effective. To clarify this distinction, ***ethics*** refers to our ideas about what is right and wrong, our code; ***morals*** refers to our conduct, the degree to which we live up to and by our code. If the code is not sensible, it does not produce wise results and is less likely to be

---

[17] Psychologist Milton Ericson developed powerful suggestive processes that became one of the main inputs to NLP or neurolinguistic programming.

adhered to. We want to advance in both aspects, toward higher ethical codes and more consistent moral conduct.

By teaching people how to defend psychologically against their inner critic (superego), we will be able to reduce some of the internal pressures that can drive people to self-destructive or antisocial acts. We will also learn how to teach parents ways to provide structure without producing unnecessary degrees of neurosis. Over the decades, this will result in increasingly healthy populations, especially when this knowledge is magnified by electronic distribution technology, such as web, virtual reality, video webcasting, and so forth. These tools will work catalytically with real-world experiences, such as gardening and other nature work. It is not an either/or choice; both media and real-world experience can provide integrated support for educational goals.

Of course, some will try to use these emerging psychological techniques to manipulate others. We can expect to see them abused for purposes of advertising and electioneering, but the longer term will see positive social effects that we can only guess at. We can imagine, for example, internet-based VR programs aimed at soothing people who are suffering from frustrated rage and helping them envision more positive outcomes. All of this could be subtly embedded within fantasy programs designed to attract positive psychic traits. On the surface, it might look like a shoot-em-up style video game yet contain subliminal suggestions and plot structures that encourage the development of positive emotional resources. Most of the capabilities for this kind of experiment are already available.

What is needed is clarity of vision and motivating factors to mobilize investment in developing these kinds of packages. Short-term drivers range from simple business acumen recognizing an opportunity to public funding driven by the war on drugs, the war on terror, and the war on disease and poverty. We are waking up to the fact that we need something new to cope with the strains of our complex lives. First-tier solutions are failing mostly because they do not know how to address complex realities effectively.

As with many other trends, once seeds have been planted, the conditions of our responsive feedback society automatically cause movement in positive directions. This characteristic of networked, free-market societies is one of the most encouraging signs. The market gravitates toward the "improved" product. In the short term, this may mean products with good production values, but longer term, positive qualities tend to overwhelm negative ones just because people ultimately prefer positives.

For example, parents will prefer to buy VR software packages that teach responsible attitudes toward violence, rather than pure shoot-em-up games that provide only negative programming. There is also no reason that healthy entertainment can't be made just as attractive to kids as products that pander only to baser instincts. The differences can be subtle and derive from deeper understanding of the motivations that attract people, especially post-pubescent boys, to violent forms of entertainment. (Over the centuries, an enormous amount of socialization effort has gone toward addressing the basic problem of testosterone control in young males, which is associated with the Red—Blue shift.)

Programmers will learn to appeal to the urge to express rage and experience empowerment while also subconsciously developing deeper resources for dealing constructively with these feelings. Eventually this approach will dominate and drive the unhealthier types of game software, movies, and TV shows from the market. Government regulation also may play a role in this transition. The movement will be furthered by our growing understanding of how the addiction-recovery model applies to rage and power issues. Greater psychological knowledge will drive subtler and wiser legislation regarding these areas.

One reason we have a hard time seeing the effect of a preference for positives is because our own psychology suffers from a defensive cynicism that is largely unconscious. We resist the idea that things get better to avoid having our hopes dashed or being perceived as foolish, childish, or gullible. People may resist some of the concepts in this book for exactly these reasons. However, simply looking at what has changed since, say, the year 1000 should provide perspective. Who in their right mind would want to go back and live even one hundred years ago? We may like to fantasize about the advantages of applying our advanced knowledge in a less developed age, but what about all the advances we would have to do without, not to mention the quality of conversation likely to be available?

The simple and obvious fact is: we do progress. Life does get better. A list of things that have positively changed in recent centuries (at least in the West) includes the end of slavery, women's rights, increased literacy, and widespread growth in psychological understanding, just to mention a few nontechnological developments.

Do we imagine that the social progress of the last few centuries will come to a standstill while technology evolves? It is not logical, nor does it accord with history, to take such a pessimistic view, but emotionally that is just what we tend to do.

In the twentieth century, we went through two of the worst wars in all human history, yet, despite the death and devastation, the net effect was to bring the world closer together, to end colonialism, and to increase social justice in most of the world. Both world wars strengthened the hand of international cooperation in such bodies as the United Nations. The fact that nuclear weapons could annihilate the world caused the next war to be something new, a "cold" war. As bad as this was, it was better than having a hot war between nuclear powers. It is also notable that it ended (after various regional proxy wars) in a negotiated peace. Nevertheless, we all have endured great shocks; we all are suffering from "future shock," so it is not surprising that we respond out of instinctive cynicism about the intractable evils of human nature, even though many facts demonstrate positive change.

A careful examination of the facts of history might lead us to conclude that something beyond any individual human consciousness was moving us forward despite our best attempts to return to barbarism. We are drawn toward the light despite our attachment to the dark.

We have been transforming under the impact of global telecommunications media, beginning with radio and ending no one knows where. Such media, especially the interactive media components of the internet, web, blogs, and email, are educating us about ourselves. We are just beginning to get to know what humanity is as a real and specific whole.

Self-knowledge is the very heart of all spiritual, psychological, and philosophical inquiry. It seems that a self-organizing process is emerging from within us, beyond our individual understanding and control, and that process is educating and transforming humanity to bring forth the true flower of its heart. We are becoming what we have always wanted to become. We are striving to fulfill the deepest longings of our souls and this striving is taking us beyond our hopes and fears into a future of wondrous vision and glory.

Multi-Q: Quotient of Multiple Intelligences

What are the components of being smarter? What makes one person smarter than another? What are the categories of greater ability? As we deepen our understanding of these factors, we will develop a more complex and subtle model. Instead of IQ, we will think in terms of multi-Q.

The list below presents some of the developmental areas we associate with the concept of "smartness."

- Logic, reasoning, analysis, critical and systems thinking
- Symbolic processing: linguistic, numerical, graphic
- Language skills: reading, researching, writing
- Numerical skills: quantity, relationship, algorithm
- Creativity in various domains: innovation and invention
- Musical skills: song, instrument, composition
- Artistic skills: color, line, volume, texture, geometry
- Mechanical intelligence: spatial perception, dynamics
- Manual skills: dexterity, strength, speed, precision
- Physical skills: strength, speed, agility, hand-eye-body coordination, flexibility, somatic intelligence, health
- Knowledge: information, know-how, process understanding
- Wisdom: discernment, intuition, perceptivity, synthesis, discrimination, application, integration, insight, ethics
- People smarts, emotional intelligence, street savvy, intelligence about power, instincts, negotiation
- Speaking skills: charm, persuasion, clarity
- Presentation: style, charisma, beauty, distinctiveness, boldness, dignity, personal congruence, character
- Presence: magnitude, authority, power, peace
- Spiritual intuition: meditative skills, integral metasystemics, holistic consciousness, moral scope

Superneural integration will increase multi-Q along all of these dimensions and more, joining the different intelligences into a mutually reinforcing whole. As higher consciousness emerges in an individual, a vast range of essential qualities becomes available, and a new range of assessments apply.

Developing Multi-Q

Table 5 below shows one idea for how basic skill sets might be grouped for education and assessment purposes. This model is not presented as an end-point, but more as a thought-provoking restructuring of the way we think about educational curriculum and skill-set development.

Skill Quotient Domain	Natural Ability or Aptitude	Training or Educational Record	Experience Application Record
Symbolics Language, Math, etc.			
Logics Reasoning Skills			
Creativity Inventiveness			
Sensorium Perception, all senses			
Mechanics Physical Materials			
Somatics Body Skills			
Empathics People Skills			
Ethics Moral Awareness			
Essential Qualities Spiritual Unfoldment			

Table 5. Multi-Q Assessment Grid

Each general domain contains many constituent subdomains. For example, under "somatics" we might consider: strength, speed, agility, flexibility, dexterity, fine-motor coordination, health, internal body control, and so forth.

In assessing skill sets, we consider the basic equipment a person is endowed with by nature—their aptitude—and then consider what they have gained through training or education. Finally, we can measure how well an individual uses what they have learned and the depth of experience they bring to practical application of a skill.

> *"Not Christian or Jew or Muslim, not Hindu, Buddhist, Sufi, or Zen. Not any religion or cultural system. I am not from the East or the West ... My place is the placeless, a trace of the traceless. ... I belong to the Beloved, have seen two worlds as one and that one call to and know..."* [18]
>
> —Jalaluddin Rumi 1207-1273

Chapter 5. Spiritual Culture (S·C)

Awakening and Cultural Integration

Two major cultural shifts are emerging that define and lead us toward the coming Great Transformation society, an outer shift and an inner shift. The outer shift is the change from a world of separate cultures to an integrated planetary culture containing many subcultures. The inner shift is the transformation of the leading segment of humanity from egoic personality levels (first tier) to awakened soul levels (second tier).

Cultural Synthesis

Every culture in the world is being studied and explored at great depth. The history and mythology of all peoples enters the global media and becomes part of all of us. Cultural synthesis becomes an increasing trend in music, art, cuisine, and movies.

This convergence of global cultures will increase and become so much a part of life in future eras we are hardly able to imagine its impact. Media developers and psychologists will study the mythologies

---

[18] From *The Illuminated Rumi*, translated by Coleman Barks, 1997.

of all cultures and weave themes into new transformation stories as part of integrating popular entertainment into education and social transformation.

In the advanced media of the later twenty-first century, every scientific knowledge of human psychology and sociology will be combined with advanced technology and art to produce the most profound experiential works. These will entertain, educate, and transform all at the same time. As with other social functions, culture and media will blend into politics, learning, work, and family life.

We can imagine families and whole communities joining in extended virtual reality adventures aimed at resolving intercultural conflicts. But such events and activity will not be separate from the constant web of similar experiences. It will simply be how life is then—just as TV, MTV, portable music, cellphones, and internet are normal parts of life experience today.

We will know the whole Earth much more intimately than we do today. When we zoom over a real-time satellite atlas, we will actually see each other living our lives, and everyone will see us.[19] We will know the details of every local situation on the globe, and these facts will be cross-checked and vetted. It will be much harder to manipulate the news and lie about real situations because everything will be so much more transparent. All views will be known and considered in the global bodies and by all citizens.

It will be very hard to reconcile brutalities, exploitations, thefts, and poverties with any acceptable civilized worldview. We simply will not be able to allow the suffering of others without doing something about it and, as a consequence, there will be less and less gross suffering. This will in turn make each incident of violence, bigotry, or unfairness that much more repugnant. When we see ourselves so clearly, tolerating ugliness in human interaction will not sit comfortably with our values, especially since we will experience media events as if we were there in person.

The heart and soul of humanity searches always for common ground, which will fuel efforts to blend and combine all cultures as part of one metaculture. We will appreciate the best of every culture, and those aspects of traditional cultures that are repellant to modern sensibilities—inequality for women, mistreatment of children,

---

[19] I wrote this before the "Google Earth" application became available … and here it is!

repression of minorities, racism, ethnocentrism, and the like—are already dissolving under the impact of a world that talks to itself. On the news, we see battles of race and religion, but under the surface, humanity is rejecting these kinds of conflict.

In the same way, economic inequities and the attitudes that sustain them will not stand the test of time. Perhaps it seems amazing and unbelievable now, but those with extreme economic advantage will find they just don't want to maintain the separation, and those disadvantaged will strive to learn and demonstrate their value. We will increasingly understand what each individual needs for greater fulfillment and also increasingly be able to deliver it, both materially and in the form of media experience.

Stories derived from mythology are an effective way of giving people experiential understanding to help them transform. These stories will be developed in vast new global industries and stored in great interactive databases. Imagine a subtle "pharmacopoeia" of story experiences. When a person or group is diagnosed as having a particular kind of problem—intertribal disputes, family arguments, addictions, adolescent destructiveness, ethnocentric arrogance, trauma recovery, and so forth—the media system will tell them healing wisdom stories.

Actually, they will participate in these stories from every point of view and feel what it feels like on all sides of the events. At the same time, the database is interactive and collects experiential data from each person for the benefit of later participants in similar therapeutic dramas. As such, the participants are also "workers in psychological media" and are compensated both for their efforts and for exceptional breakthroughs. This will be one of the accelerating economic benefits of the all-recording, information-media system. Every use refines the tool for subsequent use.

The cost-benefit multiplier of the software-enhanced idea economy will be by this time accelerating rapidly, and this is why it will have a profound effect relatively quickly. It may take a while to get the system initially developed, but once it gets going, it will multiply its power and effectiveness quickly and almost effortlessly. In a small scale, we have seen the same thing with our first-generation internet. This will be information-media network exponentially multiplied.

To get a sense of where this is going, we have to think in terms of intersecting synergies. The main one this chapter focuses on is spiritual-cultural integration. Add advanced depth psychology, mythology research, storytelling, conflict resolution, therapeutic processes, global transparency, art, and entertainment—all accelerated by media technology—and you begin to get a glimpse of how profound this change will be and how quickly it will manifest once underway.

Culture Preservation

The other side of cultural integration will be cultural preservation. The specifics of all cultural strains will be seen as a valuable resource for humanity as a whole. Efforts will be made to preserve cultural enclaves and records. Some will elect to work in these preserved environments and their experiences will be captured and integrated into the media archives.

The Treasures of Religion

A most significant aspect of the cultural integration going on today is that all the religions of the world are becoming available to spiritual seekers. We are drawing the wealth from these great repositories of wisdom and weaving it into one beautiful garment.

Each of the great teachings throughout history brought unique treasures. It is only on the surface that they seem to contradict each other. To the wise, every report from the inner world is valuable. Think of a map maker pulling together pieces of information about a newly discovered continent by weighing the reports of many explorers. The resulting map will reflect elements from all of the explorers.

Each teaching presents knowledge about three major categories of wisdom:

1. Knowledge of God or ultimate reality
2. Knowledge of true human nature
3. Knowledge of the relationship between these two[20]

We must begin by seeking to understand something about the second kind of knowledge. Until we understand more about what we are as human beings, we cannot begin to really understand even a small amount about the Supreme Being. Ultimate reality has both a personal

---

[20] The revered Sufi sage, Bawa Muhaiyaddeen, with whom I studied for many years, often drew illustrations from different religions. These categories of knowledge are from his oral teachings.

face, emphasized by some traditions, and an impersonal face, emphasized by others.

Our learning process goes through a series of stages:

1. Ignorance: We take things only at face value.
2. Intellectual knowledge: We start to gather information about ourselves and about human being in general.
3. Practice: We engage in efforts to understand.
4. Breakthrough/Insight: We *realize* a particular insight or quality, and we recognize what caused the insight.
5. Manifestation: Deeper practice over time allows us to *actualize* in our daily being the insight or quality we previously realized. This implies stabilized embodiment of the quality or insight.

This cycle goes on at many levels and repeats itself over and over again for different qualities and insights. Through practices of spiritual study, we gradually accumulate riches of deeper being.

Every religious or spiritual teaching uses some variation of these phases of practice and fulfillment. Some use more steps and some fewer, but the basic principle is the same. In all this work, we are seeking to reach a fuller appreciation and realization of reality. Through self-observation we are able to come to some understanding of the vehicle or instrument through which we live and know and be. Since the presence of Ultimate Reality exists within all things, we can only approach knowledge of this mystery through investigating how we know. We have to investigate our experience of Presence within our own being.

Along the way, we encounter all the barriers to knowing and being our true self.[21] Through the process of resolving these barriers, we begin to experience the relationship between our own being and Being itself. Jesus is said to have taught these two principles: "The Kingdom of heaven is within," and, "Seek first the Kingdom of heaven, then all this shall be added unto you." What is added are the qualities, graces, and virtues that rise up from that inner kingdom.

---

[21] A.H. Almaas, *Space Cruiser Inquiry* 2002. The Diamond Approach uses a precise method of investigative inquiry to carefully work through each barrier and unfold the essential quality hidden behind it.

Clearing the Well of the Soul

The soul is like a well that has been covered over with many layers of dirt and leaves. In our state of ignorance, we see only the surface of life, and the illusory debris from this world obscures the divine image within us.

To dig this well within our hearts, first we have to scoop out all kinds of mud and junk. At a certain point, a breakthrough occurs, and a little bubble of fresh water pushes through. This is the first realization, that there really is a well here, but we still cannot drink the water because it is too muddy. To complete the process, we have to dig further and clear the well. Then we have to line the walls with stone and let the impurities flow off. In the final stage, we reach actualization: the water is clear and available to drink from whenever we want and also to provide water for others.

The many different traditions from around the world are like different wells, and each gives its own method of digging and clearing. Each well has a distinct flavor and treasure, but all are fed from the same deep aquifer. On the surface, every individual prays to a different god, because we all have subtly different understandings of what it is we are praying to. In truth, there can be only one God, one Ultimate Reality, and this One is not bounded by *any* of our ideas about It.

One of the most stubborn barriers we face in seeking to realize universal truth is our attachment to our ideas about it. Even though it seems obvious that we cannot hope to encompass the whole of reality with our limited thoughts, we have been conditioned to cling to the surface forms of whatever tradition we have been brought up in.

We not only cling to ideas of religious exclusivity, but also, if the truth be known, we all cling to a sect of one. We are convinced that our personal way of looking at things is the best and any other ideas (even from within our familiar tradition) are seen as threats to our ego structure. That is why it is not so easy to dig out the well. Most people do not want to give up their own mud; we are attached to it. We think, "This is MY mud they are asking me to dig out. How can I be sure there really is a well of clear water underneath? Maybe the teacher just wants to steal my MUD!" And, in this way, we defend our ignorance and run from the arduous task of digging out the well.

To compensate for the wound of loss of contact with true Self, we make up stories about how our religion is better than all the others and how only *we* have the well (that we don't actually have, although it is hidden right where we are). We are aided and abetted in this delusion by the power structures that have built up around each religious tradition. Those teachers and priests who are most vociferous against other religions are always the ones who have not dug out their own wells. They teach ignorance because it is all they have. Their wells are covered over with leaves and they purvey muddy water. But in every religion, a careful examination of the meaning of the teachings will lead us to peace and universal love and away from hatred, rejection, and exclusivity. It is the mud of our own ignorance that we need to reject, not the universality of truth.

Every religious tradition houses great treasures of wisdom. Wise seekers learn from all, then go beyond into the school within where we can learn directly from reality by confronting our own delusions and clearing them away. In fact, the simple act of awareness brings help. The water within pushes up, breaks through, and washes away the mud and leaves. God wants to reach our awareness and has many ways of pushing through the dramas and delusions of our daily lives.

Some of us work through theistic traditions and some through nontheistic traditions, but truth is both and neither. There is great wisdom to be found in religions, such as the various forms of Buddhism, which teach that the ultimate nature of reality is beyond all forms of deity and that realization comes only from releasing all imaginings about any form. Yet, naturally, many good souls who seek on this particular path of enlightenment cannot help but substitute ideas of Buddha as their deity. It is not so easy to let go of all attachments to form. The Zen aphorism, "If you meet the Buddha on the road, kill him," means to let go of delusions about true nature.

Even within theistic traditions such as Christianity, mystics engage in meditative practices that are not unlike some of those in Zen Buddhism. The anonymous author of a famous book of Christian contemplative instruction, *The Cloud of Unknowing,* counsels his student to tread down every idea that intrudes on his contemplation beneath a "cloud of unknowing" to reach a place of communion beyond the ideas and images of the mind.

Theistic traditions offer access to the personal face of the ultimate reality, while nontheistic traditions offer access to the impersonal aspect of ultimate reality. The personal aspects open deeper compassion, love, gentleness, and healing. It is through the personal face that we learn to embody and actualize these qualities. Those in anguish may receive support from the Universal Comforter.

As we gain deeper wisdom, we may come to see that these paths need not be mutually exclusive, rather that being able to experience both domains of realization provides an even fuller form of enlightenment.

Periodically along the way, if we proceed with sincerity, we will go through the essence of all the traditions. This is natural, because all traditions are pointing at some aspect of universal truth. The truth is built into life as an aspect of being; teachings only reflect this reality and seek to bring the hidden knowledge to light. If we are serious seekers, we will respect all traditions as being houses of treasure for all humanity.

Hinduism has preserved from ancient times the Vedic tradition and many scriptures including the *Mahabharata,* the *Ramayana,* and the *Bhagavad-Gita.* The Yogic teachings of sages, such as Patanjali and Shankara, brought us wisdom about the subtle centers within the human body and various practices for attaining union (yogam) with the Divine. The renowned saint Ramana Maharshi exemplifies the "Advaita" or oneness teachings of Shankara in recent times.

Taoism brought subtle understandings of the way of balance between natural opposites (yin and yang). The classic *Tao Te Ching* is reputed to have been written by the Chinese sage known as Lao Tse or "old master." Taoists tended to reject social proprieties in favor of direct, free experience of the "tao." The teachings of Confucius and his followers, emphasizing social order and moral structure, provided another pillar of ancient Chinese culture. One ancient Chinese teaching that is widely known in the West is the *I Ching,* or *Book of Changes.* It has been commented on by Taoists, Confucians, and Buddhists.

Judaism has brought the traditions and prophetic books that are the foundations of both Christianity and Islam. The religion of Abraham, Moses, and the prophets brought monotheism into a world that was immersed in worshiping idols and demonstrated the power and truth of this essential principle, the unity of the divine: "Hear, O Israel, the Lord is One." The mystical Kabbalah teaches of the ten spheres (sephirot) on the Tree of Life as a way of understanding the transformative process in man and the universal law in creation.

Jesus brought two great commandments: "Love God with all thy heart and soul and mind and strength" and "Love thy neighbor as thyself." The Gospels telling the story of his life have been the foundation of Christianity.

Islam brought the Qur'an and the traditions of Muhammad. This rich tradition also brought the many teachings of the saints and sages, the spiritual science of Ibn Araby and the mystical poetry of Jalaluddin Rumi.

The revered Sufi sage, Bawa Muhaiyaddeen, with whom I studied for many years, taught that Sufism was beyond all the worldly divisions of religion, that it was for all people, not just some. He taught these principles: "One God, one religion, one human family." From this perspective, he said we should never think in terms of "your religion, my religion;" we should always look beyond all thoughts of religious differences and see the common humanity in all people. This is completely in the spirit of love, compassion, and charity and fully in accord with the commandment of Jesus to "love thy neighbor as thyself." Bawa's disciples came from all nationalities, races, and religions, and he taught from all traditions according to the needs of his students.

There is both wisdom and delusion to be found in every tradition, and there is not room here to mention them all. The long-term trend will be for us to understand spiritual practice and mystical reality as existing beyond all divisions. We will learn to actually practice the love, tolerance, and unity that all religions profess.

Today, many organizations, such as the World Council of Churches and the World Parliament of Religions, work to build ecumenical reconciliation and harmony between the religions. While some still cling to rigid concepts of religious exclusiveness, the work of moving to unity continues and may spare us the worst of religious wars. We will come to a time of peace, and we will repudiate fanatical intolerance so that our children and grandchildren may live to grow old in a harmonious world.

At deeper levels of practice, we learn that there are states that move beyond knowing. In his teachings on the nonconceptual state, A.H. Almaas guides us first to distinguish between the awareness of a thing and the "naming" that almost instantly follows.[22] He guides us to become aware of the awareness itself, independent of any content, then leads us to the devastating experience of the realm of The Nonconceptual, also known as The Nameless. We learn experientially that all our knowing, including the knowing of ourselves as a separate

---

[22] A.H. Almaas, Oral teachings in a retreat on the nonconceptual state, Sacramento, California, 2001.

identity, is composed of mere concepts. This is one path beyond the delusions of separateness. As the founder of the Diamond Approach, Almaas teaches a way of spiritual practice that leads to an integration of many essential qualities as one many-faceted diamond.

This book cannot do justice to any of these traditions or teachings. Its point is only to show that the process of integration is an ongoing trend and that out of it will come an increasing shift toward a deeper nonsectarian spirituality which will not only bring greater peace to our social world but also greater treasures to our inner practices. This is one of the most important cultural shifts unfolding in this millennium.

We will see much of this accomplished within the next hundred years. This is not to say that we will lose our spiritual traditions, rather that we will lose our taste for violent fanaticism and offensive bigotry. True spirituality will grow, because people in all cultures are hungry for true experience and true knowledge. It is only the hypocrisy of using religion as a vehicle for greed, manipulation, and divisive politics that will change.

Spiritual-Religious Transformation

Despite the appearance of increased religious strife in the world today, the longer-term trend is toward greater harmony between the major religions. This is happening on two distinct levels: the level of conventional organizations (churches, mosques, temples); and the level of mystical spiritual experience (practices and outcomes). All religions have these two levels internally.

At the level of conventional organizations, the ecumenical, interfaith movement works toward social harmony, peace, and an end to religious strife. The purpose is mainly social, expressed as the desire to get along side-by-side, but distinct and separate in terms of religion itself. This level of religion concerns itself with doctrine and organization.

At the mystical level of spiritual experience, there is an emerging movement toward greater integration of the teaching concepts themselves. Explorers from many religions are reaching out and discovering fellow mystics from other religions, often realizing a greater unity among mystics than between mystics and orthodox doctrine, the law versus the spirit. Mystics are reaching for greater integration of knowledge for a different purpose than are ecumenicists at the conventional level. They seek exchange of knowledge to deepen and enrich the completeness of their connection to Divine Reality.

Also emerging are dialogs between spirituality and science, between religion and philosophy, and between cultural pluralism and integral psychology. These conversations are the most potent directions of transformation for the way we will view spirituality in the coming decades and centuries.

Worldview Struggles

Each of the first-tier players are feeling vulnerable and defensive, which is why the situation seems more like a poker game than the civil conversation which will eventually evolve. What is at stake is the question, "What is a human being?" Each stakeholder has a part of that great answer that will affect the unfolding of humanity for centuries.

Traditional religion (at Blue) is feeling attacked on all sides by science, philosophy, culture studies, and from within by its own transformational mystic levels.

Modern science (at Orange), for all its technological prowess, saw many of its pretensions to absolute truth crushed some decades ago.[23] It has always felt misunderstood by nonscientists anyway, and so it tries to keep the barbarians from the gates. It fears that science could be lost to popular irrationality, and this fear is confirmed every time a research budget is cut.

Postmodern culture (at Green) has risen far on the strength of sharp intellectual arguments capable of deconstructing the premises of both patriarchal religion and reductionist science. However, although its view is emergent, Green has yet to gain broad political power outside the academy and feels that all could be lost at any moment.

These three players (Blue, Orange, and Green) have been struggling for control for a couple of centuries now. Conventional religion has slowly lost ground and fought a rear-guard action. Science has gained the preeminent position by playing the technology card to win the support of business and government, although often this alliance is strained.

Postmodern cultural criticism has emerged out of postcolonialism, two world wars, and in reaction to the struggle within Orange between

---

[23] For example, Gödel's work, *On Formally Undecidable Propositions*, destroyed the pretensions of mathematics to absolute truth, thus diminishing the worldview founded on mathematical physics.

capitalism and communism. As each of these three entrenched players has adapted to the positions of the others, we have come to the present post-postmodern mélange, which has left most of the population of the developed world semicomfortable, semifearful, semiconfused, semialienated, and seeking cures for a malady they can't even name.

Emergent Waves

Two more players are at the table, and both are the real emergents of the present situation, though for very different and opposite reasons. The first is transformation spirituality (Golden Olive and Yellow). This is the real edge of human evolution, and although still just beginning to make its presence felt, it is clearly the only force that can effectively include and integrate the other positions and forge a coordinated worldview that will carry us into our transformational future. This book is all about this emerging reality.

The other player is emergent in an accidental way, as a result of globalization and communications technology. This is the great underdeveloped world that has been mostly left out of the game during the colonial period and the cold war that followed it (the Beige, Purple, and Red waves). Traditional religion has seen it as an army of potential converts; science and business as an object to study and a market to exploit; and postmodern pluralism as a voiceless client to represent. But this large section of the human population is increasingly gaining a voice and its growing presence in the world is posing a challenge to the whole "game" by saying, in effect, "You may be playing your power games but we are dying. Pay attention to us; we are more than half the world."

The transformation message from Golden Olive, Yellow, and Turquoise encourages the three main players—Blue, Orange, and Green (the BOG)—to integrate and transform for two benefits: one, to resolve their own alienation and gain the focused effectiveness of unity; and two, to give their lives greater meaning by addressing the needs of the half of the world that has not yet caught up with all the progress that the rest have enjoyed. The internal alienation is resolved by allowing for a much larger perspective on what a human being is and what each of us can grow into.

The Transformation Model of human development includes the values of traditional religious community, the precise rationality of science, the pragmatic effectiveness of business, and the egalitarian inclusiveness of constructive pluralism, plus a vast spiritual vista beyond all of this. No other worldview can offer so much, and that is why transformation spirituality continues to grow. This is the story of the next few centuries as the Great Transformation society becomes our planetary reality and opens doors to unimagined unfoldments beyond.

Integrating Worldviews

I believe that world efforts to establish peace in the regions where religions collide will ultimately be successful. To move beyond the stage of negotiated truce, those who have the capacity to analyze these religions in detail will need to publish new and carefully validated studies comparing core doctrines and methods (see Wilber, *Integral Psychology*). This effort will be a cooperation between academic cultural studies, comparative religion, integral psychology, and the integrative capabilities of those who have reached second-tier consciousness.

The net effect of this work will be an integrated picture of human spiritual development and a clearer understanding of how each religion, or more specifically, how each detailed practice works to develop human consciousness. Some spiritual teachers are using, and will increasingly use, integrated approaches derived from many of the ancient traditions. Science will also play a role in evaluating those aspects of human development that can be registered with newly developed technologies.

Science and Spirituality

The conversation between spirituality and science is creating a fertile exchange of information that is changing both. The medical model of the human being, for example, is undergoing a significant revolution from a purely material view of the body to a holistic view that incorporates the effects of psyche and spirit, as well as social and environmental factors.[24] It is becoming increasingly clear to at least some scientists that living things, and especially human beings, cannot be fully understood from a purely material point of view.

At the same time, the scientific challenge to spirituality is bringing out better explanations of the truly scientific nature of various spiritual practices. The results have included more detailed comparative phenomenological research, neurological studies of meditative states,

---

[24] Laurence Foss and Kenneth Rothenberg, *The Second Medical Revolution*, 1987.

and an enormous contribution from developmental psychology to the continuum of human development. This two-way conversation has just begun. The important thing is that serious practitioners of spiritual disciplines and qualified scientists are exchanging information and ideas. Many of the gaps are being bridged.[25]

Transformationism

The transformationist view is also challenging Green "culture studies" to address human developmental research in a more receptive way. Cultural relativism has made a valuable contribution in breaking down assumptions based on ethnocentric prejudice, but there is a need to go farther. After deconstruction, there has to be reconstruction. Some hierarchies represent stages of progressive growth, as opposed to dominance hierarchies, and this reality needs to be digested by Green so we can move forward to second tier.

The message transformationism tenders toward postmodern pluralism is: There is progress; we do develop; our development has stages; and we progress in a positive direction. In this case, "positive" means that at higher stages of consciousness development we are more aware of, and able to identify with, wider and wider groups of humanity. What is interesting is that this understanding has actually been unfolded in large measure by the postmodern stage of growth (Green), which took us beyond ethnocentric views to higher more world-centric views. Yet the same worldview often denies and resists the idea that any view is "higher" and that there is any such thing as development.

After we arrive at the horizontally deconstructed network of equivalent values, we need to reconstruct the vertical dimension of conscious integration, otherwise progress gets halted by relativist fragmentation. This harms the very people it tries to protect. Golden Olive is the body of transformation that awakens this vertical dimension.

Over the next several decades, these dialogs on both horizontal and vertical dimensions of the model will create a synthesis that moves us into a fuller perspective on what humanity is and where we are going.

---

[25] To offer a few examples: Peter Tompkins and Christopher Bird, *The Secret Life of Plants 1973*; Itzak Bentov, *Stalking the Wild Pendulum* 1977; Fritzjof Capra, *The Tao of Physics,* 1975; Duane Elgin, *The Promise Ahead,* 2000; and James N. Gardner, *Biocosm,* 2003.

The result will be the emergence of the Great Transformation worldview and its constituent social institutions.

Spiritual Qualities and Virtues

One way we approach apprehension of the divine nature is through studying spiritual qualities and human virtues. As our spiritual awakening increases, we begin to become aware that divine qualities, such as wisdom, compassion, and power, exist as objective realities. These realities are objective, eternal existents compared to which even such vast physical phenomena as galaxies are transient wisps. Divine qualities are the causal control structure of the manifest universe on all its levels. We will increasingly integrate them as the core of our scientific study of reality.

Divine qualities are also the deep structure of the human spirit. This is what is meant by the teaching that we are "created in God's image." The qualities are the image of the Divine Being. During the development of the soul, the virtues awakening within the human heart are "superluminated" by these radiant powers from the level of spirit. Thus we can distinguish between levels of realization of a human virtue and the divine quality that is the source of that virtue, even though ultimately they are the same. While we are developing a virtue, such as patience or forgiveness for example, we can see clearly how different our qualities are from God's. Only when we have realized that we are not separate from God do we truly understand that the qualities at all levels come only from one source.

Word Space, Idea Space, and Being Space

In the beginning of our study, we are only aware of the words. We might begin to think about various values that we appreciate, such as truth, love, justice, peace, and so forth. For many, these terms are passed around as social tokens with little awareness of their depth. For example, the word "peace" is treated as meaning merely the absence of war or conflict. This is what I call the "word space," in which we start to become slightly aware of these realities. The token words as dictionary entries are the dimmest shadows of the realities they name.

If we begin to contemplate what these words mean, we may start to cluster groups of value words together to deepen our understanding of their meaning and relationships to each other. For instance, consider the words "wisdom," "knowledge," "understanding," and "truth." We may recognize a kind of kinship within this cluster and distinguish it from other clusters: ("love," "compassion," "mercy," "kindness,") or ("power," "will," "capability," "strength,") and so forth. We may recognize ideas that seem to exist between and among the words without being entirely captured by them. This is the awareness I call "idea space." We begin to sense the power and influence these ideas have on our lives. We begin to sense that they truly are "holy ideas."

At a deeper level of spiritual contemplation, we come to know that these qualities and the names associated with them are reflections of profound realities. As this awareness opens in the Sapphire realm, we come to experience the actual presence of the divine attribute that resides within the name, and the word becomes radiant for us. We experience it as the name of a vast world. In this awareness, we are experiencing what I call the "Being space" of the divine names.

Patience: A Journey toward the Mansion

When I first began studying with Bawa Muhaiyaddeen, he spoke often about the importance of developing the quality of patience and also about the dangers of hastiness or lack of patience. He also taught several stages of developing this necessary quality. This teaching seemed eminently reasonable to me; after all, how would I be able to learn if I was too impatient to study?

Thus began a journey of unfoldment that continues to this day. What began as a word and unfolded as ideas eventually became a deep contemplation of a vast mansion surrounded by a beautiful garden. In my vision, I saw myself praying on a road rising up toward this mansion of divine Patience. From this I learned that divine qualities may be progressively unfolded within us, but they always remain the property of God. We can never say that we "have" them, but through God's grace, they may be loaned to us in varying degrees. We are in a state of continuous approach to the divine qualities until we are utterly dissolved within them. As long as we have a body, we have more to learn.

This is a natural state for human beings. It is good to be aware of being on a journey of approach, and it is good to make efforts to cultivate virtues. We should not say that we do not have patience or any other quality. These qualities are not something we either have or don't have. They are potentialities within us that we can build and develop. We can use a small amount of patience (even if it is only the idea of patience) to develop a little more.

Spiritual Culture | 115

The reason for developing virtues is not because some authority says you ought to; the reason is because they are intrinsically valuable and beneficial. We don't need anyone to tell us to eat a tasty meal, it is natural. Developing virtues is the same way; once we get to know the taste, we want as much as we can get.

Divine Qualities

Bawa Muhaiyaddeen wrote a profound book about the divine qualities called *Asma'ul-Husna* (The Names of The Holy). The 99 beautiful names of God described in this book are also understood as qualities given to the true human being. Bawa's teaching was that we must find this treasure within our innermost heart and water it with our intention and prayer until it bears fruit. These gifts have already been given to all of us, but it is up to each of us to unfold the gift and bring it into fulfillment.

The Enneagram of Holy Ideas

"Enneagram" refers to an ancient teaching associated with a diagram of nine points on a circle. In *Facets of Unity: The Enneagram of Holy Ideas*, A.H. Almaas presents his inquiry into the nine Holy Ideas originally taught by Oscar Ichazo and transmitted to students in the United States by Claudio Naranjo. Almaas explores the Holy Ideas from the perspective of his Diamond Approach teaching. This is a detailed investigation of how loss of contact with essential being results in the specific complexes of each of the nine personality types and how the Holy Ideas unfold as these complexes are resolved.

Ichazo, in the preface to Almaas' book *Facets of Unity,* associates the concepts of the enneagram teaching with Plato, the Neoplatonists, and Pythagoras, the tenth Pythagorean number being understood as the unity of the other nine. It is also associated with secret Sufi orders by way of G.I. Gurdjieff.

Today it is used as a guide to spiritual direction in many spiritual traditions. The enneagram as a tool for transformation is described further in Chapter 11, Individual Transformation. The Holy Ideas are associated with the nine enneagram points as follows:

1. Holy Perfection
2. Holy Will
3. Holy Harmony
4. Holy Origin
5. Holy Omniscience
6. Holy Strength
7. Holy Wisdom
8. Holy Truth
9. Holy Love

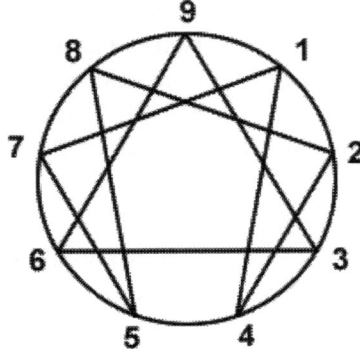

Figure 6. Enneagram of Holy Ideas

The Enneagram of Virtues

In *Understanding the Enneagram,* Don Richard Riso and Russ Hudson describe the virtues for each personality type:

1. Serenity
2. Humility
3. Truthfulness
4. Equanimity
5. Nonattachment
6. Courage
7. Sobriety
8. Innocence
9. Action

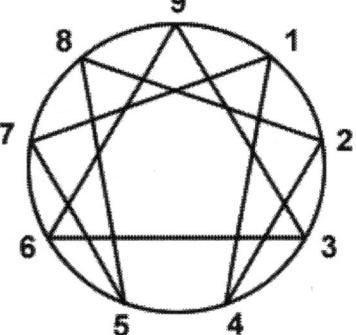

Figure 7. Enneagram of Virtues

The point of this teaching is that each of us has a particular personality trap and a specific virtue that frees us from that trap. The divine attributes can help us develop many virtues as we evolve, but one of these nine virtues will be central for each individual, depending on the structure of the personality.

Sapphire: The Realm of Attributes

One way of understanding our progress through history and our evolution during the millennium ahead, is as a gradual unfolding of deeper embodiments of the divine qualities. We journey from ignorance to a vague awareness of the words. Then we see the words as representing desirable virtues. Slowly we begin to experience the words as powerfully transformative and radiant ideas. And eventually we experience them as profoundly real beings, vast stars in the heavens, brilliant mansions and gardens, each more beautiful than the last.

Along the way, we seek to embody these aspects of the divine at progressive levels of actualization. Throughout the stages of soul development these powers illuminate us and influence us by the degree of their presence as we unfold. In the third-tier realm I have called "Sapphire," these divine presences directly touch and guide the whole fabric of human society. Although many individuals will still be unfolding earlier waves of development and others will have gone on to higher stages, by the end of this millennium, the main focus of society will be to learn the divine realities.

Every phenomenal manifestation, everything we can experience with our senses and our minds, is governed by the divine qualities. They are the causes revealed on the causal level of consciousness. The divine qualities are the control center of creation. No matter how we organize our understanding of them, no matter how many books we write, our knowledge remains yet very young. There is no coming to the end of this learning other than by becoming utterly dissolved in the One Being that is the unity of reality beyond emptiness and fullness.

There always remains an infinite amount to be said about the realm of the divine attributes. We can never exhaust the explanation, nevertheless, it remains valuable to express some little glimpse. The history of all religion, philosophy, and science consists only of such glimpses.

Transformation Philosophy

In practical terms, what is most sensible is to start where we are. What is compassionate is to work at the awakening edge with those who are struggling to wake up, while also keeping in view the needs of the whole. Nothing is more important to the whole of humanity than to support the awakening of more people to second-tier awareness. The complex challenges we face will need every degree of soul awareness we can muster. Transformation philosophy takes human development, and especially soul awakening, as the greatest good at this time in human development and organizes thought and action around that end.

Awakening and Transformation

The coming new awareness awakens us to the holistic integration of all culture and to the direction of human evolution. It is the awakening of the soul and the whole. This is the transformation worldview.

"**Awakening**" means, first, becoming aware of wider unities and identification with those unities. Then, we actualize the understandings of each level of awakening, disidentify with limitations of the earlier level, and open to greater degrees of awareness. Awakening is closely associated with maturity. As we become more aware, we become more adult. We also become more connected to wider integrations with the universe around us and thus less alienated and more relaxed.

"**Transformation**" literally means to "moving across and beyond the form" of the new levels of realization we have achieved. All things change this way and that, but transformation means change in a direction that is positive, constructive, and progressive, in that it encompasses all that was before plus new levels of integration. Transformation is profound evolutionary change, not just passing, surface change. By "moving across" (trans) the form that is realized, we move from realization to actualization; that is, we internalize, digest, and embody what we have first experienced.

Awakening and transformation are indicators and signposts of advancing levels of consciousness. By becoming more conscious of wider domains of experience, we become more connected to reality. This connection makes us simultaneously more powerful, more compassionate, and more imbued with wisdom. How could it not?

This is the very essence of growing up, but most people stop the process halfway and become imprisoned in frozen lives. Life has meaning only when we are growing and transforming. This is what keeps us connected with the spirit of life, or Essence, that is both within the universe and also beyond it. When we are awakening and transforming, we are alive and full of meaning. That's the point.

Millions of people are in the process of shifting to a new tier of development, and millions more are on the brink of making this shift. Of course, at every wave level there is also a general moving forward, but I am especially speaking here of the emerging edge of human awakening, the group of people who represent the highest level that humanity as a whole has reached. We know there are levels far beyond this because of the few extraordinary beings that have appeared as spiritual leaders throughout history. Those great teachers pointed in a direction, and gradually humanity has been moving in that direction.

Now, a significant forward edge of humanity is discovering a new way of being, the tier of soul awakening.

Beyond this are many levels of spiritual unfoldment, but what is important now is building roads, bridges, and maps for this awakening edge of humanity. We are moving from mind to higher mind to soul illuminated by spirit.

The process of awakening to a life beyond the prisons of the ego shell has always been a difficult and hazardous journey, as attested by the writings of spiritual pilgrims.[26] Those adventurous few who have sought to escape from Plato's cave have faced many traps on the road to enlightenment.[27] The majority of humanity has not even been aware that there is a journey to take, being for the most part content with conventional worldviews. Those few who tried to make the journey were sometimes fortunate to find guidance in the form of books written by other explorers or, if very lucky, a personal guide who has already taken the journey. Unfortunately, among the hazards are false guides who have not made the journey but relish the power and respect granted to a guru or spiritual director.

The Spiritual Journey and the Teacher

Over recent centuries, a story of how the spiritual journey ought to proceed has taken shape. One studies, prays, prepares, talks with other would-be pilgrims, and, above all, seeks long and hard for the blessing of finding a true teacher. Sincere seekers eventually find the teacher when they are ready, or more accurately, the teacher finds them.[28]

Then the real work begins. Through a variety of practices, the teacher helps the student to see through various levels of false identifications, knots, and imprisonments. The student grows more devoted to the teacher and experiences progressive degrees of liberation. There are many variations on this story and many detailed lessons, but the central theme has always been the teacher-student relationship.

Success on the spiritual journey is nearly impossible without a guide. There are just too many pitfalls. Some few great ones are

---

[26] John Bunyan, *The Pilgrim's Progress*, 1678, for example.

[27] In *The Republic*, Plato described the egoic prison using the metaphor of the cave, thus the phrase "Plato's cave" has been used as shorthand ever since.

[28] "When the student is ready, the teacher appears." This dictum reappears throughout various esoteric writings.

reputed to have achieved liberation by themselves through extraordinary efforts, but for most of us, the way of the disciple is the only way. Without guidance, we are unlikely to reach our goal. For one thing, we do not know what the goal actually is! Those who have not experienced liberation cannot know what it is they are seeking, only what it is they do not want (and even that only in hazy form). Seekers can experience the state of imprisonment and frustration they have, but not the state of freedom they do not have. If they could, there would be no need to seek it.

Problematically, the mind of a seeker is divided and pulled this way and that by all sorts of neurotic nonsense. Even with a guide, they will succeed only if their soul is strong enough to convince them not to listen to all the nonsense from their mind. Otherwise, they will say that the work is too hard and not continue.

Another problem that arises quite frequently is that the state and qualities of the guide may not match the needs of a particular student. Almaas describes this problem in some detail in his writings.[29] Different paths emphasize different qualities of Essence, such as will or love or truth. If the student needs to develop will and is working with a teacher like Gurdjieff whose teaching emphasizes will, then all is well, but the same student on a path that emphasizes devotion (bakti) may not get what is needed. Another student who is seeking to clarify understanding may need a teaching that provides a lot of detailed explanations[30] rather than one that emphasizes only surrender, and so forth. This is why the Diamond Approach integrates many essential qualities as facets of the diamond, and why Bawa Muhaiyaddeen spoke from many different traditions according to the needs of the particular disciple he was responding to at any given time.

Truly, no challenge is more worthy and no work is more difficult. The challenges of worldly achievement are nothing compared to climbing the mountain of the ego self to discover the greater Self beyond.

Something new is beginning to emerge in this time of transformation we are entering. The old stories of the need for guidance remain true, but many more people are seeking to make the journey to a higher level of awakening. There are more good teachers emerging and

---

[29] Almaas, *The Inner Journey Home*, 2004, and others.
[30] Bawa Muhaiyaddeen referred often to the level of wisdom called "Qtubiyyat," the voice that gives the explanation.

Spiritual Culture | 121

improved teaching processes but, even so, the demand for guidance is growing much faster than the supply of good guides.

A huge, self-organizing pilgrimage is emerging, and its pattern is somewhat different from the traditional stories. Naturally, many false gurus are attracted like wolves to the flock, but seekers also communicate among each other and thus a reporting network is also emerging of who is good and who is not. Also, even among true teachings there are different approaches to the work. Students can explore more options to find out what works for them and what does not. Even though seekers cannot really know what they need, an inner sense can intuit whether there is affinity to a teacher or not. Some seekers only shop around and never settle down to do the work, but those who are determined to succeed eventually do find a path and proceed to walk on it.

The main thing I am saying here is that the general conditions have changed. What was once a thin stream of pioneers is becoming a great migration of settlers. Although it is still a small percentage of humanity as a whole, estimated at 1 or 2 percent, even 1 percent of six billion is sixty million people. There is a huge need for support structures for this flood of spiritual travelers. Especially there is need for a vision affirming that the process of awakening has evolved from a story of small numbers of intrepid pioneers to a story of much larger proportions.

Leaders of all kinds need to know that a new worldview is emerging that will have a profound and positive effect on all of humanity. The Transition is largely the period in which this emerging group organizes itself, becomes aware of itself, and discovers what its nature and role in the world is to be. From all the combined influences I am seeing and describing in this book, I am estimating that this group will reach at least 5 percent of the population within the next four to five decades—a huge change.

Awakening is a natural phenomenon of humanity at this stage in our evolution. It is as unstoppable as the coming of spring, although some may unwisely try to thwart this movement. The awakening will simply wash over or around any barriers set in its way. Although it is irresistible, no one should fear it, for it is the fruition of humanity and will serve the well-being of all humanity. This is not a partisan movement, but a holistic movement that is needed so that humanity can integrate the more complex reality we are entering. Without this awakening movement and its new worldview, humanity would perish or decline into barbarism. Fortunately, it *is* emerging and growing just when it is needed.

People in every walk of life, in every social and cultural group, are realizing that they want this awakening, that they want to fulfill more of their human potential, and that they want to serve humanity as a whole. The effect is to move every worldview and every level of consciousness forward a little faster. People in every part of society are finding new ways to support this unfoldment, though mostly we don't recognize it as a single movement in any formal sense.

The Meaning of Awakening

So, given that this self-organizing process is occurring, what does it mean? When I say "awakening," what do I mean? What are we awakening to? We can compare the process of awakening to the development of a child, of which it is a continuing part. An infant is totally unable to care for itself and is "awake" only to its needs for food, holding, proper temperature, and so forth. Some time during the second year, it becomes "awake" to itself as an ego. It differentiates from the mother and seeks to move out on its own. In the third year, during the rapprochement phase, the child suddenly becomes "awake" to how large the world is and comes running back to the mother.

Gradually the child gets accustomed to being an independent person and becomes "awake" to a larger society outside its home. During the preschool and early school years, it "awakens" to the society and community of its peers. The school years include a series of awakenings of physical, emotional, and intellectual capacities. The young person learns to be part of society and to conform to its norms. This is the basic conventional worldview. For much of humanity, this is as far as consciousness awakening goes.

You may notice that at each level of developmental "awakening," the human being becomes aware of, and responsible to, a larger whole: the body, the self, the family system, a larger local society, a community of peers, and the concept of society as a whole. In each of these environments, the capacities to function and achieve are awakened. Some people go on through higher education or other processes to develop the scientific or "rational" worldview (Orange). And some develop a further perception and understand cultural relativity and the pluralistic worldview (Green).

The Orange and Green worldviews represent the leading edge of human awareness (for most of humanity). The scientific worldview awakened us to being systematic about the material world and the use of intellectual logic. The postmodern worldview awakened us to the plurality of cultures and made clear the relativism of different cultural perspectives. Now the Golden Olive wave is emerging as the carrier of the disciplines and practices of soul awakening.

Transformation Memetics

In his book *The Selfish Gene,* Richard Dawson proposed the concept of units of cultural evolution that he called "memes," analogous in function to the units of biological evolution we call genes. The study of how ideas, or memes, propagate by getting copied has come to be called "memetics."

The Transformation vision and the Human Flowering are stronger memes than their memetic alleles, that is, than any counter vision of the future. As ideas (memes), they are more effective at spreading than other competitive ideas (memetic alleles).

Of course, I am speaking in general concepts, but it should be clear that "apocalyptic doomsday" is a different idea of the future than the Great Transformation vision. "Global dictatorship" and "financial oligarchy" are pictures that also are clearly distinct from the vision of a system that works explicitly to elevate (transform) all of humanity both materially and spiritually. The Great Transformation and the Human Flowering represent a completely distinct track from those visions that see us descending into anarchic barbarity or authoritarian control.

Quite simply put, the big vision of transformationism is more interesting and more compelling than any alternate vision, therefore it will win the idea competition. In detail, there will be an ongoing development of many of the component ideas, or memes, that work together to bring this vision into reality. It will evolve, with some component memes winning and some losing as the larger memetic system grows more robust and widespread. It is precisely because transformationism is better at evolving that it will emerge victorious against any opposition. Yellow is naturally adaptable and flexible. There is no need to worry overmuch about periods when the ideas of transformationism come under attack. It is built into the "DNA" of the transformation vision that it will improve by coping with challenges.

Anyone who has brains, money, charm, creativity, energy, spiritual development, or any other personal resource to bring to this effort should understand something fundamental:

There is something profoundly meaningful to be accomplished in this era.

Only one really important thing is going on in the world today, the transformation of human society into an integrated, wise, and compassionate planetary system. The progressive transformation of each individual who is ready to evolve to second-tier consciousness will be a significant part of this shift, unfolding throughout our lifetimes.

The transformation worldview is integrative and embracing of prior worldviews (the conventional, rational, and postmodern). Everyone should understand that it is part of normal life and is going on around us all the time. People from all walks of life are gravitating in the direction of this vision, without intending to do so, because the ideas and ways of life associated with transformationism simply work better for them. Almost all movement to understand oneself or to make something better in the world leads in the direction of the transformation.

The main prior worldviews (Blue, Orange, and Green) inevitably find themselves drawn together and integrated by the most advanced explorers from each of those realms. At the same time, we see much conflict between these worldviews put forth by the entrenched power interests within them. But these interests tend to die out in a generation or two. Without the renewal of the best minds there is no energy to sustain the conflict.

The vital edge of every major human movement will find itself moving in the direction of transformationism, because this is where all the convergence is leading. This is where the energy is. Transformation is built into where we are in human history at this time; therefore, regardless of where you start from, you wind up moving in the same direction (provided only that you are questing and truthful).

The very qualities that make any person promote a philosophy of life tend to draw them toward the transformation view. The most advanced people from the conventional religions find themselves reaching out toward ecumenical movements (because ideas of unity are inherent in all religions). The most advanced thought leaders in the business world are speaking and writing more about integrative concepts. The most advanced scientists are bringing out ideas that are converging on transformationist perspectives. And the most advanced cultural thinkers are moving beyond the limitations of deconstructionist views toward integrative and constructive views.

One visible aspect of this process is that the most cooperative (and thus most influential) people are cooperating and building bridges.[31] It's what they do. Since bridge-building between worldviews is inherently a way of becoming more influential, the memes for bridge-building tend to spread more rapidly. Bridge-building is another name for, or at least a precursor to, integrating, which is the essential movement that is making transformation consciousness emerge.

Transformational integration is not about creating vague and muddy compromises between conflicting worldviews. Rather, the attempt to resolve meaningful philosophical conflict pulls us up to a metalevel perspective. It pulls us out of the exclusivist insularity of any of the prior worldviews and into a truly new worldview that includes the best of what went before and also transcends all of it.

The transformationist orientation is pragmatic, transpersonal, metasystematic, self-referential, and spiritual. It seeks to engage the whole community through practical solutions. It creates a large enough map to see the whole process that is converging toward its center. It is able to see itself and thus includes the "relativistic" factors. And, it is illuminated from above by higher spiritual consciousness.

When second-tier consciousness begins to emerge, individuals are pulled away from their comfortable "normal" identities and into the "wilderness" of questioning the fundamental meaning of their lives. This is when they begin to make real contact with their souls. When this new level of consciousness begins to influence them, their way of looking at life will change significantly. This profound sense of change and its effect on people's lives is rightly called "transformation."

Until recently, there was little available support for people who were having experiences of higher consciousness. A person might be cloistered away in a monastery, burned as a heretic, locked up in an asylum, or ridiculed as an eccentric "nut." For every person who managed somehow to integrate this new consciousness, many were simply destroyed by it. The emergence of a much larger group of awakening people is beginning to form a growing social nucleus of support. There are more schools, seminars, communities, and so forth, made up of people who have had such experiences and are researching

---

[31] Ed Keller and Jon Berry, *The Influentials*, 2003

their meaning. A powerful and varied culture is arising from this new level of consciousness.

Being sorted out presently are the distinctions between truly second-tier ideas and residues from earlier levels, especially from the pluralist worldview (Green). Green's great gift was showing the importance of embracing with compassion all cultures and social positions, especially those that have been left out. It has deconstructed power hierarchies that have created much of the world's inequality. Unfortunately, it has not deconstructed itself and does not see the ways in which it nourishes conflict in the world by supporting fragmentation rather than integration.

From the point of view of emerging transformation consciousness, it is important to distinguish between the lower level of preconventional development and the higher levels of postconventional development. Postmodernism has not gotten clear on this distinction and generally rejects developmental concepts. Transformationism clearly and explicitly embraces the concept of development and asserts that some levels of consciousness are actually "higher" than others. This does not imply any condoning of dominance hierarchies. Transformationism recognizes that such hierarchies exist and works to reduce their exploitive effects.

Absolutist egalitarianism is almost always a mask for surreptitious exploitation, as the communist societies have so vividly demonstrated. There are, and always will be, unequal distributions of all sorts of properties and goods. People have varying capacities. What transformationism proposes, is to mute the extremes on either end and to support universal education and opportunity, that is, true meritocracy as opposed to enforced pseudo egalitarianism, which is mere lip service.

Green postmodern pluralists who are beginning to experience the awakening of higher consciousness need to realize that compassion is not antithetical to clarity and truth. We do progress. Consciousness *does* develop stage by stage from lower to higher levels, both in the individual life cycle and in the social collective. This does not imply that those in higher levels are justified in exploiting those in lower levels, but it does mean that higher levels of consciousness will tend to set the agenda. It is not in the interests of true compassion and humanitarianism to confuse levels of development in service of a supposed political correctness.

Transformation consciousness brings the establishment of very precise metasystems that address realities *as they are* in order to ameliorate them. We cannot correct and elevate if we pretend that there is no high and low. It is not "correct" to say that an illiterate person is equal to a literate person. The two are not equal, and the situation can only be "corrected" by teaching the illiterate one to read. They are equal in the sense that all persons deserve the opportunity to learn (and it is of selfish benefit to everyone for all to have that opportunity). To pretend that illiterate culture is equal to literate culture in today's world is a false compassion that serves only to maintain real inequalities.

Transformationist views tend to be direct and pragmatic about transforming and elevating human consciousness. There is not a lot of sentimentality in this view for the kind of cultural preservation that enshrines primitive customs just because they are ancient. Male dominance systems are an obvious case in point. They are on their way out and good riddance. At the same time, transformationism is far more subtle and delicate in initiating change than rational materialism. It is not the transformationist way to bomb people into the "modern" world.

Transformationism succeeds where the rationalist worldview, represented in a majority of modern institutions, often fails. It succeeds because its orientation is gentle, subtle, and penetrating, like water seeping into cracks in dry ground. Transformationism knows it is emergent, thus it does not need to move aggressively, and it understands that aggression creates opposition. This is something that the three prior worldviews do not understand, which is why they are exclusivist and why transformationism is integral.

There is no "enemy;" there is only awakening. Ignorance is not the enemy of awareness, and darkness is not the enemy of light. Before light, darkness cannot stand. When the Sun rises, the dark simply fades away amidst the glorious beauty of dawn. Transformation is the time between the first fading of the dark and the rising of the Sun. With the sunrise, we come to liberation and the full Human Flowering. It is the promise of these future stages that is the "illumination from above" that nourishes the spirituality of the transformation way.

To quote my beloved teacher, Bawa Muhaiyaddeen, "a man of wisdom has no enemies."[32] He also spent a considerable amount of time teaching the wisdom of learning how to "escape." The Transition, which may last much or all of our lives, is like the early dawn, a time in

---

[32] Bawa Muhaiyaddeen, *Come to the Secret Garden*, 1985.

which carnivores hunt; thus we must use wisdom to escape. Increasingly, the transparency of the emerging world is making it difficult for predators to hide. A new and more civilized world is quietly being built behind the scenes of conflict and drama.

Chapter 6.
Emerging Technology (E·T)

Technology evolves out of the level of consciousness that creates it. First-tier personality consciousness can manage only a certain degree of technical complexity. To go beyond that, second-tier consciousness is necessary. Until we reach integral and holistic levels, we can never truly understand the technologies these levels produce.

What also grows, along with the greater subtlety of these levels, is a wider holistic ethics. This chapter discusses emerging technologies and the ways they affect, and interact with, human social change.

My primary goal in looking at technological futures is to investigate *what* we will do rather than *how* we will do it. The ends rather than the means define the major directions of development. Technological means evolve over time and may influence direction in the shorter term, but in the end, the story is directed by what we want to do. The things we want to do today, but can't because of limitations of technical means, tomorrow we will discover the means to do. Technological development is ultimately guided by what we value.

Intersecting Technologies

One way to envision the story of the next millennium is to explore the interactions between major areas of advance. We can think about the structure of technological evolution in terms of four interdependent major categories:

1. Physiotech
2. Biotech
3. Humantech
4. Mediatech

In this context, we are not separating the sciences from the technologies that emerge from them. Although they are not the same, we can consider them under the same umbrellas for the purposes at hand.

The common denominator is that everything is viewed as technology; even the humanities come increasingly under this umbrella. The other side is that everything becomes humanized. Humanity in all its dimensions becomes our focus, major study, and interest. We see all things by the human measure.

Each category is an area of convergence on its own. The whole four-category domain also represents a grand convergence in which systems thinking will analyze any particular development in terms of how it affects, and is affected by, other developments across the domain.

Physiotech

This category loosely contains all the technologies of physics, materials, and mechanisms of all kinds—everything from orbital dynamics to nanotechnology.

Technologies related to mechanical systems and material stuff provide the support substrate for the other technological domains. This is the area we usually think of today as technology, things like new gadgets, robots, space shuttles, personal computers, and so forth.

A primary trend in the area of physiotech is a movement toward dematerialization. We will look for material systems with less material in them to provide solutions with lighter, subtler packages. Physiotech will work increasingly with films, membranes, composites of many-layered stuff, and plasmas. We will use energy fields and subtle molecular modeling to give thin material structures powerful properties and capabilities.

Another trend is to incorporate more intelligence into the substance of materials. We will want materials that adapt automatically to environmental changes, are responsive to commands, remember their shape when deformed, and generally are subtler and more variable than anything we can think of today.

The demands of space exploration will drive new physiotech developments. We will look for solutions involving lift out of gravity wells, strength without weight, shielding from harmful radiation, variable gravity management, and other problems that will emerge as we spend more time in a space environment.

Another primary driver is the need for alternative sources of energy as fossil fuels dwindle. As we begin to feel the painful impact of wasteful practices, all of our technological systems will be reinvented with an eye toward sustainability.

A significant application for new physiotech solutions will be environmental protection and remediation. We will want to clean up the pollution of the transitional period and develop systems for preventing generation of new pollution. Therefore, we will develop smart materials that can be easily recycled, cleaned, and redeployed. We will also be looking for membranes that can selectively sift substances on one side from other substances on the other.

To protect ourselves more effectively, we will develop multilayered systems of protection from a variety of threats. I refer to these as "envelope systems" because they envelope what we are trying to protect, first and foremost, our bodies. This will mean better cities, better houses, better vehicles and transportation systems, better clothing, and better systems inside our bodies, all focused on keeping us healthy and alive.

We will also learn to do more with common materials: earth, rock, water, air, and garbage. By applying intelligence, we will spin the most abundant materials into a variety of wonders and do it cheaply enough that everyone can have what they need.

Nanotechnology: The Power of the Small

We are on the verge of an enormous technological revolution that is currently summed up by the word "nanotechnology," which simply refers to the ability to manipulate matter at the molecular scale, from one billionth of a meter (1 nanometer) to one hundred billionths of a meter (100 nanometers). This is the scale of molecules. Being able to move atoms around and build molecules by design means we will be able to control an almost unlimited array of material and chemical properties.

Nanotechnology is real-world alchemy. This emerging revolution will supercharge all existing technologies and drive developments in all industries for the rest of this century at least. It is almost impossible to overstate its impact.

All major governments and most large corporations are pouring research and development money into nanotechnology because they know that breakthroughs in this field will control almost everything. Already, laboratories are being set up and stocked with nanoscale microscopes and molecular modeling software. Big breakthroughs are just over the horizon.

Within the next five years, nanomaterials will be in common use, new discoveries and applications will explode, and the prefix "nano" will be on everyone's lips. Word of this revolution is spreading faster than the spread of the internet in the 1990s. What is amazing about nanotech is that it is not just a passing phase and not limited to one industry. It is a genuine, across-the-board revolution in human capabilities, somewhat like the industrial revolution but even more far-reaching. As this revolution matures, it will create major fireworks every couple of years for decades to come.

Amazing new "nanomaterials" will provide almost magical control over properties and abilities. Superhard, ultralight, almost indestructible building materials and metal alloys; self-cleaning fabrics, glass, and ceramics; smart-materials that automatically adjust to environmental conditions or programmed instructions: these are just a few of the possibilities. Hexagonal carbon rings can be assembled into tiny nanospheres called Fullerenes, or "Bucky balls," after Buckminster Fuller (inventor of the geodesic dome). Carbon also can be grown into strong carbon nanotubes for all sorts of applications.

Nanotechnology will allow us to create nanoscale factories for turning out custom-designed molecules as fast as we feed them raw materials. Products can be designed to be "self-assembling." Perhaps more importantly, we will be able to create molecular robots for disassembling molecules we don't want, such as pollutants, viruses, and arterial blockages. The byproducts of such disassembly will be ready-to-use raw materials for anything we have the ingenuity to dream up.

Landfills will be turned into fuels, houses, cars, clothing, whatever we need. After all, everything that exists is made of the same basic elements and, with nanotech, we are discovering how to rearrange those building blocks according to our requirements. Carbon, hydrogen, oxygen, nitrogen, silicon, metals, and a few trace elements can make almost every material thing that we need.

Nanotech will provide vast information storage in tiny spaces and lightning-fast processor chips that will make virtual reality and ultrahigh bandwidth communication available worldwide in the very near future. This technology will be pressed into service to solve many of our energy needs by providing synthetic fuels and cheap, efficient solar cells. We will be surprised to discover that energy is abundant when you know how to capture it. Nanotech also will lead to increasingly greener industry and effective pollution cleanup.

The biggest boon, though, will be nanomedicine, which will soon conquer all our most feared diseases: cancer, heart disease, AIDS, stroke, arthritis, Alzheimer's, and a host of potential epidemics such as avian flu. Nanomedicine will remove almost all our aches and pains, not by deadening pain signals, but by curing the underlying physiological causes. Most symptoms of the aging process will be arrested and eventually even reversed. We are on the brink of discovering the real fountain of youth and, despite our most cynical fears, nanotech will be able to make it available to almost everyone.

It is quite likely that most ill-health will be eradicated by the end of the century, if not sooner. We do not know how long we will be able to live once we have achieved these breakthroughs.

The impact of this emerging revolution on our psychological state will be profound. To begin with, it will be disorienting to live in a world where ordinary matter is as programmable as a computer.

Our homes will have appliances we could call "nanofabs" that will make whatever we need based on instructions downloaded from the internet. We might have one fab for foods, another for clothes, a third for electronic devices, and so forth. What we will buy are design programs that will always be changing—new menus, new styles, new features. Our old clothes, garbage, and obsolete devices will get tossed into the recycling appliance to be converted back into raw materials.

When matter itself is programmable, our whole idea of a world of stable objects will shift. This is one more force moving us in the direction of transformation consciousness.

Nanotech will provide capabilities to solve many problems we now see as intractable. We will address climate change with subtle weather control technologies, including new ways of extracting greenhouse gases from the atmosphere. Energy shortages will be a thing of the past. Above all, nanotech will create an enormous expansion of wealth. Of course, this will be lopsided and upsetting at first, but the sheer volume of wealth will cause a spreading effect.

Also, because of nanotech's prodigious productive capacities and ease of distribution, products and benefits are likely to become cheap and widespread. It will take us a while to adjust to this wondrous but disruptive reality. We will soon live in a world that is free of material scarcity.

Megamolecule factories will turn out molecule factories by the millions whenever they are fed the right atomic ingredients. These precisely designed molecule factories will in turn generate the desired substances, medicines, fabrics, metals, artificial wood or marble, foods, or computer chips.

As we become more skilled at molecular design programming, we will be able to produce better and better things at lower and lower costs. As fabricators become widely distributed, there will be less need to ship actual products. Instead, we will send the code for their automatic assembly. In some cases, we might deliver molecular assemblers designed to use ambient materials. For example, factory "seeds" to produce emergency housing out of rock and fallen wood for disaster areas like Pakistan or the Gulf Coast.

These ideas may sound impossibly fantastic, but they are really only decades, not centuries, away from reality. Transforming the way humans treat each other is a challenge that will take a bit longer. One of our most difficult challenges may be to remain patient as we see solutions emerging that are just out of our reach.

Biotech

The biotech category covers all technologies related to life and living organisms. It includes everything from planetary ecology, agronomy, and exo-biology to microbiology, genetics, and pharmaceuticals. This major area of synergy is just beginning to emerge, but it will be accelerated by nanobiology. It will have two interacting poles: the human body and the biosphere environment.

Biotech is sometimes divided into three colors: red (medical biotech), green (agricultural biotech), and white (industrial biotech). In the "white" domain, biotech is also convergent with physiotech, where it is increasingly performing industrial work by using biological organisms to grow, rather than make, new materials.

In the area of the human body, we are seeing advances in pharmaceuticals, medicine (including many alternative practices), instrumentation, prosthetics and bionics, genomics, proteomics, physiology, metabolic systems, and nutrition. These are moving forward both in the scientific laboratory arena and also in the independent consumer arena, where people are exploring all kinds of diets, supplements, exercises, and alternative treatments while learning new ways to manage their own health.

As the future of the body unfolds, we can expect these two forces, laboratory and consumer, to affect one another in many ways. The healthy trend is toward consumers who are more informed of the latest research and who are taking charge of their own bodies. Most major breakthroughs in human bioscience will emerge from the laboratory, but they will be vetted and evaluated by the public, which has the market power to reject directions it does not like.

We have yet to see the most amazing new technologies that will emerge from genomics, proteomics and physiological process research, and new areas at the boundary between biotech and physiotech. Two areas that show extraordinary potential include nanomedicine and material science, which will devise replacement tissues, trauma repair solutions, health monitoring garments, media interfaces, and the like.

From biotech we can expect much longer, healthier lives, less pain, stronger bodies, new and better sensory powers, quicker learning, smarter brains and better memories, manual and full-body skill enhancements, closer interfaces between body and machinery, embedded hardware of all kinds, and other things at the border of today's imagination. One direction of future body enhancement will involve adaptation to other environments, including undersea, space, other planets, and so forth.

Our clothing will become more intricately interfaced with our bodies. We will develop cloth and tissues that monitor internal physiology and adapt accordingly to regulate temperature, breathing filtration, eyesight, hearing, resistance to traumatic impact, and, of course, can adapt to style and occasion. Our outer wearable systems will interact with internally embedded systems, including nanomedical systems. We will also use clothing as part of our interface to the global information media net, and this interface will be moderated by complex and subtle biotech solutions.

The demands of biosphere system management will integrate physiotech, nanotech, biotech, mediatech, and humantech to develop a range of system solutions that will become the "spiritual science" of 2110: using our human power to nurture all life and to garden Earth. The micro-organismic world will be much better understood, and we will know how to cultivate it for greatest harmony, both within our bodies and in our soil and water. We will come to a time of much greater dominion over, and harmony with, all forms of life.

As our understanding of complex ecosystems grows, we will learn how to manage them, and our own effects on them, more harmoniously. New life forms will become our robots to transform Earth into a garden. Our bodies will be pervasively integrated with hundreds of nanotechnology and nanobiology systems. Already nanotechnology is being combined with traditional natural medicine to increase bioavailability of herbal medicines. We will use living organisms to clean up pollutants and reclaim deserts.

Advances in biotechnology also will affect all aspects of conception, gestation, birth, and child rearing. The genetic material for fertilization may be woven together from many contributors, rather than just two as it is today. Already, conception can occur in vitro; in the future, gestation may occur in artificial wombs. Even in human wombs, it is likely that the growing fetus will be constantly monitored and its intrauterine environment managed by advanced biotech processes. Every aspect of fetal development will be adjusted to produce the healthiest babies possible.

Today's social constraints on biotech need to be understood and accepted as part of a cautionary slowing down of experiments that have the potential to escape and impact the whole biosphere in unforeseen and possibly negative ways. Science must take such caution seriously, exercise due diligence, and communicate more effectively with other parts of society. Scientific arrogance only annoys the public and makes for more restrictive legislation.

The scientific engineering community needs to embrace a new ethic affirming that not everything that *can* be done, *should* be done. The very power of science to effect irreversible changes in the biosphere mitigates for a careful and cautious approach. Putting career advancement or money ahead of human welfare will not be acceptable, particularly after we experience a series of negative consequences. We will need to develop wisdom in evaluating which programs to advance and which to restrain. Orange rational materialism will inevitably give way to the Yellow integral view of science and eventually to the Turquoise holistic view as human technology advances.

Humantech

The category of humantech considers the confluence of social sciences, humanities, and cultural applications as an integrated domain that is understandable as "technology" in the broadest sense. Indeed, it is one of the premises of this book that all technologies will become humanized and integrated with psychological and human factors. Software is a simple example. Humantech includes everything from spiritual psychology to cultural integration and conflict resolution. Chapter 4 is devoted to the convergence of many disciplines into the broad category of human science, which also results in "human technology."

Humantech will become the centerpiece of the whole transformation enterprise and is today one of the least clearly perceived of the synergies. Cultural activities, humanities, all the social sciences, government, management, economics, religion, and spirituality will converge in this intersecting synergy. Today we see the social sciences engaging business, government, education, and spirituality, with psychology at the focal point.

At the same time, transpersonal psychology is incorporating and exploring many aspects of human spiritual aspiration. It is investigating the barriers to human spiritual realization and methods of overcoming them. As this movement gathers deeper experience, a new form of human wisdom school is emerging. We are understanding the spiritual practices of the ancient traditions as a form of spiritual technology, a wisdom of how to clarify the soul, experience essential qualities, and ultimately realize our true nature. The commitment to truth will inform all of our activities in this realm and will be part of what leads to universal transparency. We will learn to become more comfortable with truth and to refrain from harshly judging ourselves and others.

The further we move into the future, the more clearly we will see that the major work of all people in the world is the transformation and elevation of every human being. We will increasingly see the progress of human realization as the world's work, and no other task will take precedence. All technology and physical exploration will serve our great spiritual path.

We will experience human transformation in every part of our lives, and it will always be the focus of our attention as we do our jobs, learn, raise children, play, and engage in all our activities. We will consider conscious activity and ethical behavior the most important endeavor, and it will guide every other process. This will not be a petty morality that is focused on judging ourselves and others. We will learn to work with the shadow side of the human personality and, by neither rejecting nor acting out, to heal it.

As this psychological and spiritual process dominates our reality, economics and governance will move toward greater equity, freedom, and justice, as well. Under the pressure of spiritual renewal, human technologies of management and organization will continue to evolve. We will learn how to function effectively without heavy-handed coercion or compulsion. Increasingly, leaders will lead by inspiration, mentoring, encouragement, and especially, by example. This does not mean that second-tier management cannot be directive, only that it does so more wisely.

A significant aspect of human technology will be discovering and developing new forms of organizational process. From the level of small teams of two and three all the way up to world governing bodies, we will explore ways to improve team communication and effectiveness. Instead of the dysfunctional sluggishness seen in most organizations today, we will see businesses, government agencies, professional associations, and schools that function like joyous ballets. We will learn to interact beautifully, happily, and effectively.

This may sound less utopian and more probable if you consider all the synergies coming to bear on human technology. We will understand each other psychologically much better than we do today. We will form group process teams from before birth, and children will learn this way from early infancy. We will fit our professions better because we will select them based on what we love to do and where our natural abilities are. We will form organizational teams in almost the same spirit of sacredness that we form marriages, and with far greater understanding than is possible today.

On this foundation, we will add to our relationships deep practices of inner inquiry and truth-telling. No issue will be able to arise and fester. As a matter of ingrained habit from childhood training, any strain that occurs will be addressed immediately and resolved directly between the people involved. If necessary, a team mentor will help to mediate and resolve difficult issues. Since groups will self-select from global databases based on shared interests, personality qualities, and complementarities, we will know that we are with the right people. This will be reinforced by our spiritual commitments, and we will see the resolution of difficulties as good and sacred work rather than as an impediment to the team's work. In fact, the first real work of any team will be to grow in harmony.

People will be part of many intersecting teams, work teams, study teams, family groups, civic groups, arts and recreation groups, and so forth. Of course this is true today, but in the future the intersecting structure will be much more effectively organized. A significant part of future human technology will involve the study of group numbers and group interactions. We will understand in greater detail the dynamics of pairs; triads; groups of four, five, six; and so forth. We will use software scheduling to ensure that all members of every group interact and communicate regularly.

Transformational psychology involves learning to use interpersonal exercises, shared experiences, and meeting management processes to ensure deep and engaging interactions between people. We will know each other far better than most married couples do today, and that knowledge will be combined with love, compassion, and humor, which is why tomorrow's teams and organizations will be so effective and joyous compared to so much of what we see today.

Even today we are starting to see management practices that incorporate transformational thinking at an elementary level. When they are undertaken with commitment, some of these first steps are proving quite successful. Other times they can degenerate into lip-service exercises.

Although today most of us are familiar with, and have participated in, communication seminars, conflict resolution, motivational exercises, and the like, these kinds of trainings will become a much bigger part of future life, and they will be far more profound and effective than anything we know today.

Mediatech

This category integrates aspects from physiotech, biotech, and humantech. I have made it a separate category because it will play such an important role in the changes of this millennium. Mediatech includes everything from internet, TV, and phone to holographic virtual reality and bio-interface technologies. This technology category is rapidly redefining the human social sphere.

Mediatech is the most visible driver of future change. The primary medium through which other synergies are experienced and known, it will become the amazing virtual reality internet (VR/I) that will absorb and contain almost all of human activity. VR/I will be ubiquitous. It will record and store virtually everything. In it we will work, play, communicate, learn, teach, create, and explore. VR/I will create the experience of transparency and intimacy throughout the human family.

Already, our primitive first-generation internet has integrated almost all other media. Only bandwidth and technical limits are holding it back. It is integrating phone, TV, movies, music, video, email, software of all kinds, databases, art, and so forth, and providing the universal glue for all human activities and institutions. Mediatech will increase in variety at the same time as it increases in integration. All of the various component systems will be linked within it. Chapter 7 describes this technology category (and its hazards) in greater detail.

The synergy of all four categories (physiotech, biotech, humantech, and mediatech) represents the "hyper-technology" that is a prime driver of change for the coming millennium. Every aspect of our lives will be more densely intersected with technologies than we can currently conceive possible. Eventually, many aspects of life that we have not considered technological will be considered in that light.

Technological Evolution

Technology Evolution Dimensions

As technological solutions to human problems evolve, they develop along evolutionary dimensions of change. In each growth wave, any particular technology is progressively transformed. I have defined four major dimensions of technological evolution:

1. Progressive subtlization
2. Progressive convergence
3. Progressive complexity
4. Progressive universality

These dimensions can be used to track an emerging technology through a series of stages and to anticipate evolution of technologies within developmental stages.

Progressive Subtlization
Over time technology gets more subtle, lighter, more ethereal. There is a progressive dematerialization as the technological solution becomes less physical, more energy-oriented, more mental, smaller, and more pervasive.

Progressive Convergence
Over time all categories of technology, including the major categories presented earlier, becomes increasingly intertwined. As convergence progresses, we tend to look at the whole system through the lens of new, more integrated models, such as complexity theory. There is a deep trend toward a one-tech system (or perhaps a one-system technology) in which everything is seen as an aspect of a single technological web. Life takes on the character of whatever wave is

Emerging Technology | 141

passing through the unified technosphere. The most recent wave was the worldwide web; the next will be nanotechnology.

Progressive Complexity
Technology evolves towards ever greater complexity. Lower orders of complexity become components of higher orders of complexity. Very high tech becomes the ground for ultra high tech. Complexity management tools, such as the capability maturity model (CMM) for system development, guide all technology development.[33] The ground of technology disappears from view. Physiotech, then biotech, then mediatech becomes the ground, and only human evolution remains as figure. Technology is everywhere but is unseen and ignored. We become the technology; human unfoldment becomes our sole focus of attention.

Progressive Universality
As technology becomes more widespread, the goals of new technology become increasingly humanitarian and oriented toward benefit for all humanity. Technology becomes more universal in nature. What we want changes and becomes less egocentric. The nature of new technology pervades the whole planet. The emergence of the internet is a prime example, and ecological thinking, which is still emerging, is another.

The kind of grid shown in table 6 can be used to analyze particular technologies, products, and industry spaces in greater detail, as well. For example, we could make a large grid to explore developments in specific software applications or healthcare services over the next ten to fifteen years. Similar models, using condensed symbol systems within metasystemic matrices, allow more effective complexity management. This particular grid shows how the technological environment interacts with waves of consciousness and dimensions of technological development to define the whole social experience of a time period.

---

[33] Kim Caputo, *CMM Implementation Guide: Choreographing Software Process Improvement*, 1998

Estimated Era:	2000	2015	2030	2050	2090	2200
WAVE:	OR	GR	GO	YE	TU	CO
Physiotech:						
Space Exploration	SPX_1	SPX_2	SPX_3	SPX_4	SPX_5	SPX_6
Energy	ENR_1	ENR_2	ENR_3	ENR_4	ENR_5	ENR_6
Nanotechnology	NAN_1	NAN_2	NAN_3	NAN_4	NAN_5	NAN_6
Biotech:						
Body Somatics	SOM_1	SOM_2	SOM_3	SOM_4	SOM_5	SOM_6
Environment	ENV_1	ENV_2	ENV_3	ENV_4	ENV_5	ENV_6
Humantech:						
Management	MAN_1	MAN_2	MAN_3	MAN_4	MAN_5	MAN_6
Education	EDU_1	EDU_2	EDU_3	EDU_4	EDU_5	EDU_6
Mediatech:						
VR/I	VR/I_1	VR/I_2	VR/I_3	VR/I_4	VR/I_5	VR/I_6
Software Tools	SWT_1	SWT_2	SWT_3	SWT_4	SWT_5	SWT_6

Table 6. Technology Categories, Dimensions, and Waves

Subscripts show snapshots of dimensional development, which may, or may not, correspond with waves.

This kind of grid can be used to analyze particular technologies, products, and industry spaces in greater detail, as well. For example, we could make a large grid to explore developments in specific software applications or healthcare services over the next ten to fifteen years. Similar models, using condensed symbol systems within metasystemic matrices, allow more effective complexity management. This particular grid shows how the technological environment interacts with waves of consciousness and dimensions of technological development to define the whole social experience of a time period.

Technology and Social Diversity

In the earlier world, which was more divided into separate social communities, experiments with new technologies, processes, and concepts had more options for development because one orthodoxy was less likely to prevail. Furthermore, the dangers of various choices were more contained. Each society could learn from the mistakes and discoveries of other societies. We had more "social diversity."

In an increasingly integrated planet, we will need to find ways of preserving this value. Planners of the future will find this issue significant. The question is: how can we gain the values of unity, cooperation, and peace while also preserving (and developing) the benefits of social diversity?

In his seminal work *The Structure of Scientific Revolutions*, Thomas Kuhn showed how established theory tends not to give way to new data until the generation espousing that theory dies out. Scientists with new ideas might find support from groups in other nations, but as we become more integrated globally, variety diminishes.

Two examples from recent history illustrate these concerns:

1. The pervasiveness of flawed software code precipitated the worldwide Y2k crisis. We should anticipate similar problems arising from many types of pervasive *monoculture* technologies.

2. The ability of industrial pioneers, such as W.E. Deming, to find an eager audience in Japan (when US manufacturers were not listening) gave the world a fertile laboratory for great advances in manufacturing theory and practice.[34]

In a more integrated world, such options and their benefits may be easily squashed. If everyone is believing the same philosophy, where does a new idea find room to grow and prove itself? Future social planners will have to create that room artificially to replace the losses of natural social diversity inherent in the emerging global integration.

The curve of adoption will, of course, show emergent technology first used by early adopters and later accepted by a majority of the mainstream, and finally widespread throughout the planet. As universality and pervasiveness progress, technologies will roll out across the planet in ever more rapid deployments. Eventually new technologies may be adopted everywhere almost instantly. We will need to adapt to the dangers of this trend by more careful

---

[34] W.E. Deming, *The New Economics for Industry, Government, Education*, 1994 and Mary Walton, *The Deming Management Method*, 1986

predeployment testing and artificially phased roll-outs. Sadly, we will probably have to learn this by responding to disasters.

Direction of Technological Emergence

Technology will emerge along several lines that will integrate in a cohesive direction. Technology will:

- Become more universal and humanitarian
- Move up the levels of consciousness
- Reflect understanding of systems ecology thinking
- Apply complexity theory more widely
- Show understanding of the interdependence of life
- Show continuing convergence
- Face the ecological cleanup task
- Emerge from early twenty-first century disasters
- Expand into the solar system

All these forces and more will drive scientific technology and human psychological spirituality together into a converged, one-tech discipline. Eventually, many physiotech and biotech elements will become so sophisticated that they will run almost automatically below the level of ordinary awareness, just as today machine code and low-level programming operate below the awareness of most computer users. Nanotechnology will become so sophisticated that it will, for most people, function below the level of our normal awareness. We will command our material environment with little thought to how it obeys. Instead, the focus will be on psychological or spiritual technology. Our new human technologies will also be re-applied to the processes and methods used in science and technology development.

We can barely conceive of a process whereby something like advanced prayer or meditation drives the entire infrastructure of planetary technology. To people of that era, it will seem completely natural and logical.

We will control our world by invisible computers, our computers with our minds, our minds by meditative practice, and our meditation by spiritual discipline. I am speaking of an evolved and scientific form of *spiritual discipline* not much like what we know today by that phrase. All this will emerge naturally from where we are today. There will be no magic leaps. For example, we will use ultra light-weight biofeedback and monitoring nets around (or in) our heads and bodies to improve focus and get better meditation results.

Scientific monitoring will allow us to learn what kinds of practices are most effective. We will also use advanced training technologies to teach new spiritual and psychological methods and practices. Most people will work in highly complex technological fields and will need the mental and emotional discipline that this training provides. We will invent new ways to develop capacities for creative problem solving, innovation, increased intelligence, stress management, and so forth.

The foundations of spiritual technology are already being laid in a number of interesting fields today. We will integrate the most mechanical physical processes with the subtlest levels of spiritual attainment for one reason: it will work best that way.

We will use spiritual technology for practical reasons, to get the results we want. For the same practical reasons, what we want will become more spiritual. We will come to understand that selfish, greedy actions are infantile, primitive, and ineffective. We will see that only holistic, ecological actions work to create the world everyone really wants. This is the highest form of self-interest, pure adult practicality.

Emergent Tech-Memes

Over the next few decades, waves of new technology will emerge at an exponential rate. As they evolve into more subtle and more complex forms, they will converge on mediatech and spread toward universality with ever more viral speed. It will become ever more difficult to separate technology from culture. To use a concept from ecommerce expert, Seth Godin, the emergence of these waves of technocultural memes will become more "smooth."[35] That is, they will be extremely easy for an end-user to spread to other users.

So what will happen to the world as these waves of emergent technology ripple across it with ever increasing speed? First, we need to come to grips with the reality that this increase in smoothness is inevitable. No technology or idea will be able to survive long without increased smoothness against otherwise equal competitors. The smoother new wave will simply overwhelm the old as it runs to stay ahead of an even smoother predator behind it that is gaining fast. Remember, "smoothness" means "easy to spread."

---

[35] Seth Godin, *Unleashing the Idea Virus*, 2001

Now, to answer the question I posed, what happens is that the particles of consciousness, us, become increasingly linked into a larger form of consciousness, the world-brain. The planet wakes up, and we become its brain cells. I am not predicting some sort of hive-mind, just a more conscious global community that functions figuratively like a "world-brain." As individuals, we will continue to function freely.

When that happens, and it has already begun, the old egoic level of consciousness will simply stop being able to run things (or should I say, ruin things). An awakened planet will not allow the kind of depredations that Orange "globalism" considers business as usual. The planetary consciousness will starts moving in different directions, and the majority of people will simply flow along in the new meme-stream: "Game over" for the exploitive world-dominator program. Awakening planetary humanity will yawn, shake its collective head, blink away the nightmare, and get on with the new day. In fact, part of what is triggering the shift is our exhaustion with first-tier egoic leaders and the wars they can't seem to stop fighting.

Connected networks can be induced to go along with self-destructive behavior only as long as they remain asleep. Increasing smoothness means rapid communication between all the human neurons in the world-brain, which inevitably leads to waking up. We will become aware that we are asleep, not unlike what happens in the movie, *The Matrix*. Little irritants will begin to intrude on our consciousness and propel us into waking up. Despite all attempts to maintain our drugged dream-state, it will become impossible to suppress the increasing volume of irritants that we call daily life in the postmodern world. There is no way to stop the awakening, and it won't be merely a few people who wake up, as depicted in the movie; that era is already over. Today, vast numbers are waking up to what is going on, and the smooth waves are coming more rapidly. Anyone who does not wish to be drowned had best try to learn how to align with the emerging transformation.

The concept of "alignment with emerging transformation" is itself a smooth idea virus. It has this property: the more people awaken to second-tier consciousness and awareness of universal connectivity, the more easily this idea virus spreads; that is, it automatically becomes smoother as it grows. Following Godin's terminology, we could call this property "deep acceleration." "Acceleration" because of the exponential increase in smoothness (it begins to make more and more sense to people), and "deep" because it is nourished by emergent planetary drivers. Second-tier consciousness is an emergent planetary driver because it is the cutting-edge level of consciousness that is now in process of manifesting.

Some have talked about the possibility of humanity downloading consciousness into silicon and, in essence, becoming artificial intelligence machines. This idea is a reflection of Orange-Green alienation. The fantasy that artificial intelligence machines, AIs, actually can be made "conscious" and, in effect, human, is a narcissistic dream of neurotic egos. Now, of course, we will probably be able to create a *facsimile* of a person, a simulacrum like a 3-D moving photograph, but it won't actually *be* the person. The result of such research probably will be war robots that cause much devastation before higher consciousness redirects the technology into healthier channels.

We also should remember that unconscious people generally behave like robots. And unconscious systems are mechanical automatons, as can be seen, for example, in the so-called "invisible hand" of free-market capitalism. This robotic "daemon" works to consolidate wealth in the hands of ever fewer people. Transparency is making the "hand" much less invisible. What is missing in such automatic systems is human compassion, wisdom, and a flexible sense of good judgment.

The more likely scenario is that we will gradually intermingle with the intelligent machines we use until it becomes impossible to tell where human begins and system leaves off. Increasingly the smarter thinkers in the AI crowd are focusing on IA, or intelligence augmentation, that is, augmented humans, rather than artificially intelligent machines. We will humanize our intelligent computer system because we will get tired of it trying to mechanize us.

Progressive advances in biotechnology, nanotechnology, and cybernetics would seem to make this integration of human and machine highly likely. When we combine them with the drive toward smoothness of idea transmission, likeliness approaches inevitability. Any social order that tries to suppress this movement will almost certainly be overcome by others that embrace it. Whether we think it is a good thing or not, it is going to happen. The good thing to recognize is that mechanistic, authoritarian systems are neither smooth nor adaptable.

What I am suggesting is that the marriage of human and "computer" is both a side effect and facilitator of awakening planetary consciousness. The more we become part of our systems, the more we become part of each other. It is not so much that we will lose consciousness of ourselves as distinct entities and become part of some neo-fascist, collective hive-mind, rather that we will gain—and are gaining—greater consciousness of each other. Beneath all the reactions and contractions, wars and intolerances, a different and truer story is unfolding. Humanity is falling in love with itself and with the living planet from which we emerge.

When we see pictures of the planet from space and hear stories of peoples from all around the world, we know in our deepest core that we are in fact one. We know that the ethical teachings of every true religion are not theory but fact. Our lives depend on each other and are enriched by each other. We are not separate. This is not some soft-minded fantasy but the highest form of science.

At the same time, we wish to maintain our autonomy and freedom, and this also is a truth.

To be human is to be both part of a great planetary whole and also a distinct and independent being. We are in process of discovering how to maximize both.

Technologies Distort Perception

The technologies we adopt tend to shift how we see the world, and this shift is not always toward greater reality. Technologies can distort our views in many ways. We may imagine that we are more powerful than we are, as was classically illustrated by the Titanic disaster. We may fear the potential hazards of a new technology more than necessary, or ignore potential dangers because we like the benefits.

Familiarity tends to diminish our sense of fear. For example, automobile accidents are responsible for far more deaths than result from terrorism, but we largely ignore the danger because we are familiar with it. We don't think we are wielding deadly force every time we get behind the wheel, but that is actually the case.

As we experience more new technologies coming into use in ever shorter time frames, we will need to expand our efforts at technology assessment. Our present degree of evaluation and future planning is equivalent to driving full speed down a dark highway and only occasionally glancing at the road. This attitude will probably change only in response to a series of technosocial collisions, because it is in the nature of the Transition to respond mostly after the fact.

Organizations smart enough to look ahead more comprehensively will benefit. A classical example is how Royal Dutch/Shell used the newly evolved tool of scenario planning to prepare for the OPEC oil embargo in the mid 1970s.[36] Their superior futurism moved them from near the back of the pack of competing oil companies to near the front in just a few years.

The natural progression will lead to examining the 360-degree impacts of emerging new technologies and interacting systems of technologies on various aspects of our lives. Eventually, we will come to view the **impact sphere** as an integral part of the technology and will design for this reality. A key element of effective analysis will be examining how technologies distort our perceptions of the world and consequently of the technology itself as an element within that world.[37] We will need to develop new disciplines, new methodologies, and new ways of modeling the technosphere.

Adoption Cycles

Technologically-induced perception shifts are visible in our changing attitudes over the course of the technology adoption cycle. At the forefront of every emerging technology comes an idea that is generally greeted as a wild-eyed dream. The nascent technology is perceived as crazy, impossible, something that will never work, is not feasible, is pure science fiction, and so forth.

Eventually, when a few working models appear, interest picks up. Early adopters start to imagine the possibilities of the new wonder, often leaping too quickly over the remaining hurdles, which produces results but also "bugs." As the bugs get worked out, the public starts to wake up to the new thing. What once was crazy becomes a craze: everybody has to have it, and if you don't have it you feel one-down. This is when perception shifts to enthusiasm, the "WOW!" stage. Suddenly, the new technology takes over a disproportionate percentage of our attention, and all other technologies are virtually ignored. The wild-eyed dream has turned into the solution to all problems, as we

---

[36] Gill Ringland, *Scenario Planning*, 1998

[37] Marshall McLuhan, *Understanding Media*, 1964 and *The Laws of Media*, 1988, (with Eric McLuhan)

have seen with plastics and the internet, and soon will see with nanotechnology and other such dramatic advances.

As adoption passes a certain critical threshold and more of the general public becomes familiar with what a particular technology can and can't do, people go through a period of complaining about the various frustrations they have in getting the new wonder to live up to expectations. The "wow" loses its luster, and the technology becomes just another one of life's obligations, something you have to deal with because everyone has it. This is the "ho-hum" phase, where perception tends to distort away from the reality of what the technology really *can* do and toward a blasé attitude of pretending that the former wild dream was always obvious and no big deal.

When we consider the adoption cycles of technologies that have made big impacts on the way we live and perceive reality (television, photocopiers, personal computers, digital cameras, and the internet, for example) do we see that we still have not fully grasped their impact on us?

Mostly, we are not aware of our technological environment as it really is. Like the proverbial fish who cannot see the water he swims in, we tend to experience technology unconsciously. New waves of technology sweep over us, shifting our perceptions and attitudes almost without our awareness. What we experience is a variety of disorientations which we try to put behind us. We want to perceive ourselves as cool and unaffected by the repeated impacts of technological change. To be overwhelmed is to feel vulnerable, so we repress our true experience of disorientation and feign nonchalance. We thus opt to be blind to the actual impact of the technology on our personal and social lives.

Usage Modifies Development Direction

Another interesting phenomenon of technological emergence is that user responses are fed back into the engineering cycle and influence the way the technology develops. A technology planned as the solution to one problem winds up getting used in a completely different way for other purposes.

A particularly curious example is how the DARPA[38] net escaped to become the prototype for the internet. It was developed to link American military centers, high-tech labs, and universities in a

---

[38] Defense Advanced Research Projects Agency (DARPA)

decentralized and robust network that could withstand a nuclear attack. Surely linking the whole world into one uncontrollable network of free information exchange was not part of the original military specification.

We can track other kinds of feedback loops in the development of automotive technology. Particularly noteworthy is the example of Detroit's failure to read the interest car buyers had in small, economical cars, thus handing over more than half of the industry to foreign auto makers before finally following suit with their own compact vehicles. Students of technology adoption may want to consider the general failure of early "teletext" systems, when first introduced, contrasted with the unexpectedly wild success of the worldwide web when Netscape software made web surfing easy. (Note that handing control to users was one key difference.)

The point of these phenomena is that attempts to foist a technology on the public rarely work out as planned. Ultimately, the way a technology is adopted, plus how and when it is adopted, is always driven by the customers and the ways they choose to use it, or not use it. We have more control over outcomes than we believe we do.

The trend in marketing new technologies is to test trial ideas and follow the lead of users. We are seeing more products developed in tandem with public input. Successful developers are both more insightful about what the public wants to play with and more responsive to new uses within the market. If the public wants to use a product in an unplanned way, the manufacturer is generally inclined to follow if they want to keep their market.

Government, on the other hand, may want to establish various restrictions when new, unforeseen usage threatens impacts outside the original plan. Once new technologies have been developed, they are difficult to contain; they tend to escape, causing disorientations that may require legislative attempts to constrain usage. Generally, corrective solutions come in the form of yet newer technology designed to fix problems caused by a technology that got out of control.

It is in the nature of human imagination for people to be quite inventive about finding unforeseen uses for new technologies, products, services, and ideas. The law of unintended consequences affects all things, including things like books about the future. No writer can predict with certainty how the ideas he publishes will be applied in novel ways, some of which may be quite contrary to the original intent.

We live in an ocean of human inventiveness that drives, redefines, and elaborates on every invention brought forth from a scientist's lab or a designer's studio. None of us, despite our creative pretensions, controls the end result of our work. Even as one inventive user develops a novel use for a product or idea, other users take that modified idea and change it still further, taking off in new directions from the first modification. This is the nature of culture, and our global metaculture is becoming more scientific, more educated, more diverse, more creative, and more spiritually evolved all the time.

The human family will find a way to meet its needs regardless of plans made by global financiers and authoritarian governments. The wise designer works with this reality. As organizations of all types learn to listen more closely to what people want and what they are doing with what the organization produces, new skill sets are forming new disciplines.

Complexity theory[39] and the concept of self-organizing systems will become increasingly applicable. We will learn to look for the system that is already trying to emerge, and then to support and shape that emergence. When our efforts to "shape" overstep the bounds of what can be controlled, they generally fail.

Analyzing Technology Impacts

All these trends, cycles, and evolutions mean that anticipating where technologies are going is more important than ever. Organizations need new ways of modeling the technological environment, preparing for technological impacts, and developing awareness of a whole new set of principles guiding technological evolution. Individuals also need to learn creative new ways of adjusting to the impacts of technological change on their lives.

New technology arises mainly, but not exclusively, from the soil of scientific research. Science is a very different thing from technology, though we often confuse the two because of their intimate relationship. Where technology deals with applications of known principles, science deals with seeking out new knowledge. Most true science is also known as "basic research" and is funded (or not funded) in a completely different way from technology development. Science requires

---

[39] Complexity theory: A good introduction to this emergent field can be found at www.calresco.org, especially the papers by Chris Lucas beginning with "The Philosophy of Complexity."

investment with a long lead time to return. In fact, science itself is not fundamentally concerned with economic return. Its measure is a return of knowledge for its own sake. Scientists want to know whether or not a hypothesis is true.

In the ideal, scientific methods are slow, careful, and aimed at establishing certainty about specific details of the area of study. In practice, the realities of funding tend to tie research to some desired result that will lead to problem-solving technologies, such as cures for diseases. Pure academic science generally struggles along on very limited budgets. This does not mean that lone researchers working on a shoestring cannot do good science, because science is primarily driven by creativity and intelligence. It just means that it takes longer for such researchers to verify their hypotheses.

What we consider "science" is also constrained by the popularity, or lack thereof, of various theories and schools of thought. The scientific establishment tends to lay down rules for what ought to be studied and how. This has the beneficial effect of constraining pseudoscience and maintaining good experimental practice—at least, it is supposed to. Peer review journals are intended to expose all new theories and results to rigorous challenge by the world scientific community. While this does weed out a certain amount of poor reasoning, it also tends to reinforce prevailing biases and groupthink.

Woe to the true scientist who elects to wander off the reservation and study an area considered taboo. They are likely to be thrown out as quacks along with those who really are quacks, with the result that certain areas don't receive careful scientific study to establish whether they are, in fact, nonsense or whether there might be some valuable fruit to be gleaned from the dross.

The result is that we see the emergence of scientific undergrounds that develop theories and evidence that may lead to future scientific revolutions. An awful lot of people are researching an amazing variety of subjects in the world today, and not all of that research is visible to the scientific mainstream. The point is that predicting directions of future scientific advance without including in your model areas rejected by the establishment will likely cause you to miss many of the more interesting emergent directions.

Most futurist projections deal with evolutions of known theory and with technologies about to emerge from existing basic research. This is like looking at the world through a straw. It assumes that nothing new will emerge from the vast amount of basic research being done both above and below the level of public observation.

As we look at longer range future scenarios, we must keep in mind that the nature of science itself is changing. Science today has evolved considerably from that of a mere hundred years ago. Is it not reasonable to assume that the foundation of science itself will be quite different a hundred years from now? The emergence, fairly recently, of memetics, morphogenetics, complexity, chaos, and network theory into mainstream discourse is just a small indicator of things to come.

To get a glimpse of where science and technology are likely to go, we have to ask fundamental questions, such as "What is science?" and "What is technology?" We also have to stretch our imaginations to explore new models and new ways of modeling. We have to entertain intuitions and wild fancies. Our theories have to be "crazy enough to be true"[40] otherwise we are just stirring around what we already know. If we are not challenging our belief systems, we probably are not pushing the envelope far enough to make meaningful discoveries.

Now, when we consider that new science, along with all kinds of inventiveness in applications and usages, is what gives rise to our technological environment, we should take pause. Our technosphere has a profound effect on our daily lives, as we are constantly observing. Most new technologies, even beneficial ones, are highly disruptive; they bring change. This reality will drive organizations toward better futurological modeling and efforts to explore all kinds of creative new methodologies to help us prepare for, and respond to, technologically induced change.

Fundamentally, technology is about people: it responds to human needs and wants. However, one person's need is another person's hazard, therefore we need regulation. Because ideas are hard to contain, it is very important that we develop new ways of understanding the generally chaotic and free flowing nature of technology if we wish to guide its evolution successfully. The most important values for this intent are awareness and responsiveness. Direct control is unlikely to be successful. Technology is just not very easy to contain. We can, however, be more strategically aware and more thoughtfully responsive to what arises.

---

[40] "Your theory can't possibly be true. It's not crazy enough." Reputed to have been said by Einstein or another physicist at the Institute for Advanced Studies during the heyday of theoretical physics in the 1950s.

A cautionary example of technology run amok is given in Michael Carrol's account of the labs on Plum Island off the tip of Long Island, New York.[41] The spread of Lyme disease, West Nile virus, and other insect-born pathogens may well have been the result of poor containment practices and scientific hubris.

Models for Positive Growth

If we frustrate people's natural drive to invent new ways to get what they want, the result will be "negative" technological growth designed to get around the frustration or to get back at it. One of the best ways to guide "positive" technological growth is to support it with good models and good tools.

To use a gardening metaphor, anywhere we plant beneficial plants is a place noxious weeds cannot grow. The idea is that positive technologies that respond to constructive human wants and needs make it harder for harmful technologies and usages to flourish. When we try to repress harmful technologies without responding to the underlying drivers, we are unlikely to be successful and actually may be encouraging negative forces.

A good example is the attempt to control addictive drugs. We pass laws against them because they are harmful, but the unintended result is a flourishing criminal underground. Essentially, we have been unsuccessful. Perhaps it wouldn't be a bad idea to consider imaginative, new solutions.

Before we rush to solve a problem with legislation and policing, wouldn't it be wise to ask a simple question: "Why does this problem exist?" Remembering that technology responds to the demands of the market—what people want—we ought to ask what the harmful technology provides that makes people demand it and whether that need could be filled in a better way. To return to my example, illegal drugs help users overcome despair and provide sellers with better income than is available through legal means. By modeling other ways to respond to the despair and the need for good income, we could invent ways to fill the space with a positive and diminish the space available for the negative.

---

[41] Michael Christopher Carrol, *Lab 257: The Disturbing Story of the Government's Secret Plum Island Germ Laboratory*, 2004. Chronicles an example of technology out of control and the need for public oversight.

Modeling positive technological growth means modeling human needs at all levels. Models that are whole and sincere will be successful at transforming a problem situation into a positive solution. (Usually this means involving end-users in the solution.) Simplistic or insincere models will be unsuccessful. Over time, society will progressively relinquish its false assumptions, biases, and hypocrisies in favor of models that respond to the whole situation because we will grow tired of the problem and start addressing real solutions. For example, prohibition was completely unsuccessful at reducing alcoholism, but popular fitness programs and health consciousness have provided a positive model for moderation.

Whole models that look at all segments of society as stakeholders help to support positive solutions and the development of technologies that deliver those solutions. Such models increase public awareness of all the dimensions of a problem and the possibilities for new, imaginative solutions. It is surprising how inventive people can be when they see a problem clearly.

Communication and Creativity

One way to support good technology and good science is to work on the problem of communicating complexity. As we develop better software, symbol systems, models, and concepts, we gain better tools for grappling with complex problems and communicating issues more effectively. This is the core of good solution development. Here I speak as a professional who has spent over thirty years helping teams develop better technological solutions by improving communication between stakeholders and development teams.

Developing improved creativity tools and processes provides another support for good technology development. This includes all kinds of training in ways to look at problems from new angles, ways to free our mental constructs from standardized thinking, and ways for accessing our capacity to imagine and visualize. Most people have far more creative capability than they allow themselves to use.

Many institutions are still suffering from a bias against creativity, even in an age when it is becoming clear that creativity is the source of almost all new value. If they want to survive in the kind of environment that is rapidly emerging everywhere in the world, organizations will need to find ways to encourage creativity that is balanced by disciplined standards.

Better Thinking Tools

Supporting effective technology means building better thinking tools and processes to support how ideas are modeled, developed, and tested. It means developing greater understanding of the "theory of theories," including how to build better theories and how to link them with better experimental design. We need software that does not constrain thinking within the bounds of developers' preconceptions.

This is one of the problems with current generation "expert systems." The expertise embodied in these systems is always derived from past experience, thus inherently limiting new approaches that are more responsive to the emerging present. Therefore, software that provides a flexible range of capabilities without forcing one way of application tends to support more creativity.

There are also benefits to standardizing information structures, but such data definitions work best when they account for variations in the application of the information and leave room for evolution within the structure. It is both possible and desirable to define databases and reports in ways that are both clearly structured and also flexible. The field of knowledge management continues to explore new ways of gathering and presenting knowledge and new organizational processes for connecting people.[42] The marketplace will tend to sort for better solutions.

At a level beyond ordinary intellect and knowledge processing, we will see more emphasis on developing intuitive capabilities. When we look at how great scientists of the past came up with their discoveries, we often see a primary role for intuitive processes. Consider, for example, Einstein's famous experience of "riding on a light wave" and his concept of the "thought experiment." Developing experiential imagination and visualization skills leads to better models and greater understanding of the things we want to work on.

All of these skill sets are becoming part of a discipline of metascience, the science of how science is done. Many of the same approaches could be applied to metatechnology with a different emphasis. We are investigating new approaches to problem solving and new methods for creating and applying technology. This includes looking at how the rational processes work in relationship to other dimensions of mental and transmental faculties. Reasoning *per se* is

---

[42] The industry periodical, "Knowledge Management," attempts to document the emerging body of wisdom in this field.

only one part of the total internal process that goes into discovery and invention. Logic generally comes after the fact in scientific or technological breakthroughs. First, intuition, visualization, and imagination lead to the new idea, which is then analyzed and tested by the rational faculties.

When considering future directions of technological evolution, we should look at the theory of how we understand, how we think, and how we know. Much of this falls within the philosophical spheres of epistemology and philosophy of science. We should not conclude that these areas are not themselves evolving. New philosophical theory will certainly inform how we look at both science and technology in the decades and centuries ahead. We should not be surprised if these categories, "science" and "technology," which today seem so solid and eternal, eventually melt and transform into whole new concepts and institutions associated with new categories.

Future research will investigate the relationship between objectivity and subjectivity and question how we know, understand, and respond to the phenomena we perceive in a world that has grown phenomenologically complex. Soon virtual reality media will begin to blur the line between what is "real" in the naturalistic sense, and what is created reality. From the point of view of our perception and experience, soon there may be little difference. Actually, this is already the case, even without virtual reality proper.

The two realms of reality and created reality are likely to become deeply and inextricably interpenetrated. Even while hiking in the wilderness, our VR portable communicator will keep us linked to the virtual dimensions. When software is everywhere, we will see that what we are always investigating and seeking to understand is the nature of being human. Or perhaps we will not at first see this. Nevertheless, it is exactly this understanding that we must eventually come to, and then our journey of awakening can begin. The ultimate study of all our learning and seeking is the deepening understanding of the question, "What is human?"

Metamessage of the Technosphere

Marshall McLuhan taught us to analyze the social effects of particular technologies.[43] The questions I am asking here are: "What is the impact of the entire technological environment as a whole?" and

---

[43] Marshal and Eric McLuhan, *The Laws of Media*, 1988

"What does life in a technosphere characterized by rapidly evolving technology mean?"

The basic message of this "medium," the integrated technosphere, is that **problems can be solved.** Nothing is intractable forever. The process may be messy and frustrating, but eventually some organization or individual comes up with a solution. Whether it is true for all problems or not, this is what our technosphere tells us, and we tend to absorb the message.

The metamessage of our technosphere is to expect solutions; if you demand solutions, the marketplace will work overtime to supply them. There will always be something better on the way.

Another metamessage is that **new solutions bring new problems**. We get the internet, and along come computer viruses. So we need antivirus software, and we get it, but it needs to be upgraded constantly to keep up with the viruses. We get email, and along with it, spam. As we try to control spam, some legitimate email gets filtered out. We are trying to find ways of communicating with whom we want, when we want, and not with those we don't want.

The whole tone of living in a fast-changing technosphere teaches an attitude that is completely different from what has been the basic tone for all known history. Reality behaves differently now. We are shaking off outmoded attitudes about life and how it works.

Everything teaches us that if we don't like something we can change it. Too cold? Turn up the thermostat. Too hot? Turn on the AC. The only real question now is, "How long?" How long before I start feeling the result I want? How long will it take to implement the solution?

The notion that "things just are the way they are and we have to accept them that way" does not compute. Even when we think we believe this idea, unconsciously we reject it, because the whole environment makes us not believe it. This idea of accepting things the way they are is an old conventional wisdom that is being pitched out the window. (I'm not saying that this change of attitudes is necessarily always good, or even accurate, only that the shift is occurring.) What we get in its place is the idea that reality is up for grabs, that we can eventually get what we want, that we can change things.

In some ways, it is a good thing for people to believe they can change things for the better. One negative aspect though, is that people are accustomed to getting instant results from the technosphere and expect the same from other people. There can be a tendency to lose patience and become narcissistically demanding. Nevertheless, despite these kinds of unintended consequences, it is generally positive for people to believe in the possibility of change.

Our new orientation is universal. The technosphere affects everyone, regardless of personal style. Conservative, traditionalist, and experimental early adopter alike are touched by the pervasive tone of the new reality. The technosphere is everywhere, and its metamessages are inescapable. As we observe these effects over several generations and project into the future, the conclusion also appears inescapable: Transformation will occur and the changes will be progressive responses to what we want. We will inexorably surmount all barriers to provide ways for the largest number of people to get what they seek. This process will continually progress up the ladder of consciousness development.

Pluralism of Outcomes: Shared Space

We will create a world where pluralism of outcomes is the natural expectation. The old way of thinking is that two people can't both have control over the same space. The new way is to invent a solution so that they can. For example, headphones allow people to listen to different music in the same physical space.

The general solution to "either/or" issues will be "both/and." The "both/and" solution, which today is preached as "win-win" negotiating, will come to be understood as the only way to go. Nothing else will look like a solution, and therefore it will not even be considered. We will come to a point where the idea of one person getting their way at the expense of another simply won't be part of our ethical apparatus.

Rapidly evolving technology teaches a profoundly positive attitude. We expect solutions to problems, and we just won't take no for an answer. Since everyone gets this message, it creates the problem of everyone wanting their way. Since we expect solutions to problems, we will work to solve this one, too.

The basic ethic is: **everyone gets what they want, and no one is allowed to impose on anyone else**. If that sounds impossible, just watch and see how our grandchildren solve it. It is an old ethical problem, but we have new tools and ideas to address it.

Graduated Controls: Modulated Environment

Part of the solution will involve computer-mediated alternative realities. One element of this kind of world will be graduated controls for everything. We will create and live in a highly sensitive and modulated environment. Individual will adjust things to their liking, and most of these adjustments will be automated. We will be able to be in the same general space and experience very different realities.

Those who insist on being troublesome about imposing on others will be controlled by "graduated net-jails." The more the "criminal" demonstrates that they have learned the ethic of not forcing their will on others, the more freedom they will win. If they start going back to their bad old ways, they will lose freedom on a graduated scale. The system will be in place for all and will be largely automated. Children will absorb the lesson from the computerized environment: if you break the law, you immediately and automatically lose a degree of freedom for a little while; the more maturity you demonstrate, the more freedom you automatically and immediately gain.

In this environment, crime and criminal attitudes will become increasingly rare. There just won't be any incentive. The system wants to give you what you desire as long as you play by its rules, and these rules will also be generated out of common desire. The general consensus of the community, mediated by those elected to leadership, will determine how the social software works. **Law will be written in software.**

We will learn to treat everyone with dignity, an ethic of not imposing on others. Step by step, we will become ethically evolved people. There will be a gradation of degrees of evolution, of course, but it will be continuously improving for almost all people. At the moment, in the midst of our transitional horrors, such ideas seem a bit idealistic, but soon they will seem quite natural and logical.

The Social Architecture of the Netspace

We will accomplish these outcomes as part of the social architecture of the netspace. Because everyone and everything will be on the net and through the net, we will want to put definitions of acceptable behavior into the system. And technically we will be able to do so.

For example, we want to get rid of spam because it is a terrible waste of time and an intrusion. At the same time, we want to get selected opt-in messages. It is already possible to some degree to define specialized communication queues: family and friends, work, shopping, and so forth. Soon, when we check our email/videomail, we really will see only what we have chosen to see in each queue. So someone marketing a product will have their message pulled into our shopping queue only if we have indicated an interest in that kind of ad, and we will see only those offers meeting our specific shopping criteria. Any attempts to circumvent the controls will result in an automated Better Business protest and graduated net-jail for the perpetrators until they mend their ways.

We will define models of the netspace that combine personal values, community values, and universal values. An important factor in the effectiveness of netspace architecture definitions will be public availability of netspace demographic statistics. To make good decisions, the public needs to know what the facts and trends are.

Another factor leading to effective and desirable social behavior will be the unbiased fairness with which netlaw is applied. Since it will be written into the code, no one will get preferential treatment. When enforcement is fair, universal, graduated, and redeemable, that will encourage more widespread compliance. After testing the limits of the law a few times and finding it to be unbeatable and immediate in consequences, most people will lose all incentive to break it. Of course, it will take time to plug all the loopholes, and criminals will continue to try to find and exploit them. But learning systems tend to get progressively better, so it will be harder and harder to beat the system.

Identity Verification

One crucial technology will be identity verification and prevention of identity theft. This will not be easy because any form of identification, biometric or otherwise, is potentially stealable once it becomes digital. Most proposed solutions involve very hard encryption technology. Governments tend to resist publicly available encryption tools because they want the power to spy on people in the name of preventing crime and terrorism. Thus, the two problems are going to be butting heads for awhile until we create new solutions.

A noncryptological approach might involve analog systems that are not fully digitized and therefore less vulnerable to identity theft. The tricky part is how to convey identity verification without conveying the identifying information itself. Perhaps a biometric test connected with a card that sends out a verified signal only if the user tests true. For example, our credit card might work only if our thumbprint is holding it. The thumbprint data need not be sent over the net, only the card number and the fact that the card accepted the thumbprint locally. If the card is held by anyone else, the number is rejected.

Even with such a system, great care and ingenuity will have to be brought to bear to prevent the possibility of spoofing the acceptance signal, and this will probably involve some form of encryption.

Biotech, Nanotech, and Regulation Theory

To make biotechnology and nanotechnology safe and therefore profitable as economic engines, government needs to invest in an infrastructure of rigorous safety testing. Once established, a truly rigorous government laboratory system could give emerging technologies either license to proceed or concrete evidence of why they are not safe. Both results would be funded by the industries that use them. The successful projects would supply a continuing tax revenue earmarked to directly support the testing system.

The advantages for the industry would be greater public confidence and therefore more profitable products. It is appropriate for industries to pay for this service through direct taxation of the results, which are likely to be profitable enough to easily support this taxation. The public interest would also be served by preventing unsafe advanced technology from escaping into the environment.

This is, of course, the basic principle on which the FDA, EPA, and other such federal agencies were founded, but the specific dangers of both bio- and nanotechnologies, as well as the problems these industries are encountering in public resistance to their products, need a new system that is far more rigorous and substantial. The system also needs to be chartered in such a way as to remove it from the domain of political corruption. This means that it must be an independent agency, somewhat like the federal reserve. It also means that movement of personnel between this agency and private industry must either be prevented entirely or carefully regulated to prevent revolving-door corruption and bribery by job offer. What eventually will emerge, partly in response to disasters, is a comprehensive theory of regulation and institutional enforcement.

Space: Living in the Solar System

We live in the solar system. Although we think of ourselves as living on Earth, we have always been citizens of the solar system. Now we are becoming aware of this reality. We do not really have a choice about exploring our new extended home. It engages us and challenges us in ways we cannot ignore, as the 1993 impacts of the Schumacher-Levy asteroids on Jupiter made abundantly clear.

Near-Earth object asteroids (NEOs) represent a significant threat to human existence, but they also represent opportunity. An asteroid is a chunk of potentially useful material that does not have to be lifted out of Earth's gravity well. One of the main limitations to space exploration is the cost of getting stuff into orbit. By learning how to manipulate asteroids, we will not only protect ourselves from them, we will also be able to build things out of them in space.

The current focus in space exploration mostly concerns exploring other planets and moons. I suggest that this is basically a sideshow. The main point is to learn to live *in space*, not to go back down another gravity well. Specifically, the point is to learn to live in the solar system with the same facility that we live on our planet. If Earth can be thought of as our cradle, the solar system is like our childhood home, our neighborhood.

We will succeed or fail in colonizing the whole of the solar system based on one factor: learning to build space-station habitats in or near the asteroid belt out of asteroidal materials. The belt is our stair step to the physical universe.

We will begin to shift our perspective from looking at the solar system as an empty place with a few interesting bodies roaming around in it to seeing it as a rich, vibrant home filled with energy, solar wind, gravity, magnetism, particles of matter, and millions of chunks of rock, ice, and metals. The solar system is loaded with all the materials we need to live and prosper, all the elements of the periodic table. We may find asteroids of pure titanium, gold, other precious metals, and even huge gemstones. We will certainly find valuable resources, and we will learn to live where the most resources are: the asteroid belt.

The Value of Space Exploration

Some of the values we will seek in space include:

- Resources: metals, minerals, gases, water
- Energy: solar, hydrocarbons, uranium
- Knowledge: Earth-sensing, planetary, astronomical, health science, variable gravity, and general curiosity about the physical universe
- Asteroidal and cometary impact defense
- Global and systemic police control

- Manufacturing, research & development: micro and variable gravity, hard vacuum uses, solar and cosmic radiation studies, and applications of all space properties
- Hazard distance: remote location for hazardous projects and activities
- Hazardous waste storage locations
- New environments for social experiments: people wanting to live under different systems than available on Earth
- Adventure, challenge, and the freedom to explore

It is not a question of choosing between making things better on Earth or going into space. The two things are part of one human effort; they support each other.

Challenges to Life in Space

Major challenges include the need to:

- Create artificial gravity
- Build radiation shielding
- Manage air, water, and food biosphere
- Manage the social-psychological sphere
- Be economically profitable

These are some of the main tests we will have to meet as we crawl out of our cradle and learn to stand upright in the universe. The solar system provides a series of helpful steps that will make our maturation as a space-faring species easier: our nearby Moon, the asteroid belt, the Jovian, Saturnian, Uranian, and Neptunian moons, the Kuiper belt (asteroids and comets near the orbit of Pluto), and ultimately, the Oort cloud (a vast cloud of comets approximately one light-year out from the Sun).

Each of these steps carries us further out into our local stellar neighborhood. Each step demands that we learn new things and meet new challenges. The first step will be the creation, over the next few hundred years, of the Belt Civilization, comprised of large city stations all around the inner edge of the asteroid belt. We will find stand-off orbits that are safe from random collisions but near to mining resources.

Earth Orbital Space Management

All space is not equal. Different regions of "space" have special characteristics that are either desirable or not. Near Earth are two orbital zones of particular interest, LEO or low Earth orbit, and GEO or geosynchronous orbit. Already these zones are becoming so filled with satellites and space junk we will soon need to create international traffic zoning rules. We will also need to develop the orbital equivalent of street sweepers to clear away the nuts, bolts, paint chips, and other debris left by passing mission vehicles.

Near two orbiting gravitational masses, such as Earth and our Moon, are specific locations known as LaGrange or libration points, where gravitation is balanced and bodies can be parked in stable orbits. A space vessel parked in any orbit other than these locations would periodically have to expend fuel to maintain its orbital position. This means that the libration points, L4 and L5 in particular, are desirable space real estate.[44] Stable positions can be maintained by putting an object into what is called a "halo orbit," a tight elliptical orbit around a libration point.[45]

There are also libration points between the Sun and any of the planets, L4 and L5 being 60 degrees ahead of and behind each planet along its orbital path.

---

[44] LaGrange points are named after the mathematician Louis LaGrange. L4 and L5 are the most stable of these points.

[45] An interesting animated model of halo orbits can be seen on the web at: www.ai.mit.edu/people/wessler/halo

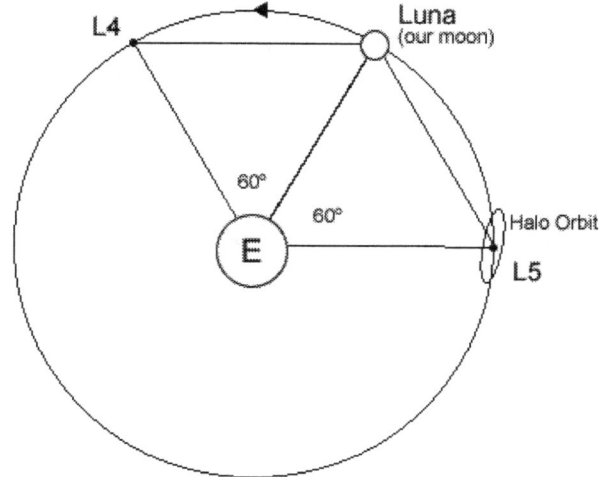

Figure 8. Libration Points and Halo Orbits

We will move asteroids into stable halo orbits around the libration points in the Earth-Moon system and hollow them out to create living and working spaces shielded from radiation by rock and metal. By connecting two such asteroids with cables and struts and rotating them around the inertial center of mass, we will be able to generate artificial gravity. Such space stations could solve two big problems for human habitation of space, the negative effects of radiation and zero gravity on our bodies.

Ultimately these spacecraft may serve as transfer stations in a larger solar system transit network as we build stations at the libration points of other planets. We will define orbital industrial zones and areas for space hotels, and for hazardous scientific experiments. Near the Sun, we will create vast solar energy collectors in the orbit of Mercury, which will transfer energy to other parts of the solar system via microwave beams. We might also build agricultural stations in the orbit of Venus. But the key to holding this system together will be creation of mining and manufacturing stations along the edges of the asteroid belt. The primary industry of the belt stations will be the building of space habitats and spacecraft for other parts of the system.

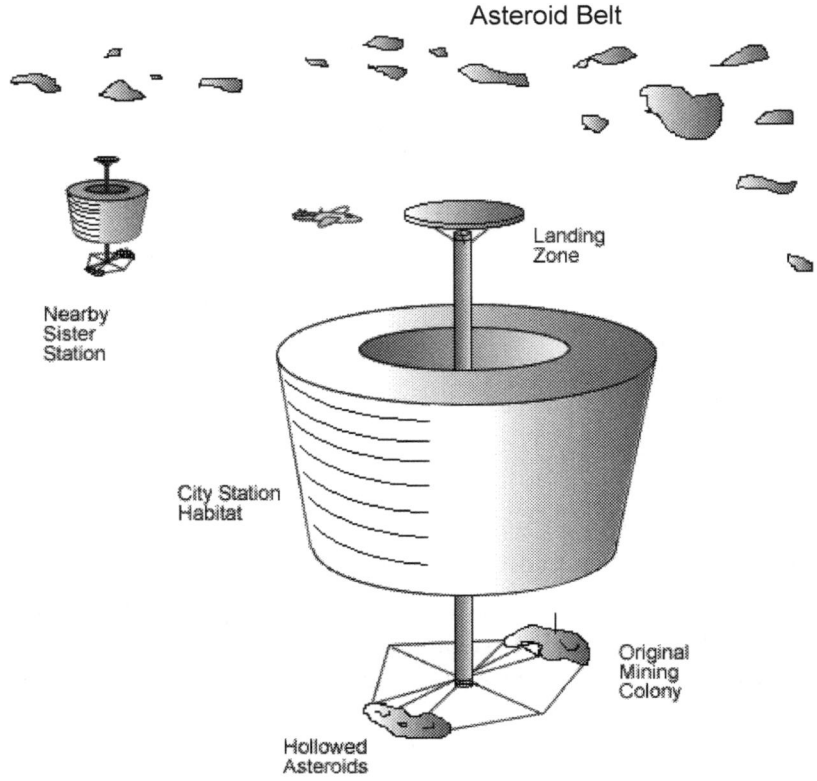

Figure 9. City Station Space Habitats

This industry ultimately will evolve into a ring of wealthy "city stations" all around the belt. These huge habitats will be created by connecting suitable asteroids and rotating them around a central spindle. The early mining colonies will live inside tunnels in the asteroids, and these settlements will grow into vast man-made environments. Picture Manhattan suspended in space, complete with Central Park.

One alternative means of hoisting large masses into orbit is the use of mass drivers on rails to hurl packages off the Moon and other smaller bodies. It might also be a way to get metals off the surface of Mercury. Another potential technology is a space elevator suspended by orbital mechanics above Earth's surface.

Generally, the easiest way to get materials in space is to find them there, and soon we will send prospecting robots scurrying all over the asteroid belt, looking for valuable materials.

The other benefit offered by the asteroid belt is that it circles the entire solar system. Thus orbiting stations and planets are always at a relatively constant distance from one part of the belt or another, even if they are on opposite sides of the solar system from each other. Establishing stations all around the belt will give us a coordination zone for all parts of the solar system.

The solar system can be seen as a magnificent living flower. As it orbits the galactic center, its various planets and other bodies transcribe nested helical world lines. It encounters new phenomena as it passes through the galactic arms and the radiant interstellar medium. We are affected by encounters with radiation from supernovae in ways we will be increasingly attentive to for the sake of our survival and also in our quest for greater understanding of the universe we live in.[46]

As we move farther from the Sun, we will face greater cosmic radiation because the shielding effects of the solar wind will decrease. Closer to the Sun, we will have to deal with greater solar radiation.

Cultural Impacts of Space Expansion

We will experience space on Earth through virtual reality media, robotic cameras, and telescopes. Orbital Earth surveillance will be ubiquitous and available to all citizens. Already, we view satellite Earth scans as regularly as the news and weather, of which they have become a component.

Orbital geo-analysis satellites will give us a more accurate understanding of our community and environment. We will be able to zoom in on any area we wish and see close detail of actual real-time imagery plus accompanying factual data that we can display at will, like an internet search but more comprehensive and up-to-date. We will be able to get detailed geographic, ecological, and demographic data at will. We will be able to pick out specific buildings and get information about the activities inside. The newly available Google Earth application is a first step toward this capability.

We will get used to the idea of open visibility and nonprivacy because the laws will be changed to prevent this information from

---

[46] Andrew Parker, *In the Blink of an Eye*, 2003; Describes the effect of supernovae on our evolutionary history.

being abused, and everyone will be exposed to the same visibility. In response, we will become less judgmental as we adjust to a culture of transparency. Judging others about personal matters will seem primitive. Only actions that negatively affect others will be subject to social sanctions.

Solar System Zones

Our last big transition was from the pre-Columbian flat-world perspective to the post-Columbian spherical world. The next will be from the globe to the solar system as a whole: the disk of the ecliptic.

There are literally tens of thousands of potentially habitable bodies, planetoids, moons, and asteroids in the solar system. These will be our new frontier.

The chart in table 7 below shows significant zones in the whole solar system civilization as it will be at the end of the third millennium. We will ultimately develop human presence, robotic stations, or both in all of these zones and subzones. This will mean a much more complex human civilization than the planetary civilization we are now experiencing.

Systemic Orbital Mechanics

We will become more familiar with the complex properties of intrasystemic space, oriented along new kinds of dimensions than those we consider "normal" today. Our "East-West/North-South" will be transferred to sidereal coordinates aligned with the ecliptic plane (the zodiac), the key stars used in astro-navigation, and the "North" and "South" ecliptic hemispheres. The center of our galaxy, at approximately 6 degrees Sagittarius, will become the ultimate point of reference.

We will think in terms of toward the Sun (sunward) and away from the Sun (outward), and in terms of the direction of orbital motion around the Sun (spinward and anti-spinward). We will also develop a subtle new vocabulary related to our direct experiences of orbital mechanics and the problems we encounter trying to master its disciplines. We will learn to think in terms of the helical pathways bodies move along as they orbit other moving bodies. Our descendents will be as familiar with orbital geometry as we are with basic plane geometry, probably more so.

Emerging Technology | 171

Zone	Subzones
Earth/ Luna (our Moon)	Continental Subzones: NA, SA, AF, EU, AS, OA, suboceanic, low Earth orbit and geosynchronous, lunar surface colonies, orbital and LaGrange point stations L4 and L5
Inner Planetary, Venus & Mercury	Venusian orbital stations and LaGrange points, Mercurian surface stations, orbital stations and LaGrange points, solar observation satellites and energy stations
Martian	Martian surface colonies, orbital stations and LaGrange points, Phobos and Deimos stations, and Martian trojans (planetoids in Mars' orbit)
Asteroid Belt	Divided into sectors and 5 lanes or rings Major robotic mining colonies and associated city stations
Jovian	16 moons: Io, Europa, Ganymede, Calysto, plus smaller moons Atmospheric robotics for extracting hydrocarbons Jovian trojans (planetoids preceding and following in Jupiter's orbit)
Saturnian	18 moons: Titan, plus smaller moons Atmospheric and surface robotics
Uranian	18 moons, all small Atmospheric and surface robotics Centaurs (asteroids and comets between Saturn and Neptune)
Neptunian	8 moons: Triton plus smaller moons Atmospheric and surface robotics
Plutonian & Trans-Plutonian	Plutonian surface stations, orbital stations Charon, Pluto's moon Kuiper belt objects (planetoids and comets near Pluto's orbit)
Other Systemic Stations	Above and below the ecliptic Mobile orbits, comet tracking stations, etc.
The Oort cloud	A vast cloud of comets and asteroids extending more than one light-year out from the Sun but still within its gravitational influence

Table 7. Solar System Zones and Subzones

We will consider solar wind, planetary shadows, gravity wells, space curvature, magnetospheres, declination, LaGrange points, halo orbits, and stationary orbits relative to various bodies and points within the solar system space. The economics of orbit achievement and maintenance will be very important to us and will define the relative value of various zones in space.

Mercury will be interesting as a source of metals. Large quantities will probably be mined and sent into near solar orbit to build solar power stations and solar monitoring stations. Venus may be too difficult to do much with in the near term but will be useful as a mass around which stable orbital stations can be established. We will ultimately use nanotechnology to transform the Venusian environment.

Mars and its moons will, among other things, serve as the stepping-off point for the asteroid belt. We will also be interested in the Martian and Jovian trojans, asteroids that follow and precede Jupiter and Mars in the same orbital path. These might provide material for stations in these zones.

Always, we will be on the lookout for water and will collect chunks of ice whenever we find them. Any ice found on the poles of our Moon or under its surface will prove very useful to lunar stations. Increasingly we will refer to the Moon as "Luna" to distinguish it from the other moons in the solar system.

Much of how we evolve in the system and beyond will depend on how well we fare biologically in low-gravity, high-radiation environments. One critical area of research will be determining how much shielding mass is necessary for long-term functional well-being. To the extent that we resolve these challenges, we will be inclined to shun gravity wells, that is planets, in favor of free space as the ideal environment. The idea here is that interacting with low-gravity asteroids and small moons requires less energy than coming and going from a planet like Earth. The other side is that Earth has enough mass to hang on to its atmosphere, something Mars may have trouble with. Nevertheless, we will probably find ways of terraforming the valleys on Mars and possibly the whole planet.[47]

The area above Earth's atmosphere will soon become "zoned" as to its uses. Already NASA and other space agencies track several thousand man-made objects, of which less than a thousand (as of publication) are functional satellites. The rest are debris or "space garbage." The lunar orbital sphere will also be zoned and managed.

---

[47] Kim Stanley Robinson, in the book series, *Red Mars*, *Green Mars*, and *Blue Mars*, explores this possibility in detail.

Increasingly, we will think of Earth, Luna, their orbital satellites, and their LaGrange points as one Earth-Luna system. This will become particularly true as we develop similar stations in the Martian system. There, the components would include orbital stations and spacecraft, as well as ground stations on Mars, Phobos, and Deimos, plus the Mars-Sun LaGrange points.

Within the next couple of centuries, the human habitat will come to consist of the five bodies—Earth, Luna, Mars, Phobos, Deimos—and the first belt stations, plus various stations and spacecraft orbiting and transiting between these points. We will want to tow asteroids, especially high-metal-content objects and ice chunks, into halo orbits around the LaGrange points in front of and behind the orbits of these bodies. The result will be a complex and economically dynamic multicentered society that will drive ongoing expansion and development of the whole solar system, particularly the asteroid belt and its valuable minerals.

Robotics

Because of gravity-well economics (the high cost of lifting objects into orbit), only high-value, low-mass objects will be dropped back down the well again. In other words, once you have a payload in space it doesn't make much sense to send it back down a gravity well, such as Earth, unless it is extremely valuable (such as a human being). For this reason and to minimize risk of loss of life, robots and remote control units will do much of the preliminary exploration, construction, and development.

Humans will nevertheless be important parts of the process, operating out of nearby remote stations as robots go into dangerous asteroid fields and identify and extract valuable objects. Robot ships deploying swarms of microbots will do asteroid mining. When the microbots find an interesting vein of material, they will spray out jets of nanobots that will scavenge the metals or minerals from the rock and pack them up for retrieval by the robot ships.

One constraint on remote control will be signal delay over longer distances. We will need to be close enough to get rapid response to our decisions. The more difficult we find the problems of protecting human bodies in space, the more we will emphasize advanced robots and the more intelligent those robots will need to be.

Earthside, people will enjoy space exploration via remote sensing devices and cameras. We will be able to maintain connection and experience each other's environments by way of the medianet. Swarms of robotic vehicles, unmanned spacecraft, and their multispectrum, 3-D cameras and sensors will make it possible for everyone to explore and become intimately familiar with the planets, their moons, the asteroids, and the comets long before any human can go there in person. The majority of human beings will continue to live on Earth for some time yet, but we will feel like citizens of the whole solar system.

Robots, with and without human companions, will also explore remote and dangerous parts of Earth—the polar regions, deserts, high mountains, and undersea regions. Virtual reality cameras will enable everyone to go along via the medianet, just as today we watch exploration shows on television and learn about remote places via the internet. The difference is that, as the VR medianet evolves, the experience will become increasingly like actually being there.

We will use robots for shopping, fetching, delivering, and personal chauffeuring. We will use personal robots in some cases, but we also will be able to plug into public robotic services (like fleets of taxis or delivery trucks). It is likely that we will become almost oblivious to the fact that these tasks are being done by robots. It will just be how things are done. We will enter our orders into the net, which is always with us, and things and people will get picked up and delivered to the specified locations. We also will not think much about how remote sensing is actually being done; we will just do it. Today, most people who use the internet or watch TV give little thought to how these things work; they just do. As I was typing the last sentence I happened to notice the software automatically correcting a typo, but normally that happens in the background, below the limen of conscious awareness.

Zero-Point Energy

Current-day theoretical physics predicts that the vacuum of space contains massive amounts of energy, referred to as zero-point energy, or ZPE. When we learn to tap into this source, we will be free from dependence on the Sun for energy. This concept is already being researched. When we unlock the secret, we will have discovered one of the essentials for being a truly space-faring species: abundant energy anywhere.

Superluminal Communication

Interesting speculations about various phenomena in advanced particle physics, such as particle entanglement, may lead to forms of communication that are not limited by the speed of light. It seems that one entangled particle responds instantaneously to changes in another entangled particle, regardless of how far apart they are. If we learn to harness this phenomenon, a whole new universe of possibilities opens up. "Superluminal" communication is a desirable goal that future scientific discoveries may make possible. The implications are that a far-flung human civilization which could remain in instantaneous contact would create a very different social environment from one which could not. This is currently considered inconsistent with the known laws of physics, thus impossible.

Health, Enhancement, Environment

Health and Pain-Free Bodies

Advanced bioscience and nanomedicine will give us an experience of life that is completely different from what we know today. We will feel vibrantly healthy, full of energy, and emotionally positive almost all the time. Because our bodies will be cleaner and more perfectly cared for than we can imagine today, we will feel very little pain. We will have been nurtured from conception to have genetically enhanced superbodies, and we will be fed on nutrients of the highest perfection.

Added to this level of natural health will be many layers of additional protection and enhancement: enhanced tough yet pliable skin linked to supermaterial clothing, internal nanotech body-defense systems, health monitoring and trauma repair systems, and automatically delivered superpharmaceuticals.

Our senses and motor skills will be augmented with embedded systems of many kinds. We will all be superhuman compared to today, just as today we enjoy much better health than the people of Neolithic times or even of relatively recent history.

Everyone will be able to climb the highest mountains, endure cold and heat easily, recover quickly from severe trauma, lift heavy weights, run tirelessly, and jump great distances. We will see very far and in different spectra, even microscopically. We will have superhearing and many other enhancements. Most of all, we will really enjoy being in our bodies.

Enhanced Elites

To what extent will financial advantage and technological enhancement devalue natural endowments? How will people with advanced abilities of various types relate to those who are merely "ordinary?" How will people with advanced abilities relate to each other? The chart in table 8 below explores some of these relationships.

Naturally Endowed	Spiritually Evolved	Economically Advantaged	Technologically Enhanced	Unenhanced Norms
Intelligence	Wisdom Vision Intuition	Nutrition Rich Environment Education Purchased Tech	Database Training Net links Intelligence Augmentation (IA)	Dullness Lack of Clarity Ignorance
Talents Creativity	Spiritual Gifts Healing	Nutrition Rich Environment Education Purchased Tech	Implants Training Drugs Net Links	Unrecognized Unsupported Unimaginative
Physical Prowess	Miraculous Powers Tumo (Heat)	Nutrition Healthcare Training Purchased Tech	Bionics Drugs Training	Undeveloped Unsupported Weak
Beauty	Charisma Attractiveness	Nutrition Healthcare Purchased Tech	Cosmetic surgeries Cosmetics	Plainness Ugliness
Psychic Gifts	Siddhis Powers	Training Freedom to Explore	Training Drugs	Hidden Undeveloped Unsupported

Table 8. Technically Enhanced Elites

Our social evolution toward universal education, greater equity and fairness, and human resource development will help all people discover unrecognized abilities. At the same time, technological enhancements will tend to devalue natural endowments. For example, beauty becomes more widespread as better nutrition, medicine, and technological enhancement become increasingly available.

While many of these forces tend toward equalitarian outcomes, some individuals will always have advantages, either naturally or from purchased technology. As technologies become subtler and more powerful, this could lead to increased dominance of society by the advantaged at the expense of the ordinary, underenhanced population. We already see these kinds of huge power differentials between people from the developed world and people from nontechnological cultures. If this trend continues, the divides may become difficult to bridge.

We may see divides between people with other kinds of advantages as well. For example, the strong and athletic are likely to become stronger, more athletic, and technologically enhanced in physical ways; the brainy are likely to become enhanced mentally; and the spiritually evolved are likely to become enhanced spiritually. The means used for this enhancement will vary from group to group, and the values of each domain may veer away from the center. Already, we say that the rich become richer. The pursuit of well-roundedness may, for a time, become supplanted by the pursuit of superspecialization.

For example, scientists may want to get some of their instrumentation embedded into their bodies, such as eyes that can see at microscopic levels, telescopic levels, and in different electromagnetic spectra. Undersea professionals will probably get implanted gills and enhanced swimming capabilities. Astronauts will get enhancements for space dwelling. Media stars will get enhancements to increase charisma and personal magnetism as well as appearance. The question is, will people with these increasingly different kinds of bodies and capabilities still be able to communicate with each other?

My career as an organizational consultant has taught me that people in different professions already have difficulty understanding each other, usually more so than people from different cultures. Engineers generally understand other engineers even when they don't speak the same language. But engineers generally don't understand marketers and vice-versa, even when they do speak the same language. That is one of the main reasons organizations hire people like me to help teams communicate more effectively between viewpoints.

Advancing technology and the tendency for technology to become more and more part of us is likely to increase interspecialty communication difficulties. This is one of the challenges that is continuing to emerge as the world becomes more complex. We can quite easily imagine conflicts between people from different technological enhancement domains because of this divergence of viewpoint.

We can also imagine the possibility that wealthy, superenhanced, supertrained elites could become completely dominant over the less well-endowed. The battles between technosupermen seen in comic books could soon become real as wealthy supercriminals easily defeat underequipped police forces. Early phases of this problem are already evident in the drug wars.

We will struggle for quite some time to control and restrain emerging technologies and thus prevent our societies from being overrun by technobarbarians. In this arms race, governments will continue to beef up police capabilities and special forces to meet criminal high tech. Those who are not inclined to be warriors will be, to some extent, caught between the forces of those who are. We already find ourselves squeezed in a confusing matrix of government intelligence agencies, terrorists, cyberhackers, corporations, politicians, and news media powers.

People wield the most enhanced kinds of power available to them based on their training and profession. Media people wield media, psychologists wield psychology, marketers wield marketing, soldiers wield the tools of military power, and writers wield the enhanced pen (word processing software). We live in a grid of techno-magical power relationships.

This kind of competitive struggle is characteristic of the Orange rational materialist system that currently controls most of our world. Toward the end of the century, and possibly much earlier, we will have shifted to a Golden Olive, Yellow, and Turquoise system with a progressively more cooperative tone. The ego-oriented consciousness simply cannot manage the complexity of our emerging reality.

**

Emerging technologies, even positive ones, are always disruptive. By remembering this, we will be better able to stay focused on the goal of overall human well-being.

Chapter 7.
Media Development (M·D)

What Are Media?

It is difficult to truly grasp media because we are so utterly immersed in a world saturated by media. Ever since humanity invented culture, we have been conditioned to see the world through the lenses of media. From the earliest media of tribal societies to the latest in electronic communications, the fabric of our experience is media. Like a fish searching for water, we are barely aware of how seamlessly surrounded by media we are.

We notice a medium when it is new. For a few moments, the shock of change makes us fleetingly aware, but almost immediately we become entranced and unable to see it. We forget that much of what we accept as natural in our world was, at one time, invented by someone.

Despite the slipperiness of the subject, we need to try to get a handle on it, because our media environment is currently undergoing such profound and rapid changes. Changes in our media environment are perhaps the single biggest factor in how our future will unfold. **When our media change, we change.**

We can say that a medium is a type of technology. According to Marshall McLuhan in *Understanding Media,* all technologies can be analyzed as media. His view was that any new technology extends an existing human capacity: a telescope extends the eye, a wheeled vehicle extends the legs, tools extend the hands, and so forth. His second insight was that these new technologies (or media) so profoundly impact us that they completely change us and our way of seeing the world. He warned us about the impact of electronic media, and we still have not caught up to his message.

We can also understand any social convention, such as law, as a medium, and all media as forms of social convention. This confluence of media, technologies, and social conventions as reflections of one thing is part of what makes the problem so tricky. Media includes everything, so it is nothing in particular. Everything has an aspect in which it functions as a medium. Thus, we can say that a medium is a vehicle for conveying impressions. Here the word "impressions" begins with sense impressions and moves on to include emotions, judgments, and thoughts.

Actually, what we are examining are the properties of the human mind. Media are technologies that extend the capacities of the human mind. For example, language and speech are some of the most fundamental media. Since we are social beings, our media are the vehicles for our social discourse and, therefore, for social transformation.

When we consider the classical art of oil painting, the "medium" is literally the linseed oil that carries the pigment. It is the transparent vehicle that supports the act of painting. Because it is nearly invisible, we tend to confuse the content, the colors, and images with the medium. This is true of all media. We think that the content of a TV show is the television medium. This is why McLuhan said, "The medium is the message;" he wanted to refocus our attention on the characteristics of the medium itself and away from the content.

In the new electromagnetic digital media, the medium itself is various applications of electricity that convey sense impressions and meaning. The characteristics of these emerging media are difficult to analyze because they are evolving so fast. Perhaps the fact of rapid evolution is their most prominent characteristic.

Media Convergence and Evolution

One aspect of the emerging media is intense convergence. The latest medium tends to absorb and integrate all the media that went before it. What were thought of as separate distinct media are now thought of as one integrated medium. We had text, pictures, music, phones, movies, computers, ATMs, credit cards, and so forth. Now we have the worldwide web, which has incorporated all of these and more. Television, print media, and internet are reflecting each other to such a degree that they are becoming part of something new.

Distinct media still continue to evolve in their own right, but they are conditioned by the new convergence. We still take snapshots, but now they are digital and we share them via email. We still write books, but we print them on demand and buy them on the web. What we have is convergence plus divergence of new spinoffs. The distinct media, each with its particular characteristics, float in a bubbling metamedium of digital electronics and software. Economic pressures and human innovation drive this mix forward toward further integrations.

Both television and internet already have gone through many generations in getting to their present states. All kinds of electronic hardware go through two major evolutionary arcs, becoming smaller and more portable on the one hand (cellphones), and larger and more immersive on the other (big screen TVs). The flow of information has become so transparent that both governments and corporations have been taken by surprise. These are just a few of the signs of the massively disruptive change that is bearing down on us all today. Paying attention to where these changes are pointing is a *very* good idea.

Definite trends and probabilities can be foreseen. The major likelihoods are already visible. Also, it is not a question of whether such changes are good or bad. The point is that they are real. The good and bad are in how we deal with these realities and, to this end, forethought is beneficial.

It is, likewise, not a question of who is foisting this media technology on us. I don't believe anyone is in a position to stop it. It is just part of what is happening at this stage in our history. However, we do have considerable latitude in how we conduct ourselves in a time that is promising many challenges.

Virtual Reality Internet (VR/I)

A major trend or metaphor for what is emerging is what I call virtual reality internet, VR/I for short. If we draw a timeline for each of the major media technologies of today and number each generation of change, we can begin to predict where they will intersect and what new capabilities they will gain. For example, TV, internet, and virtual reality:

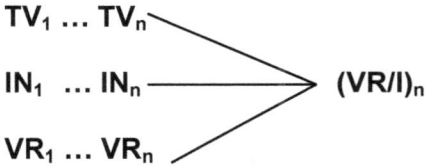

Broadband is already making webcast video a reality, and TV newscasters are incorporating internet polling and email into their shows. Virtual reality (immersive 3-D interactive environment) has evolved from a laboratory technology to applications for flight simulators and gaming. As virtual reality hardware and software improve and as bandwidth continues to grow, we are seeing the arrival of virtual reality applications that allow interactivity over the internet.

Once established, this capability will reach a tipping point at which more and more of our activities will be integrated into this new medium, VR/I. We will wear goggles, gloves, and headphones that allow us to interact in the virtual domain for telemeetings, shopping, games, creativity, work, and all of the things we use the internet for today.

As the hardware gets lighter, it will become a normal part of our mobile activity in the same way cellphones are today. The real world and the virtual world of telepresence will not be separate domains but one interpenetrating experience we call "life," with all the usual frustrations and benefits associated with new technology.

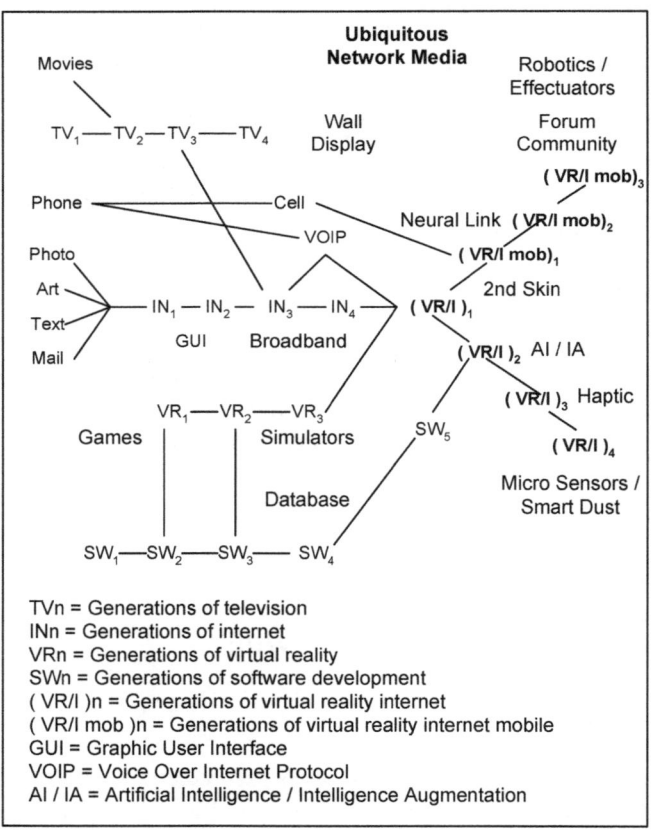

Figure 10. Media Convergence and VR/I

Second-Skin and Neural-Link Technologies

The trend toward subtlization will generate very light technology that will progressively spread over more of the body to increase the sense of being present in cyberspace. While this "second-skin" technology may be financed and pioneered by the virtual sex trade, it will also demonstrate other applications. Second-skin sensors will allow doctors to remotely diagnose and eventually even treat the wearer. Enhanced sense of touch will allow precise control of remote robotic hands for various kinds of hazardous work. Touch capabilities are today referred to as "haptic" interfaces.

This technology of cyberpresence will continue to improve, adding temperature, inertial sense plus weight or heft, and ultimately taste and smell. The perfect diet may be one in which we consume virtual meals. Healthy nutrients could be made to taste like whatever we wish. We could replay the software for a favorite meal as often as we wanted. It will be interesting to see how this capability competes with, and also integrates with healthy foods generated by nanotechnology.

Eventually, biotechnology will become so sophisticated that the interface will extend inward using "neural-link" methods to provide direct interface with the central nervous system. By this stage, virtual reality will be nearly indistinguishable from physical reality, except that we will be able to do more things in virtual space. We will be able to control the degree of our immersion in cyber-reality in such a way that the two worlds flow into one another.

We will incorporate artificially intelligent (AI) agents into our management interface to deal with all this complexity. One aspect of complexity will be the ability (and necessity) to multiply one's virtual presence. The AIs will help us manage our surrogate selves and alert us when we need to be fully present to make detailed decisions and when we can skim the summary, just as today we can choose to reply to or ignore voicemail and email. Think of surrogate selves as being like multisensory, intelligent, outgoing voice messages, such as we use on our answering machines, but far more complex.

Properties of Integrated Media

While it is not possible to define all the twists and turns of media evolution, we can anticipate and preview many characteristics of a mature medium.

The Sense/Resolution Matrix

The integrated medium must develop means of representing each of the senses plus various other sensible qualities. Development proceeds through a series of resolution stages. In the early experiments, sensory inputs will be represented at such a low resolution that the experience is essentially abstract. For example, early visual representations of simple objects in three-dimensional space were represented as wireframes showing the edges of geometrical shapes. Later, shaded surfaces were added, then visual textures and shadows. As higher resolutions were developed, the environment became increasingly "realistic," with current flight simulation and gaming spaces near the threshold of acceptance.

In the film medium, the threshold of acceptance was discovered to be twenty-four frames per second. Below that threshold, we are aware of the flickering medium; above it, we are absorbed in the experience of the movie.

The matrix in table 9 shows the component stages of a full virtual reality medium. The shading indicates where we are in the development cycle today, darker shades indicating more fully developed capacities.

Three-Dimensional Virtual Reality Development							
		Phase I		Phase II		Phase III	
Resolution Stage		Sight	Sound	Touch	Feel	Taste	Smell
4.	Hyper-Real Enhanced						
3.	Recorded 3-D Reality						
2.	Threshold of Acceptance						
1.	Abstract Experimental						

Table 9. Virtual Reality Media Development Matrix

Above the threshold at which a representation is accepted as "real," the medium needs to develop the ability to record sense data from the physical world. Here I am distinguishing between synthetic imagery, such as a realistically painted portrait, and recorded imagery, such as a photograph of the same individual (an animation versus a recorded hologram).

The highest level of resolution development takes us beyond simulation of real-world experience into the domain of the hyper-real. At this level, experience is fully malleable and enhanced with various added capabilities. For example, in a hyper-real experience we can modify many attributes to personalize the experience, such as light intensity, color, or time of day.

This level also allows various kinds of conceptual overlay, such as descriptive labels, direction arrows, and other symbolic codes. Such overlays will be useful for educational experiences by allowing the user to call up descriptions of any object. A virtual hike in a wilderness area might allow us to identify any of the plants and animals in the experience. A travel experience might provide information about architecture and history. A scientific experience, such as a journey through the human body or through a complex engineering system, could include a variety of instructional overlays, tags, and labels. Nanoengineering will be a major application of this capability. Nanoengineers will be able to build custom-designed molecules by physically moving atomic blocks. They will then be able to observe how their molecules behave in simulation, before physically generating them.

In addition to prerecorded overlays, personal note-taking capacities can be added. Hyper-reality includes the ability to "mark up" an experience with drawings and verbal or written comments. Real-world experience will also have a semitransparent media overlay that will allow us to retrieve data and to record our own experience with annotations. For example, like our virtual hike, a real-world hike might allow us to display plant and animal data as well as holo-record our experience and attach voice or text comments. We might see discrete control icons floating just at the edge of our peripheral vision.

Just as development advances along resolution levels, it also advances through sensory categories. Currently, sight and sound are the primary senses being developed. We are just starting to explore ways of adding tactile elements to our electronic media experiences through haptic interfaces. I have divided the tactile category into two sensory elements, "touch," meaning contact with the hand or foot, and "feel," meaning effects from the environment on the body. Touch includes such elements as pressure, texture, resistance, and weight. Feel includes being touched, temperature, sense of gravity and acceleration, vibration, and so forth.

Beyond the tactile, we will develop the chemical senses, taste and smell. In addition, various other sensible qualities, such as tension/relaxation, emotional state, blood pressure, alertness, and so forth, are already being explored in biofeedback experiences. A good example is the game program, "Journey to the Wild Divine," which uses clip-on finger sensors to capture relaxation and alertness indicators. Human potential guru Jean Houston was a consultant on the program development team.

As we learn more about the human nervous system and physiology in general, we will discover many more qualities that can be added to the experiential mix. For example, we may be able to induce the biochemistry of specific emotions.

Sensor/Effectuator Development

An integrated medium provides an interface between the individual and the real-world environment. Sensors, such as cameras, microphones, and thermometers, capture data about a location which can then be recorded and/or transmitted to an experiencer at another location in space or time. Sensor technology extends and modifies our sensory nerves. We are currently developing small and microscopic sensors through technologies called "smart dust."[48]

We also may wish to act on the objects we have sensed. Our motor nerves direct our muscular system to move our limbs to perform actions. I refer to technologies that extend this capacity as "effectuators." When we direct a mechanical hand to pick up an object, we are using a type of effectuator to produce an effect on that object. Any remote-controlled effect—heating, cooling, drilling, moving, and so forth—is part of the effectuator system. The integrated medium will continue to develop greater capacities for remote action of all kinds. We will extend our reach through swarms of remote microbots and nanobots (small and microscopic robots).

Communication

Integrated media will incorporate all dimensions of communication. Even when we have the capacity to communicate by telepresence

---

[48] Neal Stephenson's novel, *The Diamond Age*, 1995, explores a number of interesting concepts about nanotechnology and smart-dust sensors.

conversation, there will continue to be a need for short text-message forms, such as email, instant messages, and voicemail. Communication systems are likely to develop new tools to help us sort for what we most want to receive: keywords, summary, full message, attached VR/I documents and links. We will be able to decide how much of a given message we want to experience.

The main need this system will work to meet is the ability to communicate with the people you want to communicate with and not with the ones you don't. The system will provide a rich array of search tools for people to locate others of similar interests or special expertise who meet very detailed criteria. Much more of the presorting will be done by software than is currently the case.

The crucial technology for all forms of internet communication and commerce will be identity verification. Until we can establish certain theft-proof identity, much of the potential of the internet will remain on hold. When this issue is resolved technically, we will quickly move forward. This is necessary to protect our financial assets but does not necessarily imply loss of anonymity in all environments. We will define degrees of anonymity into a range of virtual environments.

It will be a struggle to define the balance between privacy and transparency. This is first a technical issue of being able to provide unbreakable security, which currently does not seem to exist. Second, there is the issue of what kinds of communications should be transparent and open to regulatory and news media review. For example, communications related to possible insider trading of stocks are potentially illegal and thus must be open to scrutiny.

Conversely, most people believe that the government should stay out of the bedroom. The social, legal, and technical issues related to privacy are quite complex and likely to take some time to resolve. We may always be renegotiating some of the details. There is currently a disturbing trend of government insinuating itself into greater control over our bodies, where historically we have expected sovereignty in that area.

Participation and Immersion Levels

Another aspect related to communication, but distinct from it, is participation in shared virtual space. Today we have chat rooms, multiuser domains (MUDs) for gaming, net meetings, and blog commentary. With the development of VR/I, we will experience much of the media as shared virtual reality. This phenomenon will have its own set of parameters that evolve over time.

One key parameter we will want to develop is a set of controls for managing the degree of our immersion in any given virtual reality, just as today our experience of TV ranges from being totally engrossed in a movie to casually ignoring a show playing in the background. The difference is that, with VR, the level of immersion must be intentionally set. We will want to experience some virtual realities completely, as if we were fully there. Others we will prefer to scan while remaining simultaneously aware of our actual physical location. In fact, we will spend most of our time partially linked to a virtual overlay on our "real-world" life, like a radio playing in the background.

Our normal daily experience will sport subtle icons floating in our peripheral vision, telling us the status of various monitors we have set. If an icon indicates something requiring our attention, we will flip open a small window in our visual field to check on the matter. We will fully expand the window into a virtual shared space only if it is really important, say a contact with a family member or a critical business deal.

There will be no external computer screen. The experience will be more like looking at the real world through contact lenses that can also display elements from the virtual world or completely immerse us in a selected virtual reality domain.

As a writer and visioner, I enjoy having long periods of uninterrupted solitude. Other times I am inclined to be outgoing and sociable. Most people want to control when they are accessible to others and when not, thus our media tools will evolve capacities to give us that control. Media services that are invasive are vulnerable in the marketplace to media services that give people what they want in noninvasive ways.

AI Agents and Multiple Selves

To manage the complexity of future life, we will generate multiple representations of our virtual presence. Under normal conditions, these will be operated for us by artificial intelligence (AI) agents, and routine interactions will be handled according to rules we have previously established. We will be alerted only if a matter requires our conscious decision-making ability.

In addition to software programs managing our routines, companies will offer human services for "presence management" in various VR spheres. These consultants will handle various details associated with our virtual presence, such as PR, legal, booking, accounting, scheduling, and so forth, not unlike business services available today.

Of significant importance in all interactions is the issue of who controls what aspects of a particular contact. Is it a contact that is freely chosen, a mandatory contact imposed by legal authority, or something in between? Agents will also help us manage these relationships.

Thinking/Feeling/Creating Tools

Just as computers have been applied to support thinking and creating, so too will they be supported in various evolutions of the VR/I environment. We will develop far more advanced tools for analyzing complex flows of data, for reasoning and testing alternative scenarios, and for creating expressions of our own thoughts and feelings in various integrated media.

Better processing of thoughts, ideas, knowledge, intuitions, and emotions will be critically necessary for managing future life. Just as we developed number crunchers and word processors, we will develop emotion processors to help us understand emotions, our own and those of others. We will also need consciousness processors to help us transform and to manage the extreme complexity of future reality.

Holocorder Development

As 3-D constructed realities become increasingly the norm, we will also want to develop progressively more sophisticated 3-D recorders or "holocorders." This is first a "camera" that can digitally capture a real-world environment in three dimensions, like a holographic movie. Early-stage holocorders will record visual and auditory impressions. Later, we will be able to capture weight, texture, tactile qualities, and, ultimately, taste and smell.

We will distinguish between objective recorders of environments and subjective recorders of personal experiences. The **subjective recorder** captures the full neurological detail of particular experiences. The **objective recorder** creates a three-dimensional and tactile impression of an environment that individuals can experience in various ways, like exploring different paths in the virtual space.

Media Impacts and Consequences

Now that I have covered the technical details, we need to face the absolutely devastating impacts these evolving media technologies will have on us. Currently, we have an addictive relationship with media. Our desire for new and better media technologies is like an appetite for a potentially poisonous desert. On some level, we may sense that our growing dependence on electronic media and our need for newer, fancier, more powerful capabilities is possibly dangerous, but we are hooked.

Electronic media are so useful we cannot do without them. Nor can we stay put at any level for very long. As soon as a critical number of people have adopted a new advance, everyone who can afford to is compelled to follow along, and our habit deepens. Like all addicts, we say we can stop anytime we want, but we don't stop. Very few people voluntarily give up their computers, cellphones, and TVs to go off and live the simple life. We talk about it, but we don't do it for more than a few days, and rarely do we disconnect completely.

Given this situation and the rapid spread of this addiction throughout the planet, we had best consider what the dangers are and how they are likely to affect us. It is almost impossible to overstate the depth and intensity of impact that emerging media technology will have on us. To say that these media will be "disruptive" is to distort by understatement.

Psychological Breakdowns

The primary impact of emerging media is emotional and psychological. We should not be surprised that it will lead to widespread social psychosis and mental/emotional breakdown. If we think about where we are going with these technologies, we should not be surprised, yet usually we are. We are continually surprised by the power of "the media" to shake us, despite the fact that the future has already been seen reflected in the past and the present.

Mostly we don't see that it is the media technologies themselves that are disorienting us; instead, we focus on the content that various media convey and the people who do the conveying. When we see horrible events on television, we focus our attention on the events, not the vehicle by which it is affecting us. We think, "the camera never lies," when in fact it lies all the time by only showing selected points of view.

We tend to believe so strongly that what we see on television or read on the internet is an actual reflection of reality that it becomes so by our belief. Curiously, this effect is not much counteracted by our growing skepticism. Our picture of reality is conditioned by media experiences even when we have consciously decided that they are blatantly untrue. How much greater will be our belief when we experience these things in 3-D? We will tend to think we were there in person, witnessing actual real-world facts. This belief will not change the fact that media events, such as news "stories," are artificially constructed products, even when derived from real-world events.

Effects of Artificial Reality

While we have always lived in a world of socially created reality, we have not always been confronted by so much of it from so many complex and conflicting sources. The constantly changing media environment intensifies all the other massive global change factors. It causes an exponentially increasing feedback loop that fuels global struggles between developmental waves. Some of the effects of mediatech development include:

1. Overwhelming revelations of the shadow side of the human personality force us to face aspects of our savage id drives that we had previously repressed. When we see ordinary people do evil things, it becomes harder to project these acts onto some demonic "other."

2. Every culture in the world is brought into sudden intimacy with many other, very different cultures, forcing us to learn new codes and unfamiliar ways.

3. The simple models of reality we have used to stabilize our lives break down under the onslaught of complexity. Actual reality does not fit our models.

4. The intensity and variety of sensory, emotional, and cognitive experience causes progressive overload, resulting in a habitual state of stunned paralysis. Some people are walking around appearing to be functional while whole sections of their consciousness are in shut-down mode.

5. "Fake reality" combined with revelations of deception cause us to lose trust. We lose trust in our social leaders, in the media, and, worst of all, in our own senses. We experienced it. We

believed it. And yet, we are now shown that what we were sure of was, in fact, untrue...or, maybe it was true. We are left with ambiguity.

6. The interaction of transparency (exposés), mind control, and manipulation of the media causes an experience of "loss of ground." We lose touch with what is real.

7. We tend to contract toward simple models (regress down the levels of development). But this initial reaction fails to solve the problem, so we break down in more extreme ways. For example, this state describes regressed postmodernism, in which Green regresses to Red anger, to Purple magic, then ultimately to Beige apathy.

8. Media manipulations result in real-world violence and a wide range of suffering. We experience more pervasive psychological warfare, identity theft, cybercrime, disinformation campaigns, character assassinations, invasions of privacy, and other brutalities, including actual murder and mayhem. (The Rwandan genocide was mediated by radio.)

Media technology, in both its present form and its emerging new forms, is functioning like a global blender, chopping up and homogenizing everything that has gone before in human history. This is not an effect we can avoid. It is one of the main immediate causes of the transitional stage toward the Great Transformation.

The negative effects are primarily the result of media technology that is outstripping the levels of consciousness available to manage it. Technologies and their applications are always the product of the levels of consciousness that create and use them, but to manage wisely often requires a higher level. Mediatech is no exception to this principle.

Long-Term Positive Impacts

Ultimately, the poison will be our medicine. The stresses of the VR/I world eventually will burn off many of our remaining prejudices and misunderstandings. After initial periods of regression and conflict, the pressures of our world will tend to force consciousness to evolve, partly to deal with complex realities and partly out of sheer exhaustion with all the lies and deceptions.

In the second half of this century, as we become more accustomed to our new media technologies, they will become the primary vehicle for defining a new ground. Our suffering will have taught us ways of building in safeguards and guiding this most dangerous technology in positive directions. We will negotiate generally accepted universal values and define globally applicable social ends.

The fantastic media tools we have so painfully explored will be tamed and put to positive human goals. Both the pain of the Transition and the recovery period will have taught the majority of humanity the need for tolerance and for positive social order. Bandits, exploiters, manipulators, extremists, and terrorists will all be subdued eventually.

In this environment, advanced VR/I tools will provide an enormously powerful way to move consciousness forward all around the world. As we gain more maturity, we will use these tools to support and develop the Great Transformation system. Such a system of governance and trade would not be possible without widespread availability of these powerful consensus-building tools. The very technology that threatened to destroy us will evolve into one of the means for our salvation. Its immense power will force us to mature as we learn to manage it sensibly. Part of the solution will involve the integration of mediatech with humantech and second-tier consciousness.

Transformation Media News Content

We will learn to use webcast TV to put news events into context by maintaining historical archives, abstracts, and philosophical theory as web files and downloadable documents. One problem with what we call "journalism" today is its short attention span and lack of context. "Jour" is French for "day." Yesterday's news disappears and today's is sensationalized. The effect is to distort relative significance and the consequent meaning of the news reports. Is a subject really important, or is it just a slow news day?

By refusing advertising from most corporate sponsors, web-based transformation media can keep coverage and analysis objective and focused on the needs and interests of the target audience, which is educated, middle-class, affluent, influential, centrist, literate, and committed to empowering others; these are discerning news evaluators and bridge builders.

Revenue can come from download fees, book sales, and selected advertising from products and content that is congruent with transformation philosophy. Transformation media theory encourages competition and open dialog on all issues. It wants to build and support a multichannel universe of transformation media webcasters.

The transformationist approach to news believes that extremist views will not be able to dominate when information context is fully and freely available. In open, fair debate, where historical and contextual facts are easily available, the good always wins. The detailed policies of transformationist philosophy will positively evolve in that debate.

Chapter 8.
Wealth Economics (W·E)

Weal' (wēl), n. 1. *Archaic.* Well-being, prosperity, or happiness: *the public weal; weal and woe.* 2. *Obs.* Wealth or riches. 3. *Obs.* The body politic; the state. [ME *wele*, OE *wela*; cf. well']

Wealth (welth), n. 1. a great quantity or store of money, valuable possessions, property, or other riches: *the wealth of a city.* 2. a rich abundance or profusion of anything; a plentiful amount: *a wealth of imagery.* 3. *Econ.* a. all things that have a value in money, in exchange, or in use. b. anything that has utility and is capable of being appropriated or exchanged. 4. rich or valuable contents or produce: *the wealth of the soil.* 5. the state of being rich; prosperity; affluence: *persons of wealth and standing.* 6. *Obs.* Happiness. [ME welth (see well' + th'); modeled on *health*]

Well-being (wel'bē'ing), n. a good or satisfactory condition of existence; a state characterized by health, happiness, and prosperity; welfare: *to look after the well-being of one's children; to influence the well-being of the nation.*[49]

---

[49] Definitions from *The Random House Dictionary of the English Language,* unabridged edition, 1967

Like many other categories explored in this book, ideas about wealth evolve along with the waves of consciousness. The following formula concisely expresses this understanding:

Wealth follows consciousness

This chapter explores various aspects of wealth and how these will evolve as we advance through emerging waves of consciousness. As the definitions suggest, wealth is about wholeness and well-being. Changing worldviews will mean great shifts in how we think about wealth.

Two primary sources of wealth, trade and innovation, will act as drivers for transformation and will be affected in turn as the way we look at life evolves. Peace and freedom, as significant factors for wealth development, ultimately will guide us away from wealth-destroying conflict.

We will evolve away from militarized economies that primarily benefit defense contractors and require constant war to sustain them. This kind of system is a feature of present-day societies dominated by degraded forms of the Orange worldview. We will learn to seek a harmonious balance between the freedom of each individual and the peace of all individuals.

Long-Term Transformations

1. More wealth
2. Wider distribution of wealth
3. Separation of wealth and power

During this century, a level of worldwide abundance such as humanity has never known will arise from the synergy of advances in many areas of social life. Many of the best and brightest in all nations are committing their energies to creating benefit for all of humanity and especially for those most in need. We are inventing ways to produce and distribute more and better food. Efforts to combat disease are growing as we come to understand that reservoirs of disease anywhere present a danger to everyone. New ways of building low-cost, earthquake-resistant housing are being developed. Education and internet access are spreading. We will eradicate starvation, homelessness, illiteracy, and many diseases before the end of this century.

Despite this glowing prediction, we will continue to struggle with wealth inequities, armed conflicts, and many challenging social ills. As we can see, conflicts over dwindling supplies of oil and other scarce resources are likely to severely shake the next few decades. Even so, our evolution is slowly bearing fruit. Consciousness is growing, even in circles of high finance, that the overall economy benefits when wealth is spread more widely. Comfortable, middle-class people buy more things and produce more value. New technologies, such as nanotechnology, will allow effective recycling and sustainable consumption for all.

The third transformation I mentioned, the separation of wealth and power, may seem more problematic. We have lived for a long time with the equation that wealth equals power and find it difficult to imagine that this may not be an eternal verity. Nevertheless, the separation of wealth and power will occur as a sequel to the first two trends. When most people have abundance and security, material wealth will not be scarce, and power will migrate naturally toward other scarce resources, such as wisdom, charisma, and leadership. We will come to see that allowing money to buy social policy is not healthy for humanity.

We are already inventing dozens of new technologies for delivering energy, discovering new resources and better ways of managing them, and creating new ways of using common materials including garbage. Our organizational and management wisdom is growing by leaps and bounds. And, above all, the level of ethical and moral consciousness across the globe is slowly beginning to recognize that all humanity is one family. All these forces, accelerated by global media, will cut through ancient tribal hatreds and nourish growing prosperity.

Transformation Economics

Wealth Follows Consciousness

As we develop, each wave interprets wealth-related values in its own characteristic manner as shown below in tables 10 and 11.

VALUE	Blue (BL)	Orange (OR)	Green (GR)
Profit: Increase	Harvest, the will of God, feudal-agrarian (land)	Bottom line, ROI (return on investment), manufacturing economy	Suppression of profit: profit = "money grubbing;" connections / network
Innovation: Impact Management	Suppression of change	Short-term gain, anything that works, pragmatism, amorality	Exploration of diverse lifestyles, cultural and social invention
Organization: Vision	Formal hierarchy, nobility / clergy, divine right of kings	Business structure, free market, currency	Community consensus, postmodern network
Equity: Fairness of Distribution	Hierarchical within in-group, feudal system	Capital: shares, winnings, ROI, entrepreneurial	Fairness, equality, philanthropy, socialism
Ecology: Environment	Multiply livestock, taking dominion, land as value	Exploit resources, pollution ignored	Protection of biodiversity, Green ecology, pollution restriction
Consciousness: Development	Rules and Roles, suppression of id drives, obedience to authority	Free thinking, empirical analysis	Compassion, embrace the rejected, human rights
Wholeness: Soul & Society	Salvation through conventional belief	Material substance, soul discounted, freedom from social constraints	Unity through fragmentation, relativism, retrieval of shadow
Health: Well-Being	Traditional medicine, health as blessing	Scientific medicine, healthcare as business, body as machine	Public healthcare, alternative medicine, healthcare rights
Education: Potential	Religious and patriotic education, training in rules and roles	Modern scientific and business education, degree as advantage	Public education, special ed., PC ideas, consciousness raising
Employment: HR Utilization	Loyalty to stable organizations, hierarchy, low mobility	Competition, rat race, performance, work for $ only, opportunity	Socially positive jobs, nonprofits, workers' rights

Table 10. Wealth Values Matrix, Tier I: BL-OR-GR

VALUE	Golden Olive (GO)	Yellow (YE)	Turquoise (TU)
Profit: Increase	Transformation learning, profit = growth in consciousness	Flexibility, time and knowledge as wealth, wisdom economy	Universal prosperity, harmony as wealth, economics of unity
Innovation: Impact Management	Discovery of higher cognition and values, awakening new understanding	Supercreativity, impact planning and response, vision	Holistic logic, coordinated planning for social good, planetary scale
Organization: Vision	Transformation research institutes and schools	Metasystem network, process flow, integration, complexity	The Great Transformation, holistic human development
Equity: Fairness of Distribution	Invention and exploration of transformation economics	Realistic balance, reward for skill, educate for evolution & growth	Moderate pyramid with safety net, peace and equity of distribution
Ecology: Environment	Disaster recovery, pollution control, climate change research	Balance of usage and conservation, play, parks, virtual space	Holistic ecosystem harmonization, gardening of Earth
Consciousness: Development	Leadership training, second-tier schools	Being-level experience, refinement of psychic structures	Awakening to collective needs, unified development, compassion
Wholeness: Soul & Society	Hunger for understanding, soul awakening, spiritual search	Awareness of splits, seeking unity, integrating	Wholeness of soul to build unity of society
Health: Well-Being	Healing and recovery, purification, transformative illnesses	Health refining: mental, emotional, body, and soul, super health development	Provision for universal low-cost holistic healthcare, planetary public health
Education: Potential	Seeking spiritual guidance, open to discipline and training	Learning on the fly, fluidity, complexity, dynamism, variety	Provision for universal free holistic education, paying people to learn key skills
Employment: HR Utilization	Improved income to support learning goals, develop skill-sets and capabilities	Self-employment, entrepreneur-ship, exploration of change	Provision for near universal employment, holistic resource usage

Table 11. Wealth Values Matrix, Tier II: GO-YE-TU

This matrix analysis shows how wave development transforms the way economic issues are addressed. As planetary leadership evolves, everything changes.

Social Entrepreneurs

As Green, Golden Olive, and Yellow become a larger part of the wave mix, we are seeing the rise of social entrepreneurs, people who use savvy business skills to develop nonprofit solutions to social problems.[50] These entrepreneurs are building nongovernmental organizations (NGOs) and other civil society institutions to create innovative responses to human needs. This movement will change the world over the next several decades and lead efforts to recover from transitional disasters.

This movement also will make socially responsible investing the standard by creating an independent, web-based, triple-bottom-line stock market accounting system that rates all companies on issues of people, planet, and profits rather than on profits alone. Increasingly, investors will learn how irresponsible companies hurt causes they believe in, and money will start to change hands.

The Need for New Economic Theory

The most creative young economists and business school graduates are beginning to develop new economic theory to account for and manage emerging life conditions. This new wave of post-Orange economic ideas will need to address twenty-first century challenges:

- Reducing wealth-gap imbalances between haves and have-nots
- Managing global capital and labor flows
- Coping with economic disruptions and dislocations
- Anticipating the social impacts of new technologies
- Strengthening local economies
- Building the security of the middle classes
- Providing affordable universal education
- Providing low-cost universal healthcare

---

[50] David Bornstein, *How to Change the World: Social Entrepreneurs and the Power of New Ideas*, 2004

- Providing optimal human resources utilization and near universal employment
- Nurturing the emerging innovation boom
- Increasing global prosperity and well-being
- Cleaning up the environment and gardening the planet
- Creating more successful business startups
- Balancing international economies
- Making intellectual property law workable for all people: individual artists and inventors, small businesses, larger corporations, and nations

The innovative new theories and business practices these young economists and entrepreneurs develop will take into account complexity theory and emerging second-tier values. The result will completely change our concepts of wealth and economics.

The Coming Planetary-Wisdom Economy

At some point, the leading waves of humanity will begin to identify with all of us instead of just with some of us.

We are transitioning out of the national-industrial era. Concepts of technological revolutions, information revolutions, knowledge economies, world trade/globalism, and pluralistic societies are all various intermediate forms and stages leading to the era I call the "planetary-wisdom era."

We are inexorably gravitating toward an integrated and diverse human society. The basis of our economy has already moved from agriculture to industry to information/services. Now it is evolving from information to knowledge, and it will evolve from knowledge to wisdom. We are orbiting around the intersecting attractors of planet, humanity, and wisdom. The planetary-wisdom economy will allow us to integrate peacefully and prosperously as a universal human society.

A crucial part of the wisdom aspect will be learning how to nurture diversity and variety in a nondisruptive, low-conflict way. It is desirable for us to constantly explore new concepts and ways of life. At any given time in any given environment, it is also desirable for there to be humane mechanisms for allowing selection of "preferred" processes and rejection of processes that are not working. That is, we want evolution to work, but not brutally.

A deeper understanding of complexity theory will help us nurture more effective emergent environments. The goal is an ongoing, vibrant human evolution and a robust diversity of characteristics that increase the likelihood of longer-term human survival in many diverse environments. Harmonious diversity also provides immediate benefits by deepening the richness and variety of human society.

> **Complexity =** **Evolutionary innovation maximized at the balance point between order (law) and chaos (freedom).**

The more effective this balance between chaos and order, the more creative new solutions are produced.

The Innovation Economy

Regardless of what aspect of the global economy we consider, innovation is becoming the primary driver of wealth development. Even commodity industries like oil or building materials are profoundly affected by innovations in production, refinement, and distribution. If two brick-making companies are competing, the winner will be the one that is most innovative in all aspects of the business. Perhaps, for example, we will want to make buildings out of "smart bricks" containing imbedded nanosensors. If the benefits are significant, ordinary bricks will no longer do.

Thus, to understand the future of wealth, we need to look at factors that affect innovation and are likely to be affected by it.

Innovation Factors

Maximum wealth is generated when the business climate supports and nourishes creativity. Four factors that encourage this are:

1. Business culture
2. Consciousness and values
3. Economic climate
4. Focused application

Business culture
Creative people perform best in environments that tolerate diversity. The interplay of diverse ideas stimulates the kind of experimental thinking that can lead to breakthrough concepts.

Consciousness and values
Second-tier consciousness stimulates people to expand virtues such as wisdom, compassion, strength, and presence. Such virtues and the values they cultivate are, and always have been, the true foundation of wealth. They encourage a business climate governed by a just and merciful rule of law. The social trust this generates directly stimulates increased innovation.

Economic climate
When wise governance provides the stability of an intelligent safety net, more people feel secure enough to venture entrepreneurial risk. More new businesses get started, and existing businesses explore new possibilities.

The best values of the true free-market economy can be achieved only by guarding against monopolistic restraint of trade and the special privileges of entrenched wealth. Intellectual property law and its enforcement needs to better protect smaller startup inventors from attack by well-heeled corporate powers. Innovative technologies are too often stolen by companies with superior political influence, money, and legal muscle. Sometimes innovations are suppressed by punitive market practices.

These kinds of practices essentially subvert the whole concept of the free market by turning it into a battle of raw might, rather than a fair test of product value decided by consumers (the market). Consumers, who are supposed to produce an efficient market by their buying decisions, often have no chance to become aware of an innovation.

What is purported to be an "efficient free market" is actually neither efficient nor free. What it is, currently, is wasteful and rigged. The magic of capitalism, which has brought us so much value, is struggling under a burden of lawlessness resulting from the failure of government to manage an objective and fair playing field.

Capital is also exposed to enormous risks including financial manipulations that amount to outright theft. Large companies receive too much leeway, while startup entrepreneurs, who have brought us so much new value, struggle to get capital on reasonable terms. What is needed are sources of capital for innovation combined with honest and supportive financial guidance.

Many CEOs of well-established companies would like to plough more resources into R&D, systems development, and other long-range goals, but are unable to do so because of pressure from financial markets focused only on quarterly results. The impatience of capital and the speed of capital movements tend to suppress innovation. We will need to develop better transparency to protect investors as well as greater investment stability to encourage longer-range planning.

One way to increase the justice of our economic system and stimulate broad economic growth is to provide affordable universal education for all ages. No other social policy would provide a better return on investment to society. Lifelong learning, available to all, would directly increase the number and skills of the creative workforce and inevitably increase general wealth. If we fail to grasp this point, we may have to learn it from other societies that do.

Focused application

Good organizational management provides fair incentives for focusing creativity on defined goals. Applications for innovation include products, services, processes, business models, new industries, and new markets. When organizations and societies create the right economic climate, vast new potentials for prosperity and abundance open up.

As second-tier consciousness grows more influential in our society, we will see positive evolutions in our whole economic system that will increase its effectiveness at producing and distributing wealth.

Human and Intellectual Capital

Emerging economic theory is increasingly recognizing human and intellectual capital as a new component alongside monetary capital, and discussion is ongoing about how to properly account for these powerful factors. The quality movement and international standards such as ISO-9000 have elevated the importance of defining and documenting processes.

Visibly using a well-documented set of processes can be an asset in acquisition of investment financing, in company valuation, and ultimately in stock price. The creation of strong and flexible process definitions helps to bring organizational vision into actualization.

The emerging field of knowledge management deals with effective use of "knowledge," both in recorded form and as value held in people's heads.

Human capital corresponds to what is called "tacit knowledge," knowledge that is not written down or formally defined but resides in the skills and talents of employees.

Intellectual capital corresponds to what is called "explicit knowledge," knowledge that is written down or formally defined in some fashion.

Some companies do an adequate job of managing human and intellectual capital, but almost none do it brilliantly. Effectively managing intelligent and creative employees in a rapidly changing technological environment requires great vision. There is a need to think through issues many companies are having trouble facing. For example, some technical employees may know more about, and have more control over, their company's business than the executives they report to.

When a company's human capital sees high-tech jobs shifted overseas to reduce labor costs, how can management inspire full creativity and effort? Companies that find ways of winning genuine loyalty from employees by demonstrating loyalty to them in return will win the extra effort that makes the competitive difference.

Increasingly, investors are able to find out about the human climate inside a company before they invest. In the long term, this is going to change the climate of business in profoundly significant ways.

Compensation for Contribution

When innovation becomes the prime driver of wealth, all business becomes "knowledge business." This is no longer a special category of business. Every industry and every company depends on more effectively processing knowledge to guide creative work product.

The working core of any business, no matter how large, is a series of communications between two or more individuals. These interactions are the atoms and molecules out of which value creation (a.k.a. business) is made. Every business meeting, every phone call, every email can, at least theoretically, be evaluated in terms of how much knowledge was exchanged or how much value was created. The sum of these value-creating communications, from the boardroom to the shop floor, from the engineer to the point of sale, and from the auditor to the stockholders' meeting, determine the value of a company at any given time.

The more open and honest the communication, the more efficient the flow of value creation. When knowledge sharing is incentivized by "compensation for contribution," communication produces value with maximum efficiency. When people trust that they will be rewarded for their creative contributions, they will stretch to maximize them. If they feel that their input is being ripped off, they will have an incentive to slow the speed of knowledge flow. Companies that maximize the fairness of "compensation for contribution" will get more contribution and will prosper.

It is amazing to see the lengths companies go to today to try to get people to share information while simultaneously rewarding them for not sharing information. Knowledge management systems rarely take into account that anyone who has valuable information is generally paid for keeping it close to the chest and often not paid for sharing it.

As the information systems of the future become more transparent, compensation systems will also have to become more transparent as well. In fact, it will be precisely the transparency and fairness of compensation that will catalyze the increasing openness of the system.

Automated, Value-Added, Assignment Software

The near future will see far more extensive communication analysis both within companies and throughout industry networks to convert theory into practical communication protocols and performance metrics. Innovation in management methods is becoming a great source of wealth.

As more of the communication activity of business gets done through, or is facilitated by, the media network, it will become ever more possible to automate the capture of performance valuation as it happens. Knowledge management software will increasingly be able to assign a value-added quotient to any given exchange. This will allow more precise ways of measuring the value and social impact of every element of the business and industrial process.

Automated negotiation and contribution valuation software will be offered as a feature of emerging business networks. As this software improves and develops a body of industry standards, the valuation process will become more automated and less stressful for participants.

Business discussions about possible ventures will be quicker and more efficient because every participant's role and contribution will be automatically derived from the content of the actual business development process, recorded by the system as it happens. As the efficiencies of such systems prove their power, they will merge and aggregate to become an integrated global system that includes everyone. This will tend to blur the distinction between employer and employee.

Since virtually everything will be done in the "system," everything will be automatically recorded, and therefore credit for ideas and inventions will also be automatic. When multiple people come up with the same idea or contribute to its development, as will usually be the case, contribution value will be automatically assessed and attributed to the various parties.

As this kind of software becomes part of the network worldwide, it will serve to establish a more level playing field for all aspects of business and trade. It will include negotiation modules for establishing and negotiating all the parameters of value-added valuation and will become the medium in which business is done.

Universe Modeling and Better Organizations

Communications analysis and modeling will also support the development of more effective organizational structures and processes. Analyzing communication flows by modeling comprehensive stakeholder environments will help to build better organizations.

We want to answer the question, "Who is communicating what to whom?" This provides a basis for realigning policy to more effectively achieve organizational goals.

> **Communication is the fuel that turns innovation into value creation.**

Increasingly, what I call the "Universe Model" will apply to all organizational interactions. In brief, the Universe Model defines categories of organizational interactions and tracks how those interactions affect an organization. For most corporations, the Universe Model might list the following stakeholder communication categories:

- Investors
- Customers
- Suppliers, contractors, consultants

- Employees, unions, guilds, professional associations
- Regulators, governments, standards organizations
- Media commentators, industry analysts
- Competitors
- Strategic partners
- Mergers & Acquisitions prospects and suitors

Nonprofit organizations have a slightly different but similar set of stakeholder categories. Leaders in NGOs will apply the most innovative ideas from business to the tasks of social entrepreneurship.

As the new environment comes into sharper focus, we will see ever more clearly the interdependence of all stakeholder roles. The new model will focus more on processes occurring within networks of organizations rather than on single organizations as the main locus of activity.

Almost all organizations today have fuzzy borders, and this creates new challenges that current theory and practice have not yet fully addressed.

In figure 11 below, lines between boxes define the communication flows in a high-level communications analysis model, as seen from the perspective of one organization in relationship to its environment. To model the business landscape as a whole requires a more complex network analysis.

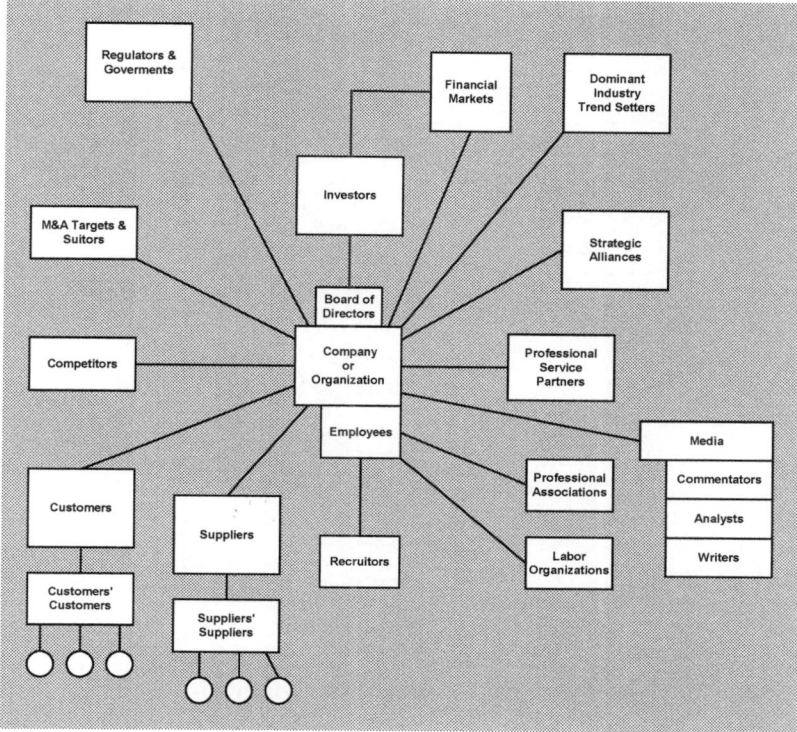

Figure 11. Universe Modeling Diagram

One such landscape diagram models the concept of value network optimization, which shows that the ideas of "supply chains" and "customer chains" are better described as "value networks." This is shown in figure 12 below.

In the value network, a supplier can become a customer and vice-versa. An integration portal, such as a shopping website, can disintermediate players anywhere in the network. Profit also migrates as different elements within the network strive to optimize the flow of value to their advantage.

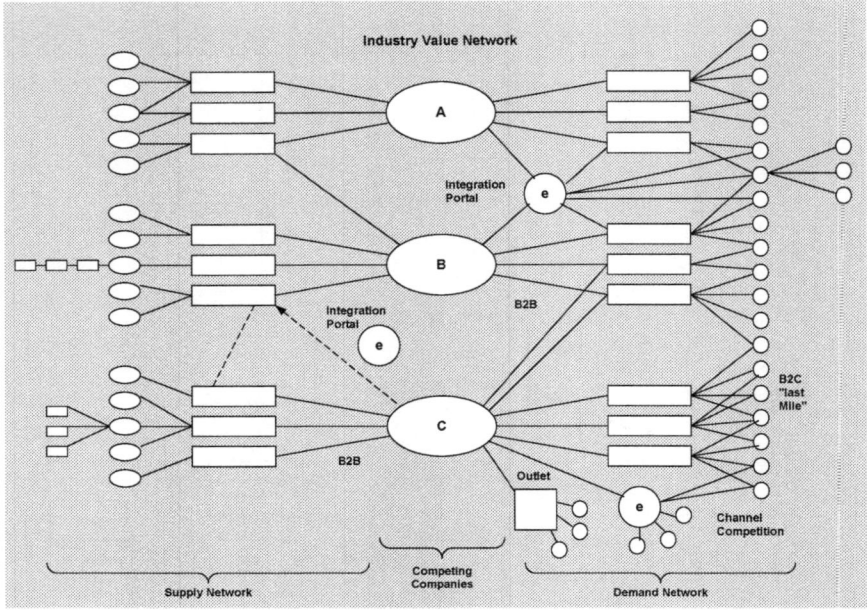

Figure 12. Value Network Optimization Diagram

The Future of Business

Business is one of the most vibrant areas of transformation in the world today. An enormous amount of innovation has occurred in this domain since the end of the second world war. The pressures of competition, the order provided by laws and regulations, and the demand for ever-increased productivity have created a climate that is fertile for emergent phenomena.

As complexity theory has posited, creative forms are most likely to evolve in the border domain between chaos (too much freedom) and order (too little freedom). This is primarily where business has operated over the last fifty years, especially in the developed world.

The result has been innovation and, despite challenges like intellectual property theft, peak oil, and offshoring dislocations, there is no sign that innovation is going to abate in the foreseeable future. This vibrant energy has put business at the center of world power, and the ideas coming out of business have integrated and defined relationships between other social functions.

We could define business as organized activity (busy-ness) focused on producing value. This is a simple formula:

Business = Activity organized to produce value

It can be applied to a wide range of activities, whether for profit or not for profit, as well as to most nongovernmental organizations (NGOs).

Although the business environment tends to oscillate between overregulated bureaucracy and anarchic lawlessness, on average it operates in the creative zone between these extremes. Whenever conditions move to either extreme for too long, government usually steps in to apply corrective measures, regulation or deregulation according to the perceived need. This social arrangement tends to ensure a certain degree of innovation over time.

The challenge of change inspires business people to take calculated risks. At the same time, they are constrained to do everything possible to mitigate risk. The result of striving for this balance over the decades is massive practical change that affects every aspect of our lives. These evolutionary conditions are certain to produce massive changes for business itself.

If we could travel ahead even fifty years, we would probably have difficulty recognizing the economic activity of that time as what we call "business" today. To manage the next couple of decades, successful business people will have to make more effective use of futurism and scenario planning. When day-to-day activity involves so much focused pragmatism, it is often difficult to grasp what "thinking out of the box" actually means.

Here are some basic concepts applicable to both short- and long-range business change:

1. Value means customer perception.
2. An influential minority guides customer perception.
3. Influential customers typically belong to many networks.
4. Customer perception is affected positively or negatively by organizational behavior.

5. Organizational behavior is evaluated in relation to all stakeholders: customers, employees, communities, investors, regulators, even competitors.
6. Ethics matter.
7. Nothing is secret; eventually everything is transparent.
8. Profitable value means unique innovations, especially innovations that reinvent industries and create new markets. Ideas are the most important product.
9. Innovation comes from creative people.
10. Profitable innovation means effective management of creative people.
11. Interesting and tolerant organizational environments attract creative people.
12. Effective communication stimulates innovation and value production.
13. Effective communication includes all stakeholders.
14. Whatever activity gets rewarded gets done.
15. People are not stupid; it pays to be honest with them.
16. Very smart people are never smart enough to understand all the complexities.
17. Managing complexity is difficult; throw all the brain-power you can at it. Some understanding is better than none.
18. Find ways to make complex things simpler, but not too simple to be valuable.

Values Create Value

When we want to understand the emerging future, we should always go to the human heart for answers. It is ultimately human longing that defines what is valuable.

> **The future of business is defined by the relationship between value and values.**

When customers weigh the value of an offering (service or product), they are comparing it to values of their own that are associated with the area that the offering addresses. The contextual meaning of an offering often has more impact on its perceived value than the substance of the product or service offered.

Every product or service is expected to meet baseline requirements. Differentiating factors have more to do with subtle contextual meanings. For example, the value of a T-shirt often has more to do with what is printed on it than with the quality of the cloth or the sewing. The same principle applies to intangible services. People buy because of what the purchase means to their identities. In this context, a single ethical failure can destroy a company's reputation.

Because trust is highly valued today, we can expect business practice to migrate in that direction. Businesses will compete to prove greater trustworthiness because that is what attracts customers. Eventually, business trends always migrate in the direction of the values most important to customers.

Of course, the market is neither as rational nor as well-informed as some suppose it to be. Therefore, there are inefficiencies that give forward-looking companies an advantage if they can envision what their customers will want before they realize it themselves. This is more effective than trying to make customers want something.

Ultimate value efficiency occurs when there is perfect congruence between the values of a company and the values of its customers. Therefore, advanced company leaders spend a lot of time identifying and describing their values, imbuing their organizations with those values, and finding customers who match those values. This long-term trend will produce business networks with shared values that will function more like families. Growing mutual trust will tend to create an atmosphere of friendly community that all members will be loath to break. As mutual trust becomes the main avenue through which business is done, the consequence of breaking trust with your network may become more severe and lead to expulsion.

Some networks may fall into the hazard of enforced conformity, which results in a loss of flexible thinking. Ultimately, selective evolution will break through enforced conformity. That is, networks that support greater tolerance will attract and nurture greater creativity, thus producing higher survival values than do more restrictive networks, which will tend to decline. Flexible (Yellow) values, because they are more adaptive, will tend to grow.

Positive human qualities will be the main driver of future business.

This has always been the case and will remain eternally so, but certain factors now are intensifying this eternal verity. Orange technological society eventually produces spiritual hunger, which leads to a longing for connection, positive qualities, and virtues.

Green alienation is attracted to the healing properties of true compassion, strength, and wisdom. At the same time, technology is increasing communication and information transparency. While it is easier to stay connected via email, cellphone, instant message, and such, it is also harder to hide personal and company data.

Therefore, there is increasing demand for honesty, trustworthiness, ethics, emotional warmth, compassion, capability, strength, dependability, wisdom, humility, humor, clarity, presence, friendliness, and a host of other positive qualities or virtues, both as personal characteristics and as expressions of organizational values.

The future of business will be defined by the emergence of virtuous qualities and research into means for expression of these qualities within organizations.

Cynical people may find such a statement unrealistic and utopian, but thoughtful executives and entrepreneurs already realize the logic in it. Developing higher consciousness is the only effective way to stabilize virtuous qualities.

Although basic truths remain true, times of great change mean looking beyond the apparent. Many science fiction movies present a picture of greedy corporate dictatorships ruling over impoverished populations. While we may see some of this in the near future, it is really more a reflection of the past and the present than of where we are headed.

Humans don't want that kind of future and, more than we imagine, we have the power to get what we want and to reject what we don't want. Even people who would never dream of engaging in any form of political activism actually exercise their power of choice every day. While it is true that people have to put up with some things they don't like, it is also true that the small everyday choices and resistances of many people over time actually do change things.

In the kind of high-connectivity environment we are building, this kind of feedback effect is becoming increasingly pronounced. The speed with which it can take effect has already startled many who have been caught at nefarious deeds. Small flaws suddenly revealed can injure even very well-meaning people. For a time the crowd enjoys throwing stones until it begins to dawn on us that we are all vulnerable. The ancient advice, "People who live in glass houses shouldn't throw stones," was never more true. Business will have to learn to live with much greater transparency.[51]

Ever increasing transparency will force us to learn ways of functioning in a diverse world of people whose ways may seem alien to us and ours to them. Intercultural communication skills are already valued in today's business environment and will continue to be so to an even greater extent tomorrow. This area is expanding into a wide range of professional skills, from the ability to express culturally neutral messages to the expertise to negotiate the nuances of specific cultures.

Flexibility and Communication

The ability to reach across all divides to forge bonds of commonality and trust will be a central business skill. It is always the market that defines perceived value, and the market is increasingly diverse. People are inventing ever more complex ways to distinguish themselves. Many individuals identify themselves as unique, a market of one. As business learns to create flexible, customizable products and services to meet the uniqueness of every individual, business itself will utterly change beyond all recognition. Many customers want to design their own products and services down to the last detail.

Businesses that learn how to create facilities that allow an almost infinite capacity for custom variation of products and services will have gained a powerful advantage. The subtlest area for this shift is the delivery of custom services. The trick will be to offer choice and uniqueness without making customers feel they are doing most of the work. Already, every salesperson has become a "consultant" because customers now need advice and guidance on how to navigate the menu of options and prices. Marketers need to ask questions like "How big a menu is needed?" and "How much consulting is beneficial and profitable?"

Network Business Models

One of the more curious shifts some business environments are going through is the evolution from supplier-customer relations to networks

---

[51] Don Tapscott and David Ticoll, *The Naked Corporation*, 2003

of partnerships where all parties are both seller and buyer. The same shift can be described in terms of employer-employee. Some industries may melt into large networks of partners all acting as owners, creators, distributors, suppliers, and customers of one another.

A related model is being explored in the virtual corporations set up to coordinate major entertainment events. Major corporations in some fields outsource an increasing percentage of their work force to contract labor, facilities managers, and consultants. Multivendor project management has become a skill set in its own right. Often teams of people working in many parts of the world need to cooperate to produce a desired result.

The network model in many different flavors is already with us. We can expect this process to continue to evolve as organizations learn more effective ways of managing network projects.

At the same time, on the individual level, networking groups are emerging for many purposes. Professionals join associations, in part, to purchase health insurance at group rates. Talent managers pull together teams of diverse talents for intensive contract jobs in advertising shoots, movie making, contract software development, interactive video, disaster recovery, contract building—any time a team is needed for short-term, intensive problem solving. The evolution of the internet will facilitate the growth of network business into new forms.

A New Business Environment

On the capital side, risk-management and risk-spreading insurance systems will offer investor pools, pension funds, and institutional managers a safer way to develop capital. There may be less chance of making a killing but also less chance of getting killed. The main body of global financial managers will increasingly opt for more efficient and stable processes. Given the profit multiplier of innovation, it still will be possible to generate significant returns, especially in a more lawful environment. Ethics, trust, and transparency will come to be seen as major value multipliers.

Capital borrowers will prefer doing business with such lending/investing institutions and will comply with the greater transparency rules because they will enjoy much more patient capital. In this environment, CEOs will be able to run their enterprises with an eye to real, long-term efficiencies and the generation of real value, rather than struggle to make this quarter look better than it really is.

Wealth Economics | 217

In such environments, investing more heavily in employee training, in systems development, and in product quality makes more sense. We can also expect more public investment in education and infrastructure to parallel this business movement.

In the new environment, the boundaries between social functions will break down at the same time the new business environment is evolving. Connections between business and government will be even greater than today. Some industries will consolidate, and the incubation of startups may become an industry-sponsored process. Free-market competition in such environments becomes atomized to the individual or small-group level.

International boundaries are also breaking down, and a new balance will emerge between a somewhat more managed economy and the free-market entrepreneurial process. The result will not be a victory for either but a new synthesis that makes new spaces for both. This is actually already underway as the G7/G8 countries, the G20, and the new emerging nations come to grips with an increasingly global economy.

The ideal of prosperity in every part of the globe is going to drive all leaders in the direction of coordinated policies. Local leaders pressing the partisan interests of their constituencies are going to be transformed by the realities of global interconnectedness.

Today, we see how most world leaders, regardless of political leaning, eventually wind up coming to a moderate global management position because ultimately that is the only position that works. The parties may elect a candidate under the rhetoric of a particular partisan point of view but, once in power, the elected official learns (after a few bumps) that the only way to get anything done is by compromise. Thus, extreme positions are voted out or marginalized and the moderate position is the ultimate winner.

Characteristics of the future business environment include:

- Information transparency
- More stable capital pools
- Automated compensation valuation
- Unimpeded knowledge sharing
- All work and communication on the system

- More psychologically healthy organizations
- Entrepreneurial free market and managed-economy synthesis
- More efficiency and lawfulness
- Real value creation rather than paper value manipulation
- International industry consolidation
- Universe Model of interdependent stakeholders

The net effect of this development will be that the world will get down to doing what it needs to do with a lot less friction and waste, for example:

- Finding new ways to generate jobs
- Establishing coalitions of business and government to create near universal employment
- Providing efficient and effective universal education
- Encouraging and rewarding employee innovation and knowledge sharing
- Creating more value for all

Value Net Wars

The next few decades will be characterized by a series of upheavals and disruptions in how we view our value networks. I am referring to this aspect of the Transition as the "value net wars." Mostly, these will be nonshooting wars, but they will sometimes be quite violent all the same, just not in a way we are familiar with.

The problem we are working out is how to distribute rewards in the various value networks that make up our global economy. Continuous changes in technology, social demographics, and shifting coalition alliances will drive a long process of determining who gets compensated and by how much. That is, we are sorting out the real question of how much value each person contributes to the value-added chain of any given product or service and how much they should be rewarded for that contribution.

The key principle to bear in mind is this: all value in the near future economy is driven by creativity.

In the agrarian economy, land ownership was key. In the industrial economy, ownership of factories, mines, oil wells, and distribution systems was key. In the information economy, information and data processing were key. Now, all of those processes plus additional new processes are being driven by environments and institutions that nurture and support creativity. All market advantage now comes from creative ideas.

First, let us look at what the "net wars" are not. They will not be primarily military in nature, though they may spawn flare-ups of violence, rioting, crime, and police actions. The net wars will not be primarily cyberwars, though this certainly will be a feature of some of the action.

The net wars will not be primarily between nations, though intergovernmental conflicts and struggles will be a factor. These will not be wars against terrorists or wars of religious fanatics, though all of these factors will arise periodically. Primarily, the net wars are commercial struggles between various components of a complex and shifting global economy. It's about money.

Partly, net wars involve guild warfare, although that term also doesn't quite capture the nature of the beast. A good example of a recent interguild struggle is the ongoing battle in the United States over healthcare dollars. Doctors and healthcare providers were prospering and consumer costs were up. Insurance providers were trying to reduce payouts. Enter the lawyers and political lobbyists, and suddenly we had a shift to "managed care" and HMOs. Although this is a vast oversimplification, the basic effect was to shift value within the network.

Another example of a value network struggle emerged out of the corporate downsizing period of the 1980s and 1990s. Information technology workers and managers were let go then often rehired as subcontractors or consultants at higher rates of pay but without benefits. Human resources agencies and consulting companies flourished as the need to fuel the dot-com boom with talented systems developers mushroomed...and then crashed. Today the issue is offshoring, but tomorrow it may well be repatriation of jobs.

While neither of these examples quite rises to the level of what we would normally call a "war," anyone who lived through them knows that they represented disruptive change in the way value is exchanged in the industries involved. Revolutions and counter-revolutions have occurred, and these struggles are far from over.

Often, these struggles are fought in the marketplace and in the courts, and there are real winners and losers. If a "road-warrior" businessman dies in a car crash from too little sleep, or a downsized ex-vice president dies of a heart attack, or an overstressed worker dies from alcoholism or drug abuse, we don't think of these as casualties of war, but perhaps we should.

Software piracy and the effect of Napster on the music industry are excellent examples of how the net wars are progressing in these early stages. The electronic trade routes are under attack, this time by thieving consumers.

In the international arena, the relationship between the global financial institutions (WTO, IMF, World Bank, etc.) and the economic structure of various developing nations has been implicated in all kinds of disruptions. Whether we believe these organizations intended to help or to enslave, the perception of global inequity has led to an environment of conflict. Affluent nations, and wealthy people in general, have come to be seen as legitimate targets by the poor and disadvantaged, and people from other, less affluent, nations. The perception is that the game is rigged.

This, of course, is not new. It is the basis of all traditional class warfare theories and practices. Labeling it "class warfare" or "socialist" does not, however, make it go away. What is new is the speed of commerce in an electronic environment. Massive amounts of capital flight can occur in seconds, leaving economic devastation in its wake. Just as rapidly, computer viruses originating on the other side of the planet can disrupt tranquil bastions of finance in the developed nations.

These are some of the factors setting the stage for the net war environment. Our trade systems are at risk, and our domestic tranquility along with them. To successfully make our way through this difficult stage, to shorten the conflicts, and to found a new planetary civil society, we will need to develop several things:

1. New economic theory that addresses the complexity of global networks, creativity as a driver, and technology as a change agent
2. Better ethics and moral consciousness about economic issues and better ways of conveying these values
3. Improved ways of nurturing increased creativity and better use of creative assets
4. More effective ways of assessing value contribution and resulting compensation
5. Better security and policing of the trade routes, including both transportation security and computer security

6. A carefully managed planetary social safety net and meaningful steps to establish a widespread sense of fairness and equity (Here, educational opportunity is key.)
7. Proper currency valuations and supports for those dislocated by global labor outsourcing and sudden capital movements
8. Globalization of political oversight and regulation of transnational business (When trade and capital flows are international but governance is not, finance gains too much power and subverts democracy.)
9. Better vision planning and strategic modeling to anticipate social and technological change

These are some of the challenges that will occupy us as we try to survive disruptions and build flourishing communities in an era of great conflict over wealth. The important thing to remember is: when social order creates a sense of fairness, peace and prosperity expand for all; when it does not, no one is secure. The welfare of the whole world is in everyone's interest.

The great wealth gaps that are features of today's environment will eventually trigger balancing international regulation. Many of the moderating transformations of finance are actually originating within the bastions of capitalism as leaders work to stave off more radical restructurings from without.

One factor that may help to ease the Transition is that new technologies, such as nanotech and other innovations, will be generating a massive expansion in total planetary wealth. The challenge will be to find wise ways of distributing this wealth to support overall social stability through the Transition.

Urban World

The world of the next few decades will be increasingly urbanized. Thus, although overall population growth is expected to level off by around 2025, the experience of population density is likely to be significant for some time to come. This suggests that planning and management of urban environments will be a growth industry for quite a while.

Although terrorist attacks on cities might exert some counter-urbanization pressure, they probably will not offset the economic draw of cities in the next few decades. Even electronic telepresence will not completely remove the advantages of living in, or near, metropolitan centers. People like the physical availability of cultural events, restaurants, markets, and other people.

The chart in table 12 shows United Nations' estimates for the largest agglomerations (cities) in the year 2015.

Rank	Agglomeration (City)	Country	Population Est. 2015
1	Tokyo	Japan	27,190,000
2	Dhaka	Bangladesh	22,766,000
3	Mumbai	India	22,577,000
4	Sao Paulo	Brazil	21,229,000
5	Delhi	India	20,884,000
6	Mexico City	Mexico	20,434,000
7	New York	USA	17,944,000
8	Jakarta	Indonesia	17,268,000
9	Calcutta	India	16,747,000
10	Karachi	Pakistan	16,197,000
11	Lagos	Nigeria	15,966,000
12	Los Angeles	USA	14,494,000
13	Shanghai	China	13,598,000
14	Buenos Aires	Argentina	13,185,000
15	Manila	Philippines	12,579,000
16	Beijing	China	11,671,000
17	Rio de Janeiro	Brazil	11,543,000
18	Cairo	Egypt	11,531,000
19	Istanbul	Turkey	11,362,000
20	Osaka	Japan	11,013,000

Projections by the Population Division of the United Nations
www.geohive.com/charts/city_agg1950_2015.php

Table 12. Estimated Population of Largest Cities 2015

Wealth Economics | 223

Compare table 12 to table 13 showing the balance between urban and rural populations for each continent in 2000 and estimated in 2030, and the trend toward urbanization becomes clear.

	Population 2000				
Continent	Total	Urban	%	Rural	%
Northern America	314,000,000	243,000,000	77.4	71,000,000	22.6
Latin America & Caribbean	519,000,000	391,000,000	75.3	127,000,000	24.5
Oceania	31,000,000	23,000,000	74.2	8,000,000	25.8
Europe	727,000,000	534,000,000	73.5	193,000,000	26.5
Asia	3,672,000,000	1,376,000,000	37.5	2,297,000,000	62.6
Africa	794,000,000	295,000,000	37.2	498,000,000	62.7
World Total 2000	6,057,000,000	2,862,000,000		3,194,000,000	

	Population 2030 (Estimated)				
Continent	Total	Urban	%	Rural	%
Northern America	396,000,000	335,000,000	84.6	61,000,000	15.4
Latin America & Caribbean	723,000,000	608,000,000	84.1	116,000,000	16.0
Oceania	42,000,000	32,000,000	76.2	10,000,000	23.8
Europe	670,000,000	540,000,000	80.6	131,000,000	19.6
Asia	4,950,000,000	2,679,000,000	54.1	2,271,000,000	45.9
Africa	1,489,000,000	787,000,000	52.9	702,000,000	47.1
World Total 2030 (Estim.)	8,270,000,000	4,981,000,000		3,291,000,000	

Source: United Nations, "World Urbanization Prospects, the 2001 Revision"
www.geohive.com/global/pop_urbancnt.php

Table 13. Urban/Rural Population by Continent 2000 and 2030

In the developed world, over 80 percent of the population will soon be living in urban centers. Inevitably, we will want to build better cities, and all aspects of urban quality-of-life solutions will be in demand. One way to analyze this is by technology sectors:

- Physical infrastructure
- Biological environment
- Cultural and psychological processes

Urban Physical Infrastructure
Design solutions for urban infrastructure, streets, buildings, bridges, tunnels, and system conduits will need to consider the maintenance life cycle of various system components. The goal will be to design modularized systems that can be repaired, replaced, and upgraded with minimum cost and disruption.

Imagine urban street units that can be repaired from below. A worn "block" gets a new unit installed while traffic continues above. When it is ready, the old unit is removed for repair or recycling and the new unit is raised into place, all in a short time and during the lowest traffic hours. Infrastructure planners and developers will increasingly be thinking in dynamic terms. The discoveries of complexity science will go into analyzing the total life cycle of the system. Some major goals will be:

- Smooth, non-polluting transportation throughout metropolitan areas
- Major reductions of noise pollution
- A clean and hygienic environment
- Safety and security
- Ease of maintenance

Producing quiet space by reducing noise pollution within densely populated areas will become a huge industry. Also, the physical infrastructure will work closely to support the biological environment.

Urban Biosphere Environment
Engineers will turn toward an environmentally sensitized new biotechnology for solutions to problems of cleanliness and hygiene. They will monitor a city's molecular climate with sensitive biosensors and systematically intervene to cultivate a healthy urban biosphere with the help of advanced nanotech and biotech molecular solutions.

Early mistakes in this area will lead to an inevitable migration away from the mechanical-chemical model and toward an emerging ecological-wellness model of biotechnology. The struggle between biotech corporations and environmental/alternative health groups will ultimately lead to the emergence of a positive and balanced outcome we could call "biotech II."

The city of the future is likely to be a much greener and quieter place. We will live in urban gardens that feel more like elegantly landscaped suburban spaces. The idea will be to create beauty, tranquility, privacy, and peacefulness within high-density environments. Improvements in nonpolluting transportation and energy solutions, advances in materials science, and the widespread embrace of ecological principles will make this possible.

We will understand that our well-being and safety depend on a healthy biosphere, all the more so in places where large numbers of people live in close proximity. Successful, healthy cities will be enormous wealth generators, and the technologies to produce them will be a huge growth industry because the whole world will want them. Who does not want to live in a pleasant environment?

The garbage dumps outside many third-world cities, currently the habitat of the poorest of the poor, will be transformed into energy resources for biodiesel fuel production and other recycled products. The poor will be given sustainable housing, and their children will be educated to contribute to a new society. We will no longer be willing to waste either resources or people.

Urban Cultural Management
The city is all about culture, communication, and synergy of imagination, that is, the wonderful interplay of lots of people. As valuable as infrastructure and biosphere will be, by far the greatest industry of the future will be the technologies of cultural exchange and human social psychology. We could call this "sociotech" or "social gardening," though by that time it will have hundreds of names and divisions.

Social gardening, as I am seeing it, means the conscious management of human culture to nurture many levels of quality-of-life solutions. These will include:

- Human services for people in all phases of life, families, singles, children, and aging people
- Neighborhood cultural ecology

- Safety and security through emotionally intelligent community policing
- Education, especially the emotional intelligence aspects of human interaction and conflict resolution
- Media overlays that increase the beauty, privacy, and utility of the urban environment
- Vision management and urban identity
- Public forum and debate
- Consciousness development
- Art and cultural entertainment

The goal will be to create environments that are brilliantly responsive to human need and that elevate human development. This domain provides a vast potential for economic growth and employment into the far future. The one challenge we will not run out of will be our own transformation. There are always greater heights to scale, and this is where our greatest value and purpose lies.

The whole purpose of having a healthy and beautiful environment is to support a human culture that helps people grow and achieve ever greater personal and spiritual unfoldment. The successful city should develop all its citizens to their highest potential. We will want to raise and educate millions of scientists, artists, healers, saints, sages, and leaders in all walks of life.

The management tools we develop to make this possible will be part of our sociotech industry and will be a valuable trade property. This is a long-term source of wealth, an international trade in processes and infrastructure tools that improve the success of human cultural environments. Many of these techniques will be applicable in rural environments as well but, at least for the near future, the majority of people will live in or near cities. Therefore, we will want to create cities that work.

Cultural Disease Monitoring
A significant part of managing the global urban/virtual environment will be to monitor for emergent cultural diseases. A cultural disease is a pattern of creating meaning through ideas that lead to negative social consequences. Some of the main variants include: extreme ethnocentrism, xenophobia, racial and religious intolerance, nihilism, lethargy, hopelessness, boredom, suicidal and homicidal tendencies,

"ghostliness" or loss of identity, alienation, robotic behaviors, machine envy or worship, militarism, addictions, extremes of promiscuity, greed, corruptions of power, and so forth.

Of course, individuals have manifested most of these symptoms for ages and, although they are generally considered symptoms of ill-health, they only become "cultural diseases" when they become part of a life style that spreads throughout a district or subset of an urban culture in ways that threaten the overall balance of the society.

To determine when a social phenomenon is part of a healing expression of shadow components in the collective psyche and when it is poised to shift into a pathological expression requires a delicate assessment. For example, the "gothic" style favored by some youth may be a natural part of coping with the difficulties of growing up, whereas a sudden increase in aggressive, neo-Nazi "skinhead" gangs would be a signal requiring interventions.

As our human science becomes increasingly subtle, we will learn how to engage cultural ecologies in sensitive and delicate ways that nourish a great variety of healthy cultural diversities while keeping the unity of the whole social space positive and integrated. It will be exactly this learning of what works and what does not that will comprise the growing body of knowledge that I have called "social gardening," which is human science applied to cultural ecologies.

No doubt there will be trends and counter-trends in this field as our experience and wisdom develop over time, but the net result will be a growing understanding of how to build societies that flourish. Such wisdom will be a major source of planetary wealth and well-being in our future world. Applied human science is our future, which is why it is the core of this book.

Fairness and Equity

The Essential Middle Class

The vast majority of creative innovations and energetic productivity comes from the broad middle classes. Aristocracies tend to be constrained by social convention and lack of incentive. The poor are busy struggling to survive. Thus, most economic transformation efforts should be focused on strengthening the middle three-fifths of our society.

Today, the economic system favors the wealthy top of society, and government assistance, such as it is, focuses on the poor. The middle is left to fend for itself. But the middle is essential to a healthy society. When the middle class gets stronger, it tends to fortify the economy in general by consuming and producing, starting new businesses, and contributing to charities of various kinds. When the middle is strong, the poor have somewhere to grow into. They see possibilities for hope.

Models of Economic Equity

The only kinds of social compacts people will continue to support over the long term are those that continually increase justice and freedom for all individuals. People across the globe expect constant improvement in conditions year after year. We will seek out new philosophies and economic theories to deliver progressively better solutions.

Which policies and legal structures will give us a stable, fair, and dynamic economy and a power structure that encourages upward mobility and meritocracy? How will the American experiment interact with the European experiment in democratic systems? How will established Western democracies interact with emerging democracies in the East and South? What new forms of democracy will India bring to the debate? How will China make the transition to democracy and in what form? These are some of the key questions for the next century of human progress. Though the process is likely to be messy, the ultimate outcome is generally clear: we are likely to have greater equity in 2100 than we do today.

Tracking Economic Quintiles

Trustworthy demographic and economic data for the whole planet needs to be available to everyone so that people can be reliably and truthfully informed about what is happening.

Measuring economic quintiles, fifths of the population, on both income and asset growth gives a fairly good picture of how people are doing over time under various administrations and policies. Quintiles represent approximately our general concepts of economic classes:

1. Upper
2. Upper middle
3. Middle

4. Lower middle
5. Lower

When everyone can see reliable figures for these general segments of the population, it becomes easier to tell what is, and is not, benefiting people in the most basic of ways—their pocketbooks. These kinds of public statistics provide an objective measure to keep political rhetoric focused on reality. That way, when a politician or pundit says that "the economy" is doing better, people can see clearly *whose* economy they are talking about.

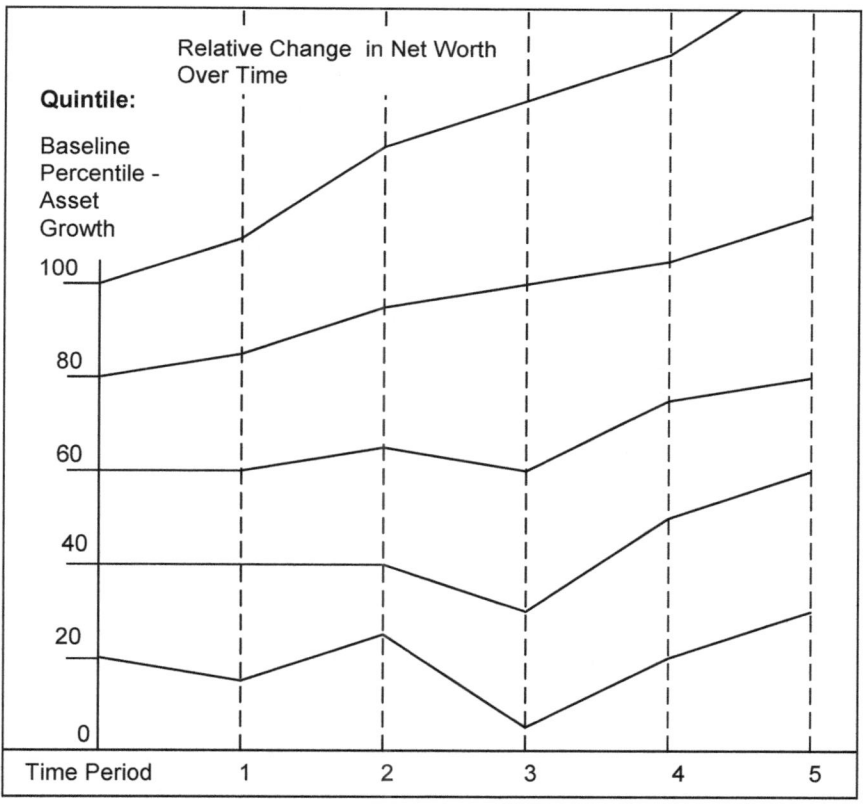

Figure 13. Tracking Economic Quintiles

To have a strong society, we need a dynamically stable pyramid that is progressively improving. The pyramid must be stable in the sense that extremes between top and bottom must even out over time rather than grow always greater. At some point, there must be balance, otherwise the pyramid stretches out like a thumb-tack and the society becomes unstable. Extreme gaps between top and bottom are socially brittle.

Figure 14 shows how the unstable "thumb-tack" model, which describes an economy with high wealth gaps between rich and poor, transforms into the stable pyramid model, an economy that all classes see as fair and equitable. The stable pyramid economy, is characterised by easy access to education and upward mobility for those who seek it.

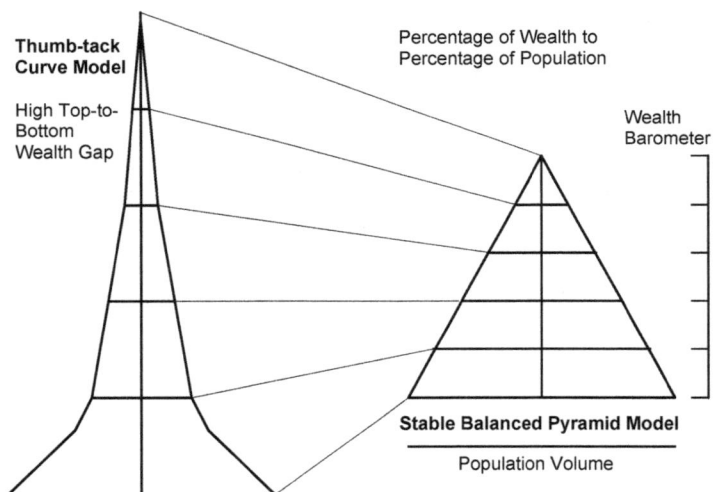

Figure 14. Economic Pyramid Models

The goal of economic policy must be to move the whole pyramid upward on a curve of economic progress that is equitable. The middle and lower classes must eventually catch up to maintain social unity.

Wealth Economics | 231

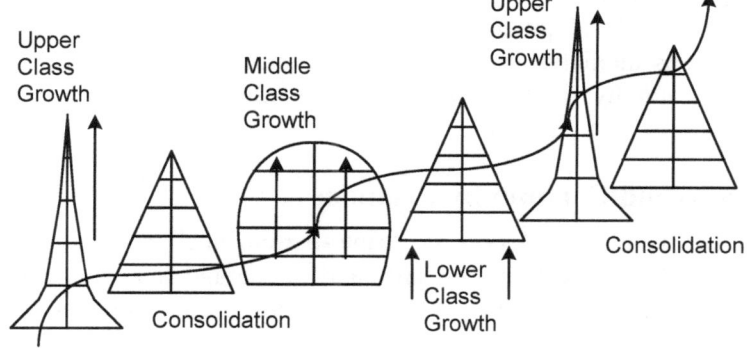

Figure 15. Step-Wise Model of Socioeconomic Growth

The system must be dynamic in providing maximum opportunity for internal mobility based on merit and effort. It is understood that societies inevitably will have hierarchies of wealth and power. The idea is to make them moderate, with the top not too high and the bottom not too low.

To make this work in a global economy, we will need to develop plans for progressively integrating national economies and making adjustments for various specific dislocations. The ultimate goal should be a fair and balanced economy throughout the planet, but achieving this will require a complex process of assimilation and adjustment.

It is unwise to allow free capital flows and jobs that move to the lowest-cost labor without providing adequate adjustments for those who lose jobs or, conversely, penalties that balance the playing field such that the jobs do not move offshore. Without some sort of balancing plan, all national societies are at the mercy of single-bottom-line capitalism (which has no mercy). This mercilessness is not necessarily the fault of individuals; it is systemic. The system must be changed to allow social virtues to express.

If free trade is globalized, especially in financial markets, political governance must also be globalized to provide a comprehensive oversight and regulatory function. Otherwise, vast accumulations of capital dictate to all nations what their social policies shall be on threat of capital flight and financial ruin.

The argument is that investors are only enforcing beneficial "fiscal discipline," but the effect is a complete subversion of democracy and brutal cutbacks in necessary social programs. While better accounting practices and reduction of corruption are indeed beneficial, when lenders dictate all social policy, that puts profit before people. We will invent better development approaches as a result of multistakeholder negotiations mediated by emerging civil-society institutions. A world of despotism by debt is simply unacceptable to moral, democratic peoples.

Business and Community Relations

The increasing prevalence of "triple-bottom-line" accounting may reduce global relocation of plants and encourage the emergence of universal labor relations. The triple-bottom-line concept means accounting for people, planet, and profits. Businesses that avoid addressing this concept will find that others have done it for them (not necessarily in the most favorable of ways) and posted the results on the web.

We can expect to see the further emergence of the triple-bottom-line stock market because investors increasingly care about business ethics, labor practices, and the environment. An evolving issue in this regard concerns how to account for human and environmental practices between businesses. There is a need to develop units of measure that will allow investors and communities to analyze and make comparisons in a balanced way. Fair and standardised measures will allow managers to make better decisions.

Chapter 9.
Wisdom Governance (W·G)

The general trend in governance is toward greater dispersions of power, that is, the continuing rise and extension of democracy. More nations are becoming democratic in nature, and those that are already democratic are becoming more so. This trend will continue to transform the nature of governance, despite occasional movements that appear to move in the opposite direction.

There are otherwise responsible adults who question the legitimacy of any government at all. Some hold the theory that "market factors" are sufficient to govern all social issues. Others believe that anarchy serves the public interest.

I suggest that both views are terribly wrong. The fact that people have different levels of wisdom, maturity, and capability provides the fundamental legitimacy of governance at the ethical level. This truth is not fundamentally altered by the fact that government usually has been exercised by persons who have seized authority through some form of power. Human beings are a social species and, as such, we have always needed leaders to coordinate our groupings.

Our history of leadership from tribal times onward has left a record of good and bad leadership that exists as a cultural sense within us, providing a conventional wisdom of how leaders should behave. Appealing to this cultural sense is what politics and political rhetoric is all about. Candidates want us to see them as having the qualities of a good leader.

The long-term future for governance will involve a progressive evolution of leadership wisdom aimed at balancing the various forces in the world such that everyone gains as much freedom and empowerment as possible without impinging negatively on others. Doing this will involve building, maintaining, and improving the sense of social contract for the common good. To function in planetary harmony, as we must and will learn to do, leaders will progressively evolve better ways of conveying to all people the sense that we owe something to the civilization we live in. Each person is responsible for living life in a way that serves the well-being of every other person. This has always been true and has been taught by every enlightened leader from the beginning. The ways in which we move through each stage of learning this truth will bring about a succession of transformations in governance.

Already we have built civil societies in larger and larger units, achieving progressively greater tolerance for internal diversity. What remains is to stabilize our system of governance for the whole planet so as to provide peace, freedom, and justice for all peoples.

Planetary Governance

Unregulated competition leads to anarchic social breakdown, which is felt most severely by the poor and disempowered but also by the privileged elite. No complex system is invulnerable to disruption, which can be accomplished with an increasing economy of means. The asymmetries favor the disruptors.

> **Emerging high tech + population explosion = anarchic war or world governance**

Empowered world governance that is constitutionally oriented toward attending to the needs of the whole is the only viable means of damping down the tendency of disaffected people to sabotage the system. Unless given reason to believe that preserving the system is in their interest, some people will continue to seek ever more effective means of disrupting it, even to their own detriment. Revolutionaries feel they have nothing to lose. Indeed, the negative impact of disruption on the powerless is seen as useful for recruitment. Therefore, if we want to avoid chaos, we must develop a governing power that is not beholden to elites or special interests from any side of the political and economic spectrum, a governance that will fairly serve the whole of humanity.

During the Transition, we are groping for ways to manifest a form of benevolent, meta-democratic control structure. This must be founded on constitutional principle, responsive to all parties, yet strong enough to take unpopular stands for the good of the whole. We must work to build a foundation of trust in such a governance structure so that we can accept granting it the kind of powers that emerging conditions require and that new technology will allow.

As we are already beginning to see, the attempt to form a world government around a financial power elite without recognizing the needs of the many will fail. Our social order can be disrupted with increasing ease as our civilization grows more complex. It is probable that, for awhile, we will continue to see periodic outbreaks of various kinds of rebellions, along with attempts to suppress them that are only partially successful. Eventually, this will lead to conditions under which a growing majority, including many among the current power elite, will demand a new authority that is less polarized.

At first, of course, this new, broad-based order will face the same problems as the oligarchic order and will require the power to restore a degree of stability. The difference is that the emerging holistic order will have better access to, and sensitivity for, the needs and views of the populations from whom the disrupters are coming. As these populations see their needs being attended to, they will show less tolerance for violence because they will have something to lose. Real reform, supported by communication and all the powers of supermodern global governance, will press this advantage, and we will begin to move into the new world for humanity.

Once fully underway, this holistic process will change everything within one generation. And within three generations after that, most problems we confront today will be well on their way to solution. Our present troubles will be history, and we will live in a radically altered world with a completely different set of problems. This shift probably will be realized between 2100 and 2200 CE, although it will begin in this century. In fact, the first moves in this direction are already underway, although not always visible.

What Planetary Governance Looks Like

The picture that is gradually forming shows a complex network of millions of small groups woven together by global communications media. McLuhan's "global village" is slowly emerging as the real location of governance. Some of the component groupings include:

- **Geographic Hierarchies**
    Township and precinct level
    County level
    State or province level
    National level
    Continental/civilizational groupings

- **Cultural / Linguistic / Religious Hierarchies**
    - Smallest to largest aggregates
    - Denominational groupings
    - Language and tribal groupings
- **Social Function / Professional Groupings**
    - By social function and subfunction
    - Industry organizations
    - Technology special-interest groups
    - Media groups and organizations
    - Business, finance, and trade groups
    - NGOs and civil society groups
- **Developmental Wave Groupings**
    - Special communication groups for each wave
    - Intermediate and transitional stages
    - Ombudsmen for noncommunicative populations
- **Issue-Specific Groupings**
    - NGOs focused on specific concerns
    - Outreach to special populations

Many of these structures and processes already exist to some degree. Although our immediate experience is often of heavy-handed, top-down authority, the future picture will include far more responsiveness to local needs.

We are in the process of reinventing government in a world of advanced electronic communications media. In the next few decades, the evolving governance software will be tracking issues and gathering views and opinions at both wider-ranging and much finer levels, and leaders will work harder to respond to what is revealed than they do now.

Kinds of Power and Social Functions

Every social function develops a power structure that organizes and purveys that function to society. The overall balance of power within a society tends to shift among social functions according to the conditions of the times and the needs of the society. Thus we can see that "power" has different flavors within different social functions. The raw power of force projection as purveyed by the military function is different from the quality of power purveyed by the political function, the religious function, and the media function. Each is different from the others, yet each has the ability to influence social direction in various ways. That is, we recognize that each function has what we call "power."

In addition to the above, we can list a few other social functions: legal, judicial, police, medical, scientific, technical, educational, financial, business, labor, diplomatic, trade, spiritual, entertainment, artistic, journalistic, communications, and so forth. Considering this list of functional labels, we also note that social functions are not neatly divided and separate; they overlap and blend. In practice, societies function as networks of individuals, organizations, and institutional structures that weave all of these functions together.

Any particular entity engages many functions at the same time. For example, a pharmaceutical company is a business that also impinges on the medical, scientific, and educational functions, and is impinged on by many other functions. Most large organizations are engaged with almost all of the social functions to some degree.

Just as profit migrates within a supply-chain value network, power migrates within the network of social functions. For example, during the Middle Ages the Church was a major repository of power; later, the national kingdoms seized back some of that power. With the rise of democracy, the nobility lost power to the bourgeoisie as political and economic functions gained importance. Science and technology, once of little account, rose to great heights with the industrial revolution, as did the power of banking and finance. Every social revolution has shifted power within the functional network.

Although periodically we may see disturbing concentrations of power during the Transition, the long-term trend is toward distribution of power. High-tech societies do not function well for very long without democracy. Creative innovation requires freedom and demands continuous redistribution of power. Social orders that resist this reality get chewed up by the laws of chaos theory to make way for new social forms that are better aligned with the processes of emergence.

The most successful social structures find the creative balance on the border between chaos and order that produces the most viable new forms. Neither anarchy nor dictatorship has much survival value in this emerging reality. Only democratic and empowered populations can produce the necessary creativity to compete in a complex world.

In the near future, every social structure, national or transnational, will be consciously searching for the optimal balance between order and chaos because it will be their key to survival. Social functions that are able to purvey freedom and empowerment tempered by civil stability and trust will become the centers of power. The specific institutions, organizations, and individuals within this network that best understand the direction of this irresistible trend will receive the privilege of guiding it. (The trend is irresistible because it generates effectiveness, wealth, and power.)

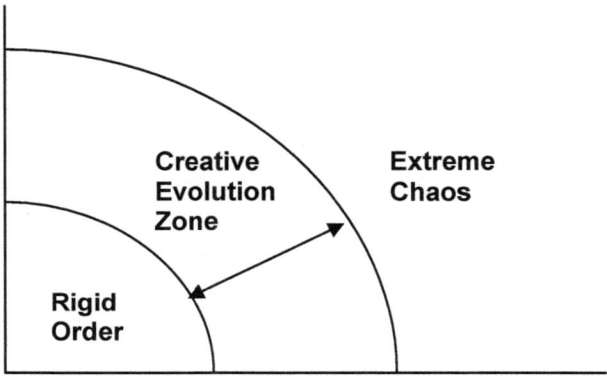

Figure 16. Complexity Theory and Creative Evolution

The basic forces driving these changes are emerging from deep within the human reality and can be redirected only in small ways. The situation is somewhat like being on a raft in a river; where the surface of the water is smooth, we can steer the raft freely, but once we enter the rapids, all we can do is avoid rocks and try to stay afloat. Until the next calm stretch is reached, the river determines the direction of travel.

We are now entering the rapids of a great transformative force. If we wish to be aligned with this force, we must work to align our individual lives, our organizations, and our social functions with two principles:

1. To be sources of empowerment for people and organizations (and to be tolerant of the creative disorder that comes along with this)

2. To nurture all forms of civic trust that provide sources of legitimate authority that reduce the need for harsher forms of policing

Eventually, organizations based on trust always defeat organizations based on force. Those who can provide civic trust and empowerment are well-aligned in the current of changing power balances. Those who resist this reality will see their structures crushed by continuing waves of change. The force that one day crushes a dictatorship becomes itself vulnerable the next day if it cannot serve the demands of the currents of change. This statement is not based on any partisan agenda. It is just the way things are at this time in human history. The human spirit wishes to be free, prosperous, and at peace. It wishes to flower. If we serve to help it grow, we are aligned with what is true. If we try to thwart it, we are standing before a tidal wave with a match stick.

Nonetheless, we must not ignore the law that every organism fights to stay alive and every old power structure resists change. It is foolish to imagine that transition happens without turbulence. Thus it is wise to be wary of the death struggle of old orders. Even a spring flood has eddies, cross currents, and rocks we must avoid.

At present, capital finance is one of the main power centers in the global social network. If those who manage the financial processes of global wealth want to continue to enjoy the privilege of being guides of change, they will need to considerably revise "free-market" capitalism to make it more empowering of more people. In fact, such revisions are already underway, but whether this function can change quickly enough to align with the emerging reality remains to be seen.

The highest likelihood is that most current organizations and institutions will be crushed in the transitional turbulence of "creative destruction." Nevertheless, society will continue to need some sort of financial management and power distribution processes. The winners will be those who can envision major change scenarios in advance and thus position themselves to serve the processes of change rather than resist them.

Population and Extended Life Spans

As biomedical nanotechnology improves our health, we will experience longer, more productive life spans. We also will see extension of the fertility period, giving people the ability to have children later in life.

Population size is a factor we will need to monitor and learn to manage, although the best ways of doing that remain to be discovered. Current estimates expect population growth to level out at around nine or ten billion by the year 2050. We don't really know if the planet can sustain that many people. We may need to find ethical ways of shrinking the population at least for a time. The education of women appears to be one of the factors most correlated with reduced population growth.

Later, we may develop sufficient sustainable resources to support even more than ten billion. At this point, we simply don't know. It is crucial to gather accurate data and to conduct significant and reliable studies to get a true picture of where we stand. To develop a fully rounded, nonpoliticized perspective, we will need to look at the question from multiple points of view and with multiple models.

A Thought Experiment
Consider the current range of fertility for most women, which is approximately from ages fifteen to fifty-five. If no women had children for forty years, the human species could become extinct.

This is highly unlikely, but it demonstrates that our vast and expanding population, while an enormous challenge today, is a mobile, four-dimensional value. It changes over time along several dimensions. Some countries, notably most of the developed world, are actually losing population. In others, the rate of growth is slowing. We will need to study in greater detail the combined effects of longer life span and negative population change on regional and global economies.

We will study and explore new ways of providing for varying needs throughout different stages of the new expanding life span. The situation probably will not become stable until we hit a new limit to how long people can live, if there is one, so we will need to continually readjust our concepts of how to best use these years.

Education and Full Employment

Work is a significant need for adults at all ages, for purposes of both income and meaning in life. An important task for the emerging global civilization will be to create meaningful jobs for all who want them. No one can deny that we have a lot of work to do. A defining characteristic of leadership is the ability to put people to work making things better. If you cannot direct human resources, you cannot lead.

Although business is the immediate source of job creation, wise government leadership is necessary to provide the conditions for economic growth. Business expansion and job growth depend on transportation infrastructure, international trade negotiations, interest rates, security, rule of law, and an educated workforce. And, as stock market fluctuations clearly attest, government leadership and policy directly impact the economy.

One area we can look to for jobs that will provide significant value to society is information gathering of many kinds. Human society will greatly benefit from seeing and understanding itself and its planet better. Many people can be usefully employed in gathering and maintaining detailed global census data. These jobs would also be nicely distributed globally; wherever there are people to survey, there will be jobs surveying them, as well as jobs analyzing and condensing the data. Another related job area will be gathering geophysical data, mapping and remapping every part of the globe in detail, and collecting shifting geological and biodiversity data.

In every field of study, it benefits human society to fund more research. Developing new knowledge will pay for itself in many ways, and each breakthrough discovery can fund new basic research, which will create foundations for further breakthroughs.

The most important enterprise for planetary civilization is to educate all of its members.

In an innovation economy, all value development ultimately stems from better educated people. Thus, teaching and learning will provide limitless jobs, and society will glean great value from *paying people to learn* as well as for teaching and other forms of knowledge sharing.

Once we recognize the essential value of the process as a whole, the only remaining part is the accounting system. Significant development is needed to work out the economic theory of paying for education and recouping value from it. Such an accounting system, and the theory behind it, are nontrivial development efforts. We will also need to work out transitional plans.

Just because an idea like paying people to learn is hard for some to accept does not mean that it is not real and necessary. We cannot fail to address the need for universal education and full employment globally. It is crucial to establishing trust in a powerful world governance system, without which we cannot survive. Retained wealth must be tied to job creation. Wealth that is put to use creating productive employment should be given tax advantages over wealth that is not put to such use.

Significant increases in education will provide enormous value in driving the emerging innovation economy. Universal education will spawn the new technologies, the new governance systems, and the new cultural creativity to make the Great Transformation a reality. Furthermore, these emergent systems and new technologies will create enormous demand for a more educated work force and will also produce the abundance to develop it.

A fountain of creativity will fuel cultural development. The rising global population will be thirsty consumers for thousands of new art forms, and this creative outflow will oil the gears of transformation by helping to sustain an optimistic mood.

We also will see a need for work in the area of global values development, which will involve gathering and synthesizing ideas and values from all cultures. This integration of all kinds of value systems will provide a necessary underpinning for the emerging global guidance principles on which planetary governance must be based. A considerable amount of work will be needed to synthesize ideas from religion, science, ethics, and law, ranging from data collection to theoretical development to practical applications in such areas as intercultural conflict resolution. However much it costs, developing global values will be much cheaper than war and will pay greater social dividends.

Authority, Legitimacy, and Wise Governance

To be given the authority to guide social units for the common good, leaders must win legitimacy. In a world of transformative communication technologies, leadership must promote vision that encompasses segments of society more comprehensive than the simple partisan majority that passes for democracy today. The true leader must holistically address all segments of society.

The free-for-all market vision that we have embraced in America in recent years will not cut it in the long term without significant modifications and transformations. The "market" of political and economic ideas will freely choose progressive changes because people are noticing that laissez-faire capitalism is not working very well. Monopolies and near monopolies always work to prevent any such thing as true freedom in the marketplace until the people (otherwise known as "the market") demand that government break up the monopolies. This process results in a roller coaster ride of boom and bust and a persistent sense of unfairness. The lack of fairness erodes unity within the social order and results first in market inefficiency and then in market vulnerability.

The theory of American democracy is that it has (as the free-market economy is supposed to) a built-in self-correction system in the form of periodic elections. If the public doesn't feel served, they can "throw the bums out" as it is often said. But three flaws in the theory are confronting us that will ultimately lead to needed change:

1. Gerrymandered districts tend to result in "safe seats" defended by powerful party machines that make it very hard to throw out incumbents.
2. Even more problematic, we often see newly elected representatives beholden to the same special interests as previous office holders. The cost of mounting an effective campaign tends to tilt the political voice toward moneyed interests.
3. Vote counting is still vulnerable to election rigging, thus voters lose trust in the system. There is a critical need for ironclad, auditable voting records and improved voting practices.

All around the world, we are struggling with a scarcity of good leadership, both in government and business. The leadership is potentially there, but various forces conspire to block good leaders and to corrupt those who do make it into positions of authority.

What we will see emerging from this condition, and the frustrations of the populace with it, will be a continuous stream of new ideas for transformation. Many of these ideas will fail, but some will succeed and cumulatively bring about transformation.

We are seeing advances in leadership training and more venues for practice. We are also seeing new ideas of leadership process and organizational structure. When any social function, government, business, healthcare system, law, and so forth, fails to evolve with the changing times, new solutions percolate up from the societal matrix to transform that function.

Technological Species and Social Loyalty

The cetaceans (dolphins and whales) are an adaptive species. They solved their problems and survived by becoming supremely well-adapted to their environments. Humans, on the other hand, are a technological species. We solve our problems by extending our capabilities through tool usage rather than through evolution of our bodies. This significant evolutionary distinction has far-reaching consequences.

From the moment we began to make and use primitive stone tools, our evolutionary destiny was set. The advantages of tool usage almost guarantees a technological evolution leading to a culture of continuously emerging high technology, such as we have today. Emerging technology implies certain metaprinciples:

- More and more power comes into the hands of individuals.
- Society relies on ever more complex systems.
- The finite spherical environment of the planet eventually becomes filled, ensuring intercultural engagement, trade, and conflict.

Therefore, emerging technology requires that we find ways to create more equitable and just social principles to engage the loyalty of all parts of society to the whole and to the systems that maintain it. If we do not, disaffected individuals will easily be able to use the power of technology to disrupt our systems of social order and peace.

Patriotism and loyalty must be won by offering a just global society that inspires devotion. Loyalty cannot be coerced, imposed, or enforced.

> **We have come to the point where we must win the loyalty of all individuals for the sake of the whole of humanity.**

The combined leadership of humanity must create a system where everyone feels proud to contribute fully to the well-being of the whole. Any leader today who is not working on this, who is pushing the narrow advantage of one small segment of humanity to the disregard of the rest, is not actually leading today. In truth, no part of humanity will be able to survive at the expense of the rest. It is now an all-or-nothing situation.

We can no longer afford to disregard even one unhappy, disaffected person. Although spiritual teachers have been warning us about this for millennia, the situation has crept up on us and caught us unawares. Now we are all living with a wake-up call. Now, one outcast person can destroy the whole system. Our systems have become so complex and interdependent that they are relatively easy to break, and no amount of fortification will be able to stop all attacks. Therefore, we must learn to truly love one another or none of us will survive.

We are an intelligent species with a strong survival instinct and a deeply embedded mammalian sense of compassion. Because we want to survive, we must and we will find ways to create a more just and integrated world society. We will be motivated to accomplish this magnificent goal because we can envision the immense joy that reaching a new planetary unity will bring. The carrot of our great potential and the stick of painful necessity will guide us to our destiny.

We will win the support of 99 percent of the world by building a social order of unprecedented justice and glory. And we will control the remaining 1 percent with unprecedented, penetrating social control. If (and only if) the 99 percent are devoted to the social order because of its universally-lauded fairness, we will tolerate the use of strong coercive means to keep the remaining 1 percent from destroying the edifice. We will not tolerate the use of these vast powers of social control for corrupt and selfish ends. Leaders who attempt such corrupt acts will be considered part of the 1 percent of criminals.

The Rights and Responsibilities of Elites

Some people have greater capacities in various areas than others. This is a natural fact of life. We have the commonly held metabelief that all people are equal before God and the law in terms of essential worth, yet we experience wide differences in individual ability and in the qualities people manifest.

This fact of qualitative inequality creates the various intersecting hierarchies in the social fabric. There are hierarchies of wealth and general social status, of intelligence, of cultural awareness, of strength, of speed, of skill in many arenas, and so forth. The top of these hierarchies constitute the elites. It does no good to say we should not have elites; they are simply a fact of reality.

The prevalent ethical attitude is that elites are responsible for helping and uplifting the rest of society. Whether we accept this ethic or not, society as a whole generally does expect leading individuals in any group to assume social responsibility. Perhaps this expectation is connected with an intuitive sense of the unity of the whole social fabric. We do not easily accept the idea of an elite that separates itself from the rest of society by not sharing some of its bounty with the rest. Where this separation exists, as it often does, we see junctures of social friction. The rejected majority reject the special elite in return.

So what are the rights of elites vis-à-vis their eliteness, their various special abilities, and their relationship to the not so well-endowed? It seems natural and right that all people should have the right and the freedom to develop their abilities to the fullest extent. At the same time, when different levels of ability encounter each other on a crowded planet, society places limits on using power to dominate others.

The Role of Wealth in Governance

Wealth and power are not synonymous. The current relationship between money and political power is based on a complex system of laws and social conventions. It has not always been so. In earlier times, kings with military power commanded wealthy merchants to do their bidding and taxed them or robbed them, more or less at will and without recourse.

All power is ultimately based on a social compact, an agreement among people to accept, or at least to tolerate, a particular arrangement. In the feudal structure, vassals gave taxes and military service to a lord in return for protection. There was an understanding based on ancient tribal law that the lord's power entailed certain duties toward his subjects. The eternal archetype of the good king has always implied a ruler who looks to the welfare of his subjects. When the people prosper and enjoy peace, a king is deemed to be good, and when not, not.

In earlier generations, wealth was understood to be a privilege that brought with it various duties toward society in the form of charity, public endowments, providing of employment, and payment of taxes to the government. But some now ask, "How can wealth be understood as a privilege when it is gained by the efforts of free individuals in a free society?"

In America, the idea has grown of the rugged individual who goes out into the virgin wilderness and carves himself an estate solely by the sweat of his brow. Is the wealth thereby created not entirely his own sacred property? How then does he owe anything to any other man (who presumptively could have done the same thing if he had had the gumption and strength of character)?

These ideas, however ingrained in the American mythos, could do with some examination. The underlying assumptions are that the individual is wholly independent of the rest of humanity and that personal property is wholly separable from the rest of creation. Both concepts are based on rather shaky ground, whether we consider them from the perspective of physics, ethics, religion, or social theory. The fact that they are currently supported by much of American law does not change the fact that they are beginning to come under fire throughout even the capitalist West. We should remember that, until it was amended, the American Constitution did not specifically prevent one person from owning another person as property.

The future trend regarding wealth and property will move away from these concepts of independent individuals and separable ownership of property. It will move toward the recognition of interdependence and the idea that all property is held in trust for the common good. This does not imply that an individual cannot own property and grow wealthy, only that in doing so he is building on a foundation of common social trust and, as such, owes something to the social fabric that sustains him. We are, after all "our brother's keepers," as he is ours in return. We all benefit from the social fabric, and we all have a duty to it. In time, we will come to paraphrase John Kennedy: "Ask not what *humanity* can do for you; ask what you can do for *humanity*."

The philosophy of the future will be that no property is truly "virgin wilderness" and thus separable. All of creation will be seen as part of the human trust. The battle over this issue will return with respect to the use of the oceans and the ocean floor, and again with regard to other planets and asteroids. In each case, the prevailing argument will be that every exploration emerges from, and is based upon, the common society's investment, first in the individual himself in the form of education and our common human lineage, and second in the means of that exploration. For example, no one would be able to explore the ocean floor without relying on centuries of common human learning and technological development, much of it paid for by tax dollars. Even more clearly, who can say that space is free for the taking when getting to the point where individuals and corporations could exploit it has cost so much public treasure, so many lives, and the brain power of millions of people?

In practice, space colonies may at times be independent of Earth, despite these arguments for unity, and they may offer a useful variety of environments for social and economic experiment. Nevertheless, the principle of unity and interdependence will always follow close behind the wild frontier. Civilization requires us to embrace the obligation to the common good, and we will come to see any other view as unenlightened.

The economic theory for planetary financial management will also have to evolve to account for this truth. In plain terms, no individual, no corporation, and no pool of capital operates in a vacuum. Wealth is built within a social matrix that includes infrastructure built by common tax dollars, an educated work force, and a common technical legacy. All private property rests on a public foundation.

It is also true that the wealth of the common economy is raised up by the efforts of individual entrepreneurs. The idea that a free market provides the necessary incentives for entrepreneurial effort, creativity, and capital support is not wrong. It has been shown that the incentives of the free market can produce a rising tide that is supposed to lift all boats. Nonetheless, the ideas and processes that define how this market works are constantly under revision.

Increasingly, the future of wealth will involve a more precise evaluation of fair value for services rendered and a marketplace that is freer and more competitive because it is more transparent and better regulated. Properly designed regulation does not stifle enterprise but, in fact, encourages it by curbing monopolistic restraints on free trade. It is desirable for society to encourage more enterprise and to support better business planning.

The failures seen in the dot-com boom and bust were not failures of the "new economy" as such, but rather failures of the financial function to practice due diligence. The rationale for a burgeoning economy based on high-tech productivity growth still exists. What is needed is better oversight and regulation of how financial services interact with both entrepreneurs and the investment community. Future trends will see a financial process that is more transparent and better analyzed for both entrepreneurs and investors. Electronic media may disintermediate financial services that do not provide sufficient "value added" to the network.

When we see wealth as a process involving large numbers of stakeholders, we begin to align ourselves with the future trend in wealth and management of asset growth. In the future, we will consider and address in greater detail and precision every part of the stakeholder community. We will be able to calculate the value of every part of the process with advanced software systems. We will compensate every contributor's knowledge and creative ideas more fairly, based on estimated value-added formulas, and therefore knowledge will flow naturally.

We will assess and balance more carefully the relationships between corporations and communities. Business excellence will flow from true expertise and not from finding an exploitive advantage or a trick to deceive investors for one more quarter. At the same time, executives will be able to count on more patient capital that is more committed to long-range plans. Achieving this depends on effective governance.

These changes will not fully show up until after the turbulence of the Transition, during which we will develop the conceptual and social infrastructure for a new way of doing business and managing capital. The sooner we achieve new economic theory that encompasses complexity theory and addresses inequities intelligently, the less we will suffer. The more we fail to develop these ideas and communicate them effectively throughout the community, the more we will need the stimulus of disasters to force us to look at what needs changing.

Power and Corruption

Where in the past power dominated wealth, today wealth buys power. Just because we have become all too familiar with this situation does not make it any less corrupt. When I say "corrupt," what I mean is undemocratic, corrupting of the agreed-upon social compact, and therefore destructive of civic trust. When a politician elected by a certain number of votes to do one thing gets coerced by a certain amount of campaign contributions to do another thing, we have rule by money, not by votes. This is plutocracy, not democracy.

When money is used to intimidate politicians, to distort issues, and to confuse the public through deceptive media campaigns, this is a form of corruption. The result is that economic power brushes the public welfare aside. The battles of the tobacco lobby, and their ultimate failure, are a case in point. This kind of manipulation of the political process creates its own adversary and eventually loses big.

Business and financial leaders who can see the future clearly will recognize that these kinds of practices are not in their long-term interest. They will align with future trends by lobbying publicly to control corruption and thereby will gain the public trust. Those who do not do so risk being swept away as public anger toward this thwarting of democratic values builds.

It is said, "Power corrupts and absolute power corrupts absolutely." This statement applies, however, only to power *over* people when no balancing values restrain it. Empowerment *of* people does not corrupt. Power within oneself does not corrupt. It is power over others that can corrupt when it is too great.

We must always seek a balance of power within the social space. Indeed, balance of power defines the social space and whether there is one or not. When power becomes stifling, the social space goes away and the people lose their voice. We become alienated when there is no free and open debate in which to explore and test our ideas, thoughts, and opinions.

Above all, there is a need for civil discourse in open public forums. This is how we learn what public opinion really is, and this is where we resolve the variety of differing opinions on the many issues that face us. The freedom to speak our ideas without fear of reprisal is what gives a society flexibility and adaptability, qualities especially important in times of great change.

Freedom of speech does not cause the kind of great change we are experiencing today. The changes come anyway. What freedom of expression provides is the social resilience and creativity to respond to change in a healthy way. Societies that restrict this freedom do so at their peril, for without it a society becomes brittle and eventually breaks under the pressure of change denied.

We need *freedom of listening* as well as freedom of speech. When channels for being heard are restricted, people are not able to gather the full sense of the public discourse. The more we can hear the full spectrum of issues and opinions, the better decisions we can make about where we are going as individuals, as organizations, and as a social whole. It is in the open forum that we discover the ideas and the leaders that can help us solve the various problems that arise as we adjust to change.

Emergence of Transformation Governance

Some of the concepts and processes required for transformation governance to emerge are outlined below:

Transition Planning
- Careful long-term study, analysis, and integration of governance forms
- Development, simulation, and testing of proposed new structures
- Establishment of universal and regional goal targets
- Development of time-phased implementation plans
- Implementation and monitoring of each phase
- Refinement of goals based on experience gained
- Use of System Development Life Cycle (SDLC) and Capability Maturity Model (CMM) tools for policy development

Planned Coordinated Diversity
- Maintenance of variety and experimentation within a universal framework
- Use of complexity theory to balance order and chaos
- Evolution of innovative solutions: a catalog of what works
- Governments as learning organizations
- Planned diversity as hedge against monoculture hazards

Rich Civil Society Networks
- Dense issue and interest-group matrix and high-connectivity networks
- Human science innovations integrated into public process
- More NGOs and associations for issue analysis, monitoring, and integration
- Planning and development of objective media standards and news reporting methods (for example, metablogs that consolidate commentary from the blogosphere)
- Incubation of social entrepreneurs as key sources of innovation

Holistic Governance Theory and Practice
- Dense, multisourced input weave from civil society and official matrix
- Computerized input analysis and decision support tools
- Scientifically developed, integral socioanalytic notational systems and terminology

- Precise policy monitoring survey systems, down to detailed local levels
- Mathematics of holistic logic applied to social governance issues
- Complexity integration flows: self-organizing structures
- Multivariate social metabolism gardening

The above concepts and processes will come together during the next few decades to establish a well-defined process for negotiating the emergence of planetary governance systems for all social functions, all developmental waves, and all cultural environments.

Means for Increasing Wise Governance

To move toward wise governance, we need to build effective means, and the first step is to develop concepts that challenge the status quo to reach for something better. Here are a few likely solutions.

Required Candidate Training
- For all three branches of government and civil service staff positions
- A period of simulated decision making for potential future office holders during which (in virtual government simulators) they shadow elected officials as they deal with real-world challenges
- Second-tier training in how to balance and integrate multistakeholder constituent views
- A scoring system with a passing grade required for candidacy

Full Public Funding of Campaigns
- Detailed candidate information provided by public media
- Standardized comparative record format and interview structure: all candidates answer the same basic questions
- No other advertising allowed in campaigns
- Standardized universal public debate formats

Full Public Funding of All Government Staff
- Standardized training requirement for staff positions
- Shielding of staff and officials from undue private influence

- Use of indirect lobbying to a special "issue evaluation" function, which communicates to staff and elected officials

Transparency of Most Government Decision Making
- Secret periods for internal preparation, negotiation, and planning
- Public airing of proposed plans and bills
- Visible legislative voting on bills and procedures: published summary of voting records that distills substance out of procedural maneuvering and rhetoric

Cleanly Structured Legislative Language
- Precise partitioning of issues for pork reduction
- Simplified legal language, with all content of a bill required to be cogent to the subject of the bill
- Standardized bill formatting using headings and imbedded summary documentation similar to that used for software code
- Computerized text analysis to ensure compliance with format and content standards and to reveal corrupt special-interest perks

Balance of Democracy and Wisdom in Governance
- More effective public information systems
- Reduction of private money influence and demagoguery
- Strengthening of a culture of social responsibility

As we grapple with these issues, management processes will emerge to provide the means for increasing the effectiveness of wise governance.

Mechanics of Governance Transformation

Transforming the way we carry out real planetary governance will require us to engage all social functions with effective transformation processes. Here are some of the practical mechanics.

Develop Detailed, Second-Tier Vision Plans
- Organize research and knowledge
- Use situation monitoring and scenario evaluation
- Analyze the Blue-Orange-Green impasse and resulting exhaustion impacts
- Engage in disaster recovery planning and preparedness

- Plan and develop negotiation methodology
- Establish a solid, detailed vision of what the Transformation society looks like at each phase

Train Second-Tier Leaders in All Social Functions
- Develop, define, and refine skill-set curriculum for Transformation Governance (TransGov)
- Define TransGov variables by social function
- Develop training methodologies: lines of development
- Apply superneural training tools to develop multi-Q

Establish Second-Tier Institutions and Networks
- Think tanks for research, theory, and planning
- Spiritual psychology schools and professional associations for training and connecting
- Networks and umbrella organizations
- Social entrepreneurship incubators
- Endowments and foundations for financial support

Create Innovative, Second-Tier Transformation Media
- New media awareness, innovation, and development
- Idea virus memetics: well-packaged content; vision congruence
- Websites, blogs, and webcast video
- Teleseminars via phone bridge and webinars; telepresence
- Print media: magazines, book publishing, databases
- Talk radio, audio recording, phone applications
- Movies, video, and television
- Software development, virtual reality/internet space

Build Transformation Power Base
- Cultivate and connect influentials and bridge builders
- Cultivate socially conscious entrepreneurs
- Develop intelligent, wave-mix appropriate communications
- Develop parallel systems for all social functions
- Capture best and brightest by demonstrating why second tier is worth attaining

- Highlight the many transformation roles available in all social functions that provide meaningful work for all

Ecological Social Gardening

Throughout the twenty-first century, a monumental research and development effort will identify governance processes that work for every social function and every level of development. We will be inventing the multidimensional social governance processes that will enable the founding of the Great Transformation system. We will study in detail every society on the planet and throughout history to determine the kinds of conditions most conducive to evolving consciousness. These researches will be integrated into refined models and simulations, then tested in many social environments around the world. This work will define the emerging discipline I call "social gardening."

Transformationism is a form of natural, ecological gardening of world society. It is not about imposing change by destroying the past, as has been the case with most first-tier futurisms. Like nature gardeners, social gardeners work gently with what is already growing, encouraging positive growth, discouraging what is negative, and creating an order that works. Transformationism is about integrating diversity into a higher context, not to homogenize culture, but to bring out the harmony.

This way is very different from Orange's imposition of Western secular culture. In the transformation way, which is well-aligned with the actual likely path, all cultures, including the West, find that they must adapt to one another. None will be able to successfully impose its culture on all the other civilizations of the world, nor would it be desirable to do so if it were possible.

In a well-guided social ecology, all life forms and human varieties have a place in the whole order and a natural evolutionary path. We will invent ways of effectively integrating high levels of freedom with necessary social order and security. People need peace as well as self-expression, and these needs must be balanced against each other.

Only an integration of the best of all societies can bring about a harmonious higher integration, and this can only be gently guided, negotiated, and evolved over time. Green is open to the multicultural perspective; Golden Olive learns to disidentify; Yellow can separate the wheat from the chaff; and Turquoise can present a fully integrated view of the social whole.

Conscious Governance

Second-Tier Transformation Policy

A new approach to governance and policy making will arise as Yellow-Turquoise leadership emerges. We will develop processes that are barely imaginable today—because we will need them and because second-tier consciousness will provide capabilities we haven't had before. The general situation in the early stages of the Great Transformation era (and the reason for it) will be a planetary network of second-tier leaders struggling to help a first-tier world to evolve.

The policies and programs developed will be far more multifaceted than anything we know today. Every major policy initiative will be supported by extremely detailed psycho-demographic data, and issue tracking processes will be based on input structures from all interest groups on the planet. Also, these efforts will be coordinated with processes that engage every social function.

Rich participatory cultural activities, music, movies, arts, and events will help to convey the benefits of a policy to the people it affects. Programs will be backed up by economic efforts, security efforts, and trained conflict resolution teams. All implementation efforts will include feedback processes and full participatory involvement, that is, they will be neither top-down nor bottom-up, but a synthesis of both. These major social gardening initiatives will be undertaken because they are preferable to war, terrorism, and social fragmentation. With a lot of struggle and some false starts, we will learn to make them work.

Suggestions that it is wimpy to psychoanalyze or understand terrorists are just plain stupid. The war on terror is fundamentally a psychological war by the very definition of terrorism. If your enemy understands you better than you understand him, you are in serious trouble. It is basic military wisdom to understand the adversary and the reasons for the conflict. Only by getting inside your opponent's decision cycle can you bring the conflict to a successful resolution and re-establish peace (assuming that is the objective).

Major program structures developed at the universal or international level will be "localized" to account for regional differences. At the same time, millions of locally developed programs will be integrated to guide global planning.

Second-Tier Policy Efforts for First-Tier Evolution
Policy efforts will have to address the issues of each wave of first-tier evolution, as follows:

1. Beige: Ending starvation, disease, and homelessness
The continued sufferings of Beige must finally be brought to an end in the twenty-first century. We can develop and implement policies to end war, starvation, disease, homelessness, and illiteracy. We have the capacity, and we will find the effort a source of healing and unification between nations and interest groups. Seeing the progress we make when we work together will give everyone great courage and faith for further planetary efforts. Ultimately, no adult person will have to struggle in the Beige wave. In the Great Transformation system, only infants and some of the very aged will represent this wave.

2. Purple: Cataloging and understanding tribal beliefs
We will need to more precisely catalog the tribal "genome" of the planet. Managing social transformation requires us to understand more exact models of intertribal dynamics in all social environments. This includes analyzing the underlying tribal dynamics within complex advanced societies as well as in societies that are more obviously influenced by Purple structures.

Though later waves generally overlay these structures, repressing them under larger categories of race, religion, and nationality, they are still present in all of us. Under pressure, communities can break down along tribal lines, even in environments that have long denied tribal roots.

The better we understand these foundations, the more effectively we will be able to develop conflict resolution strategies for all global hot spots and the more proactively we will be able to create harmonious communities. The more we understand that nations are aggregations of tribes, the better we will be able to develop coherent international policy.

3. Red processing: Purple-to-Red shift and Red regressions
This policy domain will explore ways for social groups to move through, process, and understand the learning offered by the Red wave without creating the social havoc usually associated with Red. This domain includes two sections: a) Red encountered for the first time as transition out of Purple, and b) regressions to Red from Blue, Orange, and Green waves.

Policies for the first section (a) must develop smoother ways of awakening egoic awareness out of the automatic groupthink of tribal superstition, while damping or redirecting the violence this shift usually evokes. The idea is to gain the lessons of self-empowerment without bloodshed and move smoothly through Red into positive Blue structures. For example, a disciplined (Blue) sports team can help young men channel Red anger away from gang violence and into vigorous competition.

Policies for the second section (b) must address the universal first-tier condition of unresolved Red issues that have been repressed psychologically. Red is about raw id-drive expression through the ego: sex, aggression, and ego dominance. Processing and integrating these drives and psychic structures into the mature personality is part of the transition to second tier. Yellow is able to express Red energy smoothly without violence or loss of awareness, which is what gives Yellow its characteristically fluid strength and aliveness.

Managing Red is like putting rocks around a campfire and keeping a bucket of water handy to quench any escaping flames. Using wisdom, we can have the value of fire without the danger, strength without violence.

4. New Blue: Promoting healthier universal forms of Blue

This policy domain will distill universal Blue principles and promote new forms of Blue that are resistant to the Blue tendency to focus aggression against out-groups. (Out-group aggression is one of Blue's methods for managing internal Red energies by redirecting them at the "other.")

The same rule-based, conventional thinking that is Blue's hallmark can be refocused on loyalty to all humanity. We will develop programs that curb nationalistic ethnocentrism and show the common beliefs shared by all religions. We will learn to celebrate unique cultural distinctions without turning these into causes for war. Transforming historical animosities and mythic enmities will require a great deal of healing work.

5. Orange: Regulation and culture balancing

Second-tier governance will restrain the self-centered, gaming quality of Orange organizations through regulation, accountability, change in organizational culture, and triple-bottom-line accounting systems. This will be particularly challenging when we have to restabilize the

Wisdom Governance | 259

multipolar environment as China and India emerge as major economic powers.

Yellow leadership vision can give Orange new reasons, based on self-interest, for going along with a more structured playing field. Second-tier leadership can strengthen the benefits of both trade and politics by creating a publicly transparent referee system to ensure that everyone plays by the rules and that the free-market process stays healthy.

Governance in this policy domain will soften the impact of Orange capital and Orange technology on rapidly emerging regions, such as the resource–rich nations of Africa. In the twenty-first century, there is no reason for African peoples not to be prosperous and healthy, since that continent is one of the richest on the planet in all natural resources.

In the realm of science, Orange rational materialism is already being leavened by Yellow complexity theory and repurposed by Green ecological sensitivity.

6. Green: Defragmentation and healing inspiration

As Green increasingly becomes a more dominant worldview on the planet, it will need to work with second-tier leadership to defragment the many diverse interest groups it attempts to serve. Green can attain true leadership only with the support of emerging Yellow and the Golden Olive awakening process.

The policy domain for Green healing will involve psychological investigation of repressed earlier waves: Beige, Purple, Red, Blue, and Orange. As the crown of first-tier personality development, Green includes all first-tier waves, but in a jumbled, undigested way. The Golden Olive process can help Green metabolize these elements and integrate them into a transforming personality.

Healthy Green learns to rise above postmodern absurdity and regain purpose by focusing on social transformation through self healing. The task for second-tier leadership will be to inspire Green with vision that does not reject Green's compassionate inclusiveness. Much of the healing of the later transition period will be carried out by Green and Golden Olive working together with second-tier Yellow and Turquoise to negotiate the path to the Great Transformation system.

Developing Second-Tier Consciousness

I have described how second-tier policies work to resolve the issues of each first-tier wave. One of the most important policy domains for the Great Transformation system will be finding ways to support every opportunity for second-tier consciousness to emerge. The continued well-being of our civilization will depend largely on awakening a growing percentage of the global population into second tier.

This process will engage educational efforts to awaken all lines of development into Golden Olive awareness. We will create curricula for cognitive, emotional, ethical, creative, and spiritual development. These will be supported by an increasing presence of Yellow integral ideas in the media and in the arts.

The entire Great Transformation system will be built on second-tier institutions in every social function. These structures are just beginning to emerge today, but we would do well to build them as quickly as possible. They will help us manage the Transition and recover from our first-tier struggles.

Civilizations and Nations

We are still operating in a world of nations and civilizations, but we would do well to realize that this way of looking at the world is undergoing transition. All of the divisive structures we have habitually used to categorize human groupings are socially created fictions. Nationality, language, religion, class, culture, and even race are ultimately habits of thought. These fabricated divisions are progressively breaking down under the pressure of changing life conditions.

The reality is that we are all human beings. What we have in common is far more important than the variations that separate us. As we become more conscious, these variations will be seen as enrichments rather than divisions. The sooner we embrace this truth, the better aligned we will be with what is emerging.

To see the world as a "clash of civilizations"[52] is to miss the far more interesting ways in which we are all becoming fascinated by other cultures. In all nations and regions of the world, the young and the cultured are exploring and adopting ways and styles from other parts of the world. Being cosmopolitan is clearly seen as more civilized than clinging to a narrow parochialism. This is one aspect of the movement toward Green and ultimately through Golden Olive to a more integral Yellow worldview.

---

[52] As in the title of Samuel Huntington's book, "The Clash of Civilizations," 1996. This is basically an old concept that does not accurately fit the emerging reality of planetary humanity.

Nevertheless, it is not always an easy transition. Different communities have developed distinct ways of communicating and cultural patterns that frequently are misinterpreted because we are not very well educated about each other.

What is seen as straightforwardness and honesty in Western, especially Anglo-Saxon, cultures may seem hasty, blunt, or rude in Oriental, Middle-Eastern, and South American cultures. The style of continuous renegotiation many Arabic cultures view as natural and flexible appears tricky and untrustworthy to some Westerners. In general, heavily Orange cultures tend to prize efficiency, while cultures operating more from Blue and Purple like to take their time building trusted relationships.

Beyond these generalities, we all would benefit from learning to look through subtler lenses. People, organizations, and nations are too complex to stereotype. The images that governments, media, and commercial representatives project are often very different from the realities people discover when they actually spend time in another culture. Everywhere, people want similar things for their lives. In all nations, there are people who are prejudiced and people who are more open. Although stereotypes reflect general cultural trends, the subtle variations in any society are more important than the generalities.

Everywhere there is a great need for better education about the wondrous complexity of the human family. We do ourselves a disservice when we lump people into divisive categories of race and religion. Even categories such as developmental waves or personality types can quickly become rigid barriers. If we start thinking, "This person or nation is Orange and that one is Green," for example, we have closed down the subtlety of our awareness. It would be more truthful and accurate to use such models to understand that the whole model is dynamically present everywhere, and that one or more points on the model may be more active in any given time and context.

Being aware and aligned with the emerging transformation means perceiving and supporting dynamic flexibility. Transformation is a death and a resurrection on both the individual and social levels.[53] As old conceptual and institutional structures confront challenges they are not equipped to meet, they begin to crumble and disintegrate. In an attempt to sustain their integrity, they react by becoming more rigid,

---

[53] Claudio Naranjo explores this potential for transformative rebirth in *The End of Patriarchy: and the Dawning of A Tri-une Society,* 1994

which makes them even less able to respond to challenges effectively and ultimately leads to a death struggle.

If we are identified with these old structures, as most of us are to some degree, we may feel that we ourselves are dying. But we always have the option of disidentifying. Human beings are not conceptual structures; in truth, we are free and living consciousness. The more we are open to change as a natural aspect of being alive, the more flexibly we can adapt to emerging realities. Only by embracing all of humanity can we be truly free or truly compassionate. When we identify with only one nation, race, or religion above all others, we are out of touch with the reality of human unity. The truth is that all nations, races, and religions must work together to build the new world of planetary unity.

I believe that this unity is coming inexorably out of the pressure of changing life conditions, but the rebirth does not come easily. We have lived for a long time with separative habit patterns. War and suspicion have always been negative patterns, but now high-tech weapons and cultural interpenetration have made them dysfunctional for our survival.

Although it may not be obvious because of resistance to change, such negative patterns are dying. We are no longer comfortable with killing and torture. These are still practiced, but every nation and society is becoming increasingly aware of their disintegrating effects.

As old patterns of separation, conflict, and domination begin to crumble, new patterns of unity, caring, and cooperation are emerging. The Transition is not really a struggle between the old patterns and the new. It is the period in which the old is struggling—and failing—to deal with realities beyond its capacities, while the new sprouts up in small crevices everywhere, inventing responses for which it is ideally suited.

The new patterns are simply better adapted to life conditions. While Green and Orange are often at odds, Yellow rises above the fray and integrates all the first-tier capabilities through the Golden Olive bridge. As Yellow rapidly moves toward Turquoise, it intuitively reaches out to help all the developmental waves to evolve and to live harmoniously as a unified whole.

On every continent, new powers are emerging and new waves are expanding. The rising economic powers of China and India will greatly change the global dynamic. Other nations will follow close behind them. South Africa and oil-rich Nigeria are emerging as centers of continental prosperity. As one of the richest sources of raw materials, we should expect Africa to prosper on its own terms in the coming century.

Though not all European nations may choose to join the European Union, continental cooperation and prosperity will continue and may eventually include Russia. Considering the long history of European warfare, this emerging cooperation is nothing short of a miracle.

In South America, Brazil is rapidly becoming a major regional power and other nations are emerging beside it. Despite fits and starts over the next few decades, North America will continue to integrate as Mexico continues to prosper. The Caribbean and Central America will also be progressively drawn into this regional process. The US will need to develop programs to soften the economic disruptions of cheap labor; the more effectively we do this, the quicker the region can integrate. As Central America prospers, the labor impact will subside.

Beyond continental integrations, global cooperation will continue to grow in spite of, and partly because of, periodic conflicts. The struggle to control terrorism, weapons smuggling, drugs, and crime will continue to stimulate increased international cooperation. As the US, Japan, and Europe adjust to the presence of China, India, and other emerging powers, new trade treaties and more widespread prosperity will flourish.

All of these positive developments will entail also a series of institutional breakdowns and the corresponding emergence of new processes. This will not result in Orange corporate globalism as we know it today. The coming decades will see a much more Green, Golden Olive, and Yellow orientation to planetary development.

This is the story of the twenty-first century. What is being put into place is a planetary culture for the purgation of our ancient divisions, the purification of the soul, and the healing of the nations. The completion of this process will be the work of the Great Transformation society over many generations.

Asia and the West

The old trilateral model of Japan, Europe, and the US is shifting to a multilateral model: China, India, Russia, Europe, Japan, and the US. China and India, together representing one third of the world's population, are rapidly emerging as economic power centers. The educated populations of these nations (and the extended Asian zone) have also been evolving rapidly through the Orange-wave rational materialist worldview.

Although they are studying and embracing Western ideas and methods, culturally there remains a long memory of Western colonial domination. These rising capitalists may have no reason to feel compunctions about returning the favor by seeking economic domination over the West. At the same time, China and India in particular are spurred on by competition with each other, and the whole East Asian zone in general follows along.

Meanwhile, European and American corporations compete with each other over access to the vast Asian markets they imagine they can dominate to serve their dreams of a new era of economic colonialism disguised as "globalization." They are also salivating over the huge savings obtained by exporting jobs to these low-wage regions. In their dream, the new global aristocracy represses the wage demands of "greedy" middle-class managers and workers in the West. In reality, they cut the foundations out of the Western economy while enriching Asia for their own short-term (and short-sighted) gain. If this situation continues for too long, Asian corporations will turn Western corporate CEOs into puppet governors that dominate the West just as the West once used Asian puppet governors to dominate colonial empires.

This scenario is too simplistic to fully represent reality, but at least it offers a slightly more complex model than the simple East versus West. We are conditioned by old-style bipolar concepts from the Cold War era. In the coming era, we need to realize that the struggle for democracy, economic fairness, and freedom is a multidimensional one in which our own leaders can become enemies of the very principles they proclaim to support. Sometimes this happens consciously out of greed and lust for power. More often, it happens unconsciously as a result of ignorance.

Today the West, and I will speak especially about the US, is stuck at an evolutionary impasse between three main worldviews—Blue, Orange, and Green (the BOG). Orange dominates, small percentages slowly seep toward Green, while Blue fights a fierce rearguard battle as it slowly wanes. The short-term effect of this frozen tension is to slow the development of consciousness into second-tier Yellow and Turquoise. The remedy is the emergence of Golden Olive transformation.

This situation roughly describes the social and political struggles in the United States for the last fifty years. But with the end of the Cold War and the rise of a more complex multidimensional world reality,

Blue conventional non-thinking, Orange reductionist thinking, and Green anti-Orange thinking just won't cut it.

The West cannot compete effectively with Asia Orange-to-Orange. Asian societies can field a variety of Dickensian state-private business models that we cannot match, and would not want to. To maintain our freedom and prosperity, we will need to evolve more quickly into second-tier thinking. Yellow and Turquoise holistic systems thinking can integrate the complex multidimensional solutions needed in the US and throughout the world. To accomplish this shift, second-tier development needs to be properly organized and funded.

This means forging more transformationist think tanks, institutes, networks, and developmental schools. It means defining the problem/solution matrices, as I have begun to do in this book. And it means propagating an enormous cluster of new ideas throughout all media and in all cultural forms, books, magazines, music, art, radio, movies, TV, and internet. To survive as a culture and contribute effectively to the evolution of the world, we need to move the leading segments of our society into a new worldview.

It is wonderful and beneficial to see Asia evolving into Orange; from that base, these societies will continue to progress to Green and beyond. It is not wonderful to see Orange power brokers in the West sell out their own society to increase their own wealth and power. Western business and government has got to evolve to Yellow and Turquoise to keep the whole world developing up the spiral. The leadership of our society has got to define ways of restraining Orange greed and tempering Green rebelliousness. In a word, we need new and better vision.

A book like Vision 3000 is not the end of the story; it is only the beginning. We need a new transformationist theory of economics, a new theory of governance and politics, and a new cultural movement. In America, in Europe, and throughout the developed world, we need a brand-new philosophy that captures the imagination of the intelligentsia. The old socialist-capitalist bipolar thinking has gone beyond boring and begun to stink like old fish. The new transformationist, second-tier thinking takes effort because it really is NEW.

It will not be easy to develop creative and effective responses to the rising power and wealth of Asia (or to the willingness of CEOs to kowtow for a piece of the pie). This problem is coming at us faster than we are getting ready for it; consequently, we probably will suffer some losses before we wake up and find wise solutions. The first reactions are likely to be polarized, simplistic, and lacking in sufficient subtlety. Politicians will try to present simple ideas to the people and at first may calm our fears, but when these strategies don't work and corruptions are revealed (as they always are), people will feel confused and betrayed.

Today we are dealing with a complex "war on terrorism" primarily focused on radical jihadi fanaticism, but bigger things are working behind the surface. The TV network news media is failing to adequately inform people about the wider picture in the world. As long as America allows US-based multinational corporations to behave badly around the world, the entire rest of the world will perceive us, fairly or unfairly, as the hated colonial master. Europe will be able to use this perception of US power as a convenient shield to deflect their responsibility for colonial barbarities of the past onto America. The leading power is always the one that gets the credit or the blame.

The only way for the US to stem this situation—and engage the world as the light that we are—is to clearly define limits and responsibilities. We must hold corporations, intelligence services, and arms dealers to behaviors that do not tarnish American values. This is a hard problem to solve, but we need to get working on it. We will be the true guiding light of the world when we insist that all our institutions and representatives live up to a code of conduct that truly reflects the soul of America.

Until we resolve this problem with multidimensional solutions, we will continue to suffer. If we allow our society to remain divided, those who hate American leadership in the world will exploit our weaknesses and divisions. This is precisely the message of the prophets to the kings of Israel: If the house is divided by inequities within, it is vulnerable to attack from without. We need to become more socially congruent with our ideals.

What will the long-term relationship between the US and China be? Can we build cooperative processes to work together for the good of the world? Or will we allow militarists on both sides to steer us on a glide path toward war? We need to think about these things now, not just in specialist think tanks but as a society. The whole world needs to think about how to ensure peaceful cooperation between major powers and how to drive out into the open those forces in all nations that are still playing the domination-exploitation game.

China's population is over one billion today, one sixth of the total population of the planet. It has a large land mass crossed by many rivers and a network of thriving cities rapidly being connected by modern highways. For the last decade or so, China's economy has grown at approximately 10 percent per annum, unmatched by any developed nation. China's leaders have embraced a form of state-guided capitalism that gives them formidable powers of social engineering, and their booming economy gives the government a mandate to rule.

Mainland China is also supported by a vast network of prosperous Chinese merchant communities throughout Southeast Asia and around the world. As China moves away from communism, these expatriate communities are reconnecting and building business ties with the mainland. In sum, China is a major player on the world stage and steadily becoming more so. Do we have a well-thought out vision of our future with them? It appears, from some of the evidence we have, that they think long-term and very carefully.[54] Does America? Generally, the answer is No.

The US military certainly has explored all sorts of war games for battle over Taiwan or Central Asian oil fields. In industry, US arms manufacturers are certainly eager to develop as many weapons as possible for such possible conflicts. Meanwhile, other business sectors are exporting jobs to cheap Chinese labor markets, importing Chinese-made goods, and doing anything to try to get a slice of the Chinese market. There seems to be a perfect willingness in many business circles to sell the American middle class down the river without a second thought.

If business continues to export jobs and technology and government continues to run up deficits to support a massive military, what is going to happen to America over time? We had better start rethinking these trends and get a new vision, a vision that is conscious, wise, long-term, and win-win. Mercantilism backed by military force is not going to work in the real world as it is now emerging.

India, the other great giant with a population over a billion, is also growing economically, though not as fast as China. It seems likely the world will have to contend with rivalries, conflicts, and even possibly wars between these two giants. Bhutan and Nepal have had trouble with Maoist rebels. Myanmar is a seething mess of corruption, drug

---

[54] Laurence Brahm, *China as Number One*, 1996

lords, and wild-west style business gamblers from all over the region. On the other border, India is contending with Pakistan over Kashmir in a conflict involving terrorism, conventional forces, and nuclear threats.

At the same time, there is massive trade throughout the region between India, Indonesia, Malaysia, Thailand, Singapore, Australia, New Zealand, Taiwan, the Philippines, China, Japan, and Korea. This is a very complex multilateral region. Buddhism, Hinduism, and Islam intermingle with local cultures and rational secularism.

India is also strongly represented by Indian communities in East and South Africa where they form what Amy Chua, in *World on Fire*, calls a "market dominant minority" in tension with local populations. Wealthy Chinese populations also face the same problems of backlash from poorer native populations in many areas throughout Southeast Asia.

How will the governments of China and India respond to attacks on their countrymen as they grow stronger and more influential? How will regional populations respond to the growing power of these giants? And how will Europe and the US deal with these complex tensions? We need better vision.

Although US corporations are involved throughout these regions and the US State Department has a presence, our society as a whole is very poorly informed; the news media deals only with piecemeal conflict stories. We need to change our basic social mindset from thinking of these regions as backward areas to realizing that they may be calling the shots on many issues in the very near future. We need to educate our nation away from the unconscious arrogance of American exceptionalism and toward multicultural awareness. The US is exceptional but it must export its best vision, not its worst.

Today, ethnically European populations dominate four of the six habitable continents (Europe, North America, South America, and Australia), but Asia and Africa are emerging as powerful presences in the world. Indigenous populations are also demanding to be heard, particularly in places like South America, where non-Europeans are in the majority. This is not *The Death of the West,* as Pat Buchanan would have us believe, nor is it primarily a *Clash of Civilizations*, as Samuel Huntington would say; it is simply fair and just. It is long past time for all of the human family to sit together at the table as equals.

We will not respond well to the rising power of Asia, Africa, and South America, and especially the great powers of India and China, until we develop more second-tier leaders and promote second-tier visions of the world. Orange will always tend to see things in terms of exploitation and dominance. Green will tend to export a naïve political correctness and an unconscious arrogance, the very things it purports to be against. Blue will always have an undercurrent of ethnocentrism and racism. Only Yellow and Turquoise can cope effectively with the complexities of the emergent world reality and these waves can only emerge through the transformative process of Golden Olive.

Leadership and Vision

Leadership Roles

Current conditions are stimulating new leaders to emerge in all walks of life. Ordinary citizens working within their own professions and interest groups to invent positive transformations are gaining enormous empowerment. What I am calling "governance" is being created everywhere in all social functions and areas of life.

Certainly there is a great need for transformation leadership in developing new political vision, campaign methods, and processes for moving government forward. But "governance" is larger than "government." Every citizen of every nation needs to understand that governance extends well beyond the formal structures of state.

Many people are learning that they can have a direct positive effect on society by focusing on the issues that are important to them and working from where they already are. The turbulence of transitional times and the challenges of building a new global society are calling out for more leaders. All conscious individuals can empower themselves by developing leadership skills and by learning to align with the direction of transformation. This is what the emerging Golden Olive wave is all about.

Sharing leadership wisdom with others to develop more leaders is empowering. Training and developing leaders is an important role, because we are not likely to catch up to the need for conscious leadership any time soon. This is a growth industry.

Empowering Leadership

Second-tier leadership is about empowering others. Transformation leaders have the authority and dignity that comes naturally with competence, and it is appropriate that they express this authority firmly. But the nature of second-tier consciousness is such that the goal will never be to dominate others or to keep them down. True transformation leaders always work to raise others up, to empower them with wisdom, and to guide them toward becoming empowering leaders themselves.

Transformation occurs first within individuals, and then is manifested socially. We experience ourselves as individuals, not as societies, so transformation of society is carried forward by change within individual people and through their personal relationships with others. Transformation wisdom is passed through one-to-one relationships and stabilized through small groups of relationships. Transformationist ideas are powerful, but they really come alive when they are embodied. Transformationist leaders transmit the reality of transformation through their being.

Awakening transformationist leadership is a lifetime work, a multigenerational work, and a very difficult work, but it is the most satisfying work to which we can apply our life energy. If we want to be aligned to the wave of transformation that is our emerging future, we must commit ourselves to this work every day.

In the domain of political governance, transformationist leadership works to integrate all elements of society into the political decision-making process. The multistakeholder model is the core of transformation political philosophy: Society works best when the needs of all its parts are heard and addressed. Transformation leaders look to balance the flow of resources in ways that unfold all the petals of the flower harmoniously. The needs of both the powerful and the weak must be met. In fact, both are met most effectively through integrated solutions.

Transformation leaders are bridge builders, linking various functions and levels of planetary society to encourage communication and strengthen relationships. Yellow leaders tend to become influential because their integrating impulse reaches out toward many groups that would otherwise remain closed circles.[55]

They also make connections between leaders in different groups, and all these connections allow their ideas to spread rapidly. That is the definition of "bridge builder," someone who links leaders in different circles. This pattern is studied by network theorists and is described by the emerging field of memetics.[56]

---

[55] Ed Keller and Jon Berry, *The Influentials*, 2003.

[56] Many of these ideas were developed by network theorist Mark Granavetter (coincidentally my advisor when I was undergrad at Harvard). Seth Godin's,

Thus, people who are awakening to second-tier consciousness tend to become influential, and people who are influential because they belong to many varied groups tend to awaken to the integral view of life. This is one of many reasons that the transformation worldview is so powerfully emergent now. The conditions are ripe.

The complexity of today's social difficulties has intensified the demand for transformation leaders and bridge builders, who become more influential by their bridge building and thus spread their transformationist ideas to others, who in turn are empowered to become transformation leaders.

Reverses and difficulties only make people more reliant on strong leaders who can keep the vision burning bright and guide them through trying times. Transformation leaders build conflict resolution into systems even before conflict arises. Second-tier consciousness plans systemically and long-term (as well as short-term). It is natural for this worldview to work to reduce violence and increase harmony; doing so is the very nature of the integrative motivation.

Trans-Civilizational Transformation

When we examine the historical record, we see examples of advanced Orange- and Green-wave phenomena emerging out of predominantly Red-Blue environments well before the beginning of the first millennium of the common era. Examples include the rationalism of many classical Greek philosophers, the technological and organizational sophistication of early China, and the religious tolerance of Asoka's India in 262 BCE.

Although most of the major events of the last three thousand years seem to have occurred on the Red-Blue and Blue-Orange transitions, it is interesting how frequently we see multiple waves operating in the same environments. Partly, this is the bias of historical reportage. Things that stand out as different from the background attract more attention than the vast expanse of sameness.

Nevertheless, it is noticeable that the most developed societies tend to support the most evolved waves of consciousness and the most varied wave mixes. These societies are highly influential in their neighborhoods and hence most noticeable in history. Would we

---

Unleashing the Idea Virus, 2001, provides concrete marketing applications for these ideas.

remember much about Sparta were it not for the historians of neighboring Athens?

Historians, such as Arnold Toynbee, have developed cyclical models for the rise and fall of civilizations.[57] Some have asked whether we really progress or if progress is an illusion of rising civilizational stages, which are forgotten when a civilization falls.

Perhaps these cyclical models of civilization have some merit, but when we take the Spiral Dynamics/Transformation Model to the historical record as a whole, the trans-civilizational progression is obvious. Yes, civilizations rise and fall, but humanity as a whole evolves in a progressive way.

When we focus on times and places where higher attainments were crushed by civilizational decay, it is easy to support a pessimistic view. But when we look over the broad sweep of time, progress is equally obvious. By gross measures, humanity is very successful: more people live longer and more conscious lives; we know more; we have a broader moral scope; and we are more capable with each passing millennium.

In ancient times, civilizations rose and fell in relative isolation. Later, as civilizations came into greater contact with other civilizations, they rose and fell in an apparently competitive model. Now, all civilizations are intimately interdependent to a degree that all societies are increasingly sensitive to the advancing and declining of local societies anywhere on the planet. All societies change as a natural evolution and as a result of contact between societies. Though it is popular to divide the world, it is becoming harder to determine where one society or civilization begins and another leaves off.

The state of social civility fluctuates, but the long trend is toward greater civility, more tolerance of diversity, and more harmony. It is now not so much that some societies or civilizations die, as that all societies change and the whole planet is becoming one metacivilization, integrating all diversities.

What rises is the transformational worldview, and what falls is ethnocentrism. This may seem to favor advanced societies that are already diverse and integrated over more monocultural, traditional societies, but in reality, both will change. No one can successfully resist change. The nature of the times is to integrate and to transform.

---

[57] Arnold Toynbee, *A Study of History*, 1947

In the short term, it is natural that resistance arises within everyone, almost without exception. Some few may have attained a state completely free of ethnocentrism, but most have not. Though politicians everywhere make hay by pandering to fear and cultural bigotry, they do so at the peril of their own societies. The transformational view is empowering to both individuals and societies. Attempts at isolationism only weaken a society and increase the suffering of change.

That said, it is in everyone's interest to manage the Transition carefully. Not all change serves positive transformation. Particularly at this early stage, much of the change we are experiencing is actually anti-transformation turmoil. Mostly, political leadership around the world is not managing change wisely because the necessary level of leadership has not yet been developed. Leaders generally do the best they can with what they have to work with, in themselves, in their governments, and in their societies. Change takes time and inspiration. It is difficult and often painful.

That is why preparing transformation plans and developing second-tier leadership skills ahead of time is so important—so we can minimize the suffering that inevitably comes in times of great transition. Inertia does not serve us now. We are called to a cause greater than ourselves, and we must respond. Doing so is the one thing that can satisfy our souls.

PART III.
What We Do Now

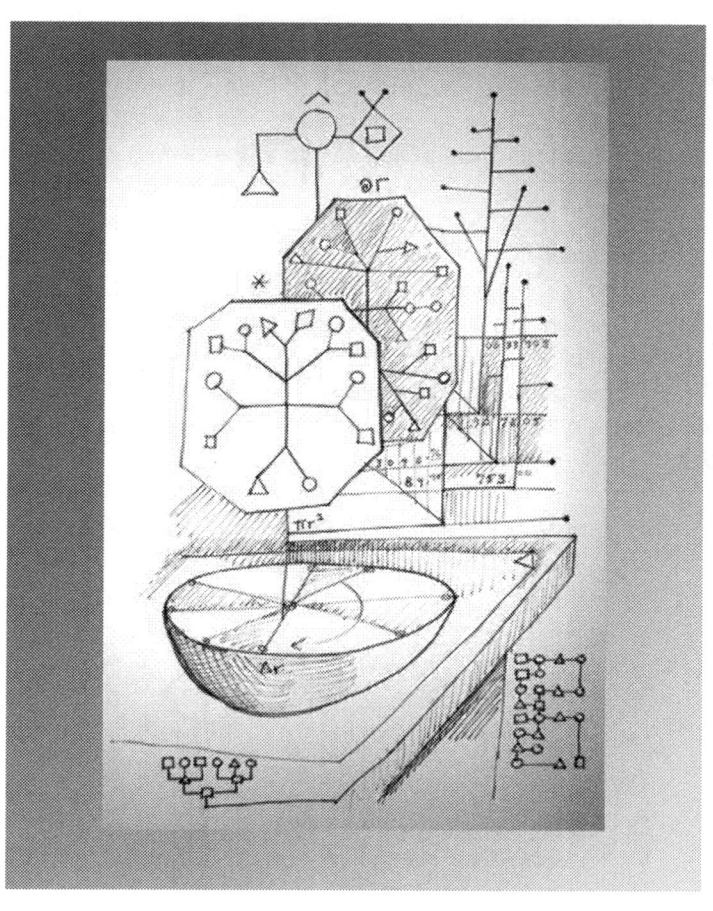

Introduction to Part III

The final three chapters integrate the social functions, the lines of development, and the waves of human evolution into the cohesive transformation vision as it applies to our present situation.

Chapter 10, The Transition, deals with how we get from where we are today to the Great Transformation society I have envisioned as emerging toward the end of this century.

Chapter 11, Individual Transformation, explores the practices and processes that are helping us to evolve, as individuals, into second-tier consciousness. It also describes the soul journeys that are the expression of that process.

Chapter 12, Social Transformation, presents the ways in which the vision is being made real within our societies, as well as the dynamically interactive elements of the transformation plan as it is unfolding.

The diagram in figure 17 below shows the Transformation Model in a form that integrates the three major dimensions described in this book: the waves of evolution, the lines of development, and the social functions. Together these form a cubic matrix that encompasses the major dimensions of human transformation.

The formula that summarizes this relationship is: ***Transformation*** equals ***Waves of evolution*** by ***Lines of development*** by ***Social functions***.

$$T = W_\varepsilon(L_\Delta)(S_\phi)$$

T = Transformation $\qquad W_\varepsilon$ = Wave evolutions
L_Δ = Lines of development $\quad S_\phi$ = Social functions

Σ = Third Tier: Spirit
Ψ = Second Tier: Soul (Psyche)
Π = First Tier: Personality

Introduction Part III | 277

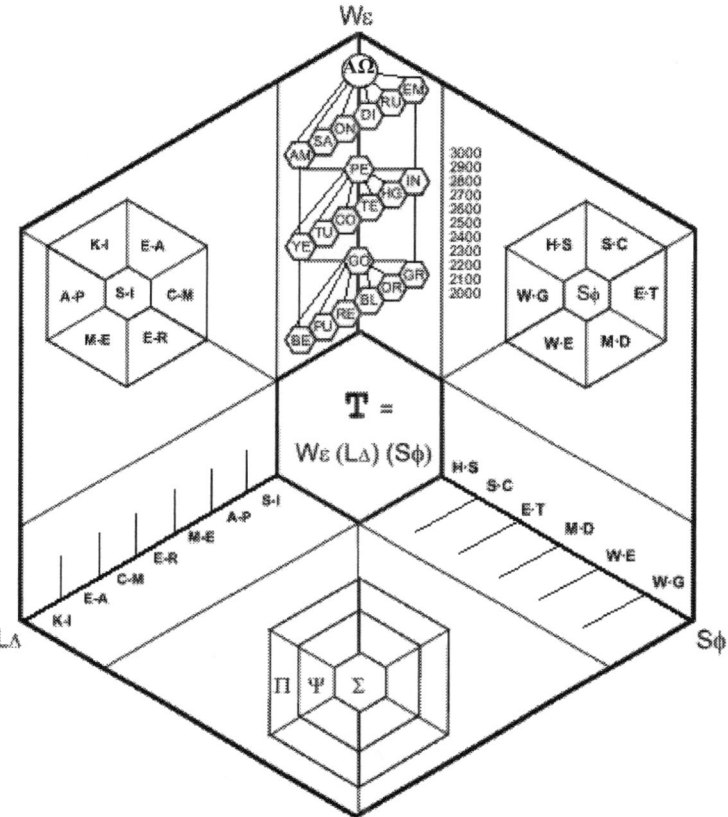

Figure 17. Integrated Transformation Model

L_Δ		S_ϕ	
K-I	Kinesthetic - Instinctive	**H•S**	Human Science
E-A	Emotional - Affective	**S•C**	Spiritual Culture
C-M	Cognitive - Mental	**E•T**	Emerging Technology
E-R	Empathic - Relational	**M•D**	Media Development
M-E	Moral - Ethical	**W•E**	Wealth Economics
A-P	Aesthetic - Perceptual	**W•G**	Wisdom Governance
S-I	Spiritual - Intuitive		

Chapter 10.
The Transition

The great message for our time is to have faith in life. So much spiritual energy is available today. Despite the many challenges to our sense of stability, the current of awakening continues and grows. Sometimes the turbulence of change may obscure that goodness from our view, but it is still there. There is a wondrous future worth building and a wondrous present worth living.

It is important that we find the creativity and love to live our lives fully. This is a good time to be alive. The challenges of every day give us valuable opportunities to grow. The shocks of life, both small and large, can help us to break free of rusty old habits that have kept us stuck. We can learn to stop expecting life to stay the same and embrace our aliveness as a continuous adventure.

This chapter examines some of the shifts that are occurring now and in the near future to help us understand the unfolding that is going on in this time of the Transition.

From What – To What

The Transition is defined by what we are transitioning from and what we are transitioning to. We can describe the world before 1900 as largely "preglobal." It had not yet been connected by electronic media and remained divided into discrete nations, languages, races, and religions. The colonial system, though worldwide, was far from a truly global integration.

After 2100, the world will be integrated into a coordinated whole under what I call the Great Transformation system. The two-hundred-year period between 1900 and 2100 is the transition from the preglobal world to the Great Transformation world.

Characteristics of the preglobal world:

- Ethnocentric national culture and religion

- Conventional and preconventional consciousness (dominated by emergent rational materialism – Orange)
- Agrarian and industrial economies
- Divided colonialized regions
- Patriarchal dominance hierarchies
- Print media and mail (disconnected time and space)

Characteristics of the Great Transformation world:

- Polyethnic diversified universal culture
- Second-tier consciousness (development of all waves)
- Creative innovation, wisdom economy, and advanced subtle technologies
- Planetary governance system
- Spiritual ethics and human value networks
- Virtual reality internet (VR/I)
  (everywhere media – integrated time and space)

The shift from preglobal to Great Transformation is the most profound change in all of human history, and we are right in the middle of it.

The Wave-Mix Model

As we move toward the Great Transformation, we encounter a series of collisions between developmental waves. Different nations and segments of society are operating at different developmental levels, resulting in conflicts and failures of communication. At any given period, we can observe a particular mix of developmental waves within a nation or in the whole world. The dominant wave will be the one representing the largest percent of population and power. The other waves will be either receding or emerging as we evolve up the ladder under pressures from social and technological change.

To simplify this presentation of the overall model, I have focused on only the dominant wave and have grouped the populations of the world into three groups: advanced, developing, and lagging. There are no value judgments here, just recognition of facts. And, of course, there are individuals at all stages in all nations. The model is an abstract map to help us understand the territory.

We can describe where we are at present by stating the current wave mix on the planet: Orange, Blue, Red. As we move forward in time, we can estimate when one of the three population groups will become dominated by a new developmental wave, as shown in table 14 below.

By considering how the worldviews of these waves are likely to react, we can get an idea about how the future is likely to unfold. The resulting wave-mix model represents a condensed integration of a large number of complex variables. This is both its strength and its weakness. Despite the difficulties inherent in abstract models, any tool that helps us manage complexity has considerable value for providing "big-picture" understanding.

The Wave-Mix Model									
	Estimated Transition Scenario								
Estimated Transition Date	< 2000	2001	2010	2020	2030	2040	2055	2065	2075	2090
Advanced Populations	OR	OR	**GR**	GR	**GO**	GO	**YE**	YE	**TU**	TU
Developing Populations	BL	BL	**OR**	OR	OR	**GR**	GR	**GO**	GO	YE
Lagging Populations	PU	**RE**	RE	**BL**	BL	BL	**OR**	OR	OR	GR
Event Periods or Phases	Struggle		Exhaustion Recovery		Negotiation		Establishment			
Wave Symbols	BL = Blue RE = Red PU = Purple		GR = Green OR = Orange				TU = Turquoise YE = Yellow GO = Golden Olive			

Table 14. The Wave-Mix Model

Caveat

The dates in this idealized scenario are pure estimates. Even the exact order of transitions is an estimation: for example, the developing populations might go to Orange before the advanced nations stabilize in Green. Some populations at Blue may regress to Red under certain circumstances.

We can consider this model in terms of geographical regions, such as nations, or in terms of transnational populations. The time scale may be off by fifty or more years, plus or minus. Nonetheless, the overall pattern is more or less "built-in" as an expression of human development.

By 2075 (2125 at the latest), the advanced populations will have shifted their center of gravity to Yellow, and the developing populations will be going to Golden Olive. This will inaugurate the beginning of the Great Transformation system.

Another factor not represented here that may speed things up is the effect of waves that are emergent but not yet dominant, especially the second-tier waves.

Phases of the Transition

The descriptions of these phases are necessarily broad-brush and subject to any number of qualifications and exceptions. Nevertheless, they do give us a big picture of emerging events that can help us navigate the coming century.

This is a difficult time, and some of what is shown here is not pretty. Anything that can help us move more smoothly through our transition to a better world should be welcomed. I would rather be wrong about much of it, but trying to avoid challenging realities does not help.

The best navigators of this time will be those who can face actualities while holding firmly to clear and positive vision. We must not lose sight of where we are going as we confront the immediate obstacles in our path.

The Transition unfolds in a progression of phases:

1. **Struggle** (wars and psi-wars)
2. **Exhaustion** (collapse)
3. **Recovery** (healing)
4. **Negotiation** (moving forward)
5. **Establishment** (the new Great Transformation system)

These phases cycle and recur in various forms throughout much of this century and also vary at different places on the planet. Each decade may see a miniature version of all phases.

As you read these transitions, remember that no wave is inherently good or bad. Everything depends on context. Evolution is healthy and regression is unhealthy, but all waves are a necessary part of development.

The Struggle: Purple–Red Violence

The pressure of globalization, literacy, and electronic media on Purple societies triggers a shift into Red power gangs and a surge of violence. The parental authority of Purple society is disintegrated by the influx of outside forces, and teenagers—especially young men—look instead to war leaders to empower their lives.

This shift may bring ethnic genocide (as in Rwanda, Bosnia, and East Timor), gang wars in inner cities, suicide bombings (as in Israel-Palestine), or terrorism (as with Al Qaeda). This is a significant component of what is now happening in the tribal societies in Iraq, especially in the Sunni Triangle. The violence inherent in the Red urge for empire building is frustrated by the presence of more powerful Orange and Blue waves in the social environment. The violence is exacerbated by the powerful weapons of Orange technology in the hands of Red.

Stagnant Blue societies also tend to decay into the Red-Purple zone. As long as there are societies transiting these developmental waves, we will see violence and probably terrorism against the more powerful societies. As more of these Red-wave populations stabilize into Blue and Blue-Orange worldviews, this kind of violence will decrease. An example of such a shift is postcolonial Singapore, which used Blue discipline to stabilize into an Orange technological economy.

The developed world, particularly as it becomes more Green, tends to view Blue societies as authoritarian and undemocratic, but we ought to recognize them as stages of development and encourage the most positive aspects of Blue. Contrary to rhetoric and popular opinion, terrorism is not primarily a function of Blue Islamic fundamentalism, but of Red anti-colonial rebellion. The orientation of jihadists is not primarily obedience to Blue discipline, but rather expression of personal power against a disempowering social environment. Terrorism is actually contrary to the teachings of Islam.

The Struggle: Collapse of Blue in the US

The United States has long had a tradition of Blue populism in the form of the itinerant preacher, the revival meeting, and fundamentalist Christianity in general, but Blue has not held dominant political power since before the American Revolution. As the quintessential experiment of the Enlightenment and the first modern democracy, the United States has always been governed by an Orange power structure. The apparent rise of Blue conservatism in recent years has been primarily a rhetorical illusion to win votes for Orange candidates.

Other forces prompting a final bloom from the Blue wave in the US are millennial apocalyptic fears, reactions to transitional pressures, advancing reproductive technologies, and terrorist attacks. The main trend, though, is away from conventional political and religious power hierarchies. Church scandals and hypocrisies from Jim Baker and Jimmy Swaggart to the priest sex-abuse disasters have weakened the moral authority of Blue religious institutions.

Blue tends to react with anger at the loss of power and lashes out. Examples are vigilante attacks on abortion clinics, rising anti-Semitism, and comments by Pat Robertson that the 9-11 attacks were God's vengeance on New York. This reversion to Red may lead to more attacks of domestic terrorism like the Oklahoma City bombing and more militia groups in the hills, but these only further diminish the power of the Blue worldview. Although foreign terrorist attacks may cause a brief resurgence, the further we get from the millennium, the more Blue will fade in the US, especially as more enlightened forms of spirituality emerge and are integrated into the Christian mainstream.

The final chapter of the Blue wave will be played out in the third world, where it will serve as a stepping stone from tribalism to the modern world. The hazard here is the potential for Blue-on-Blue violence as Christianity, Islam, Hinduism, Confucianism, and various Blue nationalisms compete in different parts of the world.

People tend to cling to Blue conventions when they want certainty in an uncertain world. Unfortunately, the price of such certainty is ignoring every aspect of reality that conflicts with established conventions and acceptance of a rigid control hierarchy. Eventually the dynamism of change overwhelms the Blue model of reality. When the final defenses crumble, many people are likely to experience major psychological breakdown.

Religious people should be comforted that this shift will not mean the triumph of a secular society, but rather a renewed spirituality emerging from second-tier consciousness. The advanced edge of Blue culture (which has already gone through crypto-Orange and crypto-Green), will actually be part of this new, more tolerant and ecumenical spirituality.

We will see a new expression of Christianity emerge that embraces the commandment of Jesus to "love thy neighbor as thyself," and that rejects the moralistic critique of others in favor of looking to correct one's own faults instead. This new second-tier Christianity is already reaching out and embracing other religions and cultures.

Of course, Blue will continue to be a part of every individual's maturation cycle, even as it becomes less a factor in future social power.

The Struggle: Decline of Orange in the West

Orange has been dominant in the West for over three centuries and has defined the modern world. It has been astonishingly successful and has brought about enormous positive change as the author of democracy, modern science, and capitalist prosperity. Increasingly, however, it is being challenged by serious difficulties:

- Charges of economic unfairness and instability
- The spiritual aridity of materialism
- Charges of ethical failures made visible by corporate fraud scandals
- Negative ecological impacts of industrialization
- The failure of reductionist logic in the face of massive complexity
- Failures of Orange scientific theory
- Competition from emerging Orange in Asia

Under pressure, Orange tends toward mercantile exploitation, leaving it even more vulnerable to challenge from emerging Green. The severe threat of terrorist attacks is turning Orange government toward militarism and police state tactics, which, if prolonged, can lead to social atrophy and regression toward unhealthy forms of Blue nationalism.

These processes eventually lead to loss of power. America's militarism has already cost us much of our ethical stature in the world.

We need to fight terrorism in smarter ways or the US will become isolated and exhausted by ill-planned strategy.

On the positive side, there are several signs of healthy evolution toward Green. The development of environmental science shows an integration of rational analysis with ethical consideration for the whole biosphere. In the business world, concepts such as team building, executive coaching, personal development, business ethics, and cultural sensitivity training indicate an understanding that human factors affect the bottom line. Increasingly, successful corporations are paying attention to social responsibilities, albeit not to the extent their critics would have them do. The negative effects of globalization are fueling a backlash for which Orange short-term thinking is ill-prepared.

Orange will either evolve incrementally toward Green or regress and become too rigid to compete in an increasingly Green environment; or, more likely, a bit of both will occur. The healthiest trend for Orange at this time is the emergence of the synthesis I have called the Golden Olive, a combination of Orange and Green evolving toward Yellow.

Psi-War and the Exhaustion

Particularly in the United States, but also in other parts of the world, the collision of waves is creating an increasingly stressful psychological environment. The collision of Blue, Orange, and Green in the courts, in the media and in politics is escalating toward a condition I have reluctantly called "the psi-war," a drawn out social struggle with negative psychological effects.

Now, in some ways, we could say this has been the case for a long time. We could even argue that the US has been in a state of semipermanent revolution since its founding and has benefited from the continuous ferment and renewal. That said, some new factors in the emerging struggle are exacerbating the problem:

- This is the first time the power center in the US is shifting to a new wave (Orange to Green).
- More developmental waves are colliding now than ever before.
- Technology has made our society more complex and more vulnerable.
- The war on terror is putting a new kind of stress on our system.
- The threat of nuclear, chemical, and biological weapons introduces new kinds of fears and challenges.

- The power of more pervasive and compelling electronic media are engaging and manipulating us more intensely.
- The militarized economy pulls energy away from more sustainable development.
- Peak oil and its economic impacts raise new fears.
- Volatile global capital and offshoring of jobs shakes people's sense of security.

The central driver is nothing new: a struggle for power and money between three worldviews. Orange maintains power by directing attention away from itself and toward the drama of "conservative" (Blue) versus "liberal" (Green). Meanwhile, many complaints from both Blue and Green are actually complaints against Orange.

If instead of looking at the last fifty years as a story of two political parties, we look at it as a story of three waves, everything gets clearer. Blue was slowly giving way, Orange was more firmly in control after World War II, and Green was emerging, challenging Orange and slowly gaining ground. This is the normal developmental struggle of one emerging wave against another established wave. Then, in the 1980s, resurgent Orange supply-side business interests linked up with reactive Blue social conservatives. Green-Orange liberalism found itself fighting on two fronts.

In part, this has been a normal social reaction to Green's rapid advances throughout the 1960s and 70s: civil rights, the peace movement, women's rights, gay rights, environmentalism, cultural pluralism, alternative medicine, and so forth. To some extent, society is just catching its breath.

We should note that periodic alternations of political party in office has not stopped, or even appreciably slowed, the successful advance of the Green worldview. For example, many Green ideals, such as social pluralism and environmentalism, went mainstream during the Reagan administration, not due to government action but because American society was ready to accept these ideas.

Most individuals today are a mix of developmental waves, and many people who would self-identify as culturally Blue are considerably Greener in viewpoint than they were twenty years ago, even as many Greens have retreated somewhat toward Orange and Blue in the wake of 9-11.

Although business conservatives and the religious right don't have that much in common, the coalition has mostly held for the last few years. Orange corporate federalists in both parties have managed to gain enormous economic and political power by playing Blue and Green off against each other without giving much political ground to either.

The result has been the transfer of vast wealth into the hands of the few and significant deterioration of social cohesion. Blue and Green are both social waves, thus by neutralizing each other's social vision, the field has been left open to Orange individualism, which has no real social vision. Orange is oriented to material power and sees life as a contest in which the winner gets the spoils.

This brings us to the present. The psychological stresses and social divisions of this situation are already fairly severe, but several factors are likely to increase the heat:

- Green, as an emergent wave, continues to gather strength, and Blue, fighting a rearguard action, gets more desperate.
- New terror attacks are likely to result in increased loss of privacy and civil liberties, along with the intended increase in fear.
- New media technologies are becoming increasingly invasive: high-speed internet, remote video conferencing, location tracking, personal data collection, surveillance and sensor technologies, and so forth.
- All technologies, as they get more complex, become more vulnerable to malfunction, cyberattacks, and other forms of sabotage, further increasing stress.
- Foreign competition from China, India, and a long string of emerging economies is creating job and wage pressure throughout the developed world. (China and India will be subject to similar pressures as other economies rise behind them.)
- Orange business and political leaders, under pressure from all sides, are resorting to more extreme measures to produce desired results. Ethics are likely to become casualties of war as we slip further down the slope.
- Increased demand for scarce resources, especially oil, tends to lead to conflicts and wars.

These are some of the forces that are stirring a psychological civil war throughout the developed world over the next decade. Every leader who cares about people should think about these problems and look for ways to reduce the damage. Psi-war attacks people's sense of hope, their feeling of civic decency, and their sense of social unity.

This is what each wave could do to reduce tensions:

Blue: We should stop trying to legislate morality. It doesn't work and usually causes greater resistance, moving it in the opposite direction. We should realize we are all being tricked into taking a judging position to increase the power of a few, but God is the judge of each person's actions. Let us look to the beam in our own eye, before we point to the mote in our brother's.

Green: We should stop being so aggressive about public sexuality and more sensitive to the pain this causes even some supporters of Green values. Disregard for public decency may ultimately threaten private freedoms. Let us work for ecumenical peace making between Green spirituality and Blue religion. Remember that both Green and Blue seek social good and sometimes Blue is developmentally healthy; it is the only possible step forward for Red. It is not *always* necessary to deconstruct the ideas of other worldviews or to transgress all rules on principle.

Orange: We should stop allowing greed and expediency to destroy the principles of freedom and democracy. Understand that the power we gain from a free society entails responsibilities to the whole of that society, not just to our shareholders. Understand that it is not rational to harm the common good for short-term gain. Unethical behavior usually comes back to haunt us. We should use our power and economic leverage to support social harmony between all waves, not to divide and conquer. The divided house cannot stand, and we are living in it.

Although it is unlikely that the majority will do what they ought, the actions of even a few in these directions can reduce the severity of our domestic psi-war and speed recovery. The television news media, both broadcast and cable, has a particular responsibility in this regard.

This is a great test for our society. If our souls are not strong, we can slide down a slope to tremendous suffering. What might come is a thing we have not seen before, and I will not tell all I have visioned. Every good person should pray, in whatever way you know how, that we do not have to experience the worst of this possibility. It is not inevitable. A few people moving boldly to make peace can set a pattern that makes an enormous difference.

If you want to do something meaningful with your life, understand that this struggle between worldviews is the most important problem in the world today. Solve this and the rest comes along. Think deeply about it and do the right thing whenever possible.

Even if this struggle is mercifully brief and relatively mild, most of us will come out at the end of it emotionally, mentally, and spiritually exhausted. This is the time I have called "the Exhaustion." The Exhaustion will create a great need for healers and spiritually strong souls.

The Exhaustion

We can anticipate the nature of the kind of "future shock" experienced in the exhaustion phase by considering the range of stress factors:

- War: the largest stress for society and individuals
- Terrorism: biological, chemical, and nuclear threats
- Crime: murder, theft, rape, muggings, and intimidation
- Economic stress: money worries, basic needs unmet
- Media invasion: manipulation of emotions and perceptions
- Political polarization: struggles without clear winners
- Technology impacts: increasing in rate and intensity
- Religious conflict: belief system strife and coercion
- Family breakdowns: relationship stress
- Illness: physical and emotional
- Competitive struggle: at work, at school, and at home
- Learning curve: speed and volume of learning demand
- Addictions: drug, alcohol, food, sexual, and others
- High mobility: frequent travel and change of domicile
- Loss of job, profession, or industry
- Sexual abuse and sex-related disorientations

The Transition | 291

- Cults and psychological manipulations
- Loss of cultural foundations, identity, self-esteem
- Loss of trust in society, authorities, and community
- Loss of positive vision of the future

These and other factors can combine to produce widespread psychological exhaustion. As stress factors accumulate, the most vulnerable people in any social environment begin to break down. We have already become almost accustomed to this reality.

What intensifies the effect of high change in an environment of conflict is that these stresses can concentrate suddenly on normally strong people. When stress accumulations burn out the leaders that others rely on for support, the impact multiplies.

Conventional kinds of fortifications, such as accumulating money and power, cannot wall out many of these stress factors. The impact of exhaustion will easily penetrate most conventional defenses. For example, some kinds of impacts, such as technology and media, may actually concentrate on the wealthy and well-equipped. Another example is when religion betrays people's trust. The very thing they counted on to support them becomes the source of trauma. It is specifically the experience of having the defense we most counted on fall apart that leads to exhaustion and loss of will to struggle.

When many of these factors combine to affect large numbers of people, whole segments of society can regress to a generally Beige-like state. Recovery support will be most critical at this stage to prevent the exhaustion from becoming so entrenched that it becomes difficult to dislodge and scars a whole generation of people.

The Recovery and the Rise of Golden Olive

The exhaustion—which will be precipitated by the cultural psi-war, the terror war, wars over resources, and the cyberwar, along with the constant disruption of new technologies—will have a profound transformative impact. We will be too tired to accept phony solutions. This will help many people to evolve to higher levels and will cut through a lot of rigid habits.

Our search for recovery will be one more factor leading to Green becoming the dominant wave. The rise of emergent Golden Olive and Yellow also will tend to move development up the ladder. Yellow can support all developmental waves and, in particular, will help Orange to accept its loss of the dominant position, since Orange tends to see Yellow as a slightly more innovative form of itself.

Green has tended to prefer the role of social critic and has some ambivalence about being officially in charge. The emergence of Golden Olive will bring more decisiveness into the mix. Orange leaders, evolving through the Golden Olive bridge, will be comforted by the guidance of individualist Yellow. Green and Blue will be comforted by the emergence of social Turquoise.

Helping people recover from the exhaustion is a task for which the Golden Olive wave is ideally suited. For healthy Green (moving into Golden Olive), healing from the psychological trauma of the psi-war is natural work; for Yellow (emerging from Golden Olive), developing new metasystem solutions is natural work.

The transition to second-tier consciousness will have greatly strengthened Golden Olive psychologically. Having already undergone a thorough psychological processing in evolving to second tier, these people will be much less susceptible to the impact of the psi-war and the exhaustion. To some degree, they will be psychologically immune, or at least better protected.

The Negotiation: Yellow-Turquoise Emergence

As the recovery process continues, nations struggling with Red will gradually stabilize into Blue, and the terror war will dwindle. The developing nations, such as India and China, will begin to stabilize in Orange, enormously increasing world prosperity. Alternative energy development will reduce the pressure of demand for limited oil resources.

Europe and the United States will need the brilliance and creativity of Yellow to compete successfully with intense economic pressure from the vast Asian populations going to Orange, particularly the "Chinese Overseas" network throughout Southeast Asia.[58]

Yellow and Yellow-Turquoise will bring great new resources to dealing with planetary problems. A significant period of negotiation and discussion will begin the process of designing the structures of the Great Transformation system.

---

[58] The "Chinese Overseas" networks, in Vietnam, the Philippines, Thailand, Malaysia, Indonesia and other nations, are described by Amy Chua in *World on Fire*, 2003, and by Laurence Brahm, in *China as #1*, 1996.

The Transition | 293

We must understand that this is much more than a negotiation between nations and governments. It will be a multistakeholder negotiation involving civil society organizations, NGOs, financial structures, corporations, media organizations, and religions, as well as governments at all levels. To be effective, all social functions and all waves will need to be addressed.

It is important to appreciate that Yellow is the first wave that can see beyond its own worldview. Golden Olive is a process of learning to see beyond first-tier limitations. Blue does not want to see beyond its worldview. Orange and Green each believe that they see beyond, but they see everything through colored lenses without being aware of the lenses themselves. Of course, Yellow is also a lens, but Yellow actually does see its own lens and can put on any of the first-tier lenses as needed, which makes a very big difference.

Individuals who have gone through the difficult Golden Olive transformative process to get to Yellow have gained considerable self-knowledge. The Yellow wave is invariably successful at whatever it tries to do because of the many strengths, talents, and virtues it brings to the task, and because these capacities are strikingly more developed than those of any first-tier wave. Yellow is flexible, flowing, and joyous in its capacity to integrate. And this is exactly what it consciously and naturally works to achieve: integrating a new synthesis of all first-tier concepts, values, systems and institutions, wherever it finds them.

Yellow is an individualistic wave, so it seeks personal freedom from all the rigid structures of the first-tier world that are so disastrously colliding during the present transitional period. Yellow either cuts through the knots or rises above the fray, surfing the chaos. Its natural response to the craziness of the Transition is to use its talent to preserve the freedom to explore and achieve higher integrations.

These qualities have a tilling, cultivating, and loosening effect on the knotted social fabric. The success of Yellow at dealing with conflicts, rising above the exhaustion, and helping in the recovery make this worldview very attractive. Yellow's ability to see things from the perspective of other worldviews also tends to make it widely popular.

As Yellow emerges, it is less obviously visible than other waves because of its chameleon-like fluidity and also because first tier has a hard time grasping the idea that there really is such a thing as second-tier consciousness. First tier tends to perceive Yellow as olive—a little bit Orange and a little bit Green—but Yellow is more spiritually awakened than either of those waves, which appeals to the advanced elements in Blue culture.

Orange appreciates Yellow's individualistic effectiveness and intelligence but tends to find its solutions "too complex," because Yellow insists on considering all parts of the system. Yellow easily sees through Orange's tendency to game the system for unearned advantage and moves subtly to check it.

Green finds Yellow's individualistic orientation somewhat less than politically correct. Yellow also tends to shock Green because its deep psychological and spiritual integration cannot be so easily deconstructed as that of Orange. A major part of the later recovery period will be newly dominant Green trying to cope with emergent Golden Olive and Yellow while these waves deftly avoid Green backlash.

To see its program realized, Green needs to partner with Yellow. Eventually Green comes to an accommodation with Yellow because it must. Golden Olive is the transition stage to second tier, and Yellow is its guide.

The Establishment of the Great Transformation

As Yellow builds to critical mass as a result of extensive Golden Olive transformation, it will establish integration of first tier conceptually, culturally, and institutionally. The integration of the parts will make it more profoundly aware of the whole, and its leading edge will begin a quest for something more. This will herald the emergence of Yellow-Turquoise, supported by the already present advanced wave of Turquoise, which, although still small, will be quite potent. Turquoise is the first social wave of second tier. As such, it is deeply concerned with the whole of world society; thus, it is holistic, universal, and planetary.

This pair of emerging waves, Yellow and Turquoise, will build the planetary governance system leading to The Great Transformation. Turquoise, in particular, will convert "internationalism," which is a collection of national fragments, into a metanational planetary network that also incorporates civil society. Building on Yellow integration, Turquoise also will create a culture that is metacultural, as contrasted with the fragmented polycultural mix of Green.

The metaculture of Turquoise will be based on universal values. It will establish a universal, all-planet philosophy and institutional system that will reign in exploitive Orange globalism while facilitating trade. It will realize Green ecological values but will modify them with emerging new science. It will promote a higher form of spirituality that advanced Blues can appreciate and grow into.

This will bring about the founding of the Great Transformation system. The weary world will experience Turquoise as a wise and loving mother who actually achieves world peace, justice, and prosperity. Since Yellow will cooperate with Turquoise, as is expected in second-tier consciousness, no other wave structure will be able to compete.

Once founded, the Great Transformation will integrate the resources of the entire planet such that, within about one century of its establishment, there will no longer be advanced, developing, or lagging nations. People in all nations will be educated to move up the ladder of development as fast as they are individually able, and the more advanced individuals will help those who are still evolving.

Nations, as such, will gradually subside into the unfolding new world system. Today, sovereign nations are still necessary, but by that time they will be mostly historical memories and ceremonial structures. We must note clearly that the planetary governance system is not at all the same as a monolithic world government. It is pluralistic, democratic, respectful of all cultures, and the very opposite of authoritarian.

Conscious Transformation

What we can do now, as we find ourselves in the midst of the Transition era, is to consciously transform. The best way to cope with the furious flood of change is to grab the wheel and guide our own transformation as consciously as we are able. The purpose of this book is to increase consciousness of what is emerging so that we can better steer our lives.

Benefits of Awakening Soul Consciousness

To give some idea of what awakening second-tier consciousness is about, here are a few of the personal benefits of attaining it.

- **Knowledge of the True Self or Soul:** Greater awareness of being; presence in your body; knowing that your being is independent of any external identity or role; ability to disidentify with personality structures; knowing and living your essential nature

- **Freedom and Flexibility:** Ability to understand and move through the whole range of first-tier skills; having a wider ethical embrace (caring about all people, not just your own crowd); freedom from inner censorship and criticism; flow

- **Peace and Aliveness:** Relaxation of most neurotic complexes; contentment with life; ability to stay calm under stress; greater sensory perception; subtle sensory differentiation; increased sensory integration; feeling of great vitality, fullness, and joy

- **Authenticity and Presence:** Knowing your truth and being true to yourself; being real not fake; knowing what you love and what is most important to you; having a sense of solidity, substantiality, weight, and gravitas; being serious about life while not taking your ego personality so seriously; showing up for yourself every day

- **Integral Vision Logic:** Higher mental abilities; capacity to integrate large metasystems; precise subtle mind; clarity; freedom from many delusions; greater wisdom and awareness of higher principles; objectivity (seeing things as they are)

- **Soul Power:** Capacity to fully mobilize your resources; strength; courage; determination; will; persistence; greater power; unshakability; restraint and self-control (not acting out, even under provocation); greater maturity and responsibility; being connected to reality

These are some of the capacities that emerge as second-tier consciousness begins to unfold. To feel these things as a whole and integrated being is truly a new category of experience beyond the confines of personality and ego defense. To stabilize this state is to know the soul. This station of development is far more valuable than having even hundreds of peak experiences. A peak experience comes and goes, but its value lies in what is retained and integrated into daily life.

There are many levels and waves of second-tier consciousness, and egoic personality remains throughout this tier, but not as the unconscious prison it is in first tier. The egoic personality is not completely transcended until third tier.

Chapter 11.
Individual Transformation

Individual transformation is the core of all transformation. A societal shift from one wave of consciousness to another happens when many individuals make this shift within their own lives. At this stage in human history, the shift involves not just the next wave but a huge leap to a new tier of consciousness. This is truly the Great Transformation.

The transformation to second tier is a movement out of the constrictive shell of the false self, or ego personality, into the freedom of the true self, or awakening soul. It is difficult for first-tier awareness to grasp how great a leap this is or even that a second tier exists.

Although every great spiritual tradition speaks of profound transformation, few of us can tolerate truly believing that real freedom exists while we are still aware of being stuck in the cage of personality. Instead, we prefer to focus on the self-improvement project of constructing a better ego.

Most of us have had glimpses of soul awakening, but as soon as we fall back into the trance of the false self, we forget the reality of the experience and incorporate the memory into our ego structure. Perhaps we believe that we have already attained "enlightenment" or that we have been "born again" and therefore need no further work. In any case, we are sure that the experience marks us as very special people, just as we always expected.

Alternatively, we may deny the transformative character of such an experience by considering it just another mental construct. Or we may focus on the voice of our inner critic, which whispers that we are not worthy of such an awakening and too incapable to attain it anyway. How we respond to these glimpses of awakening varies according to the structure of our personality and the wave in which we are centered.

Mercifully, a few of us do come to understand that such a wondrous possibility exists and that we have not yet actualized it. This is the beginning of the transformative journey, often known as "the work." The dilemma we then face is that the ego is still involved in its perpetual self-improvement project and constantly tries to co-opt the work. We identify with the ego structures and think that they are what we really are. The process of relaxing these habitual structures requires enormous support, determined persistence, time, and effort. If we are called to this work, it must become the center of our lives. Only when we understand that there is no other purpose that could be meaningful for us will we have the necessary commitment to succeed in this journey.

Once we get a true taste of what this transformation can mean for us, there will be no turning back. No other goal or activity in life will draw us so forcefully. Although we will continue to get caught up in the mechanical turnings of our old lives, they will gradually lose their attraction.

At this stage, we must guard against self-loathing, because the false self, once seen clearly, can appear quite loathsome. Attacks from the psychic structure called the "superego," or inner critic, only keep us trapped in the old patterns. We must learn to observe ourselves with curiosity and compassion, even when we are in the midst of heart-wrenching emotions.

It is precisely because the trap of the false self is so complex and so emotionally difficult to observe that we need the help of a wise guide who has already made this journey and the support of other students who are journeying with us. It can be difficult to find our way to a school and a teacher that really suits us. Usually there is a long period of preparation during which we read, meditate, explore teachings, and work to get our lives into enough order that we can set out on the inner journey.

This chapter will describe some of the structures we will need to work through, realizations we can have, and tools we can use to support our journey. Although the journey itself requires more than reading and cognitive learning, getting a clear grasp of the nature of the problem will support the more experiential and emotional work of the transformative journey.

I am not attempting to explain the whole journey to full spiritual awakening, only to indicate that there is such a journey and that it is not separate from the whole story of human life. We have to learn about the human condition and the difference between the false self and the true self.

Maps of Transformation

Maps are helpful tools for any journey. Although our actual experience is always more complex and subtle than any map, model, or metaphor, these help us recognize where we are and guide us along the way.

Many spiritual and psychological traditions provide such maps. Here I will discuss just three:

1. The Enneagram of Personality
2. The Seven Levels of Wisdom of Bawa Muhaiyaddeen
3. The Transformation Model and the Soul Journeys

These maps describe objective realities that can be directly known and verified by any seeker tenacious enough to make the inner journey.

Some other maps include: the Christian stations of the cross as stages of inner initiation; the ten "ox-herding pictures" of Zen; the sephirot of the tree of life from Kabbalah; the Yogic chakra system; and the Sufi system of the lataif. Every teaching has developed maps to describe various aspects of the transformative journey.

Modern developmental psychology has also mapped the stages of ego development. All of these provide different perspectives on various parts of the journey of human maturation and liberation.

The Enneagram of Personality

The enneagram is a tool that can help us understand the specific ways our personality gets stuck, which is particularly useful in the transition to Golden Olive. The diagram in figure 18 shows how personality manifests according to nine distinct types or identities.

The basic teaching of the enneagram is that we all become fixated in one of these nine types, each of which is a deeply ingrained style of responding to life. Thus, instead of living freely and flexibly, we live under the habitual compulsions of our type.

Gaining a deep understanding of our type will make us more aware of, and less rigidly controlled by, these compulsions. This is a simplified description of the difference between living in first-tier personality consciousness and living in second-tier soul consciousness.

Figure 18. The Enneagram of Personality Identities[59]

Over the decades since psychologist Claudio Naranjo brought this enneagram teaching from Oscar Ichazo's Arica Center in Chile to the United States and other parts of the world, many researchers have worked with it. An enormous amount of psychological and spiritual knowledge has been incorporated into the tool and the methods of working with it, and the International Enneagram Association (IEA) celebrated its twelfth anniversary in 2006.

This tool has proven to be an extraordinary vehicle for bringing together advanced thinking in many fields—psychology, spirituality, business, and medicine, to name a few. The table below shows the passions, fixations, desires, and fears of each type, the virtues they transform into, and the holy ideas that guide them.

---

[59] Don Richard Riso and Russ Hudson, *Understanding the Enneagram*, 2000.

Individual Transformation | 301

Type	Personality			Soul	Spirit
	Passion / Fixation	Basic Desire to:	Basic Fear of:	Virtue	Holy Idea
1	Anger / Resentment	Have integrity	Being bad, corrupt, evil, or defective	Serenity	Holy Perfection
2	Pride / Flattery	Be loved	Being unworthy of being loved	Humility	Holy Will
3	Deceit / Vanity	Be valuable	Being worthless or without inherent value	Veracity	Holy Law
4	Envy / Melancholy	Be oneself	Being without identity or personal significance	Equanimity	Holy Origin
5	Avarice / Stinginess	Be competent	Being useless, incapable, or incompetent	Non-attachment	Holy Omniscience
6	Fear / Cowardice	Be secure	Being without support or guidance	Courage	Holy Faith
7	Gluttony / Planning	Be happy	Being deprived or trapped in pain	Sobriety	Holy Plan
8	Lust / Vengeance	Protect oneself	Being harmed or controlled by others	Innocence	Holy Truth
9	Sloth / Indolence	Be at peace	Loss of connection, fragmentation	Action	Holy Love

Table 15. Enneagram Transformations[60]

As we evolve to higher levels of development, the passions and fixations are progressively transformed into the virtues. While the personality pattern persists in fainter form, it has less and less hold on the movement of the soul. Since each individual's fixation is centered in only one type, there are at least nine distinct transformative pathways, each quite different from the others.

---

[60] Terms and concepts from Don Richard Riso and Russ Hudson, *Wisdom of the Enneagram*, 1999; Sandra Maitri, *The Spiritual Dimension of the Enneagram*, 2000; and A.H. Almaas, *Facets of Unity*, 1998.

Although our basic type doesn't change, the more we evolve, the more we become aware of the energies of all the types within us. We become less fixated in personality and more able to experience the full range of human capacity.

When the soul is awakened, it becomes consciously receptive to superlumination by the divine qualities and the holy ideas from the third tier.

Further explanations about the enneagram and its application to spiritual transformation is provided by many books on the subject, some of which are listed in the bibliography.

The Seven Levels of Consciousness

The revered Sufi Sage, Bawa Muhaiyaddeen, taught that seven levels of consciousness need to function together in the true human being:

1. Feeling
2. Awareness
3. Intellect
4. Evaluation (Judgment or Discernment)
5. Subtle Wisdom
6. Divine Analytical Wisdom
7. Divine Luminous Wisdom

The first three, Feeling, Awareness, and Intellect, allow us to be conscious of our present experience. The fourth, Evaluation, allows us to discern which of the many things presented to us by our experience are valuable for our journey.

As we awaken to higher consciousness, Subtle Wisdom begins to function as an intelligence that is much faster and finer than ordinary Intellect. Subtle Wisdom clears a space within us into which Divine Analytical Wisdom can descend to provide the guidance of profound explanation. This level of Wisdom can distinguish the finest speck of light within darkness and the finest speck of darkness within light. Finally, Divine Luminous Wisdom comes as the radiant face of God

Individual Transformation | 303

before which all darkness is dispelled.[61] Although each of the seven levels unfolds progressively, they must also function together.

Similarly, in the Transformation Model, all waves exist simultaneously, even as one wave is the center of emphasis, while others are either undeveloped or subordinated. In the enneagram of personality, there is a similar dynamic pattern in which all points are active to some degree while one point is the main center of focus.

In all of these models, the more awakened we become, the more elements of the model function as fully developed capabilities. We grow into wholeness.

The Golden Olive Journey to Soul

At a certain point in their lives, some people begin to question the validity of the postmodern condition and to look around for something more meaningful. The presence of Green means that they know too much to accept either material science or conventional religion as adequate answers.

The Golden Olive Journey is the movement out of first-tier egoic levels and into awakened soul consciousness. Although it is a journey between tiers, I group it as a second-tier wave because it is ruled by the quest for soul. Throughout most of this journey, people are still swayed by first-tier impulses, but they are ultimately ruled by the longing to awaken to second-tier. Golden Olive inevitably seeks guidance from teachers who have awakened to second tier.

The main third-tier spiritual influences come from Amethyst, Sapphire, and Onyx. The primary movement is upward as Golden Olive seeks to disentangle from lower waves and imbibe enough spiritual qualities to awaken and stabilize in Yellow.

Golden Olive must learn to stop identifying with the lack of structure and discipline that is so characteristic of postmodern Green. The path of awakening specifically requires us to embrace a structured set of practices and the guidance of a teacher. To be mature is to dedicate ourselves to discipleship. No one can *make* us do these practices; we have to choose the discipline voluntarily. Then the teacher can provide guidance and help us move through the various barriers that arise.

---

[61] These levels of consciousness are referenced in many of Bawa Muhaiyaddeen's books and tapes. They are described in *Zikr: The Remembrance of God*, 1975.

Green hates being told what to do because it arose as a reaction against the Orange and Blue power hierarchies. It interprets almost all rules and structures as inherently anti-liberation. Green is ego freedom. Since the ego has no point of reference beyond itself, the postmodern condition has a lost quality about it. Green society agrees with a vague "rule" that everyone should be "free" to do whatever they want as long as it doesn't negatively affect anyone else's freedom.

Golden Olive realizes that awakening to true freedom means doing the hard work to overcome automatic habits, robotic behaviors, and animal instincts. It increasingly understands that the journey requires a guide and a willingness to engage in disciplined effort.

A difficult lesson for Golden Olive is to refrain from intruding on their fellow students' processes. This involves learning to restrain the urge to give advice, to "share," and to seek consensus, which keeps us trapped in Green ambiguity. When we learn to keep silent and simply act as neutral witnesses, our focus gets redirected to observing our own reactions. We learn to mind our own business and thus we begin to progress.

When Golden Olive has learned to stabilize its practice in a mature way, many of the traps of first tier can be seen through. We learn not to act out negative emotions and to defend against the inner critic, which frees us to pursue serious self-inquiry. The more clearly we can see ourselves, the more we awaken to deeper realities.

As our journey rises out of the jungle of ego identifications, we clear the tree line and a bright new vista opens up. Now we can see for ourselves the nature of the journey. A new autonomy emerges and the light of Yellow dawns. Now we know from direct experience that we are soul, the clear and spacious awareness that is not identified with any particular form.

The Soul Journeys

The soul moves in a dynamic play of energies between third-tier illuminations and first-tier integrations. In the first true soul journey, Yellow receives gifts of spiritual awakening from Amethyst and Sapphire. In a parallel lower movement, Yellow investigates into the internal first-tier structures that are holding frozen energies left behind from childhood traumas. Some of this work has already been done in Golden Olive, but, in Yellow, it becomes a self-directed and conscious part of every moment.

There are no fixed sequences in this process, but at each wave a particular set of issues arises and specific integrations are achieved. For example, one noticeable step in the Yellow soul journey is the investigation of repressed Red energy and the recovery of lost strength. This journey begins as the first tinges of Yellow emerge in Golden Olive. The early stages, which are the most difficult, carry us over into second tier and gradually establish the full presence of Yellow.

Each of the stations of soul from Yellow to Pearl make a complete tour of the third-tier spiritual domains and of the first-tier psychic structures. This recurring journey through the upper and lower realms brings about a progressively more complete awakening and a deeper integration of being. The idea that the journey is repeated helps to explain how people can have similar spiritual experiences but at very different levels of maturity. It also offers a way of differentiating between many grades of spiritual realization.

To understand how these transformative journeys manifest in daily life, picture something like an electrical current flowing between the soul station and each of the waves of first tier and of third tier, as shown in figure 19 below. At any given moment, our dominant experience may emphasize one or another of these waves, as though we had received a pulse along the open circuit.

Golden Olive is the journey *to* soul. The process of awakening into Yellow and integrating its lessons is the first true journey *as* soul. The second journey repeats this process, but now we are experiencing the spiritual domains and the personality structures through the holistic awareness of Turquoise, and so on through each of the stations of second-tier consciousness.

Although our actual experience moves back and forth between first- and third-tier content, we can describe the process as a lower and an upper journey. The upper journey provides spiritual resources from third-tier spirit realms which are then applied in the process of resolving first-tier personality contractions. As first-tier barriers get resolved, we become more open to deeper spiritual influence. The upper and lower halves of each soul journey work together to support our transformation.

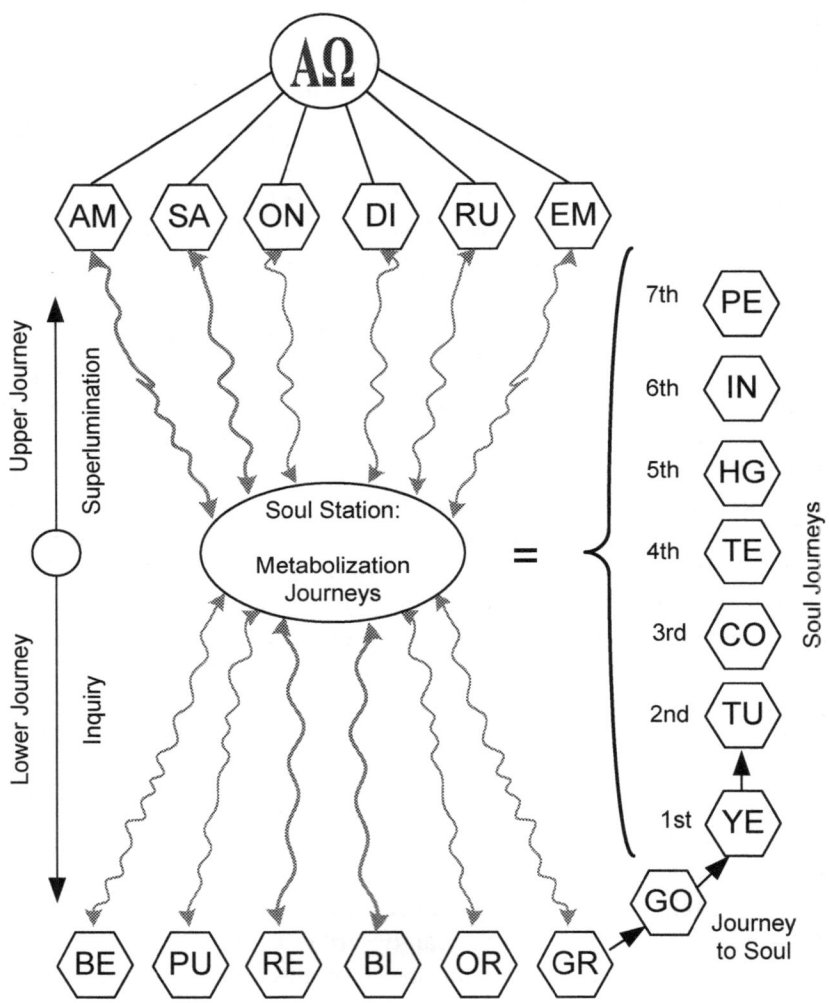

Figure 19. Journeys of the Soul

The Yellow Journey

The Yellow journey of integration encounters various issues and awakenings as it explores first-tier domains. The summary below provides a high-level overview of processes covered in depth in the writings of A.H. Almaas[62] and others. I have combined the structures

---

[62] A.H. Almaas, *The Inner Journey Home*, 2004.

Individual Transformation | 307

of Spiral Dynamics for the lower levels with the structures of other spiritual teachings for the upper levels, then mapped what I learned from Almaas, Bawa Muhaiyaddeen, and my own experiences onto the Transformation Model.

The Lower Yellow Journey

We must remember that earlier stages overlap developmentally and remain within us as we evolve, thus integration means going back and metabolizing material that remains undigested.

Beige The primal domain holds our most primitive inner structures, the deepest and earliest impressions laid down during infancy and even in prenatal experience. These may involve experiences of struggle for survival, hunger, feelings of abandonment, and also the positive experiences of pure contentment. These depths generally are not touched until late in the process of integration. By then, we have integrated experiences closer to the surface and gained the capacity to penetrate into deeply repressed feelings. Integrating these deep, primal structures gives the soul a fundamental connection with Being that heals the sense of alienation typical of first-tier egoic consciousness.

Purple The archaic domain corresponds to a slightly later stage when the infant has begun to achieve an integrated sense of mother, what developmental psychologists call "object constancy." The mother, or primary caregiver, represents the entire world at this stage, and the infant's identity is also merged as part of this world, which is sometimes called the "dual unit." The infant often feels blissful, merging love when it is fed and content. Also, every negative feeling that goes through the mother at this stage is absorbed by the baby as the state of its own world. Even with the most perfect mothering possible, we will inevitably hold various repressed experiences from this time.

For example, there is a psychic structure in which we experience ourselves as "the small empty one" in contrast to the breast, which is "the big full one."[63] Resolving issues from this level allow us to know our

---

[63] Alia Johnson, oral teachings at Emerald Mountain retreats.

true nature as love, connectedness, bliss, and fullness. We learn that love exists within us as our own true nature and that we do not need to get it from another person. We can also see that the relationship with the mother is the template for all relationships.

Until we have resolved this structure, we unconsciously expect everyone, male or female, to act like our mother. Mother is the prototype for all our concepts of other: Mother = Other becomes our false equation. Thus, in first-tier consciousness, our relationships all have underlying neuroses until they are metabolized by the soul journeys. When we learn that other does not equal mother, our relationships become free and natural. When we learn that mother does not equal the world, our reality becomes larger. This part of the soul journey teaches us that love and connectedness are not dependent on mother, or on any other, but are natural parts of our own being.

Red

The mythic domain corresponds to the developmental stage called "differentiation-individuation," during which the infant differentiates itself from its mother and begins to develop the sense of individual identity. The need for autonomy calls up enormous essential strength as the child learns to say No to mommy and Yes to its own emerging ego. This is the period known as the "terrible twos," during which the child is discovering its ability to do what it likes, to walk and talk, and to make an impact on the world.

In the process of becoming a self, we lose our sense of blissful connection with the world, which we mistakenly associate with mother. In the early phases of differentiation, we imagine ourselves as emperors with magical power over all things. We charge out into life until, sometime in the third year, we suddenly become overawed by the immensity of the world and seek to return to the condition of infancy in what is called the "rapprochement" phase.

Issues having to do with strength, repressed anger, and autonomy generally get trapped within the Red domain. As we resolve them, we are able to experience greater integration of these qualities.

Blue	The conventional domain is all about learning rules, beginning with the process of potty training, learning to feed ourselves, and learning to obey basic parental expectations. In the process, we absorb the concept of roles and authority figures. The father begins to play a greater role at this stage. We resolve the fear of the world expressed in the rapprochement phase in part by internalizing parental guidance in the psychic structure Freud called the "superego," which is a child's-eye view of parental authority and concepts of right and wrong. The nature of the superego is particularly visible when we see a child imitating the parent while bossing around a younger sibling. Unfortunately, this primitive program continues to function within adults as a vicious internal critic long after its usefulness has been outgrown. During the grade-school years, most children go through a deeply conformist period where conventional rules and roles are defined by peer pressure. Until we learn to defend against the superego, we will not be able to see ourselves clearly because this structure is directly involved in maintaining the walls of repression. The Blue developmental stage represses the feelings connected with Beige, Purple, and Red in order to keep parental love and approval. Spiritual growth depends on our ability to face primitive internal structures without beating ourselves up. We can grow only by devotion to the truth, which does indeed set us free. Unfortunately, many religious structures have gotten tangled up in this kind of superego repression of "bad" thoughts and thus have become barriers to real spiritual transformation.
Orange	The rational domain corresponds with the awakening of reason and expanding awareness of the wider world. Adolescents struggle to learn to "think for themselves." In the process, egoic reasoning processes transcend and repress aspects of the Blue rules and roles we learned from our parents. The child no longer sees father and mother as gods. Nevertheless, at this stage we remain vulnerable to all kinds of conditioning and programming from the environment. We are searching for our philosophy of life and trying on a variety of ideas to see if they fit.

We are also testing our capacity to influence the world around us through our mental abilities.

In reintegrating this stage, we may confront a range of issues associated with how confident we feel about our own intelligence and the early messages we received about this. Some of these messages may be connected to our family's position in society and whether or not our intelligence was supported. Resolving these issues gives us greater access to spiritual wisdom and the essential aspect Almaas calls "brilliancy."

Green The relativistic domain corresponds with the breakdown of confidence in reason initiated by the postmodern experience. The deluge of ideas, philosophies, images, and emotions that is the normal experience of most people in the contemporary world tends to overwhelm conventional rationality. As we attempt to make sense of the world, we are confronted with a steady stream of lies and hypocrisies.

The emerging young adult sees how rational leaders are actually driven by irrational drives. As Green consciousness struggles to deal with the cruelty and mechanical nature of modernity, it sees through attempts by Blue and Orange to repress primitive emotions.

At this stage, we reject both the conventional rules and roles of Blue and the mechanistic calculations of Orange. Green's embrace of primitive structures is actually a disorganized attempt to retrieve repressed psychic material from Beige, Purple, and Red, but because we do not yet have the conscious capacity to digest and integrate this material, the result tends to be fragmentation.

Green tries to repress/obsolesce rationalist alienation and conventional fanaticism, both of which cause pain to the postmodern soul, but this attempt is generally unsuccessful. We are disgusted and depressed by the spiritual vacuity of an arrogant science that reduces life and consciousness to a pile of rushing molecules. We are incensed by the smug intolerance of a judgmental and loveless religion that breaks all its own rules and by a patriotism that professes to advance freedom by military adventure and suppression of civil liberties.

At this stage, however, we are not able to put together a viable alternative. Green is not yet integrative because it has not yet grasped second-tier consciousness. It is disintegrative in nature. This is its strength and its purpose as the final phase of egoic development.

In the usual course of development today, people who reach Green consciousness often regress slightly as they get older and reabsorb parts of Orange and Blue from the social environment. They compromise in order to raise families and survive. But this mix of disparate worldviews, which is so widely prevalent today, leaves people feeling inauthentic, confused, and even sick.

The olive is not golden until it reaches the point of choosing to enter the olive press of spiritual search.

The Golden Olive journey involves the process of emerging from Green into Yellow. The Yellow journey later returns to reintegrate and resolve structures left over from the Green wave experience. As we do, all of these painful issues need to be investigated and digested.

The progressive integration of all these first-tier structures is the lower half of the journey that stabilizes us firmly in Yellow and begins our advance to holistic Turquoise.

The Upper Yellow Journey

Soul's journey to work through first-tier barriers occurs symbiotically with its experiences in the spiritual realms. These journeys are like experiencing Dante's *Inferno* and *Paradiso* at the same time.[64] The contact with spiritual energies often triggers personality-level issues and also provides resources for resolving them.

Availability of spiritual qualities further opens as personality barriers are resolved. These third-tier realms are vast, and whole libraries are insufficient to encompass them, thus the descriptions given here are necessarily simplified.

---

[64] Dante Aligheri, *The Paradiso, The Purgatorio, The Inferno*, first printed 1472.

Amethyst   The causal-angelic realm awakens awareness of living spiritual presence within us. The many planes of this dimension represent the domains where spiritual beings reside, angels as well as human beings, including the great teachers of humanity, sages, saints, and immortals. When we experience guidance from Jesus, Buddha, Muhammad, or any of the multitudes of divinely inspired holy beings, we are receiving illumination from the Amethyst realm.

Amethyst is also the domain of the seven heavens. As our understanding becomes even more awakened, we may experience this realm as the living presence of the Logos moving dynamically throughout the manifest universe as the one cause.

Sapphire   The causal-attribute realm awakens awareness of the divine qualities, essential aspects, and holy ideas. These are the experience of Divine Presence in the form of specific attributes or powers. Each power is like a vast universe, and the Sapphire domain encompasses thousands of these radiant qualities. They shine throughout the universe; without them there would be no manifestation. We can refer to them as names of God or aspects of Essence, but their reality infinitely transcends description.

Some of these names are: The Compassionate, The Merciful, The Beneficent, The Supreme, The Highest, The Praiseworthy, The Subtle, The Gracious, The Refined, The Vast, The Most Noble, The Generous, The Lord, The Forgiving, The Patient, The Holy, The Truth, The Powerful, The Capable, The King, The One, The Eternal, The Peace, The Living, The Wise, The Loving, The Pure, The Just, The Enricher, The Nourisher, The Omniscient, The Light, The Glorious, The Majestic, The Kind. These are some of the qualities taught by Bawa Muhaiyaddeen. The divine attributes are the original sources for human virtues. As our contact with this realm deepens, our ability to embody these qualities also increases. Virtue grows.

The Sapphire domain also can be viewed through the aspects of Essence described by Almaas: Strength, Will, Joy, Peace, Compassion, Presence, Merging Love, Brilliancy, Diamond Guidance, and others.

Many different systems from all the ancient traditions talk about qualities of Being or elements of Divine Presence. Descriptions of these realities vary, partly because they are translated from different languages and cultures, and partly because mystics and enlightened beings have a wide range of experiences and a wide range of degrees of skill in being able to describe what they know.

The Transformation Model merely indicates that a domain exists in which the Divine is experienced as attributes. When we experience even a small part of this domain, we understand that all conceptual systems are utterly inadequate; nevertheless, we need them to support our journey.

Onyx

The absolute-void realm awakens awareness of the ground of consciousness as emptiness or space. In this domain we encounter the Absolute directly, beyond all aspects of manifestation or causality. Here there is nothing to cause, just Being in its absolute nature. Nonetheless, a surprising amount has been written about the infinite nothingness at the foundation of ultimate reality.

Almaas describes six grades of space or emptiness:[65]

Grade of Emptiness:	**Dissolves Boundaries of:**
1. Clear Space	External self-image
2. Black Space	Internal self-image
3. Clear Dense Space	External body image
4. Black Dense Space	Internal body image
5. Annihilation Space	Experience of existence
6. The Void	Individual experience

Within this domain we might also place the encounter with nonconceptual reality, referred to as The Nameless or The Mystery.[66] In this encounter, we come to understand that all our ideas about life, self,

---

[65] A.H. Almaas, *The Void*, 1986.
[66] A.H. Almaas, *The Inner Journey Home*, 2004.

and even our ideas about God and ultimate reality are just concepts. When we encounter The Nameless dimension, awareness continues but the entire conceptual function of the mind is frozen out of consciousness. This is experienced as a cold freshness that liberates us from the mind.

Diamond The absolute-plenum realm awakens us to the absolute fullness of Being that is always present within the great stillness of nonbeing. This is encountered as gradations of light: a vibrant luminosity within the void, a deep sense of power, the pregnant potential to become, then an awareness of all Being exploding eternally out of nonbeing like fireworks. (Actually, there is no "nonbeing," only Being as formless emptiness and Being as fullness.)

As we go deeper into this domain, we meet an effulgence, and within that a more concentrated brilliancy, and within that a radiance. Each grade of light is more brilliant as we move inward; this brilliancy comes from the increasing density of pure Being, which contains everything in the smallest point within which is a smaller, more brilliant point. There is Grace containing Love containing Wisdom containing Light, and "within that light is God, and within God is Man, and within Man is God."[67] The power of this light overwhelms and dispels all darkness of separations and differences. Here, there is only One.

As Moses before the burning bush, we fall dead here. We can be revived only because we can never completely remember that overwhelming unity of Being. Though only God can know the absolute unity of Being, much liberation and transformation occurs in this encounter and in the domain of nearness.

The Diamond domain also brings clarity—seeing through all things. When all forms are known as light within emptiness, they are understood as the transient flow of universal life. We come to the omniscient clarity that everything is just a passing wave within one eternal being. Nothing is separate, and no form stays unchanged for even a nanosecond. We come to know

---

[67] Bawa Muhaiyaddeen, *The Divine Luminous Wisdom that Dispels the Darkness*, 1977.

that everything we thought was solid and substantial is illusory, a passing dream.

We may identify, for a time, with the detached universal witness, seeing all but unmoved by anything. The absolute realms, both Onyx and Diamond, can become a kind of peaceful trap, which is why some wise spiritual traditions teach about the awakening of nonduality. This is the journey to integrate the unborn, undieing Absolute with the relative manifest world of human relationships.

Ruby The relative nondual realm awakens the understanding that the Absolute is not separate from the relative self. In this realization, we return to the world of everyday manifest reality, but with the depth of experience that has come from our encounters with the Absolute. We are able to know ourselves as an ordinary, everyday person and as the presence of the Absolute, both at the same time.

The final stage in the Zen ox-herding pictures[68] is sometimes called "entering the marketplace with helping hands." The enlightened sage is shown as a casual fellow sharing wine with ordinary people while secretly guiding them in the direction of the great spiritual journey. In this stage, there is no trying; everything is just as it is. Yet, even with no effort to attain, many layers of awakening emerge spontaneously in this realm.

Emerald The universal nondual realm awakens the understanding that not only is the Absolute not separate from the relative self, it is not separate from the entire universe, and neither are we. Emerald is the domain of the fully mature, realized being, the true human being and the True Gnostic Guru described by Bawa Muhaiyaddeen. At this stage, performing any miracle is a trivial matter. All of creation obeys the completely actualized one in the station Bawa called "God-Man/Man-God."[69]

---

[68] Myokyo-ni, *Gentling the Bull: The Ten Bull Pictures*, 1988.

[69] Bawa Muhaiyaddeen talked about this state frequently in his recorded oral discourses and in many of his books, particularly, *The Divine Luminous Wisdom That Dispells the Darkness* , 1997.

	This station is not realized until the end of the final journey, but even in the early journeys we may experience rays of grace emanating from the Emerald realm.
Alpha & Omega	The ultimate reality simply is. There is only One here. There can never be two. Thus "we" never truly encounter this One, for the instant it is seen, all separateness dies. At best, we draw near, are annihilated, and then resurrected by the One Power that is behind all reality. Every other level depends on this One.

Though it may take many years, the Yellow soul journey integrates only a basic level of experience in the domains I have described. When the accumulated wisdom of the Yellow journey reaches a certain threshold, the soul's station begins to shift upward into the holistic Turquoise level, and the next journey begins. Essentially this is a repetition of the Yellow journey, but all things are seen from a higher vantage point.

The summary below outlines some of the distinctions between the stations of the soul, or waves of second tier, and how each station experiences its journey.

The Yellow integral station described above struggles to bring all the elements of its experience together. Its purpose is to integrate and stabilize its awakening as a soul. The fruit of the Yellow journey is the emergence of Turquoise consciousness.

The Turquoise Journey

The holistic station of the soul begins the second journey in which all first-tier waves and all third-tier realms are seen as parts of a continuous whole. Turquoise is wholesome, healing, and compassionate. As it experiences the various dimensions of the spiritual realms, it tends to view things through the prism of universal love and the characteristic thinking of holistic logic. All experiences and objects are understood as elements emerging from the whole. Its journey brings a deeper unification within the depths of the soul, leading to an awakening energy.

The Coral Journey

The station of zeal and fervor launches the third journey as the flame of a powerful new capacity energizes the soul. The being glows with vitality, and the soul stretches to find out what it can do. This journey through the spiritual realms draws on the qualities of divine power, strength, and precise discrimination. There is a fierce sharpness to the soul in this station. It wants to penetrate to the core of all experiences. Its action on the personality waves is to exhort with intensity, like a coach.

The soul drives forward and expands its range of experience to vastly greater depths until the zeal burns out. As the Coral journey comes to its threshold point, we experience a new "dark night of the soul." A sense of disorientation arises as the full magnitude of the reality we have encountered begins to touch the soul's core. The fruit of our great expansion is a longing for stability and logic.

The Teal Journey

The station of order and restraint opens the fourth journey as the soul's desire shifts toward wanting to make sense of its experience. The being now expresses a tone of sobriety. The Teal journey seeks a greater lawfulness in its actions and draws on its considerable spiritual capacities to bring discipline and structure into its life process.

The soul now works to settle, regulate, and embody the territory that has been so energetically explored. It begins to pay attention to those elements within the personality levels of first tier that are still not fully comfortable with the great advances that have been accomplished.

In this station, the soul restrains its prior drive and redirects its energy toward cultivating and stabilizing virtue and orderly life supports. Every part of the personality structure is regulated and scheduled.

From the spiritual realms, the soul draws in detailed wisdom, practical knowledge, and a deeper attitude of prudence. The Teal journey attains a kind of God-fearing stability and even a hum-drum placidity that eventually leads to a renewed longing for exploration.

The Honey Gold Journey

The station of fullness and experience stretches out into the fifth journey as the soul seeks to explore its inner capacities for variety. The personality levels are by now no longer reactive, and the soul experiences all feelings, thoughts, and sensations as curious and interesting.

It seeks joy, personalized uniqueness, and creative richness of experience. There is a desire to go over every part of the terrain of human potential and examine every possibility to discover its full range. The Honey Gold journey is the soul's attempt to know itself and all of its manifestations as fully as possible.

In its depths is a dark amber sadness that Almaas refers to as "objective sorrow." This is related to wanting to be true to one's authentic being and knowing that doing so may cause suffering to those we love. On a deeper level, the sorrow is related to not wanting to be separate from God, yet knowing that the death of the self means the loss of personal connections. This spiritual sorrow, laced with a deep and mature kind of love, leads to the next journey.

The Indigo Journey

The station of emptiness and longing unfolds into the sixth journey as the soul comes to recognize its essential poverty. It begins to understand that none of the spiritual qualities belongs to it; that none of the spiritual experiences it has been collecting belongs to it, either; and that it is impoverished by nature.

This sixth journey involves layer after layer of surrendering the experience of selfhood. Here is the first stage of the final death process, not only of the last residues of ego, but of the idea of a separate soul itself.

There can be a sense that the Absolute now pursues us,[70] that we are being drawn into a final dissolving, simultaneously resisting and longing to completely surrender. This process can seem like a game of tag or hide-and-seek between lovers.

When Indigo has brought the soul to a sufficient level of nonattachment and disidentification with the forms of the phenomenal world, the Pearl journey begins.

The Pearl Journey

The station of blending and weighing fulfills the seventh journey to prepare the soul for the life of pure spirit. There is a survey of all the soul has learned from every level of its experience. The surrender achieved in Indigo allows Pearl to judge its states with complete

---

[70] Bernadette Roberts, *The Path to No Self*, 1985.

objectivity and nonattachment. The dross is discarded and the purest colors are blended and refined into a pearly luster. The faculty of evaluation sorts and filters all that the soul has gathered from its experience in life. Subtle wisdom and divine analytical wisdom purify and refine the fruit of experience still further.

All is made ready for the approach of spirit, and the soul offers itself to God. This is what the alchemists referred to as the *coniunctio,* or heavenly marriage. In the end, the soul lets go of everything it has prepared, giving everything back to the divine source. The process of subtle judgment makes it aware that all its achievements belong only to the One. With this realization, the soul passes through the gates and dissolves into spirit. As Amethyst blooms, the final journey as spirit within spirit begins. This journey beyond soul will ultimately culminate in the full nondual realization of Emerald. In the final journey, we come to know that existence as the presence of the Absolute co-emerges with personal being as one nondual reality.

As is true of all models, the Transformation Model is only a way of explaining a process that is far subtler and more multidimensional than could ever be completely captured.

Its virtues are that it integrates a vast range of dimensions into a simple structure and it shows that complete actualization of spiritual realization can come only after a series of ever deeper immersions. By combining the journeys of the soul with the lines of development, the enneagram personality types, and the levels of consciousness, we can begin to get a rich picture of how human development progresses and of what our unfoldment promises.

While this model cannot resolve all differences between religions, philosophies, and sciences, it does provide a broader domain in which to situate the discussion. In so doing, it actually begins to accomplish a gentle form of integration in which all perspectives are seen as parts of a complete spectrum that contains them as elements of a greater whole.

We must always remember that all maps and models are abstract things. Creating a model is like describing a garden by drawing a picture of it: a good picture shows approximately where the flowers are, but we can appreciate the beauty only if we actually go there. There is only one reality, but there are many ways of representing it. These differences of representation do not ultimately matter much. What matters is getting to the garden.

The Awakening of Soul

Enjoying the fruits of the garden is easy. What is difficult is letting go of the habit of the false self, which is very tenacious. It clings to us, makes us believe that it *is* us; and, if we do not see through its tricks, it is all we will ever know, which would be a waste of our human life.

In theory, the breakthrough into the contentment and authenticity of the true self can occur suddenly. In practice, most people find themselves involved in a long and protracted struggle. Thus, it is important to begin the journey to self-discovery with a strong conviction, a firm determination to persist, and a good support structure. We need to understand clearly that there is no meaningful life outside this struggle. The alternative to being awake is being asleep. The alternative to being free is being imprisoned. The alternative to being a mature human being is being an aging child. The alternative to being true to yourself is being false.

In other words, there is no real alternative. If we wish to be fully alive, free, adult, awake, strong, joyous, and peaceful, we must work to overcome the many barriers of the egoic personality. We are not trying to "get rid of" the ego, but rather not to be ruled by it. We seek to relax the ego into submission.

Finding a Path

Fortunately, we do not have to fight entirely alone. Many supports are available in the form of written teachings, fellow seekers, classes, and above all, awakened teachers. A good guide is all-important and, of course, also the rarest resource. If we are sincere and persistent in our quest, however, we will find a teacher to work with.

Teachers and teachings come in many flavors and levels of experience. Some approaches are considered "tougher" and some "gentler." Ultimately, these labels refer only to relative distinctions of surface style. Facing the false self is hard. Thus, all teachings that actually address the work are tough. An authentic path involves both pain and joy, therefore if a teaching always makes you feel good and never challenges your delusions, it is not worth pursuing.

It is generally best to work with the most challenging teaching you can handle, as best you can assess it. The problem is, we cannot assess very well until we already have traveled a long way, we must rely on our best wisdom and intuition. In reality, the path finds us when we are ready.

If you find a teacher that you feel an affinity with, it is best to stick with that guide for as long as possible. While there might be some good reasons to move on, there are also lots of bad reasons. The ego gets challenged in this work; often it is emotionally uncomfortable. This is sometimes referred to as "getting cooked," and is not a good reason to leave the work.

Some teaching approaches emphasize one essential aspect more than others, such as will, love, or wisdom. Others are more comprehensive, such as the teachings of Bawa Muhaiyaddeen or A.H. Almaas' Diamond Approach. I believe that Americans, and Westerners in general, do better in schools that offer a significant amount of explanation. We are not inclined to engage in a long practice without some understanding of the reason for it.

Also, because the level of narcissistic wounding and neurotic reactivity is generally quite high in the West, we are likely to do better with a teacher who shows a great deal of compassion, especially in the early stages of the work. I cannot speak knowledgeably about this aspect in other cultures. It seems probable that our conditions are becoming more similar as technological rationalism (and postmodern reaction to it) moves through other societies.

Studying and working with a transformative practice takes time and effort, so we need to organize our lives to support the work. I believe it is better to maintain a normal life while studying than to withdraw from the world. This is called "fourth-way" practice[71] and enables us to integrate what we learn into our daily lives. Otherwise, we could spend several years attaining a state of peace while in seclusion only to lose it the first time we experience rush-hour traffic again. Best to learn from the beginning to be peaceful in the midst of traffic.

We will need to listen to teachings and read books in order to develop a basic cognitive understanding of the terms and concepts of a particular approach. This is generally more difficult than pursuing ordinary academic study because the ideas we are absorbing are subtle, and they put pressure on us in many dimensions.

---

[71] This phrase was applied by Gurdjieff to work within the context of a normal worldly life. It was the method of his work school and of many others using this approach.

The Struggle with the False Self

As we learn about the qualities of the awakened soul and the problems of the false self, we will confront personal issues concerning how we feel about ourselves. It is not easy to see one's faults clearly and often we have to pass through a long period of emotional psychodynamic work to resolve what arises.

Different teaching paths approach these issues in different ways. My own experience has taught me that it is possible to have many advanced realizations without resolving the emotional foundation. This is called "spiritual bypass." Eventually, the psychodynamic issues have to be addressed or the spiritual work has no foundation. Doing this work may involve years of emotional turmoil, fear, shame, grief, anger, and remorse, but when fulfillment comes, there is no joy like it. After a certain point, we become more relaxed about our feelings. Negative emotions come and go, but we don't get stuck in them.

Each individual comes to the work with a unique history and unique issues. Although the general picture of this path is well-known and documented, what is most significant is coming to terms with our own particular experience—investigating our own specific personalities and coming to understand our own distinctive challenges. This is a kind of archeology of the soul. We are digging to unearth the structures that are blocking us from full spiritual experience.

Developmental Stages and Egoic Contraction

We come to understand that the soul is always present, but our connection to it is blocked by the contractions that form our egoic personality. Personality habits are tensions caused by our reactions to the loss of contact with Essence during early childhood development. We can think of Essence as the natural state of consciousness. When it is flowing freely, we experience a sense of connection to the Divine Being. This connection is present in the infant, albeit in an undeveloped form.

As the infant discovers itself to be a distinct identity, it begins to develop a personality. This is a necessary process, but it leaves us alienated from the source of life. We fill the loss with false qualities—false love, false strength, false will, false intelligence, and so forth. The ego contracts around a particular pattern of personality habits, as the enneagram of personality so clearly illustrates.

Superego/Ego Identity Traps

As children we internalize the authority figure of the parent in the form of the psychological structure called the "superego," or inner critic. This is a natural part of maturation. Parents need to discipline children, for example, to keep them from running in front of cars. Unfortunately, along with such practical wisdom, we absorb other ideas that are not helpful in later life. While we learn not to run in front of cars, we also learn that we are too stupid to keep ourselves alive in a world of dangers. We learn that we are weak, not very smart, and generally deficient relative to our godlike parents, who can drive cars and who know everything. For a child, this is the truth of how things are, so we need parents to guide us through the dangers of the world and tell us what to do.

As we grow older, we internalize the parental figures. We hear the inner voice reminding us to "look both ways before crossing the street." This is valuable in that it keeps us alive when the parent is not around. Then, we grow up and become adults, but the internalized authority figure, the superego, continues to function automatically, as if we were still children and severely limits the growth of the soul. For transformation work, the superego is a major barrier.

For adults who have developed a true conscience, the superego is only a hindrance. Its basic message is, "You are bad!" or "You are just not good enough!" Such messages from the inner critic hinder almost all adults, making spiritual progress difficult by repressing our recognition of the truth and keeping us stuck in ruts of ego identity. This automated inner critic keeps us from observing either our inner demons or our inner angels. It is often projected onto outer authority figures, moral authorities such as church leaders, political figures, or even our boss at work.

When the soul begins to discover its wider potential, the superego screams at us and punishes us. "Who do you think you are to go beyond the bounds of established identity!" We have to learn to defend against this inner structure if we want to be able to observe ourselves objectively.

The soul's potential contains all creation, every animal quality and every angelic quality, every heaven and every hell. Our awakening journey follows Virgil and Dante through the seven hells, the purgatories, the seven heavens, and beyond these to the Absolute and the nondual states. To take this journey, we must be able to observe ourselves neutrally, without acting out negative emotions and without repressing what we see; that is, we must reject the superego's judgments.

The superego is not the wise judge it pretends to be; it is a child's view of the archetypal parent. This is the source of moralistic judgments toward ourselves and toward others. Ultimately we must understand that it is a primitive and automatic psychic program, not the all-wise authority it pretends to be.

Not Acting Out

Some people think that the way to liberation is to let go of all restraints and "express our feelings" no matter how negative or who might get hurt. Experience and careful self-observation reveals that this does not work.

Just as repressing feelings puts us asleep to the truth, so does acting out negative feelings. Aside from the fact that acting out is unethical because it hurts others, it also has the surprising effect of keeping us from actually experiencing the feeling! If we act out instead of observing a feeling as it arises and discovering what it has to say to us, we embroil ourselves in an external drama with some other person. Now we are paying attention to the drama and our reactions to it instead of really feeling the feeling.

For example, if we feel angry and lash out at someone, they are likely to react, and our feelings will shift. We may feel apologetic for lashing out or fearful of their reaction or something else—but not our original feeling. If we had stayed still and followed the anger as it burned within us to see what it had to say, we might have recognized what the anger was about and learned something. By acting out, we lose contact with our truth and get tangled in a drama. Not repressing combined with not acting out is the only way to stay with our feelings and learn from them.

Transformative Practice, Soul, and Essence

In transformation practice, the investigation of our repressed traumas progressively relaxes the ego contraction. This allows the soul more freedom and flexibility to receive the illumination of divine qualities, which is its natural function.

The soul is like a substance or fluid that is aware, spacious, and impressionable. It is the substance of awareness itself. When the soul is free, it feels full of strength, peace, joy, love, wisdom, and all the qualities of Essence that emanate from Being. This is a progressive unfoldment.

We may feel weak and want strength, so we investigate how we got attached to that identity as the weak one. We may feel a lack of love, a sense of alienation or disconnectedness, a lack of clarity or intelligence, a lack of courage, and so forth. As we look into these things, we will re-experience old wounds, and gradually, through conscious presence, they are healed; we cannot force them to heal. We must stay with the truth of our experience and allow the truth to set us free. If we try to force it, we just wind up filling the wound with false qualities. This is exactly what the ego structure does and how it blocks us from the experience of open soul contact.

There are many kinds of practices to support this work: reading, journaling, prayer, meditation, conscious work practices, group work, exercises in pairs and triads, and so forth. Different practices can help us to develop specific qualities or awakenings.

There are practices for increasing awareness, developing our sense of connection to life, deepening presence, awakening aliveness, strengthening autonomy and authenticity, inspiring a sense of service, increasing our ability to allow all of our experience, unfolding compassion and appreciation, and bringing out our wisdom and vision. There are specific practices suitable for each individual's needs.

The direct presence of a teacher can provide subtle energy in the form of "transmission" as well as specific wisdom counsel. Transmission is the direct radiation of spiritual qualities to the student and is supported by the visible example of those qualities in the teacher. The degree of transmission depends on the teacher and the receptivity of the student.

I was blessed to spend many years in the presence of Bawa Muhaiyaddeen, whose radiant aura completely filled his room and extended for a long distance beyond his home. His presence was a constant transmission of spiritual qualities that could be palpably felt by anyone within the field of his gaze. Sometimes this would feel like profound peace, sometimes like a pressure, sometimes like being washed, sometimes like wisdom, sometimes like love. Anyone who came near him knew they were in the presence of a man beloved of God.

What Transformation Is Really About

When we look at what "transformation" really is, a number of key recognitions and processes stand out.

Key realizations:

1. Recognizing soul as pure awareness, the vehicle of experience: This is usually realized through meditation.
2. Recognizing the falsity of our ego identity: We become aware of our act as phony, fake, robotic. Eventually, we discover true authenticity, our real being.
3. Skillful defending against superego attacks: We realize that the inner critic that insists we are "not good enough" is just an automated program and a barrier to spiritual growth.
4. Practicing constant inner inquiry into the truth of our immediate experience: Observation and investigation become transformative.
5. Experiencing presence: Sensing our arms and legs, looking, and listening increase the awareness of being present.
6. Allowing the awakening of Essence in the form of various essential qualities: strength, will, merging love, joy, peace, compassion, brilliancy, and so forth.
7. Developing fierce determination for the work and disciplined practice: Precision and impeccable balance build support for the work.
8. Learning etiquette toward teachers and toward fellow students: Developing restraint and not acting out negative emotions awakens respect for others.
9. Developing the positive effects of transformation on daily life: We begin to see it in our relationships, in the work environment, in finding work we love, in dealing with troubles gracefully, and in experiencing joy and appreciation of life.

These are some of the key realizations, especially in the early stages of transformation. To experience what I am calling "transformation," a student must go through each of these realizations, processes, and learnings.

The Fruits of Awakening

The eventual outcome of this transformative process is the flowering of the soul. Where before we were like robots on autopilot, controlled by our ego habits, now we are free. We are no longer at the mercy of automated programs. We will continue to feel the tug of old habits for a time, but they are no longer in charge. Of course, we must first recognize that our patterns are automatic, which most people in first-tier levels do not.

Once awakened, we feel real, full, authentic, natural, and spontaneous. The awakened soul is no longer alienated; it is connected to all of life and full of love. The contented soul always feels that there is enough; even during the most miserable of days in the most difficult of circumstances, there is enough.

We are relaxed and natural, responding spontaneously as events arise. In this state we no longer hold onto old feelings. What we feel arises authentically and appropriately from objective perception of reality. We feel present and magnificently alive. The awakened true self is receptive to essential qualities and filled with flowing virtues.

There are later stages where we face deeper learning and may not always feel positive graces, but our spiritual capacities in general continue to grow.

Awakening in Chaotic Times

In today's transitional period, personal transformation is less of a luxury and more of a requirement for life. We need a degree of awakening to help us live through the challenges of the Transition. Building survivalist shelters or large financial nest eggs won't shield us from transitional stress. Only personal transformation will provide the inner resources we need to live with a degree of balance in turbulent social environments.

We must learn the length of our reach. The measure from the center of our chest to the tips of our fingers is a clue. Before we can effectively help others, we must clean up our own house. This is not to discourage anyone from doing "good works," but to encourage us all to practice self-observation as we work. Self-knowledge may help us to heal our own blindness so that we do not become arrogant and judgmental of others.

If we can gain some understanding of our own automatic behaviors without falling into self-flagellation, we may be able to see ourselves more clearly. This can show us the way to exercise a little gentle restraint, which is a far greater service to the world, and to our own souls, than we might imagine.

As we learn to observe the motion of our own awareness, we may begin to see that the true center of our being is not our mental concepts of who we are, but a free and responsive consciousness. This helps us to bring a little peace into our lives. When we remember to stay present to the immediate truth of our experience, transformation is already happening.

The best practice is to investigate with relaxed curiosity into whatever is arising, even when we are feeling difficult emotions. Such practice awakens deeper self-knowledge and greater freedom for our soul. Persistence in this practice of inner inquiry is a royal road to transformational awakening.

Transformation in Daily Life

We will notice transformation most clearly in our family relationships, with our spouse, children, parents, and siblings. We will learn to communicate more effectively, be more understanding of others' suffering, and show more gentleness in how we treat people. Transformation also may bring many difficulties to light. Restraint is important. The truth we learn is for our own understanding about ourselves, not for correcting others.

If we can stay with the truth of our experience while dealing calmly with difficult situations, we may come to see difficulty as a blessing for our own transformation. In truth, everything that occurs in our lives is perfectly designed to help us unfold. If we see it in that light, our hearts will bloom with gratitude.

Developing transformative attitudes helps us to deal with difficult relationships at work, and to develop the vision and creativity to attract the kinds of work we love.

As we learn to deal with troubles gracefully, the normal stresses of life—health problems, deaths in our families, problems with finances, children in trouble, neighborhood conflicts, and so forth—become much easier to bear. We are able to maintain steadiness by practicing appreciation for life and gratitude for the opportunity to awaken.

Emergence of Transformation Leaders

Transformed people often become examples, helpers, and leaders in their communities. Even when they are not in positions of official authority, their influence is subtly felt.

Personal Vision

As we become more aware of our awakening capacities, we need to seek and develop our personal vision. By understanding who we are and what we came here to do, we begin to actively live our lives from our true being. There are practices and processes that can help us to find and build our vision: journaling, creating drawings or collages, and focused meditations are examples.

Actively seeking to define personal vision also tends to challenge us to go beyond ego projects and find the thing that is greater than ourselves. When this begins to emerge for us, it can be a great source of liberation.

Emerging Groups and Leaders

An increasing number of transformation groups are emerging composed of people engaged in various aspects of transformation practice. Some of these groups are beginning to form networks such as the International Enneagram Association and the Integral Institute. More people are teaching various kinds of transformational practices, and more leaders in all social functions are beginning to look at their jobs from an integrating perspective.

The emergence of greater numbers of transformation leaders is a key factor in social transformation, which brings us to the next and final chapter.

Chapter 12.
Social Transformation

We are in a time when the need for social transformation is vast. In every society on the planet and in every social function, we are faced with challenging issues that demand solutions. At every level of society, people are suffering because of the failure of old ideas to solve complex social problems.

I have argued that transformation is being thrust upon us by a vortex of powerful new life conditions. I have said that we cannot avoid being transformed no matter how hard we resist. The forces of change are far too strong. But this does not mean that there is nothing we can do to navigate the process of transformation more successfully.

By developing new visions and extending them into detailed policy implementation, we can achieve a lot for our organizations, our societies, and our world. It is precisely the emergence of new ideas and new worldviews that has guided humanity through the many passages that have brought us this far.

Social transformation engages the following points:

1. Social transformation means movement from separative divisions to greater degrees of planetary unity.
2. This movement is thrust upon us by changing conditions that make unity a necessity for survival.
3. It will happen whether we work for it, against it, or do nothing, but our experience of it will vary according to how well we align with this great opportunity.
4. Societies and organizations that do not prepare for this transformation will experience greater suffering and possible dissolution.
5. Societies and organizations that do prepare will also experience the stresses of the Transition, but will be far better positioned to

turn them into something positive. Either we grow willingly or life punishes our inertia.

6. Transformation occurs as a process of disintegration of old structures and integration of new, more flexible, structures.
7. Preparation to use the opportunities for positive transformation requires research, planning, and development of new concepts and new social institutions now, before the full crisis hits.
8. Like a child in the womb, or a bud about to burst, when the time comes, the change is rapid and undeniable.
9. If we wish to minimize suffering, we must dedicate our lives to engaging the emerging transformation. That is why we are here at this time in history.

Transformation is the cause that integrates and advances all other worthy causes. Only actions that are aligned with the greater transformation will flourish.

The Importance of Vision

Vision matters and policy matters. In recent history, enlightened social policies have made enormous differences in gaining positive outcomes for disease control, for population stability, for increased literacy, and for economic development, to name a few. Life is not simple and will not respond well to simplistic social policies. There are also many examples in history of bad policy leading to social decline. The challenges we face are complex and require subtle policies.

While we cannot engineer life exactly to our wishes and the challenges are not entirely of our choosing, we can make decisions about how we will respond. Seeking greater wisdom can be the difference that makes the difference. Vision can help us better understand our passage through the rapids of a convulsive transition. We may have no choice about the passage, but it is better to arrive on the other side upright and afloat than capsized and drowned.

Vision is most effectively developed and communicated from a more integrative and holistic perspective. Such a perspective takes into account all waves of development, all economic levels, all social functions, and the technologies and media operating in these varied environments. Thus, one crucial lever for transitional guidance is the training, development, and coordination of more second-tier planners, communicators, and leaders.

Social Transformation | 333

Another crucial lever is the development of specific strategies for encouraging positive evolution throughout the entire range of developmental waves. Basic vision elements, such as resolving racial and religious conflict, need to be planned and communicated through each of the waves from Beige to Yellow, in each cultural environment and each social function.

To accomplish this, we will need to coordinate more detailed demographic and psychographic data. Building and publishing survey data on the wave percentages for every county, tribal region, town, and urban district on the planet would provide the social equivalent of whole Earth photos. We might think of the endeavor as a mapping of the social genome. It will enable us to see ourselves more clearly and track the effects of policy changes over time with greater objectivity. This would show which policies are serving positive transformation and which are not. No single set of metrics is sufficient, but the combination of many views, many factors, and many sources can bring to light a more objective image.

The Aggregates of the Social Fabric

Social transformation begins with individuals and spreads through a series of relationships; these relationships lead to the formation of larger and larger groups that are increasingly open to transformative processes.

As people gain more self-awareness, they are better able to form mutually supportive relationships. They become better spouses and better parents, creating families that are more loving, more truthful, and therefore stronger and more resilient in responding to shocks. They become better friends and better business partners. Just one awakened individual can transform a family, a small business, a circle of friends, or any social grouping. Every positive interaction increases the likelihood that participants will continue to interact positively with others, and the beneficial effects spread like rings from a pebble tossed in a pond.

Transformative ideas get mixed with positive emotions and gradually become part of the conventional wisdom of a society. For example, fifty years ago racism was widespread in the US and segregation was the norm. Today, although racism continues to exist, it is no longer socially acceptable and, despite periodic backsliding, integration is increasingly the norm. These are the qualities and the bonds that form the "fabric" of society.

There is a nested progression in the social fabric:

- **Individuals:** self-understanding and virtues
- **Relationships:** love, friendship, and trust
- **Groups:** families, businesses, circles of friends
- **Communities:** neighborhoods, churches, networks
- **Towns/Districts:** groupings beyond the circle of acquaintance

The progression continues to include counties, states, nations, regions, and eventually the whole of human society. All small groups tend to model family dynamics, all organizations model village or community dynamics, and all societies model tribal and intertribal foundations.

Modeling Transformation Reality

We need to develop better dynamic models to track social evolution in every major issue area: economics, security, education, health, civil rights, democracy, and so forth. We need to invent effective ways to communicate reliable knowledge about where we are, where we want to be, and how various policies are performing to get us there. The more aware society is, on both local and planetary levels, the more effectively we can reduce the dislocation and suffering caused by rapid change. Greater awareness makes societies more adaptable at all levels.

Social Function – Wave Matrix

One way to describe social transformation is to model the dynamic movement of emerging consciousness waves across social functions. The matrix in table 16 below is a condensed and abstracted example of such a model.

Wave	Social Function (S$_\Phi$)					
	Human Science	Spiritual Culture	Technology	Media	Wealth / Economics	Governance
TU						
YE						
GO						
GR						
OR						
BL						

Table 16. Social Function – Wave Matrix

I have selected the functions described in Part II of this book, but any set of social functions or subfunctions can be analyzed in such a matrix. For example, we could study components of healthcare as subfunctions: medical (doctors, nurses, technicians), hospitals and clinics, insurance providers, pharmaceutical firms, biotech companies, instrumentation developers, research and medical science, medical education, government policies and legislation, and various economic elements of healthcare.

Similar analysis could be applied to the arts, law, the military, education, the energy industry, communications, transportation, homeland security, counterterrorism, or any specific set of social functions or industries. Each cell of such a matrix represents substantial documentation on how each wave looks at the functions being analyzed and their dynamic interplay. We can also envision a relational database describing each cell in such a matrix. Of particular interest in such a database view would be which entities and attributes change and which remain stable as we evolve from wave to wave and from first to second tier.

What such a matrix reveals is that the discussions and debates over social policy vary considerably depending on participants' waves and worldviews. An integral (Yellow) view will work to create more effective communication across wave perspectives and more comprehensive ways of describing both problems and alternative solution sets.

As survey companies begin to incorporate these kinds of psychographic models, we will begin to get an increasingly detailed picture of the world by region, by nation, by province, and by county or municipal district. We will also see how these wave components are distributed across other demographic categories. The more accurately we can see ourselves, the more flexibly we will be able to respond to the strains of transitional change. Knowledge, though sometimes uncomfortable, always supports real transformation. We are greatly benefited by facing reality, however disturbing the picture.

We can generalize social transformation down to the shift from first-tier to second-tier perspectives. Table 17 shows this shift from the perspectives of the individual and the social unit.

Perspective	1st-Tier Transitional Challenge	2nd-Tier Transformation Process	Vision Aims / Goals Ultimate Outcome
Individual	Freedom becomes anarchy, then despotism; Lack of awareness inhibits personal life processes	Leader training; Psychodynamic practices; Lines of development; Multi-Q education	Awakening and evolution of consciousness; embodiment of virtues; Maturity and spiritual freedom
Society	Unity becomes groupthink, then totalitarianism; Fragmentation creates conflict; Social processes remain primitive	Ideas and culture; Institution building; Resource positioning	Diversity within unity nurtures awakening, peace, and harmony; Social solutions emerge from enlightened wisdom

Table 17. Tier I to Tier II: Individual & Society

Social transformation builds on four key elements:

1. **Trained Leaders**
2. **Ideas: Vision and Plan**
3. **Institutions**
4. **Resources**

The movement to second tier society integrates these elements. This shift can also be analysed by social function as shown in table 18.

Social Function:	1st-Tier Transitional Challenge	2nd-Tier Transformation Process	Vision Aims / Goals Ultimate Outcome
Politics & Governance	Corruption and injustice; Ineffectiveness; Repression; Unwise, antidemocratic rule	Planetary multistakeholder model; Complexity "gardening;" Regulation of monetary power	Wise governance; Consciousness growth; Advanced democracy
Economics & Wealth	Unfairness; Instability; Debt; Lack of productivity; Poverty and stagnation	Innovation and productivity Globalized political controls Civil society building	Abundance; Equitable distribution; Stable growth
Media & Journalism	Invasiveness; Sensationalism; Fomenting crisis; Disinformation	Reorientation to service to society; Decommercialization of news; Providing of context	Tool for Transformation; Educational vehicle; Medium of community
Science & Technology	Disruptiveness; Orientation toward wealth; Lack of ecological balance	Impact assessment; Complex systems ecology; Futurism; Disaster Recovery planning	Humanized technology; Metasystemic impact assessment; Wise forethought
Religion & Spiritual Culture	Dogmatic religion tends toward ethnocentrism and war; Unawakened	Integration w/ psychology; Evolution of spiritual science; Ecumenical harmony	True spiritual science; Pure ethical conduct; Awakening and tolerance
Human Sciences & Education	Fragmentation; Narrow scope; Disconnection from policy; Partisanship	Integration w/ spirituality; Applied to policy leadership; Multistakeholder training	Whole human model; Wisdom education; All levels served

Table 18. Tier I to Tier II: by Social Function

Transformation Drivers by Social Function

The interaction of developments in all social functions are driving these shifts from first-tier to second-tier worldviews:

Human Science	• Enormous advances in understanding human nature, both individually and collectively
	• Superneural education; multi-Q development
	• The Transformation Model
Spiritual Culture	• Comprehensive integration of spiritual wisdom from all traditions
	• Integration of scientific and religious perspectives
	• Divine attributes and awakening of virtues
Emerging Technology	• Molecular science, nanotech-biotech: stronger, healthier bodies and longer lives
	• Gardening of Earth through desert reclamation, environmental cleanup
	• Space habitat and asteroid control
Media Development	• Increased intensity and involvement of emerging media
	• Virtual reality internet(VR/I)
	• Increased transparency and visibility impacting all social functions
Wealth Economics	• Increased demand for equity and fairness
	• Abundance generated by innovation and wisdom
	• Values generated by value: spiritual economics
Wisdom Governance	• Greater democracy and wise governance
	• Planetary multistakeholder governance
	• Emerging second-tier leadership

These drivers will press consciousness transformation forward, partly in response to transitional pain and partly in response to the attraction of emerging vision. All of these forces ensure that the rapids of change are unavoidable. Only a shift to second tier will be able to manage the complex demands of change.

Developmental Lines – Wave Matrix

Another way to describe social transformation is to model how particular lines of development (or sublines) evolve as we move from wave to wave. The matrix below provides an abstract of this form of modeling.

W_ε	Developmental Line (L_Δ)						
	Kinesthetic Instinctual	Emotional Affective	Cognitive Mental	Relational Empathic	Moral Ethical	Aesthetic Perceptual	Spiritual Intuitive
	K-I	E-A	C-M	R-E	M-E	A-P	S-I
TU							
YE							
GO							
GR							
OR							
BL							

Table 19. Development Lines – Wave Matrix

Such a model is particularly useful for analyzing, planning, and developing transformative education processes—for example, leadership development seminars and training programs. One of the things this view reveals is that people develop unevenly along different lines.

One goal of transformation studies might be to look for distribution patterns and to develop hypotheses concerning the change dynamics involved. Why do certain people advance along one particular line and remain stagnated along another? For example, how do personality types correlate with developmental lines? By investigating the barriers, we shed light on how to release the contraction and allow transformation to occur.

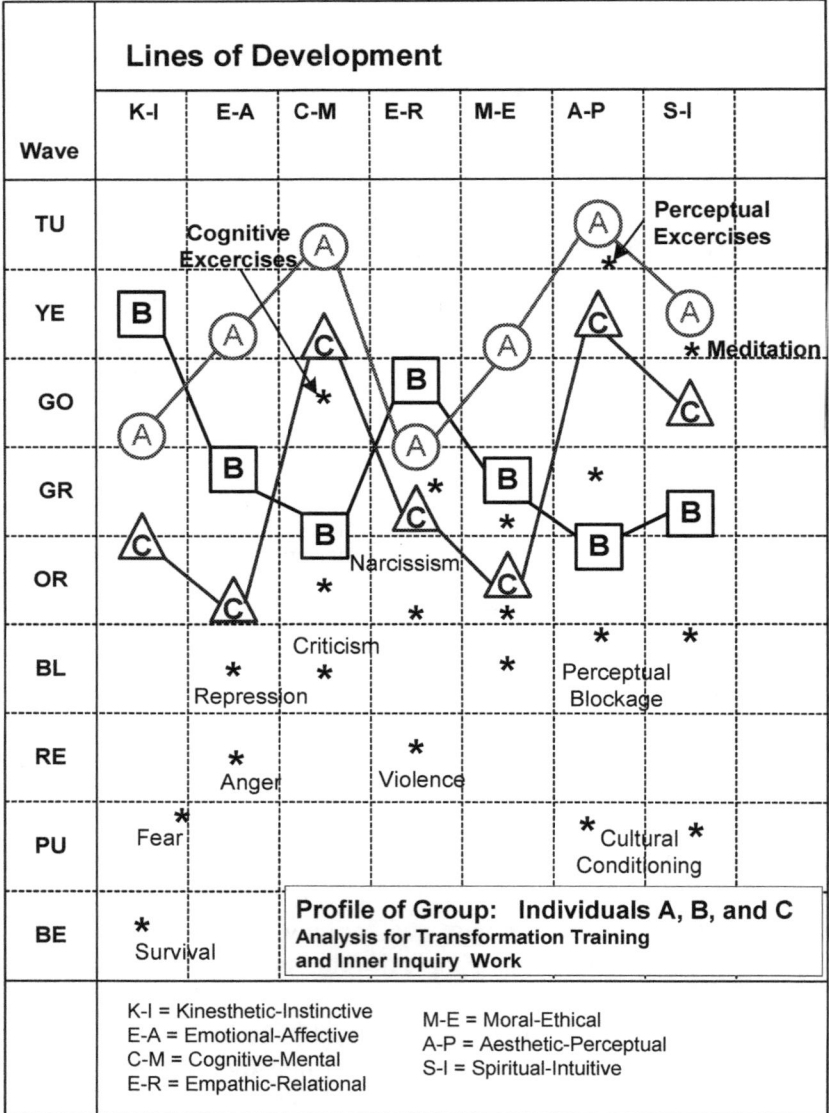

Figure 20. Group L$_\Delta$ Profiles

We should also look at how the interplay between different lines of development affects social change. Lacking specific research data, I would anticipate that cognitive lines, in our mentally oriented society, would tend to develop in advance of other lines, particularly in the Green to Golden Olive to Yellow transformation. This is the kind of hypothesis that psychographic research could actually test and verify or reject.

Such analysis also can be applied organizationally to assess how developmental waves and lines are distributed across organizational departments and to evaluate the impact of change programs.

For example, most organizations today want to increase creative innovation and cognitive flexibility, what is called "thinking outside the box." Relational and emotional intelligence is another area that many organizations have found important for effective performance. Leaders who are able to function on second-tier levels will be able to guide their organizations more effectively through challenging times. Clear models help.

Survey Instruments and Problems of Knowledge

Having suggested the value of wave-related psychographic research, I have to add that the problems of accurately capturing and interpreting such data are not small. Survey instruments are often ambiguously designed, resulting in poor data. Acquiring well-randomized sample groups poses many hazards. Small flaws in the details of how data are collected can be easily compounded during aggregation. Collection models may contain hidden assumptions and design flaws that skew results.

Social scientists and professional polling organizations are certainly aware of these problems, but this does not stop bad surveys from being done and bad results from being disseminated in the media. Adding to the problem, selfish interests often manipulate data and selectively quote results that support a particular view.

Even when there is no intentional bias, getting clear information about the world is a difficult scientific task. Many more studies are performed than there are brilliant social scientists to perform them. As in all other things, second-tier awareness brings to this problem a distinct sharpening of the lens.

The problems are ultimately epistemological, that is, they are problems of knowledge and of how we know things. One aspect of this is that we tend to see whatever we are looking for. Our perceptual lens, our worldview, distorts the picture of what we are trying to see, sometimes completely.

To take a current example, the failure of the world's intelligence agencies to accurately assess the presence of weapons of mass destruction in Iraq was distorted in at least two ways. Because the Iraqi military were internally deceiving themselves about the weapons, intelligence services became deceived, as well. Additionally, policy makers wanted to believe, and desire has long been known to be a source of knowledge corruption.

This is why intelligence reorganization studies have stressed the need to separate intelligence collection and analysis functions from political functions to prevent skewing facts to fit theories. More imagination and creativity in some areas is often valuable; in other areas, it is disastrous. We need to be 100 percent honest about facts.

Continuing the analysis to the "war on terror" (a distorting misnomer to begin with), if we are looking for terrorists and rewarded for finding them, we are likely to find more than there really are. What might have been classified as nationalist conflicts or intertribal disputes may get reclassified as "terrorism." Certainly, all violent conflicts produce terror, but where do we draw the line? Are all guerrillas to be considered terrorists? We may be in complete agreement about particularly horrible acts against civilian populations, but definitions tend to get blurred to fit policy preferences, often with dangerous consequences. In the worst case, social dissent gets redefined as support for terrorism, thus justifying repression.

For another example of how definitions can skew data, consider medical research. If we fund cancer research more than general disease research because it is perceived as a more dangerous threat, the definition of "cancer" may grow broader so that researchers will qualify for funds, and therefore the disease will appear to be more prevalent; or, if powers within the medical research bureaucracy need to show progress, rates of "cancer" can be made to appear lower by narrowing the definition of "cancer" and/or broadening the definition of "cure." These realities about data and interpretation do not necessarily imply nefarious intent. Such distortions are an unconscious fact of life for all of us in all circumstances. We see what we expect to see, what we want to see, or what we fear to see.

Elected officials and political parties often intentionally manipulate the interpretation of economic data up or down for political purposes. CEOs may engage in creative accounting to make profits look bigger or debts look smaller. This is exactly what got Enron and other disgraced corporations in trouble. Self-interest leads people to manage perceptions, thus making it difficult to get a clear picture of objective reality.

First-tier consciousness is generally not as awake to the value of objective truth; it tends to function in a kind of sleepwalking state. Second tier learns to examine knowledge on many levels: our perceptions (how we gather information), our concepts (how we interpret what we perceive), and our knowing (how we know what we know and what we don't know). The transformative process teaches us to penetrate many levels of false knowing, internal self-deception, and misinformation. There is a growth in subtle perception, discernment, good judgment, intuition, and an expanding depth of true wisdom.

Organizational Change

Social functions are expressed through networks of organizations, each consisting of divisions, departments, teams, and ultimately of individuals. Most of what we do in life is mediated through organizations. Thus, one way we can think about social transformation is in terms of organizational change.

Types of Organization

I like to use the word "organization" because it is more general than the various forms of business companies, corporations, partnerships, or proprietorships. Organization includes every form of structured human collective: public, private, profit, nonprofit, small, and large; social, professional, religious, educational, and so forth.

Government organizations are differentiated into executive, legislative, and judicial branches, and are gradated into international, regional, national, state, and local levels. In addition, there are temporary commissions, long-lived authorities, boards, and committees of various kinds. There is also an enormous variety of nongovernmental organizations (NGOs) that are focused on issues that generally involve the many topic areas that government agencies address (or fail to, as some would have it.)

Private business organizations are divided into various industries and sizes, each further defined by global, national, or regional markets. Today, organizations are far less distinct than they were a century ago, being now comprised of loose networks of intersecting organizations. For example, consulting firms, contract labor suppliers, professional associations, investor groupings, mergers and acquisitions in progress, joint ventures, spinoffs, supply chains, and customer networks. Terms like "market," "network," "landscape," and "community" provide a more accurate picture of the complexity of modern business. In fact, almost all organizations today have similarly fuzzy borders.

Healthy societies are held together by complex networks of social organizations, clubs, associations, cultural centers, and special interest groups. Many of our leisure pursuits have international organizations associated with them. These international civil society networks are a significant source of global cohesion and peace.

Religious and spiritual organizations are also structured on multiple levels and in many denominations, geographical distributions, and special purposes. Educational organizations are divided by age group and by specialty. Even our families and communities consist of complex webs of organizations and ad hoc gatherings.

All organizations are ultimately modeled on family and tribal structures. When we are considering organizational change, regardless of organizational type, we should bear in mind this multidimensional model of how organizations are structured.

Organizational Landscape

All organizations are continuously evolving whether we intend them to or not, and this constant change occurs within an organizational environment or "landscape." Defining this in terms of market niche alone fails to account for the full complexity of reality. To get a more multidimensional view of organizations, we need to model them within the full social matrix, taking into account developmental waves and all the dimensions of organizational interaction.

Modeling communication flows is a particularly good way of understanding how organizations are functioning within their environments and especially for determining where communication is not working effectively. Universe Modeling provides an effective tool for guiding this kind of communications analysis.

Vision Planning

Organizations can discover new opportunities to align with major trends by developing more effective vision plans that connect broad vision with operational activity.

Every organization today would be well-advised to develop thorough organizational contingency plans to ensure continuity of functioning under the broadest range of probable disasters. A well-conceived disaster model and an effective recovery plan can go a long way to making an organization more robust in challenging times.

Both vision plans, which identify opportunities, and contingency plans, which protect against risks, work best when defined within the broadest organizational landscape and aligned with long-term trends.

Transformational Tools

Types of Media and Applications

Leaders need to become more conscious of the transformative use of all types of media and of the impact of the media themselves. Every time anyone expresses themselves in any medium, including everyday speech, they are either consciously or unconsciously promoting a particular worldview and an attitude, positive or negative, about how things are going.

To the extent that we are operating from first-tier personality levels, we are mostly controlled by habitual attitudes of the wave we are expressing, that is, our worldview is controlling us, rather than the other way around. Because second tier can work through any of the first-tier levels at will, these waves will naturally produce more effective transformation leaders.

Transformational Language and Communication

Developing improved communication forms, structures, and processes is a metasolution; that is, any improvement in the symbol systems we use for communication has a positive impact on all social problems.

Every social function has a set of documentary formats, operating from the most global level down to the finest rules of language and terminology. At the highest level of governance, for example, we have documents such as the United Nations Charter, the Constitution of the United States of America, the constituting documents of the European Union, the Bretton Woods System (IMF, World Bank, WTO), and so forth. Religions are founded on basic scriptures, religious law, and interpretive practice. Economic systems are based on writings of foundational philosophy and contract law. Sciences are built on structures of theory and experimental verification, often expressed in formal languages such as mathematics and chemical notation.

Each social function and specialized subfunction has defined methodologies and protocols for how its processes are managed. Communication formats, procedures, and rules of logic are always a central component of these methods. Thus, when we refine communication theory and practice, we affect all social functions. For this reason, I call such developments "metasolutions."

The development of transformation processes requires careful analysis and integration of the conceptual language formats and protocols that govern our social institutions. This includes creating more refined systems for shifting from more formal levels of language to less formal levels and vice-versa. We need both the precision of formal definitions and the flexibility of natural language.

There is an implicit metastructure of language hierarchy from the more formal to the more casual levels. Developing a refined theory and notational/linguistic structure for cross-functional communication processes provides a powerful medium for social transformation. Components of such a metasystem include:

- Common terminology principles: vocabulary taxonomies
- Document formats: structure and content rules
- Processing methodologies: how documents are developed, distributed, and applied to change processes
- Rules for shifting between formality levels
- Refined grammar and syntax rules
- Symbolic notation and diagrammatic modeling systems
- Applications of emerging media

Such metasystems facilitate great transformations.

Metalanguage and Transition Phases

Applications of second-tier communication metasystems occur at all phases of the Transition:

- Disaster Recovery Planning   (Struggle Phase)
- Preservation of Resources   (Exhaustion Phase)
- Recovery Implementation   (Recovery Phase)
- Negotiation Management   (Negotiation Phase)
- New Charter Definition   (Establishment Phase)

The Great Transformation system itself will refine and elaborate its symbolic language processes at a level beyond our wildest imaginations. If we could leap forward to the year 2150, the density and subtlety of these systems would be completely incomprehensible to us while entirely normal to virtually everyone of that era.

General literacy in these sophisticated systems will be near 100 percent at that time. These symbolic systems will simply be the medium in which life is carried out in the twenty-second century, just as today a large population understands a new language of technology control icons that did not exist thirty years ago.

Cognitive Tools for Policy Development

The immediate necessity for conscious social transformation arises from a series of challenges that cannot be successfully met by existing social structures and processes. We need new solutions. The "business as usual" approach cannot even maintain the status quo. The threat of terrorism is only the most recent challenge. There are, and will be, many others that demand social change.

We need new cognitive tools for social policy development and new processes for modeling and managing complexity.

Instead of just patching the fence after the horses have gotten out, we need new kinds of fences to deal with complex social problems.
The self-aware society is one in which social reality is made visible. Some tools we will use to achieve greater social transparency include:

- Super databases
- Advanced text analysis software
- Refined data validation systems

We will see abstracted data analysis performed on the full text of the US Congressional Record (as well as the legislative records of other nations). More sophisticated text analysis is likely to reveal most of the special interest legislation, pork barrel projects, and political corruption schemes, resulting in their diminishment. This will also help legislative staffs better inform legislators about what they are voting on. Over the next few generations the likelihood that we will develop integral government processes approaches certainty.

All social functions and organizations—including business, news media, government, military, medicine, law, and education—will be made more transparent and ultimately more democratic by this kind of technology. Everything will be revealed and condensed into understandable patterns for easy public consumption. The inevitable attempts to game this system will ultimately fail. Such systems will help us better manage complexity.

For example, when we consider issues of public health, many new concerns are arising. We have to consider factors of bioterrorism from both foreign and domestic sources, as well as natural pandemics. The Center for Disease Control, the World Health Organization, and other health monitors have to work more effectively with local healthcare providers to track diseases and deliver treatments. They use syndromic surveillance techniques to identify emerging clusters of diseases such as West Nile Virus, Lyme Disease, SARS, Rift Valley Fever, and Avian Flu. Some of these pathogens may even be originating from our own laboratories. Better modeling can help to anticipate and reduce such problems in the future.

Other examples of multidimensional challenges include cybercrime, identity theft, narcotics trafficking, addiction health problems, immigration challenges, economic disruptions from global trade dislocations, and political corruption. All these challenges need new thinking.

Common Problems

Each of these challenges and others like them already have large networks of people and organizations trying to deal with them, mostly with mixed success or sometimes outright failure. Even very intelligent and capable leaders are repeatedly faced with common problems that seem to cross all subject matter areas. The first common problem is *complexity*, or what is sometimes called the *"interweave problem."* Every problem seems to interweave with an enormous number of other factors outside the range of the specific challenge any given team is trying to solve.

Another common difficulty is the *"power preemption problem,"* in which a team comes up with a brilliant solution that threatens people in positions of power who then squash it to keep their power. An example of this is illustrated in the film *The Arrow*, about the Canadian aerospace firm, AVRO, that developed a magnificent fighter jet in the 1950s. Just as this jet was surpassing all flight records, the American government prevailed on the Canadian government to shut the program down to protect the secret of the U2 spy plane, which was not as capable as the Arrow. Narrow interests prevailed over technological excellence. (The flight capabilities of this plane had still not been surpassed in 1997 when the film was made.)

A similar example is shown in the film *Tucker*, about an advanced automobile suppressed by the power of existing auto makers. They didn't want the competition and managed to block it by sheer financial muscle. A counter example is how Apple liberated computer power for the use of ordinary people. Prior to the Apple IIe personal computer, only corporations and governments had effective computers.

A third common problem is the *difficulty in gaining social acceptance* for new ideas, new technologies, and new solutions. People on all sides of the political spectrum tend to fear change because of likely unforeseen consequences. And this leads to the fourth common problem: systemic solutions tend to have *unintended consequences* and side effects that cause new problems.

The above examples illustrate that effective social transformation can best be facilitated through development of metatools for dealing with universal problems. The key is to create new tools for managing complexity.

When we create new methods for managing complexity, we solve many problems with one effort.

Metatools can be applied to all social challenges because they address problems common to all policy development domains. They are not primarily limited by subject matter (though any tool tends to get adapted to specific problem domains). Metatools deal with knowledge management, innovation facilitation, human interactions, and issues of political and financial power.

When solutions are developed using the wisdom inherent in integral and holistic consciousness, they are more robust in dealing with complex issues and unintended consequences. Developing social structures to support these kinds of solutions is the single most important task for guiding our society through the hazards of the next several decades.

People focused on pragmatic problem solving need to recognize the value of developing higher levels of consciousness, and people focused on spiritual awakening need to recognize the necessity of bringing higher consciousness to bear on complex social problems.

Developing transformative tools, methods, metaphors, and concepts is absolutely crucial to our survival as a free and democratic society. Current approaches to most of our pressing challenges are just not up to the task. The thought processes are too cognitively limited to deal with the complex realities. We can recognize this now and act to prepare new approaches, or we can learn from the pain of disaster. Preparedness is better.

Theoretical Work versus Applied Work

The hazards of theoretical work need to be balanced against the hazards of applied work. One danger is that theory can become estranged from practice and therefore not applied effectively. The alternative danger is that solutions can become too specific and thus not flexible in responding to changes over time, resulting in what are called "legacy systems." Also, specific solutions are not reusable and thus represent expensive effort.

The integral approach works to combine data from specific research with higher level metaconcepts. Early applications of conceptual models provide feedback from real-world tests. Conceptual modeling creates a broader environment "outside the box" to provide better preparedness for unusual contingencies. There are, in fact, ways of anticipating 99 percent of what more limited thinking deems unforeseeable. Too often people call some situation "unforeseeable" because they don't *want* to foresee.

Integral thinking combines three main functions:

1. Analysis
2. Synthesis
3. Creativity

These three work best when used simultaneously. We can gather millions of data points to analyze, but we will miss the picture if we have not used creativity to develop models for what data to collect and how to collect it. We can analyze till the cows come home but it will be of little use unless we can "connect the dots" in an effective synthesis.

Holistic thinking is the ultimate in working "outside the box" because holism begins with the biggest box and works inward, rather than gathering bits and integrating them into a whole. But holistic thinking is much more than top-down thinking, because it works with wholes at all levels.

When holistic and integral thinking work together, we get transformative thought.

Transformative Thought

Transformative thought (a.k.a. second-tier consciousness) combines many human processes that first-tier consciousness considers separate:

- Thought and action
- Feeling and thinking
- Sensing and intuition
- Models and realities

It combines these functions into integral wholes while simultaneously maintaining precise awareness of all distinctions, such as between map and territory.

Transformative being means that the complete range of human capacities fully engages the present in ways that first-tier personality consciousness cannot see or understand. But the results this level of consciousness produces are powerful and easy to understand, or at least, to appreciate. Transformative second-tier solutions simply work much better. Thus we may not grasp how they were arrived at, but we can clearly see their effect.

The more we develop second-tier consciousness and apply it to managing complexity and building effective social policy, the better we will survive the challenges of this transitional period. We will reach the other side when second tier has become the dominant mode of thinking for the majority of world leadership. By this I don't necessarily mean heads of state. One can hold authority and power without actually being a "leader." Conversely, many individuals act as leaders in everyday life without holding any official position.

The Great Transformation Vision

Transformation Goals

The main goal, at this time, is to move global leadership and culture to integral and holistic levels of development. This will be accomplished within the next 50 to 150 years.

Moving **leadership** means ensuring that at least 80 percent of the individuals in charge of governmental, business, religious, media, educational, and scientific organizations worldwide are people who have reached second-tier awareness (Golden Olive, Yellow, or Turquoise). Also, the majority of the creative and innovative class will be functioning at those levels by then.

Moving **culture** means ensuring that the ideas, theories, and processes in all social functions are based on transformative worldviews. What makes this viable in a complex world, which includes large groups of people at every level of development, is that second-tier awareness is naturally able to understand all levels and to support their continuing healthy development.

The immediate process for the next twenty to thirty years is to develop, refine, and disseminate detailed **vision plans** and **institutional structures**. We are doing the massive research to collect the knowledge, develop the ideas, and design the institutions that will catalyse this social transformation.

This effort is needed to align humanity with the transformation that is already under way. It is not a matter of *creating* a transformation in a world of over six billion human beings; that was set in motion thousands of years ago. The dynamic awakening is a reality. We need structures to support and guide the emergence and to align humanity with it. Otherwise, its emergence will be more chaotic than necessary. A new way of being is emerging for humanity in any case. The only question is how much suffering is entailed.

This vision is about minimizing suffering and maximizing the health of the transformation process. To that end, part of the near term, twenty-year process includes analysis and planning for predictable disaster recovery. Great change, such as we are undergoing, shakes all human institutions and individuals to the core. Recovery planning means developing resources, procedures, and healing processes for a full spectrum of anticipated social disruptions and deploying them in advance.

Building for Transformation and Recovery

We are already beginning to experience a slow-motion catastrophe that is growing and, to some degree, predictable. This predictability means that we can still prepare, thereby mitigating the catastrophe's worst effects and speeding the recovery.

The catastrophe is the result of the planetary tug-of-war between the various worldviews associated with the first-tier developmental waves, particularly the struggle between Blue, Orange, and Green. These worldviews tend to be exclusive, all-or-nothing views.

The remedy is to build the second-tier transformation waves, through Golden Olive to Yellow and Turquoise. Second-tier worldviews are integrative and holistic. They bring views together instead of pulling them apart. They are inclusive, all-and-everything views.

If we do nothing, the catastrophe itself will demonstrate the limitations of first-tier worldviews and could ultimately lead to recovery and progression up the developmental levels. However, an enormous amount of unnecessary suffering can be avoided by working more consciously now.

We build transformation and recovery capacity through a methodical, phased process. First, there is the necessity to develop and elaborate the philosophy, ideas, and plans, as this book begins to outline. We need to conduct further research and step-by-step extend the detail of transformationist theory to every social function and every social issue confronting us today, testing and correcting the theory as we build it. This stage is not easy and will require us to create and build supporting institutions in the form of transformationist think tanks, foundations, associations, and so forth. To some extent, this is already underway, but it needs to be consciously expanded and networked.

As a close and overlapping second phase, we need to develop and apply transformational practices, with theory and practice effectively linked so that feedback and learning occurs between both. What works in one social function may not work in another, but the overall picture must be continuously reintegrated into a unified whole.

Especially important is to develop and nurture a transformation economy that supports the development of Golden Olive, Yellow, and Turquoise, which are the strength of the developed world and the leading edge of human evolution. Without social and economic supports for these assets, we will lose our leading position to less democratic emerging economies, such as China. In such event, transformation would still proceed, but more slowly and painfully.

The liberal democracies of the West were founded on, and have been maintained by, a free and prosperous middle class. Today, two forces are threatening this middle-class foundation, automation and offshoring of jobs to cheaper labor markets. If we do not plan ahead, we may be faced with more sudden disruptive changes, leaving lots of potentially productive people out of work or underemployed.

The internet economy tends to be a winner-take-almost-all economy. When people can order any product or service online, they naturally gravitate toward one in every field that is perceived as "the best." Under our present rules, the winners of these "natural monopolies" try to spread the width of their power as far as possible, often preempting what should be competitive zones by sheer economic might. In these circumstances, the market fails to bring the newer "best" solution to consumers. The other consequence, of course, is that fewer employers can compete, hence, people lose jobs.

Orange so-called "free-marketers" say that this is just "creative destruction" at work, the "invisible hand" guiding the market to the most efficient production of goods and services for the benefit of all. A lot of people are questioning such faith today, even from within the capitalist bastion. I am suggesting that, absent a thorough top-to-bottom review of how our economy works in today's (and tomorrow's) social and technological environment, we stand a very high chance of experiencing a series of sudden meltdowns and disruptions. One result of these disruptions could be the loss of our cherished democratic way of life, at least for awhile.

Consider, for example: How shall we plan for the possibility of a high-tech corporation or network developing the capacity to provide almost all products and services people need practically (or literally) for free? Although this would create an enormous shift from scarcity to abundance for all, it also would be highly socially disruptive as it unfolded. Perhaps such an event seems impossible today, but nanotech, robotics, and advanced internet, combined with changing worldviews, make this scenario quite possible within this century. What would be the effect on our social stability? How could we prepare for gentler transitions and better responses to disruptions? This is not so much a prediction as it is a thought experiment designed to shake up our thinking.

It is to our advantage to find a better approach. Second-tier consciousness, by its nature, is able to process levels of multidimensional complexity that are beyond all first-tier thinking. First-tier waves usually deal with complexity by applying various forms of reductionism. Anything that cannot be understood within the constraints of each peculiar reductionism is left in the hands of fate, God, nature, or social consensus. This condition is a natural part of our human adolescence, but we do not have to suffer the worst aspects of the transition phase. Transformationist theory can and will develop subtler, complexity-friendly solutions. But to get solutions that can mitigate our transitional crises, we need to build the ideas, the practices, and the institutions that support them.

On these foundations, the transformational leading edge can build networks and systems to soften the impact and speed recovery from various predictable disasters that loom in our near future. This is the most meaningful work anyone can support right now. Our near future, which will soon be our present, depends on it.

Before the founding fathers created the United States as the first democratic nation in the modern world, most of the leading thinkers in Europe and America had already shifted to a new way of thinking by reading the works of the philosophers of the day. The theory was also tested and worked out in colonial parliaments, the houses of burgesses, and the various colonial charters. Other experiments and ferments had been underway in Europe for the previous couple of centuries. We are experiencing a similar, but more dramatic, evolutionary leap today.

Disaster Recovery Planning

If we want to continue to enjoy the relative peace, freedom, lawful rule, and civic order we in the developed West have come to expect, we must look ahead and prepare intelligently for the predictable crises and recovery from them. We must develop more detailed and precise models that show the full scope of hazards inherent in our transitional period.

First-tier thinking too often believes that this task is impossible. Second-tier thinking is already busy doing it. Essentially, we need a multidimensional disaster model and a disaster recovery plan to match. This task is completely doable, it will greatly mitigate the danger ahead, and it is already underway. All clear thinking people should support it.

We must understand, however, that first-tier perspectives still control most decision-making bodies, and therefore we are likely to remain vulnerable to poor planning and execution of recovery efforts for a considerable while. We will experience more 9-11s, Katrinas, financial corruptions, wars, and pandemics. The next two or three decades will present a difficult learning curve as we develop better ways of recovering from disasters and eventually preventing them or mitigating their effects to near zero. We *will* learn, but it won't come easy.

Leadership Development Training

To build transformation and recovery, we must also build educational capacities and media capacities for training and disseminating both theory and practice. We need to train leaders in the basic principles of second-tier consciousness.

These trainings must include:

First   The cognitive aspects of second-tier metasystems (how to be comfortable with dynamic, multidimensionally complex models)

Second   The distinction between habit-driven personality states and freer, being-level consciousness

Third   Ethical and moral implications of second-tier awareness

Fourth   Emotional barriers to realizing full second-tier consciousness

Fifth   The embodied experience of essential presence

Although other elements are present in this leap of consciousness, these are some key lines of development that can be taught to those who are ready to expand. The result of these preparations and others that will stem from them will be:

1. Trained second-tier leadership
2. Supportive institutional infrastructure
3. Broadly developed transformational theory

4. Detailed practices and policies for every social function
5. Emerging economic systems founded on a strengthened, creative middle class
6. Accessible and affordable lifelong educational systems
7. Detailed crisis models and disaster recovery plans with resources in place
8. An emerging transformational culture

A primary goal of this book is to encourage the development of these capabilities and preparations, which will carry us through our transitional crisis. This work will occupy organizations in all parts of the world over the next several decades.

We have a glorious future ahead of us, but first we must get through the transitional crisis. Leadership training, concept development, and institution building are part of how we do that. We will not escape all difficulty, but we can greatly diminish the worst of the disruptions.

This vision foresees a future world as full of consciousness development and transformation schools as today's world is full of universities. Just as today cognitive education prepares people for related professional work in industry or public service, transformational education will prepare people to advance into the social institutions of the next era. That future time will value soul awakening and higher capacities in the same way we value intellectual development today. We will come to see that development of higher capacities includes intellectual development because we will understand the need for the full human capacity and not just today's ordinary mental abilities.

We will apply to the realm of cognitive development a much higher level of intelligence than is normally known in even advanced institutions today. This level of intelligence exists now, but social and mental limitations blind the majority of people to it. It moves through the world almost invisibly, but not without beneficial effect.

Second-Tier Problem-Solving Consciousness

Awakened leadership embraces humanity with the fierce compassion of a mother protecting her children. But this fierceness is tempered by second-tier emotional calm and a mind illuminated with subtle problem-solving genius. Eventually, second-tier leaders in every small organization and town will have attained this level of capacity. Even with only five percent of the global population moving into second tier, which we will reach in the next few decades, one out of every twenty people will have this awareness. By the end of this century, we should be approaching at least 15 percent at, or above, Golden Olive, more than one out of seven. This assumes less than a doubling in each generation (25 years), therefore I believe it to be a conservative estimate.

It is natural for human beings to develop every ability to a high level. Creative geniuses will be the norm. The majority of influential people will act ethically toward the whole of human society, transcending ethnocentrism and partisanship. After the transgressive nature of Green has eroded the rigid structures of Orange and Blue hierarchies, Golden Olive training will reawaken flexible forms of courtesy and good manners in a transparent world.

The soul journeys through Amethyst awaken awareness of all time and space as living substance. The experience of Sapphire awakens awareness of the divine source of virtues. The passage through Onyx shows the spacious emptiness within all structures that relaxes identifications with any particular form. The journey through Diamond shows how all potential forms are present in every part of reality.

Such an illuminated awareness sees the living fluidity and creative potential of every situation, where first-tier consciousness sees only limitation. Because of these capacities, awakened leadership will solve problems with a power never before seen.

Multidimensional Dynamics

The integrating process of Golden Olive and Yellow emergence develops new ways of thinking and a culture that supports this consciousness. We invent ways of bringing together more dimensions of information to better understand the social situations we are working to transform.

By combining the consciousness dimensions of the Transformation Model with geographic details, demographic data, and dynamics over time, Yellow can see precise patterns of change—space, time, consciousness, and social distribution in one model. Such simulation models reveal the multidimensional universe of possible change scenarios and allow for more accurate planning and monitoring of vision manifestation. This style of policy implementation is complexity-responsive, hands-on, and fluidly adaptive.

Second-tier-devised **transportation** systems will reduce accidents to near zero because all parts will be in communication; cars, trucks, planes, ships, trains, highways, buildings, and bridges will "talk" to each other and a system will integrate this communication. This system will also reduce or eliminate traffic congestion while speeding transit flows.

Second-tier **health and wellness** systems will integrate the needs of the whole society, creating ever improving levels of health along with ever subtler biological technologies and environmental public health solutions.

Second-tier **education** will use advanced media and learning theory to develop every human being to the highest possible capacity mentally, emotionally, physically, ethically, aesthetically, and spiritually. The awakening and nurturing of every individual's unique talents will be a top priority.

Second-tier **economics** will use integrated global databases and software systems to connect every problem to the human resources best suited to solve it, thus approaching full employment and economic security. All people will enjoy stimulating opportunities to contribute to society, leisure time, and continuing education. We will not separate work, family, play, and school as we do today. Working, learning, relaxing, and family life will be flexibly integrated at all stages of life from childhood to old age. We will work to better society because we want to, not because we are required to.

Self-Aware Society

As more Turquoise awareness emerges, we will understand how all social programs, policies, and natural forces interact to form the dynamic of social experience. Second-tier consciousness is conscious of the ways its own actions stimulate reactions within the system. It awakens the first self-aware society humanity has ever seen.

The levels of international communication we know today are just a clumsy glimpse of what will emerge in this century. A planetary society that is truly aware of, and responsive to, all of its members is the new reality that will come out of the troubles we are experiencing in this transitional period.

Transformation consciousness integrates:

- Multidimensional brilliancy   (Wisdom)

- Dynamic living fluidity (Vitality)
- Complexity responsiveness (Adaptiveness)
- Spaciousness within all forms (Disidentification)
- Potential presence of all forms (Possibility)
- The power of creative intention (Engagement)

A caterpillar can become a butterfly. A garbage landfill can become energy and soil. An impoverished slum can become a beautiful garden. Transformation consciousness sees the positive potential in all things and engages loving creativity to bring that potential into reality. It manifests vision.

Where Orange uses knowledge for private profit and Green uses knowledge for social protest, Golden Olive uses knowledge for personal awakening, Yellow uses knowledge for integration, and Turquoise uses knowledge for the well-being of the whole society. One reason first tier is resistant to change is that it does not fully realize what is possible. As second-tier consciousness emerges, it manifests a whole new reality.

Emerging Transformation Science

Ongoing research must examine the social functions at every developmental stage, particularly Blue, Orange, Green, emerging Golden Olive, and Yellow. By studying the details of how various functions at different wave levels dynamically interact, we can better understand where dysfunction occurs and how to transform it. Currently, all social functions are stuck in the "BOG" impasse of the Blue-Orange-Green struggle, while new Golden Olive-Yellow energies naturally seek out any available open space to flow through.

The goal must be to develop more sophisticated interventions to support emerging second-tier capacities. When individuals learn to observe themselves objectively, without emotional self-criticism or self-delusion, they begin to see the spectrum of psychic potentials: animal qualities, robotic qualities, and divine virtuous qualities are simultaneously available to the soul. Through compassionate inquiry, the barriers impeding unfoldment of higher capacities are gradually seen through and released.

We learn to restrain and tame the primitive lust, aggression, greed, and fear of our animal nature. We learn to interrupt and deprogram the automatic behaviors of the robot and to disidentify with programmed conceptual structures. As these patterns are seen through and the contractions of personality structures relax, the greater capacities of the soul can unfold.

Similarly, the collective social contractions relax and unfold, partly as a cumulative effect of individual transformation and partly as an effect of second-tier ideas moving through the social space. Detailed inquiry into contemporary social dynamics is clarifying the nature of our transitional struggle. Through compassionate investigation that transcends blaming, we are learning more about how our social structures become stuck in contraction and about what societal illnesses result from these contractions.

As we examine the dynamics of how contractions in various social functions move through the whole domain of planetary society, we also see signs of how the social body attempts to heal itself. What is emerging is a new science of human transformation at all levels, from the individual to the collective whole. This science must address both small and large aggregates: one-to-one relationships, families, organizations, social milieus, nations, civilizations, and transnational interest groups of all kinds. Although transformation science is still in its infancy, it is the hope of our future, and we must nourish it.

We must not underestimate the power of awareness to heal. By bringing our planetary social dynamics into the light of day, we will be better able to see ourselves. When awareness and compassion are brought together with wisdom, positive transformation is highly likely.

We do not have to make the entire journey in one step. The goal is not to promote the notion of a utopian earthly paradise, but just to take the next step. This step is a big one, and it is time for us to take it. There are many steps beyond it, but we need only focus on this one. Through inquiry we increase awareness. Through awareness we clear a small space in the jungle of our human struggle. Clearing that space is all we have to do. That is the one great effort, and it is being carried forward at this very moment by people all around the world, including you who are reading this page.

We do not have to clear the whole jungle by ourselves because, once we have cleared one small space, the power of divine wisdom and guidance has room to come through and help us. This is true in individual transformation and also in the transformation of human societies. Taking one small step awakens our spiritual DNA and calls down the support of divine powers, illuminations, and mercy.

Transformation science is also practical spiritual science that learns how to respond to, and cooperate with, the light coming from above. That it is spiritual does not make it less scientific, and that it is fully scientific does not make it less than fully spiritual. Everything that is unfolding is natural. When the time is right, every seed breaks open, sprouts, and transforms into the plant it was meant to be. Some seeds awaken even in the heat of a forest fire.

We must not be distracted by the craziness of the struggle, but stay focused on the one step we are making. This next step is everything for humanity, and we are not alone in making it. There is great spiritual support near at hand.

Human Attraction Vectors

Social change occurs through an aggregation of forces moving in the direction of great human attractors. Over centuries and millennia, we move inexorably and inevitably toward the things we long for. Every human ideal, over the course of history, is made real. The nearer we come to what we yearn for, the more clearly we see it and the more we strive to bring it into being. It is the *vision* of those ideal attractors that guides us to them. Social change occurs through an integrating focus of vision.

Every individual, every organization, every leader is constantly striving toward some attractor and always trying to see that guidance more clearly. Life integrates the sum of these forces, and the whole of reality is more than the sum of its parts. There is an objective universal guidance that tilts our movement toward growth and harmonizes our hopes and fears toward ever higher ideals. From the beginning of the universe, more complex forms have been developing, progressing from stars, to life forms, to human beings. We are guided and, as human beings, we can see our way. That is the function of vision—to seek guidance and to light the way.

As each individual and each organization seeks vision, social transformation is made real. Even though the process is often turbulent, it should be obvious to anyone willing to look without prejudice that evolutionary progress is the constant long-term reality.

The direction is there; the ideal is there; the guidance is there. The job for leaders (and we should all see ourselves as leaders) is to find the focus of vision and align with it. When we align with the greater reality that is emerging, all our efforts are made valuable. Our lives are made good.

The Vocabulary of Wholes

Where does one civilization or society begin and another leave off? Though we recognize different national and regional societies, all societies today are inextricably linked. No nation, language group, or religion can be considered completely in isolation because we all affect each other so profoundly.

Samuel Huntington's *Clash of Civilizations* metaphor is an old way of thinking about things.[72] Many of the world's conflicts stem from the fact that people are operating from old metaphors that no longer fit the reality of life. How, for example, can fundamentalist Islamists expect to create a society of isolated Islamic culture in a world so utterly interconnected? There is no way to accurately model victory for this worldview, and the same could be said for many of our metaphors.

America cannot create a realistic scenario for the victory of our ideas of capitalist democracy without understanding that we will be equally affected by other cultures. It may be politically effective in the short run to persist in developing policy as if we could, but in the long run it is a recipe for certain failure. Eventually, all societies will have to embrace each other as one human family, living together as diversity within unity.

Complexification leads to large-scale integration. Natural selection operating in an environment of increasingly transparent awareness leads us to progressively select the emergent Golden Olive-Yellow-Turquoise solutions to environmental pressures. This kind of evolutionary advance toward higher order integrations and greater harmony within the emergent larger structures (in this case planetary humanity) has been "the Law" since the beginning of our universe. The universe is increasingly revealing that it is "tuned" for such integrations: stars, galaxies, life, consciousness, and so forth.[73] Slight variations in the fundamental physical values present at the origin of the universe and none of this would be possible. It seems that evolution is a pretty intelligent design.

The idea of the League of Nations was idealistic and it failed; yet here we are less than a century later with not only the United Nations but thousands of international organizations. Even if the UN were to "fail," the overall situation of international, transnational, and metanational planetary integration would continue to exist and grow.

---

[72] Samuel Huntington, *The Clash of Civilizations*, 1996.

[73] Rees, *Just Six Numbers*, 2000, and Gardner, *Biocosm*, 2003.

The UN cannot really fail, because we would need to immediately reinvent it if it did. It is a necessary reality. Nevertheless, we are building something more than just the uniting of governments.

All parties in human society will be heard, and ultimately no single party will be able to dominate without accommodating the others, despite temporary appearances to the contrary. The conquerors are metabolized within the domain of the conquest, and the conquered re-emerge within the same domain.

Institution Building: Think Tanks and the Creative Class

We are seeing an increase in the number and influence of think tanks and networks of think tanks. This is co-emergent with growing understanding of the power of ideas and the science of memetics, the study of how ideas get propagated.

Much of the policy planning function is moving away from government structures and toward these networks of thought leaders. In similar fashion, the strategic function in the private sector tends to be outsourced to consulting organizations. This parallels a rise in the number of NGOs, social entrepreneurs, and civil society organizations. Increasingly, professional organizations and special interest groups are refining and propagating the work of thought leaders.

This landscape is the institutional reflection of a growing creative leadership class. Second-tier awareness concentrates in these environments and will grow rapidly through them. The thought-leader/strategic-planning function is also becoming ever more international and metanational in flavor. In this social dimension, world unity and harmony are growing. It will become more politically centrist and universal in philosophy as its clientele becomes broader, more global, and less Orange.

When we examine every social issue from the perspective of each of the six first-tier waves, the second-tier integrating view naturally unfolds. When we open ourselves to the influence of third-tier realms, our understanding is informed by the full spectrum of spiritual guidance. The fruition of this integrative process is to see the whole of human needs in every social issue. This wholeness is the leaf for the healing of the nations. Wholeness heals.

The goal of integration is not to homogenize everything into one nondescript syncretic gruel, but to clarify the spectrum of colors into their prismatic purity and unity. In wholeness, we see both variety and unity as harmonious expressions of one reality. The parts are made to function together smoothly, as when a conductor integrates an orchestra to produce a symphony.

When the health of the whole is cultivated, every religion plays its part, every science is used, and every wave can evolve. Science must be restrained by spiritual ethics, and religion must be informed by science. When every culture, every nation, every social function, and every wisdom are seen as an integrated living whole, we can harmonize the garden and recover from the destruction of conflict.

The Challenging Transformation

The transformation of one individual from the state of neurotic ego personality to the state of conscious being is very difficult. It is so challenging that only those with great determination and persistence have succeeded. Yet here I am, declaring that the social order of all humanity will make this shift, which would seem to be even more difficult. Some authorities have said it can't happen, that only a rare few attain realization. I am saying it will happen. It will be so. It is a great blessing for it to be so. Make it so.

To be among those who commit to fulfilling this amazing transformation is to experience the greatest bliss possible for a human being, like achieving something never before achieved: climbing Mount Everest, landing on the Moon, flying in the air—only far greater. *It is the one great achievement of humanity.* Once it is done, the opportunity will never come again. It is a one-time hurdle we are crossing.

It is not even about succeeding. It is about committing to the goal. Once we determine to be responsible for transforming human society into the level of being that serves to awaken all human beings, the moment we make that determination, we begin to experience a profound liberation. Only by aiming for the one greatest and most desirable goal can we know the experience. Because this taste is so attractive, we will attain the objective. The seemingly impossible will become real.

It can be done. It must be done. It shall be done. Make it so. That is what vision is for.

We who love all that is good and true and beautiful must understand that this cause is the root cause: transform consciousness and all other ills will be healed.

If you love God, if you love your neighbor, if you believe that life is about more than self-gratification, you must embrace the cause of the

Great Transformation. Some say that only good people deserve salvation and that bad people should be sent to hell. But who is good? People who speak so may be condemning themselves. Even Jesus asked, "Why call thou me good when only the Father is good?"

All of you who contribute to any good cause, all of you who seek to fill your days with good deeds, why not add this determination to believe in and seek the Great Transformation? Why not hold this faith even in the face of war and disaster?

I do not profess to be particularly strong, but small, persistent steps and openness to divine grace have blessed me with some degree of transformation. What I can do, I do, and intend to continue to do while I am alive. Many people are moving in the same direction. What seems impossible to achieve in one go can be done in small, cumulative moments of each day, by more and more of us.

When we put our shoulder to the wheel of the Great Transformation, and we give with all our faculties and capabilities, suddenly we know, directly and certainly, that we ARE. Knowing our true being is the greatest satisfaction, peace, and joy possible. We begin to experience that it is the sincerity and intensity of our striving that awakens that profound, magical sense of extraordinary reality. Everything becomes vivid and real. We know our true reality in the core of our being. At first it may be fleeting, leaving behind a thirst for more. In time it stabilizes, and it becomes our passion to know our true reality ever more deeply.

This is how transformation arises: great effort, then the taste, followed by renewed effort that expands as it unfolds. What is true for the individual is true for the collective. At first, it seems impossible; but after great effort by many, a tipping point is reached, and the transformation gains momentum by itself.

One of the easiest ways to experience individual transformation, awakening to the deliciousness of Being, is to dedicate a fierce effort to the greatest cause, the transformation of the whole. When we engage the cause that is greater than our self, suddenly, we know we are alive. When we give of whatever we have—time, wealth, effort, creativity, our whole lives—we begin to experience life directly. When we dedicate ourselves to the greatest good, the awakening of Being, we suddenly know we are part of that Being, that greatest good. Now we are an instrument of divine grace. We are real.

No fear, sorrow, or pain matters to us. No defeat is possible. Even if we witness great catastrophe, our core remains at peace, because we know the reality and truth of Being. Even in death, there is no death. We are real, and to be part of Being is to be eternal, unshakeable. This is how the true becomes manifest even as the false crumbles.

The goal of the Great Transformation is not to make the world a paradise, but to refocus it on its true and original purpose: to be a school for souls to learn and grow into union with God. Of course, this is already and always true for those who can see, but now, for the first time in history, we have the capacity to destroy the school. We also have the capacity to rebuild it, unify it, and transform it. We must choose, now. Those who know can accept God's will either way. So, why not try to transform the school? Why not build the Great Transformation?

Summation

The vision presented in this book describes the stages of the Human Flowering during this millennium. In particular, it focuses on the next major phase of human evolution, which I have called the Great Transformation.

The Great Transformation addresses the most pressing problems facing humanity by establishing a planetary governance system committed to fostering the development of human consciousness on all levels. Both aspects that make up the Great Transformation are necessary: one, the continuous commitment to lifting human consciousness to higher levels; and two, the integration of all human civilizations into one cooperative unity.

From the present until this new system is in place, we will go through a period of transition as we come to terms with the necessity for this change. Many aspects of this transition will be painful and difficult, but we will also begin to appreciate the enormous hopefulness the Great Transformation offers. We will come to understand that no other solution is viable, and so we will proceed to overcome the difficulties.

The immense potential that will become possible through this new integration will spur us on and give us the patience and the will to complete the task. Relief from the troubles of the Transition, plus the promise of peace, health, prosperity, and soul fulfillment, will motivate the whole world to surrender a degree of sovereignty for the sake of greater cooperation. Only leaders who can demonstrate that they have attained mature transegoic consciousness will be trusted to make this work. We will have suffered too much at the hands of ego-driven power brokers to accept their dominance.

The Great Transformation system will last for several hundred years and will completely transform humanity into the flourishing wonder we know in our dreams to be our true destiny. Only long after all the great problems facing us today have been solved will the Great Transformation system break apart. But in breaking, it will reveal an even greater brilliancy in the Great Liberation. This new humanity, transformed and free, will go forth to populate the galaxy in millennia to come.

Though we can barely imagine humanity as it will be at the end of this millennium, we can know that it is coming and appreciate the next great step we must take in the direction of our magnificent potential. Committing to this cause is greater than the highest patriotism and the purest spirituality. The best and the brightest of all nations will embrace this cause and will struggle throughout the next century to bring it into reality, because no other ideal can solve humanity's problems.

In this century, the West must lead the way by expanding the growing wave of higher consciousness within American and European civilization, and by supporting and encouraging democracy and equitable prosperity in every other part of the world. The growing web of international connections, both organizational and personal, is forming the initial fabric of civil society from which the new garment of fair planetary governance can be sewn.

Advances in transpersonal psychology are leading to an unfoldment of transformational sociology, economics, and politics. The Transformation Model provides one initial foundation that we can build on. We will need to develop and validate survey instruments and gather new psychographic data in every nation and region to assess the unfolding evolution of consciousness around the world. We will discover how to build consciousness development into all aspects of our cultural expressions—movies, television, internet, music, and so forth. Once a sufficiently large number embraces the higher vision, the spread of these cultural memes will happen rapidly. We will also need to plan for, and respond to, a series of aftershocks throughout the period in which the Great Transformation structure is emerging.

All these processes are occurring and will continue to unfold no matter how difficult some of the transitional times may be. Whenever we need courage, we need only focus on the vision of the brilliant Human Flowering. Its light will guide us and lead us on through even the darkest night. Nothing will prevent the Human Flowering, for it is built into us. It is our highest expression and our destiny, our spiritual DNA.

Onward to the Human Flowering! Onward to the Great Transformation!

***

The vision is laid before you. The old world passes away. The world dominated by heartless money and mechanistic science crumbles from lack of human love. The world of patriotic jingoism and religious fanaticism tears itself to pieces, having forgotten God. The world of postmodern decadence disintegrates into depressed fragmentation and confused indecisiveness. Our lifetimes are witness to the destruction of the false, robotic, and animalistic phase of man. We are seeing the beginning of the destruction of this world.

Do we have the inner peace, the honor, and the courage to found the new world on higher ground? Why not do it? Some people have the capacity to know that loving God is peace, not war. Some of us understand that loving our neighbor means embracing the whole of humanity as one family. Some understand that becoming truly human requires a lifetime of work to subdue the animal, toss the robot onto the scrap heap, and awaken to the life of freedom, maturity, and wholeness. Once aligned with true guidance, we will be at peace with our duty to help all who are able find their way back to the true nature of Being.

Those who can do this will be guided and protected always. If we can come to this state, there is the possibility of fulfilling the vision of humanity's true potential. It is difficult, but what other goal is worthy of our life energy? Why not choose to build a part of the new world within your own life? Will you take the journey? Why not decide to become part of the transformation?

Selected Bibliography

The references below comprise a small fraction of the sources that have informed this work, but should be sufficient to allow interested researchers to investigate further.

Aburdene, Patricia. *Megatrends 2010: The Rise of Conscious Capitalism.* Charlottesville: Hampton Roads, 2005.

Addison, Howard A. *The Enneagram and Kabbalah: Reading Your Soul.* Woodstock, Vermont: Jewish Lights Publishing, 1998.

Alcaly, Roger. *The New Economy: And What It Means for America's Future.* New York: Farrah, Straus and Giroux, 2003.

Alder, Vera Stanley. *The Fifth Dimension: The Future of Mankind.* New York: Samuel Weiser, 1974.

Alighieri, Dante. *The Paradiso of Dante Alighieri.* London: J.M. Dent and Sons, 1932.

———. *The Pugatorio of Dante Alighieri.* London: J.M. Dent and Sons, 1929.

———. *The Inferno of Dante Alighieri.* London: J.M. Dent and Sons, 1932.

Allee, Verna. *The Future of Knowledge: Increasing Prosperity Through Value Networks.* New York: Butterworth-Heinemann, 2003.

Almaas, A. H. *Diamond Heart, Book One: Elements of the Real in Man.* Berkeley: Diamond Books, 1987.

———. *Diamond Heart, Book Two: The Freedom To Be.* Berkeley: Diamond Books, 1987.

———. *Diamond Heart, Book Three: Being and the Meaning of Life.* Berkeley: Diamond Books, 1990.

———. *Diamond Heart, Book Four: Indestructible Innocence.* Berkeley: Diamond Books, 1997.

———. *Essence with The Elixer of Enlightenment: The Diamond Approach to Inner Realization.* York Beach: Samuel Weiser, 1998-1986, 1984.

———. *Facets of Unity: The Enneagram of Holy Ideas*. Berkeley: Diamond Books, 1998.

———. *The Inner Journey Home: Soul's Realization of the Unity of Reality*. Boston & London: Shambhala, 2004.

———. *Luminous Night's Journey: An Autobiographical Fragment*. Berkeley: Diamond Books, 1995.

———. *The Pearl Beyond Price: Integration of Personality into Being: An Object Relations Approach*. Berkeley: Diamond Books, 1988.

———. *The Point of Existence: Transformations of Narcissism in Self-Realization*. Berkeley: Diamond Books, 1996.

———. *Spacecruiser Inquiry: True Guidance for the Inner Journey*. Boston & London: Shambhala, 2002.

———. *The Void: Inner Spaciousness and Ego Structure*. Berkeley: Diamond Books, 1986.

Andreas, Connirae, and Tamara Andreas. *Core Transformation: Reaching the Wellspring Within*. Moab, Utah: Real People Press, 1994.

Andreas, Steve, and Charles Faulkner, et. al. *NLP: The New Technology of Achievement*. New York: William Morris, 1994.

Aschenbach, Sarah. *Relationships Made Easy: How to Get Along with All Kinds of People*. Coatesville, Pennsylvania: Inspired Solutions, 2004. www.Inspired-Solutions-sm.com

Asimov, Isaac. *The Foundation Trilogy*. Garden City, New York: Doubleday, 1951, 1952, 1953.

Arntz, William; Betsy Chasse; and Mark Vicent. *What the Bleep Do We Know!? Discovering the Endless Possibilities for Altering Your Everyday Reality*. Deerfield Beach, Florida: Health Communications, Inc., 2005.

Bachelard, Gaston. *The Poetics of Space: The Classical Look at How We Experience Intimate Places*. Maria Jolas, trans. Boston: Beacon Press, 1964.

Bakhtiar, Laleh. *God's Will Be Done: Traditional Psychoethics and Personality Paradigm*. Chicago: Institute of Traditional Psychoethics and Guidance, KAZI Publications, 1993.

———. *God's Will Be Done, Volume II: Moral Healer's Handbook: The Psychology of Spriritual Chivalry*. Chicago: Institute of Traditional Psychoethics and Guidance, KAZI Publications, 1994.

———. *God's Will Be Done, Volume III: Moral Healing Through the Most Beautiful Names: The Practice of Spriritual Chivalry.* Chicago: Institute of Traditional Psychoethics and Guidance, KAZI Publications, 1994.

Bales, Robert F., and Stephen P. Cohen, with Stephen A. Williamson. *SYMLOG: A System for the Multiple Level Observation of Groups.* New York: Macmillan, The Free Press, 1979.

Barthes, Roland. *The Pleasure of the Text.* Translated from the French, *Le Plaisir du texte*, by Richard Miller. New York: Hill and Wang, 1975.

Beck, Don Edward, and Christopher C. Cowan. *Spiral Dynamics: Mastering Values, Leadership, and Change.* Malden, Massachusetts: Blackwell Publishing, 1996.

Bennis, Warren, and Patricia Ward Biederman. *Organizing Genius: The Secrets of Creative Collaboration.* Reading, Massachusetts: Perseus Books, 1997.

Bennett, J.G. *Enneagram Studies.* York Beach, Maine: Samuel Weiser, Inc., 1983.

Bentov, Itzhak. *Stalking the Wild Pendulum: On the Mechanics of Consciousness.* New York: Bantam Books, by arrangement with E. P. Dutton, 1977.

Berry, Adrian. *The Next 500 Years: Life in the Coming Millenium.* New York: W.H. Freeman and Co., 1996.

Berry, Thomas. *The Great Work: Our Way Into the Future.* New York: Bell Tower, 1999.

Bierlein, J. F. *Parallel Myths.* New York: Ballantine Wellspring, 1994.

Bornstein, David. *How to Change the World: Social Entrepreneurs and the Power of New Ideas.* New York: Oxford University Press, 2004.

Brahm, Laurence J. *China as No 1: The New Super Power Takes Center Stage.* Singapore: Butterworth-Heinemann Asia, 1996.

Breton, Denise, and Christopher Largent. *The Paradigm Conspiracy: Why Our Social Systems Violate Human Potential and How We Can Change Them.* Center City, Minnesota: Hazelden, 1996.

Brin, David. *The Second Foundation Trilogy: Foundation's Triumph,* Authorised by the estate of Isaac Asimov. New York: Harper Torch, 1999.

Brockman, John, edited by. *The Next Fifty Years: Science in the First half of the Twenty-First Century*. All new essays from 25 of the world's leading scientists. New York: Vintage Books, Random House, 2002.

Buchanan, Mark. *Nexus: Small Worlds and the Groundbreaking Theory of Networks*. New York: W. W. Norton and Co., 2002.

Buchanan, Patrick J. *The Death of the West: How Dying Populations and Immigrant Invasions Imperil Our Country and Civilization*. New York: Thomas Dunne Books, St. Martin's Griffin, 2002.

Bunyan, John. *The Pilgrim's Progress*. London, New York: Penguin Books, 1965, 1987. Originally published 1678 and 1684.

Capra, Fritjof. *The Tao of Physics: An Exploration of the Parallels Between Modern Physics and Eastern Mysticism*. Boulder: Shambhala, 1975.

Caputo, Kim. *CMM Implementation Guide: Choreographing Software Process Improvement*. New York: Addison-Wesley, 1998.

Carroll, Michael Christopher. *Lab 257: The Disturbing Story of the Government's Secret Plum Island Germ Laboratory*. New York: William Morrow, HarperCollins, 2004.

Cashdan, Sheldon. *Object Relations Therapy: Using the Relationship*. New York: W.W. Norton and Co., 1988.

Casti, John L. *Complexification: Explaining a Paradoxical World Through the Science of Surprise*. New York: HarperPerennial, HarperCollins, 1994.

Chabreuil, Fabien, and Patricia Chabreuil. *Comprendre et Gérer les Types de Personalité: Guide de l'Ennéagramme en Entreprise*. Paris: Dunod, 2001.

Chua, Amy. *World on Fire: How Exporting Free Market Democracy Breeds Ethnic Hatred and Global Instability*. New York: Doubleday, 2003.

Cleary, Thomas, Translated by. *The Buddhist I Ching*. By Chi-hsu Ou-I (1599-1655). Boston and London: Shambhala, 2001.

———. Translation and commentary by. *Dhammapada: The Sayings of Buddha*. New York: Bantam Books, 1995.

———. Trans. *The Flower Ornament Scripture: A Translation of The Avatamsaka Sutra*. Boston and London: Shambhala, 1993.

———. *Kensho: The Heart of Zen*. Boston and London: Shambhala, 1997.

———. Trans. *Living and Dying with Grace: Counsels of Hadrat Ali*. Boston and London: Shambhala, 1996.

———. Trans. *The Taoist I Ching*. By Liu I-ming (1796). Boston and London: Shambhala, 1986.

———. Trans. *The Tao of Organization: The I Ching for Group Dynamics*. By Cheng Yi (eleventh century China). Boston and London: Shambhala, 1995.

———. Trans. *Zen Lessons: The Art of Leadership*. Translation of teachings by Chan adepts of tenth to thirteenth century China. Boston and London: Shambhala, 1989.

Cloud of Unknowing, The. A version in modern English of a fourteenth century classic, a book of contemplative guidance by an anonymous monk to his student. New York and London: Harper and Brothers in association with Pendle Hill, 1948.

Corbin, Henry. *Alone with the Alone: Creative Imagination in the Sufism of Ibn 'Arabi*. Princeton, New Jersey: Princeton University Press, Bollingen Series XCI, 1969.

Critical Review: An Interdisciplinary Jounal of Politics and Society. Vol. 16 Nos 2-3 P.O. Box 1085, Emmett, Idaho, 2004. www.criticalreview.com

Csikszentmihalyi, Mahaly. *Flow: The Psychology of Optimal Experience*. New York: HarperPerennial, HarperCollins, 1990.

———. *Good Business: Leadership, Flow, and the Making of Meaning*. New York: Viking, Penguin Books, 2003.

Davenport, Thomas H. *Information Ecology: Mastering the Information and Knowledge Environment*. New York: Oxford University Press, 1997.

Davis, John. *The Diamond Approach: An Introduction to the Teachings of A.H. Almaas*. Boston and London: Shambhala, 1999.

Davis, Stanley M. *Future Perfect*. New York: Addison-Wesley, 1987.

——— and Christopher Meyer. *Blur: The Speed of Change in the Connected Economy*. Reading, Massachusetts: Addison-Wesley, 1998.

Dawkins, Richard. *The Selfish Gene*. New York: Oxford University Press, 1976.

Deming, W. Edwards. *The New Economics: For Industry, Government, Education.* Second edition. Cambridge, Massachusetts: The MIT Press, 1994, 2000.

Dilts, Robert, and John Grinder, Richard Bandler, Judith DeLozier. *Neuro-Linguistic Programming: Volume I, The Study of the Structure of Subjective Experience.* Cupertino, California: Meta Publications, 1980.

Dobbs, Lou, with H. P. Newquist. *Space: The Next Business Frontier.* New York: Pocket Books / ibooks, 2002.

Eco, Umberto. *A Theory of Semiotics.* Bloomington: Indiana University Press, 1979.

———. *Semiotics and the Philosophy of Language.* Bloomington: Indiana University Press, 1986.

The Economist: Pocket World in Figures, 2006 edition. London: Profile Books, The Economist Newspaper, 2006.

Elgin, Duane. *Promise Ahead: A Vision of Hope and Action for Humanity's Future.* New York: HarperCollins, 2000.

Evans-Wentz, W. Y., edited by. *The Tibetan Book of the Great Liberation: Or the Method of Realizing Nirvana Through Knowing the Mind.* With psychological commentary by C. G. Jung. London, Oxford, New York: Oxford University Press, 1954, 1968.

Florida, Richard. *The Rise of the Creative Class: And How It's Transforming Work, Leisure, Community and Everyday Life.* New York: Basic Books, 2002.

Foss, Laurence, and Kenneth Rothenberg. *The Second Medical Revolution: From Biomedicine to Infomedicine.* Boston, Shaftesbury: New Science Library, Shambhala, 1988, copyright 1987.

Freud, Sigmund. *The Basic Writings of Sigmund Freud.* Translated and edited by A. A. Brill. New York: Random House, Modern Library, 1938, 1995.

Fromm, Erich. *The Art of Loving.* New York: HarperCollins, 1956.

Gardner, James N. *Biocosm: The New Scientific Theory of Evolution: Intelligent Life is the Architech of the Universe.* Makawao, Maui, Hawaii: Inner Ocean Publishing, Inc., 2003.

Garreau, Joel. *The Nine Nations of North America.* Boston: Houghton Mifflin, 1981.

Garten, Jeffrey E. *The Big Ten: The Big Emerging Markets and How They Will Change Our Lives*. New York: Basic Books, 1997.

Gerzon, Mark. *A House Divided: Six Belief Systems Struggling for America's Soul*. New York: Tarcher / Putnam, 1996.

Gilbert, Mitchell. *An Owner's Manual for the Human Being*. With an Introduction by Bawa Muhaiyaddeen. New York: Samuel Weiser, 1980. New Edition, Merion Station, Pennsylvania: One Light Press, 2005. info@BMF.org

Gilpin, Robert. *The Challenge of Global Capitalism: The World Economy in the 21st Century*. Princeton, New Jersey: Princeton University Press, 2000.

Gleick, James. *Chaos: The Making of a New Science*. Great Britain: Cardinal; Maxwell Macmillan Pergamon Publishing, 1987.

Glenn, Jerome Clayton. *Future Mind: Artificial Intelligence: Merging the Mystical and the Technological in the 21st Century*. Washington: Acropolis Books Ltd., 1989.

Gödel, Kurt. *On Formally Undecidable Propositions of Principia Mathematica and Related Systems*. Translated by B. Meltzer. New York: Basic Books, 1962; originally published in 1931 as a paper in the *Monatshefte für Mathematik und Physik* entitled *"Über formal unentscheidbare Sätze der Principia Mathematica und verwandter Systeme I"*.

Godin, Seth. *Unleashing the Idea Virus*. New York: Hyperion, 2001.

Goldberg, Michael J. *The 9 Ways of Working: How to Use the Enneagram to Discover Your Natural Strengths and Work More Effectively*. New York: Marlowe and Co., 1999.

Goodman, Nelson. *Languages of Art: An Approach to a Theory of Symbols*. Indianapolis and New York: Bobbs-Merrill, 1968.

Graves, Clare. *Various papers and seminar handouts*. www.claregraves.com. See also: www.spiraldynamics.org and associated other sites.

Green, Michael. *Zen and the Art of the Macintosh: Discoveries on the Path to Computer Enlightenment*. Philadelphia, Pennsylvania: Running Press, 1986

Grof, Stanislav. *The Adventure of Self Discovery*. Albany, New York: State University of New York Press, 1988.

Gurdjieff, G. I. *Beelzebub's Tales to His Grandson: An Objectively Impartial Criticism of the Life of Man: All and Everything / First Series*. New York and London: Viking Arkana, 1992. Translation under the direction of Jeanne de Salzmann first published in 1950.

———. *Views from the Real World: Early Talks in Moscow, Essentuki, Tiflis, Berlin, London, Paris, New York and Chicago as Recollected by His Pupils*. London, New York: Penguin Books, Arkana, 1984; Original talks given between 1914 and 1949.

Halevi, Z'ev ben Shimon. *A Kabbalistic Universe*. New York: Samuel Weiser, 1977.

Hall, Calvin S. and Gardner Lindzey. *Theories of Personality*. New York: John Wiley and Sons, 1957, 1967.

Hamel, Gary. *Leading the Revolution*. Boston: Harvard Business School Press, 2000.

Hampden-Turner, Charles. *Maps of the Mind: Charts and Concepts of the Mind and its Labyrinths*. New York: Collier Books, Macmillan, 1981.

Harrison, Albert A. *Spacefaring: The Human Dimension*. Berkeley: University of California Press, 2001.

Hartmann, William K., Ron Miller and Pamela Lee. *Out of the Cradle: Exploring the Frontiers Beyond Earth*. New York: Workman Publishing, 1984.

Hesse, Hermann. *The Glass Bead Game (Magister Ludi)*. Translated from the German "Das Glasperlenspiel" by Richard and Clara Winston 1969. New York: Henry Holt and Co., 1969, 1990. Original German version published in 1943.

Hiriyanna, M. *Outlines of Indian Philosophy*. London: George Allen and Unwin, 1932.

Hixon, Lex. *Mother of the Universe: Visions of the Goddess and Tantric Hymns of Enlightenment*. Wheaton, Illinois; Madras, London: Quest Books, The Theosophical Publishing House, 1994.

Holland, John H. *Emergence: From Chaos to Order*. Reading, Massachusetts: Perseus Books, 1998.

Honderich, Ted, edited by. *The Oxford Companion to Philosophy*. Oxford, New York: Oxford University Press, 1995.

Honeycutt, Jerry. *Knowledge Management Strategies*. Redmond, Washington: Microsoft Press, 2000.

Houston, Jean. *A Passion for the Possible: A Guide to Realizing Your True Potential*. New York: HarperSanFrancisco, HarperCollins, 1997.

Hubbard, Barbara Marx. *Conscious Evolution: Awakening the Power of Our Social Potential*. Novato, California: New World Library, 1998.

———. *Emergence: The Shift from Ego to Essence*. Charlottesville, Virginia: Walsch Books, Hampton Roads Publishing, 2001.

Huntington, Samuel P. *The Clash of Civilizations and the Remaking of World Order*. New York: Simon and Schuster, 1996.

Hutchinson, G. Evelyn. *A Treatise on Limnology: Volume IV, The Zoobenthos*. Edited by Yvette Edmondson. Editorial assistance by Anna Aschenbach. New York: John Wiley and Sons, 1993.

Hutton, Will. *A Declaration of Interdependence: Why America Should Join the World*. New York, London: W.W. Norton and Co., 2002, 2003.

Husserl, Edmund. *The Phenomenology of Internal Time-Consciousness*. Edited by Martin Heidegger and translated by James S. Churchill. Bloomington and London: Indiana University Press, 1964.

Ibn al'Arabi, Muhyiddin. *The Bezels of Wisdom*. The *Fusus al-hikam* translated by R.W. J. Austin. New York: Paulist Press, 1980. The original was composed in 1230 CE (A.H. 627).

———. *Journey to the Lord of Power: A Sufi Manual on Retreat*. The *Risalat-ul-anwar fima yumnah sahib al-khalwa min al-asrar* translated by Rabia Terri Harris with an introduction by Sheikh Muzaffer Ozak al-Jerrahi. Rochester, Vermont: Inner Traditions International, 1981, 1989. The original was composed in 1204-1205 CE (A.H. 601-602).

International Enneagram Association, 2004 Conference Proceedings: 10th Anniversary Conference. Cincinnati, Ohio: Internationa Enneagram Association, 2004. www.internationalenneagram.org

Izutsu, Toshihiko. *Sufism and Taoism: A Comparative Study of Key Philosophical Concepts*. Berkeley, Los Angeles, London: University of California Press, 1983. First published in Japan 1966-1967.

Johnson, Steven. *Emergence: The Connected Lives of Ants, Brains, Cities, and Software.* New York: Simon and Schuster, 2002.

Jung, C. G. *Psychology and Alchemy.* Translated from the German *Psychologie und Alchemie* by R. F. C. Hull. Princeton: Bollingen, Princeton University Press, 1968. London: Routledge, 1953-1989; Original published 1944.

Kaku, Michio. *Hyperspace: A Scientific Odyssey Through Parallel Universes, Time Warps, and the Tenth Dimension.* New York, Oxford: Oxford University Press, 1994.

Keller, Ed and Jon Berry. *The Influentials.* New York: The Free Press, Simon and Schuster, 2003.

Kelly, Eamonn, Peter Leyden and members of the Global Business Network. *What's Next?: Exploring the New Terrain for Business.* New York: Basic Books, 2002.

Kim, W. Chan and Renée Mauborgne. *Blue Ocean Strategy: How to Create Uncontested Market Space and Make the Competition Irrelevant.* Boston: Harvard Business School Press, 2005.

Knapp, Stephen. *The Vedic Prophecies: A New Look into the Future, The Eastern Answers to the Mysteries of Life, Volume Three.* Detroit, Michigan: The World Relief Network, 1997, 1998.

Kuhn, Thomas S. *The Structure of Scientific Revolutions.* Chicago and London: The University of Chicago Press, 1962, 1996 (third edition).

Kurzweil, Ray. *The Singularity Is Near: When Humans Transcend Biology.* New York: Viking Penguin, 2005.

Lachman, Gary. *A Secret History of Consciousness.* Great Barrington, Massachusetts: Lidesfarn Books, 2003.

Laing, R. D. *The Politics of Experience.* New York: Ballantine Books, 1967.

Langer, Susanne K. *Philosophy in a New Key: A Study in the Symbolism of Reason, Rite, and Art.* New York: Mentor Book, New American Library, 1948.

Lapid-Bogda, Ginger. *Bringing Out the Best of Yourself at Work: How to Use the Enneagram System for Success.* Foreward by Helen Palmer. New York: McGraw-Hill, 2004.

Lawrence, Robert Z., Albert Bressand and Takatoshi Ito. *A Vision for the World Economy: Openess, Diversity, and*

Cohesion. Washington, D.C.: The Brookings Institution, 1996.

LeBoeuf, Michael. *The Greatest Management Principle in the World*. New York: G. P. Putnam's and Sons, 1985.

———. *Imagineering: How to Profit from Your Creative Powers*. New York: Berkeley Books, 1980.

Lee, Wayne. *To Rise from Earth: An Easy-to-Understand Guide to Spaceflight*. New York: Checkmark Books, 2000.

Levin, E. L. *The Road to Infinity*. San Rafael, California: International Association of Sufism, 2005.

Levine, Rick, Christopher Locke, Doc Searls, and David Weinberger. *The Cluetrain Manifesto: The End of Business as Usual*. Cambridge, Massachusetts: Perseus Publishing, 2000.

Lorie, Peter and Sidd Murray-Clark. *The History of the Future: A Chronology*. New York: Doubleday, 1989.

Lilly, John C. *The Deep Self: Profound Relaxation and The Tank Isolation Technique*. New York: Warner Books, Simon and Schuster, 1977.

——— and Antoinetta Lilly. *The Dyadic Cyclone: Autobiography of a Couple*. New York: Pocket Books, 1977.

Maitri, Sandra. *The Spiritual Dimensions of the Enneagram: Nine Faces of the Soul*. New York: Tarcher / Putnam, 2000.

———. *The Enneagram of Passions and Virtues: Finding the Way Home*. New York: Jeremy P. Tarcher / Penguin, 2005.

Marcus, Sharon. *My Years With The Qtub: A Walk in Paradise*. (A first-hand account of life as a disciple of Bawa Muhaiyaddeen.) Toronto, Ontario: The Sufi Press, 2005.

Marion, Jim. *Putting on the Mind of Christ: The Inner Work of Christian Spirituality*. Forward by Ken Wilber. Charlottesville, Virginia: Hampton Roads Publishing, 2000.

Maslow, Abraham H. with Deborah C. Stephens and Gary Heil. *Maslow on Management*. New York: John Wiley and Sons, 1998.

McLuhan, Marshall. *Understanding Media: The Extensions of Man*. New York: McGraw-Hill, a Mentor Book, 1964.

——— and Bruce R. Powers. *The Global Village: Transformations in World Life and Media in the 21st*

Century. New York, Oxford: Oxford University Press, 1989.

────── and Quentin Fiore. *The Medium is the Massage*. New York: Simon and Schuster, a Touchstone Book, 1967.

────── and Eric McLuhan. *The Laws of Media: The New Science*. Toronto, Buffalo, London: University of Toronto Press, 1988.

Marchand, Philip. *Marshall McLuhan: The Medium and the Messenger*. New York: Ticknor and Fields, 1989.

Meier, Dave. *The Accelerated Learning Handbook: A Creative Guide to Designing and Delivering Faster, More Effective Training Programs*. New York: McGraw-Hill, 2000.

Merrell-Wolff, Franklin. *Pathways Through to Space: A Personal Record of Transformation in Consciousness*. Introduction by John C. Lilly. New York: Warner Books, 1973.

Micklethwait, John and Adrian Wooldridge. *A Future Perfect: The Challenge and Promise of Globalization*. New York: Random House, 2003.

Monk, Linda R. *The Words We Live By: Your Annotated Guide to the Constitution*. New York: Hyperion, 2003.

Muhaiyaddeen, M. R. Bawa. *Asma'ul-Husna: The 99 Beautiful Names of Allah*. Philadelphia: The Fellowship Press, 1979. www.BMF.org

──────. *Come to the Secret Garden: Sufi Tales of Wisdom*. Philadelphia: The Fellowship Press, 1985.

──────. *The Golden Words of a Sufi Sheikh*. Philadelphia: The Fellowship Press, 1981.

──────. *The Guidebook: To the True Secret of the Heart, Volume 1 and 2*. Philadelphia: The Fellowship Press, 1976.

──────. *The Divine Luminous Wisdom: That Dispels the Darkness*. Philadelphia: The Fellowship Press, 1972.

──────. *The Tree That Fell to the West: Autobiography of a Sufi*. Philadelphia: The Fellowship Press, 2003.

──────. *To Die Before Death: The Sufi Way of Life*. Philadelphia: The Fellowship Press, 1997.

──────. *Zikr: The Remembrance of God: An Explanation by His Holiness Shaikh Muhaiyaddeen M. R. Guru Bawa*. Philadelphia: The Fellowship Press, 1975.

Murphy, Michael. *The Future of the Body: Explorations Into the Further Evolution of Human Nature*. Los Angeles: Jeremy P. Tarcher, 1992.

Myokyo-ni. *Gentling the Bull: The Ten Bull Pictures, A Spiritual Journey*. Comments taken from talks by The Venerable Myokyo-ni. Boston, Rutland, Vermont, Tokyo: Charles Tuttle Co., 1996. First published 1988.

Naisbitt, John. *Global Paradox*. New York: Avon Books, 1994.

———. *Megatrends: Ten New Directions Transforming Our Lives*. New York: Warner Books, 1984.

———. *Megatrends Asia: Eight Asian Megatrends That Are Reshaping Our World*. New York: Touchstone, Simon and Schuster, 1997.

——— and Patricia Aburdene. *Re-inventing the Corporation: Transforming Your Job and Your Company for the New Information Society*. New York: Warner Books, 1985.

Naranjo, Claudio. *The End of Patriarchy: And the Dawning of a Tri-une Society*. Oakland, California: Amber Lotus, 1994.

———. *The Enneagram of Society: Healing the Soul to Heal the World*. Translated from the Spanish, *El Eneagrama de la Sociedad—Males del Mundo, Males del Alma*, by Paul Barnes. Nevada City, California: Gateway Books and Tapes, 2004.

Nirenberg, John. *Power Tools: A Leader's Guide to the Latest Management Thinking*. New York: Prentice Hall, 1997.

Nöth, Winfried. *Handbook of Semiotics*. Bloomington and Indianapolis: Indiana University Press, 1995.

Ostrander, Sheila and Lynn Schroeder. *Psychic Discoveries Behind the Iron Curtain*. New York: Bantam Books, 1971, 1970.

——— with Nancy Ostrander. *Super Learning*. New York: Laurel, Confucian Press, Dell Publishing, 1979.

Ouspensky, P. D. *A New Model of the Universe: Principles of the Psychological Method in its Application to Problems of Science, Religion, and Art*. New York: Vintage Books, 1971.

———. *In Search of the Miraculous: Fragments of an Unknown Teaching*. New York: Harcourt Brace and Co., 1949.

Palmer, Helen. *The Enneagram in Love and Work: Understanding Your Intimate and Business Relationships*. New York: HarperCollins, 1995.

Parker, Andrew. *In the Blink of an Eye*. Cambridge, Massachusetts: Perseus Publishing, 2003.

Pearce, Joseph Chilton. *Magical Child: Rediscovering Nature's Plan for Our Children*. New York: Bantam Books, 1980.

Peebles, Curtis. *Asteroids: A History*. Washington and London: Smithsonian Institution Press, 2000.

Peirce, Charles Sanders. *Peirce on Signs: Writings on Semiotic by Charles Sanders Peirce*. Edited by James Hoopes. Chapel Hill and London: The University of North Carolina Press, 1991.

Perkovich, George. *India's Nuclear Bomb: The Impact on Global Proliferation*. Berkeley, Los Angeles, London: University of California Press, 1999.

Pert, Candace B. *Molecules of Emotion: Why You Feel the Way You Feel*. Foreword by Deepak Chopra. New York: Touchstone, Simon and Schuster, 1997.

Peters, Tom. *The Circle of Innovation: You Can't Shrink Your Way to Greatness*. New York: Vintage Books, 1999.

Popcorn, Faith. *The Popcorn Report: Faith Popcorn on the Future of Your Company, Your World, Your Life*. New York: HarperCollins, 1992.

——— and Adam Hanft. *Dictionary of the Future: The Words, Terms and Trends that Define the Way We'll Live, Work, and Talk*. New York: Hyperion, 2001.

Pound, Ezra. *Confucius: The Unwobbling Pivot, The Great Digest, The Analects*. Translation and Commentary on the "Stone Classics" by Ezra Pound. New York: New Directions, Penguin, 1951.

Preston, Richard. *The Hot Zone*. New York: Anchor Books Doubleday, 1994.

Radhakrishnan, Sarvepalli and Charles A. Moore. *A Sourcebook in Indian Philosophy*. Princeton, New Jersey: Princeton University Press, 1957.

Ratey, John J. *A User's Guide to the Brain: Perception, Attention and the Four Theaters of the Brain*. New York: Vintage Books, Random House, 2001.

Rees, Martin. *Just Six Numbers: The Deep Forces That Shape the Universe*. New York: Basic Books, 2000.

Restak, Richard. *The New Brain: How the Modern Age is Rewiring Your Mind*. N.p.: Rodale, 2003.

Rhodes, Peter. *Observing Spirit: Evaluating Your Daily Progress on the Path to Heaven with Gurdjieff and Swedenborg*. West Chester, Pennsylvania: Chrysalis

Books, Swedenborg Foundation Publishers, 2005. www.swedenborg.com

Ringland, Gill. *Scenario Planning: Managing for the Future.* New York: John Wiley and Sons, 1998.

Riso, Don Richard and Russ Hudson. *Understanding the Enneagram: The Practical Guide to Personality Types.* Boston, New York: Houghton Mifflin, 2000.

———. *The Wisdom of the Enneagram: The Complete Guide to Psychological and Spiritual Growth for the Nine Personality Types.* New York: Bantam Books, 1999.

Roberts, Bernadette. *The Path to No-Self: Life at the Center.* Boston: Shambhala, 1985.

Robinson, Kim Stanley. *Red Mars.* New York: Bantam Books, 1993.

———. *Green Mars.* New York: Bantam Books, 1994.

Roche, William. *A Conversion of Manners: The Spiritual Legacy of Saint Benedict.* Devon, Pennsylvania: Trefoil Publications, 1998.

Rumi, Mevlana Jelaluddin. *The Essential Rumi.* Translated by Coleman Barks with John Moyne. Edison, New Jersey: Castle Books, 1997.

———. *The Illuminated Rumi.* Translations and Commentary by Coleman Barks; Illuminations by Michael Green. New York: Broadway Books, 1997.

———. *Unseen Rain: Quatrains of Rumi.* Translated by John Moyne and Coleman Barks. N.p.: Threshold Books, 1986.

Rush, Locke. *The True Marriage: A Guidebook for a Lifelong Journey.* N.p.: 2003. www.thetruemariage.com

Ryan, Michael. *Knowledge Diplomacy: Global Competition and the Politics of Intellectual Property.* Washington: Brookings Institution Press, 1998.

Sanders, Irene T. *Strategic Thinking and the New Science: Planning in the Midst of Chaos, Complexity, and Change.* New York: The Free Press, 1998.

Schwartau, Winn. *Information Warfare: Cyberterrorism: Protecting Your Personal Security in the Electronic Age.* New York: Thunder's Mouth Press, 1994.

Schwartz, Tony. *What Really Matters: Searching for Wisdom in America.* New York: Bantam Books, 1995.

Scotton, Bruce W., Allan B. Chinen and John R. Battista, edited by. *Textbook of Transpersonal Psychiatry and Psychology.* New York: Basic Books, 1996.

Searle, Judith. *The Literary Enneagram: Characters from the Inside Out*. Portland, Oregon: Metamorphous Press, 2001.

Seeds, Michael A. *Astronomy: The Solar System and Beyond*. Pacific Grove, California: Brooks/Cole, Thomson Learning, 2001.

Senge, Peter M. *The Fifth Discipline: The Art and Practice of the Learning Organization*. New York: Doubleday Currency, 1990.

Singer, June. *Boundaries of the Soul: The Practice of Jung's Psychology*. New York: Anchor Books Doubleday, 1972.

Soros, George. *George Soros On Globalization*. New York: Public Affairs, Perseus, 2002.

Stapledon, Olaf. *Star Maker*. Foreword by Brian Aldiss. Los Angeles: Jeremy P. Tarcher, 1983.

Stallman, Richard M. *Free Software, Free Society: Selected Essays of Richard Stallman*. Edited by Joshua Gay. Boston: GNU Press, Free Software Foundation, 2002.

Stephenson, Neal. *The Diamond Age: Or, A Young Lady's Illustrated Primer*. New York: Bantam Books, 1995.

Sterling, Bruce. *Schismatrix Plus*. Includes *Schismatrix* and selected stories from *Crystal Express*. New York: Ace Books, Berkeley Publishing Group, 1996.

Sullivan, Patrick H. *Value-Driven Intellectual Capital: How to Convert Intangible Assets Into Market Value*. New York: John Wiley and Sons, 2000.

Tapscott, Don and David Ticoll. *The Naked Corporation: How the Age of Transparency Will Revolutionize Business*. New York: Free Press, Simon and Schuster, 2003.

Teilhard de Chardin, Pierre. *The Phenomenon of Man*. With an introduction by Sir Julian Huxley. New York: Harper and Row, 1959; (original in French 1955, translation by Bernard Wall).

Terrill, Ross. *The New Chinese Empire: And What It Means for the United States*. New York: Basic Books, Perseus, 2003.

Thomsen, Erik. *OLAP Solutions: Building Multidimensional Information Systems*. New York: John Wiley and Sons, 1997.

Tillich, Paul. *The Courage To Be*. New Haven and London: Yale University Press, 1952.

Toffler, Alvin. *The Third Wave*. New York: William Morrow and Co., 1980.

———. *Future Shock*. New York: Bantam Books, 1971.

Tolle, Eckhart. *The Power of Now: A Guide to Spiritual Enlightenment*. Novato, California: Namaste Publishing and New World Library, 1999.

Tompkins, Peter and Christopher Bird. *The Secret Life of Plants*. New York: Avon Books, 1974.

Toynbee, Arnold J. *A Study of History*. New York and London: Oxford University Press, 1946.

Tulku, Tarthang. *Knowledge of Time and Space*. Berkeley, California: Dharma Publishing, 1990.

———. *Skillful Means: Patterns for Success*. Berkeley, California: Dharma Publishing, 1978, 1991.

Wacker, Watts and Jim Taylor, with Howard Means. *The 500-Year Delta: What Happens After What Comes Next*. New York: HarperCollins, 1997.

———. *The Visionary's Handbook: Nine Paradoxes That Will Shape the Future of Your Business*. New York: HarperCollins, 2000.

Walsh, Roger. *Essential Spirituality: The 7 Central Practices to Awaken Heart and Mind*. New York: John Wiley and Sons, 1999.

Walton, Mary. *The Deming Management Method*. Foreword by W. Edwards Deming. New York: Putnam, A Perigee Book, 1986.

Wheatley, Margaret J. *Leadership and the New Science: Discovering Order in a Chaotic World*. San Francisco: Berrett-Koehler, 1999.

Wilber, Ken. *A Brief History of Everything*. Boston and London: Shambhala, 1996.

———. *A Theory of Everything: An Integral Vision for Business, Politics, Science, and Spirituality*. Boston: Shambhala, 2001.

———. *Boomeritis: A Novel That Will Set You Free*. Boston and London: Shambhala, 2002.

———. *Integral Psychology: Consciousness, Spirit, Psychology, Therapy*. Boston and London: Shambhala, 2000.

———. *Sex, Ecology, Spirituality: The Spirit of Evolution*. Boston and London: Shambhala, 2000.

Wilhelm, Richard. Trans. *The I Ching: Or Book of Changes*. The Wilhelm translation rendered into English by Cary F. Baynes; Foreword by C. G. Jung. Princeton, New Jersey:

Princeton University Press, Bollingen Series XIX, 1950-1969.

Williams, Sam. *Free As In Freedom: Richard Stallman's Crusade for Free Software.* Sebastopol, California: O'Reilly and Assoc., 2002.

Wright, Robert. *Nonzero: The Logic of Human Destiny.* New York: Vintage Books, Random House, 2000.

Wycoff, Joyce. *Mindmapping: Your Personal Guide to Exploring Creativity and Problem Solving.* New York: Berkeley Books, 1991.

Yeats, W. B. *A Vision.* New York: Collier Books, 1966; first printing 1937.

Zukav, Gary. *The Seat of the Soul.* New York: Simon and Schuster, A Fireside Book, 1990.

Acknowledgements

No one creates a life or a book by themselves and I have had much help. To my wife, Sarah, who has been my companion for the last quarter century and who edited the final manuscript of this book, you are the sweetness of my life; thank you for all that you are. My son, Daniel, has also given me much to appreciate.

To my beloved guide and teacher, Bawa Muhaiyaddeen, who transformed my life and showed me what a True Human Being could be, you remain always in my heart.

My parents, Paul and Anna Aschenbach, raised me brilliantly with love in an environment of diverse stimulations. My father, an internationally known sculptor and professor at the University of Vermont, taught me how to make things in many media, to sail, draw, and appreciate nature, books, and people. My mother, a lifelong social activist and champion of civil rights and peace, taught me her strong sense of justice and an appreciation of diverse cultures. Both she and my sister Karen, a writer, director, and film maker, contributed materially to supporting this book and were early reviewers. My other sister, Elizabeth, and her three lovely daughters, Brittany, Jenna, and Emily, are dear to my heart and my brother, Mark, is also much appreciated.

My cousin, Jack Mills and his wife Ellen were reviewers of the Transformation Model and encouragers of the writing. My great aunt, Elizabeth Taylor Shipley, a Quaker activist who faced down the Nazis to free Jews from Germany before the war, was a great spiritual influence in early childhood. My father's second wife, June (Sahra) Aschenbach, a spiritual psychologist, helped me get into Harvard University on full scholarship. My father-in-law, Adolph Risko, was a NASA rocket scientist from the early years of space exploration and a wonderful inspiration to me. My sister-in-law, Kathleen Risko, and nephews, Adam, Andrew, and Brian Russell, and Bob Risko are also dear to me.

My early life was filled with many interesting, creative, and intelligent people including: sociologist, Paul Oren, of the Sorbonne and University of Vermont; mathematician, Victor Gugenheim, of University of Chicago, who wrote theorems in our summer house, Antoine Ferroni, civil engineer for the city of Menton, France, and many others. I am also grateful for all my childhood friends and teachers including, Steve Maeck, J.P. Oren, John Carpenter, Peter Sorensen, Jane True, David Wade, Jeanette Andrew, Mrs. Stone (who taught me to outline), Hanlyn Davies, Maria Eugenia Silva de Domenico, and her friends in São Paolo, including Marcio Sousa and Jose Marreco (both film makers).

At Harvard, I was fortunate to study symbol theory with philosopher, Nelson Goodman, and scientific modeling with James Watson, co-discoverer of the DNA double helix. One of my classmate friends was Thomas Francis Cleary, now a premier translator of Asian spiritual texts, who introduced me to "the true Chan," Chinese Zen Buddhism. Others who contributed to my experience in that era include New York Times writer, Frank Rich, James Atlas, Juan Perez, Tricia Killian, Kathy Spenser, Ruth Martin, Tom Sancton, Mark Granavetter, Jim Stodder, John Ballantine, Mark Jacobs, Richard Bach and Bob Cox, who introduced me to great science fiction (Olaf Stapleton, Jerome Brunner, and Cordwainer Smith) and the game of Go. Through my mother, I met limnologist, Evelyn Hutchinson, of Yale Biology Department (widely considered the father of ecology). We discussed multidimensional modeling and he encouraged me in my explorations.

Later on, I co-founded a privately funded research institute with mathematical physicist, Berj Ensanian, where I engaged in various interdisciplinary studies including modeling of human interaction processes. I am appreciative of the many members of this group including Denis Chernyshow, who was an early supporter of this book. Others from that era include Tony Romano, Dave MacKensie, Dave Franzoni (screen writer *Amistad, King Arthur*), Ashley Lane, Karen MacGregor, James and Maryruth Glowgowski, and Cynthia Curatalo.

I have been benefitted by many members of the Bawa Muhaiyaddeen Fellowship including Patrick Andrews, Michael Toomey, Carl Marcus, Mitch and Sonia Gilbert, Locke and Jackie Rush, Michael Green, Coleman Barks (translator of Rumi), Lou Beutler (who helped me get a job at Unisys), Herb Levin (who found us our home), Carolyn Lawton (my homeopath), Susan Growe (our dear sister and early reader of the manuscript), Jonathan Granoff (who works tirelessly for nuclear disarmament), Ann Hochberg, Aisha Stern, George Graves, and so many others. The fellowship is a Sufi family of

Acknowledgements | 393

great and enduring love. Through an invitation by Jonathan to a meeting at Bryn Mawr and Haverford colleges, I came to know Barbara Marx Hubbard (co-founder of the World Future Society) and Ashok Gangadean (director of the Global Dialog Institute).

My professional life as an organizational consultant has also brought me into contact with a long list of people who have given me much, notably software developer Charlie Cheney, a friend and early supporter of this book. Others from the business world include Bob McAllister, Bill Wright, L.J. Hainley, Pricilla DeWitt, and Bob Lubking at Unisys; Rosemary Myers at The Franklin Mint; Simon Kearsley, John Maslanski, and Richard Hull at Merck; Sandy McNair, Dan Pettine, Debbie Harnsberger, Tim Humphreys, Tom Cole, and Ray Ross at The Vanguard Group; Joel Adams, Jim Sherry, Hank Gehron, Aashish Gupta, and Barbara Keller through Devon Consulting. Through the Barter Connection, I met Mary Broussard, Lelia Broussard (a rising musical talent), David Newman, Martie Walus, and others.

Reverend Susannah Currie invited me to hold an art exhibition at the Temenos Retreat and Conference Center, where I also gave my first talk about this book. Through this I have begun to get to know various people associated with the Swedenborgian community including Pete Brakman, Deborah Foreman, and Peter Rhodes.

I am grateful to Don Riso and Russ Hudson for teaching my wife and me the enneagram and for introducing us to the Diamond Approach developed by A.H. Almaas (Hameed Ali). We became part of the Emerald Mountain School of Diamond Heart work led by Alia Johnson to whom I remain profoundly grateful. I must also acknowledge my debt to all of the Diamond Heart teachers including, Renee Moran, Hameed Qabazard, Kristina Bear, Jessica Britt, and others, as well as to my fellow students including Nancy Baker, Sam Bonasso (who first mentioned *Spiral Dynamics* to me), Max Cohen, Jeff Collins, Jan Crawford, Merlin Dailey, LeClanche Durand, Rose Felle, Sally Gottesfeld, Gary Heller, Lora Lynne Heller, Sheila Hixon (wife of Lex Hixon), Scott Hogan, Valtraud Ireland, Laura Lao (producer of the film *Open Water*), Tomar Levine, Isabelle Lorans, Scott McBride, Jeff Meyers, Bonalyn Mosteller, Suzanne Noble, Barbara O'Hara, Merle Pollak, Ken Porter, Pat Power, John Read, Marlene Reisman, Jonah Schwartz, Anne Singer, Gail and Murray Staal, Jane Strong, Tony Schwartz (author of *What Really Matters: Searching for Wisdom in America*), Cornelia Wathen, and every one of you. Diamond Heart is profoundly transformative work. Almaas and all those who work with him have done a great service to humanity in developing it.

I would like to thank the many other teachers and students of the enneagram that I have come to know through the International Enneagram Association, including Helen Palmer, David Daniels, Maria Beesing, Richard Rhor, Ann Kirby, Ginger Lapid-Bogda, Judith Searles, Rabbi Howard Addison, Walter Geldart, Andrea Isaacs, Jack Labanauskas, and so many others. I recently had the opportunity to meet with French researchers Fabien and Patricia Chabreuil, who are exploring interesting connections between spiral dynamics and the enneagram. We must all acknowledge our debt to Claudio Naranjo who first brought the enneagram teachings from Oscar Ichazo's Arica group in Chile to the U.S. and to Ichazo for discovering and developing these teachings. Hameed Ali (Almaas) and Sandra Maitri were early students of Naranjo's and have both written significant books on the enneagram.

A great many other writers and thinkers have contributed to the fabric of this book, some I know personally and some only through their writings but to all I am grateful. First and foremost, I want to acknowledge my obvious debt to Clare Graves and his disciples Don Beck and Christopher Cowan, who presented his seminal work in the book *Spiral Dynamics*, which everyone ought to read. I encountered this book after completing my second draft and immediately began incorporating many of its ideas into my thought. Any good scientist should build on the best of prior discoveries and, in the human sciences, their work is a strong foundation.

Along related lines of thought, I deeply appreciate the work of Ken Wilber and Barbara Marx Hubbard, among those who have extended and elaborated on the Gravesian model, as well as presenting their own profound insights.

The writings of Teilard de Chardin were early influences in my life and continue to inspire. Other futurists who have influenced my thought include Alvin Toffler, Joel Garreau, Mark Gerzon, John Naisbitt, and Patricia Aberdene. In the realm of transpersonal psychology, I should mention R.D. Laing, John Lilly, Stanislav Grof, and Jean Houston.

In Christian mystical thought, the writings of Bernadette Roberts are interesting. Peter Rhodes has recently published a book integrating Gurjieffian practices with the teachings of Emanuel Swedenborg. In modern Buddhist thought, the writings of Tarthang Tulku are

Acknowledgements | 395

extraordinary. Thomas Cleary's translations of the Flower Ornament Sutra and the Blue Cliff Record are both extremely valuable.

I have long been a student of communication and media and in this domain have been much influenced by the writings of Marshall McCluhan who remains underappreciated, in my estimation. In semiotics, the writings of Umberto Eco and the seminal compendium of Winfried Nöth seem the best anchors in a messy field.

The footnotes and bibliography list additional influences. Even with my best efforts, I can never begin to acknowledge all the debts I owe to those who have gone before and those who have helped me.

Finally, I would like to thank Bobby Bernhausen and the people at Virtualbookworm.com who helped get this book ready for publication, Brian and Peggy Centonze at PLH Worldgroup Communications who developed my web site, and Steven Burke, M.D. who keeps me healthy.

Some may consider it sentimental to thank everyone one has ever known. I do not. It is my sincere belief that I have learned and gained from every single person I have met, even briefly, even where the relationship was less than positive. To say so seems only courteous and true. If you are not named explicitly, your contribution is nonetheless appreciated.

About The Author

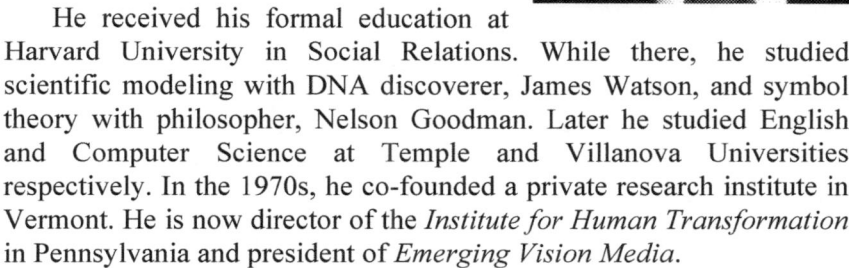

Michael Aschenbach brings a lifetime of training and experience to helping individuals and organizations gain deeper understanding and integration. His facilitation processes serve to clarify vision and create plans for transformation.

Aschenbach was born in central India of American parents, grew up in Vermont, lived in France and Brazil, and traveled on five continents.

He received his formal education at Harvard University in Social Relations. While there, he studied scientific modeling with DNA discoverer, James Watson, and symbol theory with philosopher, Nelson Goodman. Later he studied English and Computer Science at Temple and Villanova Universities respectively. In the 1970s, he co-founded a private research institute in Vermont. He is now director of the *Institute for Human Transformation* in Pennsylvania and president of *Emerging Vision Media*.

He has been engaged as consultant to a wide range of companies and non-profits including Unisys, Merck, The Vanguard Group, The Franklin Mint, Children's Hospital of Philadelphia, The Devereux Foundation, and various national, state, and local government organizations. He is principal of the consulting company, *Human Communication Systems*, and has written over 150 book-length technical documents.

He has been involved in focused spiritual work for over thirty years, studying teachings from all major religions and transpersonal psychology. He studied closely with Sufi sage, Bawa Muhaiyaddeen for many years and later spent six years studying the Diamond Approach developed by A.H. Almaas, in the Emerald Mountain School established by Alia Johnson.

Aschenbach is an accomplished artist working mainly in oil paint and print media. This life-long interest in visual media helps to inform his work in developing models of complex systems. He is also an avid gardener and nature photographer with an abiding interest in ecologically sustainable community. All of these interests contributed to writing *VISION 3000*.

Contact via: www.emergingvisionmedia.com

Lightning Source UK Ltd.
Milton Keynes UK
UKHW04f1126310718
326558UK00001B/309/P